Samuel Adams
and the Vagabond
Henry Tufts

ALSO BY NATHANIEL PARRY
AND FROM MCFARLAND

*How Christmas Became Christmas:
The Pagan and Christian Origins
of the Beloved Holiday* (2022)

Samuel Adams and the Vagabond Henry Tufts

Virtue Meets Vice in the Revolutionary Era

Nathaniel Parry

McFarland & Company, Inc., Publishers
Jefferson, North Carolina

LIBRARY OF CONGRESS CATALOGING-IN-PUBLICATION DATA

Names: Parry, Nathaniel, author.
Title: Samuel Adams and the vagabond Henry Tufts : virtue meets vice in the revolutionary era / Nathaniel Parry.
Description: Jefferson, North Carolina : McFarland & Company, Inc., Publishers, 2024 | Includes bibliographical references and index.
Identifiers: LCCN 2024012848 | ISBN 9781476694719 (paperback : acid free paper) ∞
ISBN 9781476652672 (ebook)
Subjects: LCSH: Tufts, Henry, 1748–1831. | Adams, Samuel, 1722–1803. | United States—History—Revolution, 1775–1783—Biography. | United States—History—1783–1815. | Massachusetts—History—1775–1865. | Revolutionaries—Massachusetts—Biography. | Rogues and vagabonds—United States—Biography. | Thieves—United States—Biography. | Adams family. | Tufts family. | Massachusetts—Biography.
Classification: LCC E301 .P357 2024 | DDC 973.2—dc23/eng/20240328
LC record available at https://lccn.loc.gov/2024012848

BRITISH LIBRARY CATALOGUING DATA ARE AVAILABLE

ISBN (print) 978-1-4766-9471-9
ISBN (ebook) 978-1-4766-5267-2

© 2024 Nathaniel Parry. All rights reserved

No part of this book may be reproduced or transmitted in any form or by any means, electronic or mechanical, including photocopying or recording, or by any information storage and retrieval system, without permission in writing from the publisher.

Front cover images: *left to right*, possible drawing of Henry Tufts in jail; Samuel Adams by John Singleton Copley and engraved by Charles Goodman and Robert Piggot (Library of Congress); the concluding section of the death warrant condemning Henry Tufts to hang, signed by Governor Samuel Adams; *background*: map of British America, 1774 (Library of Congress).

Printed in the United States of America

McFarland & Company, Inc., Publishers
Box 611, Jefferson, North Carolina 28640
www.mcfarlandpub.com

To my mother, Julie Tufts, who first told me Henry's story, and in memory of my dearly departed grandparents, Stanley and Cicely Tufts

Table of Contents

Acknowledgments   ix
Preface   1
Introduction   5

Part I—Rebels and Rogues   19
    1. Seeds of Rebellion   20
    2. Crime, Vice and Enlightenment   32
    3. Legitimate Lawlessness   49
    4. Escalation   65
    5. Living with the Indians   81

Part II—Incongruities   95
    6. Patriots, Slaves and Loyalists   96
    7. Spirit of '76?   114
    8. Class Divisions in the Revolution   129
    9. Alcohol in the Revolution   144
    10. Framers vs. Farmers   161

Part III—Republican Values   173
    11. We the Rabble   174
    12. Crime and Capital Punishment   191
    13. Unleashing Genius and Dismantling Patriarchy   206
    14. Heroes, Anti-Heroes and Villains   219
    15. Coming to Terms with the Revolution   235

Chapter Notes   251
Bibliography   285
Index   289

Acknowledgments

Since it was my mother, Julie Tufts, who first brought the story of Henry Tufts and Samuel Adams to my attention, I would first like to acknowledge her for looping me in on this fascinating history, as well as for the feedback she's provided throughout this project. Thanks, Mom.

I also would like to thank my distant relative and family genealogist Tom Tufts for his comments, as well as the invaluable research that he has compiled on both Henry and the more respectable Tuftses. His blog *Tufts Family Genealogy* is well worth reading to learn more about the nearly three centuries of the Tufts presence in America, most of which is far more honorable than the life of Henry—and sometimes even as interesting. To those members of the Tufts clan who might be less than thrilled about me bringing more attention to the family's black sheep ancestor, I can just offer my thanks for their understanding and my hopes that no one is too perturbed by me resurrecting a ghost from the family's past.

Daniel Allie, the editor of the 2017 reprint of Henry's *Narrative*, has my deep gratitude for not only doing the painstaking work of transcribing and publishing the book but also for providing a treasure trove of related historical documents at his blog *HenryTufts.com*. The generosity with his time in patiently answering my questions has been a huge help and is much appreciated. I also thank Neal Keating for his past work on Henry Tufts.

Writing a book that strives to provide an overview of the Revolutionary War and explore various themes of early American history would not have been possible without the scholarship of all those who have contributed to the vast historical literature on the subject. I therefore owe gratitude to all the devoted academics and researchers who continue the admirable mission of telling the story of the founding of the republic. As I immersed myself in this subject matter in researching this book, I found particularly helpful a number of resources that I would like to mention.

Michael Troy's *American Revolution Podcast* is a meticulously detailed and always fascinating account of Revolutionary War history and is well worth checking out. (He also has an accompanying blog for those who would rather read than listen.) Also worth reading is Harry Schenawolf's *Revolutionary War Journal*. Since 2006, J.L. Bell has been diligently maintaining the *Boston 1775* blog, which provides "history, analysis, and unabashed gossip about the start of the American Revolution in Massachusetts." Bell's research skills are second to none and the information he so expertly presents on his blog was useful to me more than once. And then, of course, there are the editors of and contributors to the *Journal of the American Revolution*, which is a national treasure.

I would be remiss if I didn't also recognize the biographers who have produced books on Samuel Adams in recent years, helping to ensure that this indispensable Founding Father receives the credit that he deserves in launching the American Revolution. Particularly helpful in my research were the books by Ira Stoll and Mark Puls, as well as the superb recent biography by Stacy Schiff, *The Revolutionary: Samuel Adams*. Daniel Bullen's excellent 2021 book, *Daniel Shays's Honorable Rebellion: An American Story*, was also useful in helping to round out the picture of Adams, in particular by elucidating his more reactionary side.

Thanks are also due to the archivists and curators who have made so much primary source material available online, including those at the Library of Congress, the National Archives, New York Public Library, the Metropolitan Museum of Art, and Internet Archive. I also thank the whole team at McFarland for their assistance and guidance during the writing process and for the opportunity to publish this book.

And finally, I offer my deep appreciation to my lovely wife Malene and wonderful daughters Eva and Lea, who all provided useful feedback on my ideas while working on this project.

Preface

In October 2011, I received an email from my mother that looped me in on a conversation she had the previous weekend with my brother and sister. Apparently they had been enjoying some Sam Adams Octoberfest beers, which prompted my mom to share a story about one of our ancestors, an "Indian yarb doctor" and notorious criminal named Henry Tufts. She didn't know his full life story but recalled that he was a Revolutionary War deserter who married an Indian princess. Eventually sentenced to hang for his crimes, he managed to narrowly escape the gallows by the intervention of Massachusetts Governor Samuel Adams.

My interest immediately piqued, I began searching for more information and quickly found out that Henry had written an autobiography, so I ordered a copy and began immersing myself in his narrative. While enjoying his many amusing anecdotes of heists and jailbreaks, as well as his thoughtful reflections on the ups and downs of life in colonial New England, what fascinated me the most was the timeline of his adventures—how Henry's life of debauchery coincided with momentous events taking place all around him that he clearly couldn't care less about. It occurred to me that besides being an entertaining account of the adventures of a vagabond and a peek into the underbelly of colonial life, his story served as something of an irreverent counter-narrative on the founding of the republic, offering a fresh perspective on major themes of the American Revolution. The fact that it also intersected with the career of Samuel Adams—an indispensable yet often overlooked leader of the revolution—convinced me that this story could be worth exploring further.

In any historical inquiry, of course, the trustworthiness of sources is of utmost importance, and there is good reason to doubt the veracity of some details of the autobiography of Henry Tufts. Sticklers for the truth might cringe at a historical study that heavily relies on the narrative of a known liar and thief, and a good deal of the attention his autobiography has received over the years, in fact, has focused on how seriously it should be taken as a source.

Perhaps the skepticism with which many approach Tufts's autobiography is warranted considering his dubious track record, but a fair reading would have to concede that its main thrust is one of brutal honesty. While an anecdote here or there might well be embellished or possibly even fabricated, on the whole it is a frank account of life in the late 18th and early 19th centuries in which Tufts doesn't shy away from laying bare the hypocrisies of society or revealing the loose morals of many of his contemporaries. Even when sharing stories about himself, Tufts freely offers details that cast his actions in a negative light—for instance, the sometimes shameful ways that he treats other people, in particular the women he misleads and often betrays. "In obedience to a strict adherence to truth," Tufts admits at one point, "I have left wife and children, wholly destitute of the conveniences of life, without previous notice, and without the least excuse for a conduct so inhuman."[1]

If he was making it all up, one can't help but wonder why he wouldn't have made himself look better.

More broadly, though, the way he describes the realities of life in the criminal underworld belies the general picture of this era that we are often presented with, namely the strict Puritan moral codes, the celebrated "Spirit of '76," and the patriotic zeal of the nation's founding generation. The book therefore is an insightful look into the mentality of—at the very least—a sizable minority of Americans during this time of turmoil. Whether Tufts is offering rationales for his decision to become an outlaw, providing context for the apathy some Americans felt about the upheaval taking place, or implicitly repudiating Puritan morality, he helps pull back the curtain on social realities during the revolutionary period and the early days of the American republic.

* * *

While Tufts's narrative is sometimes challenged for embellishing stories, Samuel Adams has been maligned over the centuries as a serial exaggerator who demonized his political enemies and cynically exploited events such as the "Boston Massacre" to advance his agenda, with one biographer dubbing him a "pioneer in propaganda." He is also criticized by scholars for being among the more taciturn of the founders, leaving little in the way of a paper trail, which poses challenges to historians. Adams was known to destroy his correspondence by cutting it into pieces or throwing it into the fire, and he would sign many of his letters, particularly those written during the war, with the instruction to "burn this," lest the communications fall into the wrong hands. Frustrated by this tendency, one historian even called the revolutionary leader a "neurotic" who suffered from an "inferiority complex."[2]

The complaints about Samuel Adams's reliability as a historical source and the questions raised about the trustworthiness of Henry Tufts's autobiography are among the many parallels between these two figures, reminding us of a basic truth when it comes to the study of history: scholars are often driven to explore a topic simply based on the availability of primary sources.

What these sources underscore is that history is always told from a certain point of view, and sometimes this perspective is self-serving. Just like the broader American narrative that emphasizes certain themes and downplays others, Tufts and Adams tell their stories through the prisms of their own experiences. In this way, the Tufts narrative is symbolic of the American story—just as Americans embrace the view of themselves as heroes who stood up for causes of liberty and defeated the most powerful empire on the planet, Henry Tufts didn't see himself as a villain but as a scrappy, resourceful survivor who did what he had to do to make it in an uncaring and unfair world. He personifies the sense of rugged individualism that characterizes the American spirit.

At the same time, of course, he was also a thief and a liar, and with this in mind I have striven to confirm as much as possible of his story, as well as point out where his account might not comport with the facts. More broadly, this book seeks to contextualize the narrative of Henry Tufts by exploring relevant themes and juxtaposing Tufts's life of crime with the story of Samuel Adams, who believed that "rulers should have little, the people much," according to one of his contemporaries.[3] Adams's uncompromising commitment to virtue was as strong as his commitment to the revolution, a sense of purpose that contrasts considerably with Tufts's ambivalence about the cause and his somewhat pathological devotion to vice. But if one scratches the surface, what becomes clear is that these two figures actually have much in common and more fundamentally that the revolution in which they participated was also characterized by the virtue and vice that Adams and Tufts personified.

* * *

This book is organized thematically, following a loosely chronological structure beginning with English settlement of America to the early years of the constitutional republic. Part I covers the life experiences that led Henry Tufts and Samuel Adams on their respective paths, exploring the corresponding themes that characterized life in colonial America and set the country on a course of rebellion. Part II explores the incongruities underlying what is broadly understood as a virtuous and righteous war for independence but was also characterized by class strife, vice, and disaffection. Part III covers the founding of the republic, examining the framers' wide-ranging views on issues such as the appropriate level of democracy and how to appropriately deal with the nation's criminal element, as well as the role of mythmaking in establishing a national identity.

When utilizing primary sources from the late 18th and early 19th centuries, the book preserves the writers' original voices and refrains from correcting their grammar, misspellings, and rather random capitalization styles.

Introduction

As family lore would have it, a decision by Massachusetts Governor Samuel Adams in the late 18th century to commute the death sentence of a "famous New England vagabond" was responsible for saving our family tree. A genealogy compiled in 1938 and passed down over the generations offers this account of our bad egg ancestor, Henry Tufts: "tried and convicted 1793 for stealing six silver teaspoons. Sentenced to hang Aug. 14, 1793. Commuted to life imprisonment by Gov. Samuel Adams. Escaped from Salem (MA) jail June 23, 1798, going to Lee, NH, then to Limerick, ME, where his wife and eldest son Simeon had built a home."

In fact, the year of Henry Tufts's conviction for stealing the spoons was 1794 and the escape from Salem jail seems to have taken place on November 10, 1798, rather than on June 23, but besides those small details, the summary above provides a fairly accurate thumbnail sketch of the final years of his life. My family descends from his marriage with Lydia Bickford, with whom he had nine children before being sentenced to hang and to whom he would return after his final jailbreak. Henry would later tell his life story, including an account of the stroke of luck that would have his execution date postponed and then cancelled, in an autobiography titled *A Narrative of the Life, Adventures, Travels and Sufferings of Henry Tufts*, published while he was still on the lam.

The story of his commutation holds personal interest for me, as I have wondered at times what it might have meant for my family if Governor Adams didn't take pity on my forefather and his death sentence had been carried out. Would his children and their descendants have been born? Would I be here? Why did Adams decide to commute the sentence anyway? A true vagabond, Henry Tufts married five different women and would ultimately have at least 10 children, so there could actually be quite a few Americans today asking these questions. As enthralling as it might be to imagine that Governor Adams rescued Henry's bloodline, however, it doesn't appear that he had any more children after his reunion with Lydia. The family tree doesn't appear to have been affected by Adams's decision after all.

It's possible, it should be said, that some of Henry's descendants and others bearing the Tufts name continue to hold a certain degree of embarrassment regarding their black sheep ancestor, who for generations has been treated as a skeleton in the family's closet. When his book was published in the early 19th century, family members apparently bought them up and burned them, leaving few surviving copies.[1] James Arthur Tufts, a professor of English at Phillips Exeter Academy in New Hampshire in the late 19th and early 20th centuries, even served on several local library boards for the sole purpose of preventing the acquisition of Henry Tufts's autobiography in library collections.[2]

Continuing this trend of attempted erasure, in 1963, Jay Franklin Tufts published a family genealogy which opted to exclude Henry from receiving a proper entry. "As Henry had rather a questionable reputation," Jay Franklin explained in justifying this rather glaring omission, "it is better to let old family skeletons die, and stay buried."[3] Continuing into the modern era, an article in 2012 by James Arthur Tufts's great-grandson, Tom Tufts, asks for posthumous forgiveness for even mentioning Henry's name.[4] To some in the Tufts clan, Henry appears to be an embarrassment that sullies the legacy of an otherwise respectable and distinguished family.

And indeed, there are many Tufts ancestors to be celebrated. The family name is enshrined as the handle of a top-tier school, Tufts University in Somerville, Massachusetts, which was founded in the 1840s with a grant from Charles Tufts, who was a descendant of Henry Tufts's older brother. A library in Weymouth, Massachusetts, also bears the Tufts name,[5] and a number of genealogy books and blogs hail the achievements, accomplishments, and sacrifices of Tuftses dating back to the earliest days of American history. With a presence in America since the 1630s, when Peter Tufts emigrated from England to Massachusetts, the Tufts family includes soldiers, sailors, preachers, authors, business leaders, and educators.

The Tufts clan also has numerous forebears who paid the ultimate price in fighting America's wars. There was James Tufts, who died at the Battle of Bloody Brook in King Philip's War in 1675, and several who died a century later during the Revolutionary War, including Adam, Aaron,

Opposite: **Cover page for Henry Tufts's *Narrative*, published in 1807 by Samuel Bragg in Dover, New Hampshire. Three years after the publication of this book, Bragg's printing house went up in flames, which some have since speculated was an act of arson by a mob angry over Tufts's book. No contemporary sources, however, indicate that the fire was intentionally set (Henry Tufts, *A Narrative of the Life, Adventures, Travels and Sufferings of Henry Tufts, Now Residing at Lemington, in the District of Maine In substance, as compiled from his own mouth*, Samuel Bragg, 1807).**

A NARRATIVE

OF THE

LIFE, ADVENTURES, TRAVELS AND

SUFFERINGS

OF

HENRY TUFTS,

NOW RESIDING AT

LEMINGTON,

IN THE DISTRICT OF MAINE.

IN SUBSTANCE, AS COMPILED FROM HIS OWN MOUTH.

Ab ovo usque ad mala.
OVID.
Meliora video, proboque, deteriora sequor.
IDEM.

ENTERED AS THE ACT DIRECTS.

DOVER, N. H.
PRINTED BY SAMUEL BRAGG, JUN.

1807.

Ichabod, and William. Another William Tufts died at sea during the War of 1812, and several Tuftses perished in the first and second world wars, as well as in Korea and Vietnam.[6] My own grandfather, Stanley Tufts, was a lieutenant in the Navy during World War II, sailing treacherous missions back and forth across the Atlantic to the Mediterranean Sea. His older brother Jesse was in the Army, driving a tank across France throughout the war, while his younger brother Arthur was a Marine who served in the Pacific, fighting at the Battle of Guadalcanal. Thankfully, all three returned in one piece—Grampa even used to joke that the only injury he sustained during the war was a sprained ankle from a pick-up basketball game on his ship.

Another notable descendant of Peter Tufts was Dr. James Hayden Tufts, an eminent professor of philosophy at University of Chicago, co-founder of the Chicago School of Pragmatism, and president of the American Philosophical Association. In the early 20th century he co-authored (with John Dewey) the highly influential book *Ethics*, which served as a blueprint for a generation of social scientists. In *Ethics*, which contains several passages that could be directly applied to understanding Henry's unscrupulous life, Dr. Tufts advanced ideas about the relationship of ethical development to external stimuli, noting that "new habits, the new character, embody more intelligence."[7] He was an advocate for educational reform and is credited with writing the bulk of University of Chicago's history of philosophy, as well as mainstreaming the role of psychology in political discourse, including in labor negotiations.[8]

So, basically, this is all just to acknowledge that the Tufts family includes many distinguished figures who have contributed immensely to their country over the centuries. Compared to these courageous and accomplished patriots, perhaps it is understandable that Henry is considered the "black sheep of an otherwise respectable family," as Tom Tufts put it.[9] But while Henry certainly could have been better and his opprobrious behavior can rightly be condemned, he too should be appreciated—if for nothing else than as a significant contributor to early American literature. His unique book is not only a true crime classic and a highly entertaining collection of picaresque tales of a rambler's life, but it offers real historical value as a glimpse into an underworld that existed at the time of the nation's founding.

As abolitionist, politician and soldier Thomas Wentworth Higginson sympathetically wrote about Henry's narrative in the late 19th century, his "great historical value lies … in his vices." Higginson observed that matters of historical importance, such as the difficulties George Washington had in organizing an army, the depreciation of the Continental currency, and the outbreak of Shays's Rebellion in the post-revolutionary period, "can never be understood except by studying the revelations of the reprobates."[10] In this sense, we owe Henry some gratitude for documenting a perspective that is otherwise omitted from traditional histories of the American Revolution.

* * *

Luckily, despite efforts to suppress the book, it survived throughout the 19th and early 20th centuries and was republished in 1930 as *Autobiography of a Criminal*, edited by Edmund Pearson. This version was a significantly abridged edition of the 1807 original, with entire sections cut out, including the preface, as well as Tufts's descriptions of events preceding his actions. The abridged version was reprinted in 1993 with an introduction by Neal Keating, but it wasn't until Daniel Allie transcribed the entire original text and published it as *The Narrative of Henry Tufts* in 2017 that the book as written by Henry became available for the first time for a wide audience—more than 200 years after it originally appeared.

The narrative that Henry produced (with the help of a ghostwriter, it should be acknowledged) is "a book like no other," as Allie puts it.[11] He writes that this book is "an early American narrative that did not overly moralize, and did not shy away from presenting the very worst of actions."[12] Keating is even more effusive in his praise, calling it "one of the great American books" and noting that "it is probably the first American hybrid in a venerable line of outlaw literature," featuring "autobiographical, picaresque writings about life, love and theft outside (yet alongside) the normal boundaries of legal systems and mercantile moral codes."[13] What makes it all the more remarkable is that it was published in a region of the country still dominated by Puritanical modes of thought and morality. Even today, reading the book, with its casual descriptions of criminal activity and references to sexual promiscuity, would be enough to make some people blush. One can only imagine what the prim and proper members of New England society would have thought about it in the early 19th century.

And then, of course, there are his rather dismissive references to the American Revolution that had just been fought. Henry Tufts spent the early years of the conflict living with the Abenaki Indian tribe, and unlike some of his kinsmen who earnestly embraced the cause and joined the Continental Army out of convictions and principles, he did so simply for the bounty that was paid to volunteers—and then promptly deserted once he received his payment.

The indifferent manner with which Tufts describes the revolutionary cause and his obvious lack of concern about the war's outcome calls into question some fundamental assumptions about the nation's founding.

With just a few explicit references to the war in his narrative, usually in relation to being pursued as a deserter, his irreverent autobiography reminds us that not all Americans in those days shared the revolutionary spirit—a more nuanced understanding that is enhanced by juxtaposing his worldview with that of his unlikely redeemer, Samuel Adams.

* * *

Brought together by fate, the lives of Henry Tufts and Samuel Adams symbolize the broader story of the Revolutionary War and the American narrative, urging us to consider how the motivations for declaring independence from Britain might not have been all that different from the motivations of a son rebelling against his father and compelling us to rethink our concepts of fairness, egalitarianism, and the legitimacy of rebellion. Beyond that, their story offers insight into the nature of crime and punishment in early American history, the importance attached by the colonists to property rights, the role of education in crime prevention, and the early consideration of alternatives to the death penalty in the penal system. It also elucidates the role of Native Americans in the revolutionary era and the cultural exchanges that took place between whites and their indigenous neighbors.

More fundamentally, examining the narratives of Henry Tufts and Samuel Adams illuminates the way that history is conveyed over generations and how aspects are downplayed or exaggerated, in particular the role of "minor" historical figures. While Samuel Adams continues to receive attention from historians, and his profile was given a significant boost in the mid–1980s when the Boston Beer Company introduced its flagship product, Samuel Adams Boston Lager, the reality is that both Samuel and Henry are upstaged, to varying degrees, by other family members. A number of Henry's kinsmen show up in history books, with, for example, one of his distant cousins receiving credit for playing a role in Paul Revere's famous ride to warn John Hancock and Samuel Adams and alert the colonial militia in April 1775 about the approach of British forces before the Battle of Lexington and Concord. In a book published in 1995, historian David Hackett Fischer reconstructed the Midnight Ride with an honorable mention of Samuel Tufts of East Cambridge, who embarked on his own separate ride after his neighbor had spotted the British column.[14]

Another Tufts who shows up in history books is Zachariah, who at the outbreak of the Revolutionary War was just 15 years old. Zachariah Tufts served around Boston in the beginning of the war and then signed on with Daniel Morgan's Riflemen, a unit that gained notoriety as lethally effective snipers. Zachariah's service is featured in *Massachusetts Soldiers and Sailors of the Revolutionary War*,[15] which incidentally also contains a brief record that Henry Tufts enlisted as a private in Captain Smith Emerson's Company but then deserted.[16]

Likewise, although Samuel Adams was instrumental in promoting the cause of independence, he is largely overshadowed by the accomplishments of his cousin John Adams, who played a more prominent role in securing America's independence and would become the second president of the United States. As an early indication of how history would treat the two cousins, when John Trumbull produced his famous painting celebrating the presentation of the Declaration of Independence at Carpenter's Hall, he sandwiched Samuel Adams in between Richard Henry Lee and George Clinton. Samuel is barely perceptible in the painting, but John, of course, is front and center, standing proudly alongside Thomas Jefferson and Benjamin Franklin.

While John Adams is hailed as one of the indispensable Founding Fathers, widely celebrated and even profiled in an HBO miniseries devoted to telling the story of his life, Samuel Adams in some ways gets short shrift

Declaration of Independence, **painted by John Trumbull in 1818, depicts the presentation of the draft of the Declaration of Independence to Congress in July 1776. John Adams counselled Trumbull as he worked on the painting, urging him to "let not our Posterity be deluded by fictions under pretence of poetical or graphical Licenses." Thousands of Bostonians flocked to see the painting when it was displayed in Faneuil Hall years later, only to be disappointed that Samuel Adams was nearly imperceptible (United States Capitol. Washington, D.C.).**

and his radical views are often portrayed as unreasonable or rash. David McCullough's Pulitzer Prize–winning book *John Adams*, for instance, tells the story of the Boston Massacre by noting that Samuel Adams hastily and rather propagandistically called the killings a "bloody butchery" while his more prudent relative agreed to provide legal defense to the British soldiers based on his sagacious belief that no one in a free country should be denied legal counsel.[17] In McCullough's follow-up work *1776*, Samuel Adams doesn't appear at all, while John Adams's name shows up in the pages more than a dozen times.

Other history books show similar levels of favoritism toward the more famous of the Adamses. David Reynolds's highly acclaimed general history of the United States, *America: Empire of Liberty*, devotes many pages to John Adams, Abigail Adams and John Quincy Adams but none to Samuel Adams. Likewise, the Massachusetts Historical Society's Adams Family Collection includes papers relating to John Adams, Abigail Adams, John Quincy Adams, Louisa Catherine Adams, Charles Francis Adams, Charles Francis Adams II, and Henry Adams but not Samuel Adams.[18]

One explanation for this disparity may be that all studies of the man have essentially concluded that his career peaked in 1776. As historian Pauline Maier pointed out in a 1976 article called "Coming to Terms with Samuel Adams," while he was indispensable in setting the revolution in motion, he played a relatively minor role, at least in comparison to his cousin, in the post-revolutionary period that completed the process,[19] and he came to be seen as someone who was out of touch with modernity and progress. As a conservative Calvinist whose views were rooted in Puritanism, he "belonged to another era," Maier observed, and was thus "excluded from the pantheon of Revolutionary leaders around which Americans were asked to rally" in the post-revolutionary period.[20] She notes that biographies of some revolutionary leaders began being written in the early 19th century, but the first full biography of Samuel Adams wasn't published until 1865,[21] indicating an early bias taking hold against the Boston patriot and a difficulty determining his place in the revolution. Other historians tend to agree with Maier's observations. "Samuel Adams was ultimately eclipsed by the independence movement to which he once seemed indispensable," Jack Rakove writes. John Adams, on the other hand, "was liberated by it."[22]

Yet, although history would be far kinder to John Adams than it would be to Samuel Adams, back in the 1770s, it was Samuel who was the more celebrated of the two. Thomas Jefferson alluded to his indispensable nature when he called him "truly the Man of the Revolution," and his notoriety as a rabble rouser was so widespread that other patriots were often referred to as "the Samuel Adams of" various colonies and regions.

Introduction

Christopher Gadsden, for example, was known as the "Sam Adams of the South," Cornelius Harnett was called the "Samuel Adams of North Carolina," and Charles Thomson was "the Sam Adams of Philadelphia."[23] When John Adams traveled to Paris to shore up diplomatic support for the American Revolution, he disappointed his French hosts that he was not "the famous Adams."[24] While surely humbled and possibly embarrassed by his hosts' disappointment, even John would acknowledge his cousin's essential role in the revolution. "Without the character of Samuel Adams," John Adams would say, "the true history of the American Revolution can never be written."[25]

In some ways, actually, John Adams seemed to be his biggest fan, lauding his cousin's indefatigable commitment to the cause and marveling that "for fifty years his pen, his tongue, his activity were constantly exerted for his country, without fee or reward." John regretted the way that Samuel's legacy would be tarnished and neglected in the years after the revolution. "If the American Revolution was a blessing, and not a curse," he wrote in 1819, "the name of Samuel Adams ought to be preserved." John lamented that a "systematic course has been pursued for thirty years to run him down" and often found himself defending his cousin's name against slanders and attacks.[26] At the same time, however, John knew that it would be difficult for historians to fairly describe Samuel's role or to accurately capture his personality. Reflecting on how posterity would someday treat his cousin, John wrote that Samuel's "character will never be accurately known" due to the fact that "it was never sufficiently known to his own age." Similarly, when Samuel Adams passed away in October 1803, a clergyman observed that he had "an impenetrable secrecy" that prevented him from "being loved by his friends" to the same degree that he was "feared by his enemies."[27]

Some have attempted to peel back his "impenetrable secrecy" and give him his proper credit, with Mercy Otis Warren writing in the 1805 book *History of the Rise, Progress, and Termination of the American Revolution* that Adams's life "exhibited on all occasions, an example of patriotism, religion, and virtue honorary to the human character." As one of the earliest advocates for revolution, Adams "continued firm, through the great struggle, and may justly claim a large share of honor, due to that spirit of energy which opposed the measures of administration, and produced the independence of America."[28] More succinctly, as Edmund Morgan put it in 1953, "probably no American did more than Samuel Adams to bring on the revolutionary crisis."[29] Samuel Adams is a central figure in A.J. Langguth's 1989 book *Patriots: The Men Who Started the American Revolution*, with a full chapter devoted to his role in sparking the rebellion against British authority. A PBS series called *Liberty!*, which chronicles "the birth of the American Republic and the struggle of a loosely connected group of states to become a nation," claims that "without Boston's Sam Adams, there might never have been an American Revolution."[30] In a 2022 portrait titled *The Revolutionary*, Stacy Schiff notes that he was "intrepid and unwavering, in the vanguard at the most perilous times," underlining that his "character and conduct were irreproachable."[31]

But notwithstanding these accolades, Samuel Adams generally suffers from the tendency in historical studies to elevate the contributions of certain people while overlooking others. Considering that there are so many notable figures to profile in the revolutionary period, perhaps it is understandable that Samuel Adams is often relegated to a minor supporting role, with more focus generally paid to the contributions of individuals such as John Adams, Aaron Burr, Benjamin Franklin, Alexander Hamilton, Thomas Jefferson, James Madison, and George Washington—the septuplet dubbed the "founding brothers" in the 2002 Pulitzer Prize–winning book by Joseph J. Ellis. But as Ira Stoll laments in his 2009 biography of Samuel Adams, in the 21st-century resurgence of interest in the American Revolution, "other founders have gained stature at Samuel Adams's expense." Samuel Adams, Stoll regrets, "has faded into the background … so much so that contemporary writers often simply refer to 'Adams,' assuming that the reader will understand that the reference is to John, not Samuel."[32]

Besides the fact that there are just so many other distinguished figures to compete with, one factor that has likely contributed to the downplaying of Samuel Adams's role in the American Revolution is his historical association with mob violence, including the brutal practice known as tar-and-feathering. This might not be entirely fair, however, as there is actually no evidence that Samuel Adams condoned or participated in any of the tar-and-featherings or other incidents of mob violence that he is often associated with. In fact, although he was denounced by British royal governor Thomas Hutchinson as an "incendiary" who had a "malignity of heart,"[33] when Hutchinson's home was ransacked on August 26, 1765, by a mob angry over British plans to impose the Stamp Act on the colonies, Adams publicly condemned the attack. He also kept his distance from the planning of mob actions spearheaded by his local Sons of Liberty branch that preceded the Boston Tea Party. Although Adams had led protests against the tea tax, he took pains to avoid association with violence and left the task of leading mobs that attacked the shops of tea merchants to others, men such as William Molineux and Joseph Warren.[34] He also advocated restraint from his Boston compatriots at key moments and helped quell civil unrest in the post-revolutionary period. As Stoll writes, "Adams was no Gandhi … but neither was he a Robespierre."[35]

***

While Samuel Adams's name is perhaps unfairly tarnished for supposedly inciting criminal acts, Henry Tufts's name is closely associated with the last crime that he was convicted of—stealing six silver spoons. But although Henry Tufts most certainly led a life of debauchery and crime, or "an uncommonly misspent life," as an 1888 review of his memoirs aptly described it, it is possible that he was in fact innocent of the crime that ultimately resulted in his death sentence. Although perhaps we shouldn't take his word at face value, Tufts was rather adamant in his account of the silver spoons incident that he in fact had purchased them from an associate named John Stewart. In a book filled with frank admissions of all sorts of transgressions, which actually borders on braggadocio at times, it is noteworthy that he pleads innocence to this particular crime.

Some skeptics, nevertheless, have expressed doubt over his version of events. In the book *Rogues, Rascals, and Other Villainous Mainers*, author Trudy Irene Scee says, "He may have been writing the truth, or he might have been telling yet one more lie. Henry Tufts was, after all, an infamous liar and thief."[36] An article at the website of the New England Historical Society reports as flat fact that he "got caught stealing spoons" in Marblehead, Massachusetts, noting that his reputation as a thief and a liar have diminished his credibility.[37] It seems that to many observers Henry's dishonorable reputation negates anything he might say and renders his claims of innocence doubtful.

The fact that so many continue to doubt his story might be understandable considering his track record but it also may reveal a certain ongoing bias that many hold toward him and his memoirs as a historical source. While his narrative employs common literary techniques of emphasis and omission and at times appeals for sympathy from the reader, in this way it is not all that different than many narratives of the American Revolution. Initially an oral tradition with accounts passed along by direct participants, who often embellished certain aspects and forgot others, the basic contours of this history were established early on and quickly became forged as the national mythology through countless books that told generally the same story: American republicans, oppressed by British tyrants, rose up to oppose unjust treatment and fought a glorious war for independence, which, against all odds, succeeded in establishing a new nation defined by liberty and justice for all. (The inconvenient fact of the existence of chattel slavery in this republic is usually rationalized as something that, while unfortunate, would be dealt with later in the Civil War.)

The history of America's founding narrative, essentially, has been taught for generations in a way that affirms the national identity. As the American Legion advised in 1925, the goal of education should be to "inspire the children with patriotism,"[38] which means that an agreed-upon narrative is needed to protect the national consensus. This is the function of familiar and pleasant stories such as Paul Revere's Midnight Ride and the minutemen bravely facing down the British regulars on Lexington Green. The revolutionary fervor of New England and the selfless commitment of Continental soldiers who answered the call to serve the cause of liberty are celebrated and their tales told and retold over the ages, but the stories of some people, those like Henry Tufts, seemingly have no place in this history and are thus suppressed and dismissed as lies. But the result of this approach, as James Baldwin once put it, is an American identity based on "a series of myths about one's heroic ancestors,"[39] rather than a full and accurate picture of our common past. While these pleasant stories might be important in shaping the national identity, they don't provide the full picture. Not all of our ancestors can be heroes, after all.

And, it should be acknowledged, even while based in reality, some of the more familiar stories may not be entirely true either. The earliest versions of the Midnight Ride, for example, presented a picture that accentuated the spontaneity of the event and minimized the elaborate preparations that the Whigs made to establish a network of spies, informants and fighters who were actively preparing for battle. Careful to portray themselves as the innocent victims of British aggression, Whig leaders suppressed any information that could cast them in a negative light, including the written account prepared at the time by Paul Revere who offered inconvenient details on the preparations that preceded the event and declined to unequivocally state that the redcoats fired the first shot at Lexington Green. While other depositions that advanced the Whig narrative were rushed to print and circulated widely in the colonies, Revere's deposition was returned to him and remained unpublished until 1891.[40]

With so many of our national mythologies shaped, to one extent or another, by a bending of the truth, it is the task of historians to continually re-examine them and provide fuller context. As Thomas A. Bailey pointed out in his 1969 essay "The Mythmakers of American History," most of the "pretty little stories of history are in some degree false, if pursued to their smallest details."[41] Defining historical myth as "an account or belief that is demonstrably untrue, in whole or substantial part," Bailey urged historians and teachers to resist mythmaking and instead focus on presenting the most truthful picture possible, in all of its rich complexities and troublesome ambiguities.

In this sense, Tufts's story—even if occasionally embellished—contributes to a fuller understanding of the founding of the republic. In a way that is impossible by focusing only on the many myths that have been handed down from generation to generation, the insights offered by this "famous New England vagabond" shed light on aspects of the revolutionary era that cannot be found in any textbook. In short, the story of Henry Tufts's brush with the gallows and the debt of gratitude owed to Samuel Adams challenges us to rethink American history and appreciate it as the multilayered, nuanced and sometimes contradictory cornucopia of facts, trends, currents, and ideas that it is.

Part I

Rebels and Rogues

"The criminal's cardinal sin, as he himself can come to see in his moment of repentance, is to ignore Providence."
—John J. Richetti

"What better is honesty than crime, so long as oppression is allowed to the few, to lord it over the many?"
—William Stuart

1

Seeds of Rebellion

At first glance, Henry Tufts and Samuel Adams appear to be polar opposites. One a sinful ne'er-do-well and the other a pious Christian, one a philanderer and the other a devoted husband, one a deserter and the other a revolutionary leader, they seem to have little in common other than the fact that they lived through extraordinary times in close geographical proximity to each other. In reality, though, the figures are two sides of the same coin, ultimately sharing far more in common than it might initially appear—representing the shrewd, self-interested capacity for survival as well as the lofty promises and ideals that made the American Revolution possible. They both abhorred hypocrisy and became outlaws who resisted systems that they felt were unfair. Although Adams was a revolutionary and Tufts was a criminal, they both challenged the status quo and made their own rules, reminding us that, at the end of the day, what the American Revolution came down to was a defense of liberty and property, with property sometimes being the more important of the two.

Although they would follow very different paths in life, Henry Tufts and Samuel Adams shared similar backgrounds and pedigrees, with ancestors who were among the first waves of Puritan settlement in Massachusetts. Following the initial immigration that founded Plymouth in 1620, which would establish a colony of only about 1,500 by the end of the 1620s, the much larger wave of the 1630s would come to be known as the Great Migration. It was this wave that the Adamses and the Tuftses belonged to, the settlers—mostly hailing from the eastern counties of England such as Essex, Suffolk, Norfolk and Lincolnshire—who would establish the Massachusetts Bay Colony to the north of Plymouth.[1] Unlike the earlier settlers of the 1620s, most members of the Great Migration who settled in Massachusetts were people of means. Composed of families and interrelated family groups, they usually paid for their own passage across the Atlantic—a fee equal to the annual income of a yeoman farmer—and brought one or two servants to help with hard labor.[2]

As Henry Tufts relates in his memoirs, he knew "little [of his] paternal ancestors," and mistakenly believed that his grandfather, Thomas Tufts, was the first to emigrate to the colonies from England. Henry had been told that his grandfather was born in Devonshire, England, and arrived in Boston in the late 1600s. "A worthy and pious man" who apparently was unsatisfied with his situation in England, Thomas left his homeland to improve his station in life, Henry explained. Providing a glimpse into Henry's sense of skepticism about the American dream, however, he writes that "his circumstances, … I imagine, were not greatly advanced by the removal,"[3] and notes that when he died, he "was by no means affluent."[4]

Henry, it seems, had been misinformed about his ancestry. In reality, he was the great-great-grandson of Peter Tufts, who migrated from Norfolk, England, in the 1630s. Peter was a prominent early citizen of Medford, Massachusetts, owning some 43 acres of land. In 1647, he became a ferryman on the Mystic River and in 1669 would become the first representative from Medford to the Massachusetts legislature, known as the General Court. He also appears to have played a role in the Salem Witch Trials of 1692. Based partly on Peter's complaints, Elizabeth Fosdick and Elizabeth Paine were arrested and placed in Salem jail on a charge of witchcraft. According to a local history published in 1899, "Peter Tufts of Mystic Side, who many times during a long life appears in the court records and files, and not always as a desirable neighbor, also complained of [Fosdick and Paine]," specifically that they had committed "acts of Witchcraft … on his negro Woman."[5] (It seems he may have owned a slave.)

Besides being an undesirable neighbor who went around accusing women of witchcraft, Peter Tufts was apparently an ogre of a boss, with his servant Henry Swillaway ultimately rebelling against him for the ill-treatment that he endured. As the same 1899 text describes it, Swillaway was the "unfortunate servant of Peter Tufts who 'beate his man with the greate end of A goade Sticke,' and 'said that he would tie him to a tre and beat him for he was his moneie." One day, Swillaway apparently had enough of this abuse and decided to "strike his master upon the brest with his hand," according to an eyewitness, and threatened him with a large stone.[6]

* * *

Samuel Adams descended from Henry Adams, a Puritan farmer who arrived in Boston with nine children in 1632, as well as Maria Fifield, the granddaughter of the minister who preached the farewell sermon to John Winthrop and the first wave of Puritans who set sail for America in 1620. Adams had family ties with Increase Mather and his son Cotton, who were leading Puritan clergymen in the Massachusetts Bay Colony and participated in a 1689 rebellion that toppled the royal governor of the New England colonies for "raising of taxes without an Assembly." As a nod to this heritage, Samuel Adams would later adopt the pen name "Cotton Mather" in some of his screeds against the Crown.[7] Adams never forgot his roots, recalling in his writings that the "first Settlers of New England" fled "Ecclesiastical Tyranny" in their homeland, bravely crossing an "untried Ocean & tak[ing] Shelter in a dreary Wilderness."[8]

With a strong background in Puritanism, Adams's parents had hoped that he would join the ministry. His father, Samuel Adams, Sr., was a church deacon and prosperous merchant who wanted his son to follow in his footsteps, but the younger Samuel, after a brief and unsuccessful business career, was drawn to politics instead. He was deeply religious and proud of his Puritan heritage,[9] but at the same time, tended to deemphasize his ancestry, placing little stock in bloodlines and recoiling from those who elevated themselves over their peers out of a sense of privilege and pomposity. This was based on his conviction that neither wisdom nor virtue were hereditary, and that reaching back to one's ancestry for legitimacy could be a double-edged sword. "When traced far enough back," Adams's biographer Stacy Schiff points out, "one bumped up against the inevitable horse thief."[10]

Despite—or perhaps because of—his pedigree as a member of one of the most prominent families in early American history, Adams was wary of attaching too much weight to one's surname. He warned against "family pride," particularly among statesmen, calling it "a ridiculous kind of Vanity among Men."[11] Rather than allowing his pedigree as a member of an elite family shape his attitudes, Adams's political beliefs were infused with Christian convictions, and he was seen by those close to him as a natural-born radical who was hardwired to challenge authority. As John Adams once wrote to his wife Abigail, "I pity Mr. Sam Adams, for he was born a Rebel," adding, "I hope he will not die one."[12] In his diary, John described Samuel as "zealous, ardent and keen in the Cause, is always for Softness, and Delicacy, and Prudence where they will do, but is stanch and stiff and strict and rigid and inflexible, in the Cause." Samuel, John wrote, had "the most thourough Understanding of Liberty, and her Resources, in the Temper and Character of the People, tho not in the Law and Constitution."[13] His revolutionary zeal was based at least in part on his belief that God supported the American cause, and indeed his brand of republicanism would share a number of elements of Puritanism, in effect becoming a more secular and less rigid iteration of the earlier ideology.[14]

* * *

It is not clear whether Samuel Adams and Henry Tufts knew this or not (or whether it played any role in Adams's later decision to commute Tufts's death sentence), but it turns out that the two shared some common familial relations. As a second cousin to John Adams, Samuel Adams was also a distant cousin to John's wife Abigail Adams, who was a cousin by birth and niece by marriage to Cotton Tufts,[15] who was a grandson of Peter Tufts. Abigail Adams and Cotton Tufts corresponded regularly in the late 1700s and early 1800s, and Cotton Tufts also corresponded directly with John Adams, including while he was president of the United States.

Besides these familial ties, something else that Henry Tufts and Samuel Adams had in common was that they would both be financially disadvantaged through no fault of their own, with Tufts falling victim to his father's decision to pass his full inheritance to his older brother, and Adams falling victim to a British decision to shutter a bank where his father served as director. The inability of Henry Tufts and Samuel Adams to get an early leg up would have profound impacts on their respective life paths.

At the beginning of his autobiography, Henry offers an account of his motivations for choosing the life of an outlaw, explaining that it all started when he was denied a fair compensation for the labor that he had provided his father on their farm. He explains that as he entered adulthood, he had asked his father to help him get started in life by "bestow[ing] on me some part of his property." This, Henry said, would have served as "an encouragement to industry, and towards my obtaining a comfortable subsistance in the world, in proportion as he had done by my elder brother."[16] But unfortunately for Henry, the general practice in those days was for fathers to pass on inheritance to firstborns while their younger siblings got nothing. This practice, considered by some an important way to encourage landless people to earn wealth outside the family, precluded an equitable distribution of the estate.[17]

While Henry may have hoped for his father to depart from the cultural norm of bequeathing the estate to the firstborn legitimate child, it is possible that his father's hands were tied. Some colonies followed primogeniture laws, in which issues of family settlements and division of property were prescribed by the colonial courts,[18] and generally followed the custom of "favored heir plus burdens." This meant that in practice most of the estate would go to the eldest son while the rest of the children received just a fraction, if anything.[19]

Whether he was influenced by the cultural norms of New England or because he held a particular bias toward his firstborn son, his father was not inclined to distribute his property equitably. Knowing that Henry wouldn't be happy with his decision, he stalled in providing an answer. As Henry tells it, "My father, for some time, evaded all direct answers to my requests, while I continued both solicitations and complaints." But after what must have been a rather drawn-out period of nagging from Henry, his father "finally rejected my suit, declaring it his intention, that his eldest son should possess the whole of his estate."[20]

This angered Henry, who seemed to be at a loss, initially, as to how to respond. As he explains in a rather understated fashion, "being disappointed in my hopes, and cut off from that, which had long been the ground of my only dependence, I grew angry and discontented, not well knowing what steps to pursue."[21] Perhaps understandably, Henry felt denied what he was entitled to, having "diligently served my father during minority," primarily, he says, in the "business of husbandry," or the raising of livestock for meat, milk, and other products. One can only assume that during his years of performing day-to-day, labor-intensive care tending to the livestock, that he might have dreamed of being granted some compensation for his work, and feeling cheated out of his birthright, decided that he would not passively accept this fate.

His bitterness was compounded by the fact that the amount of time that he had spent working for his father meant that he was not able to pursue other opportunities, learn marketable skills, or receive a proper education. Although he would later claim authorship of the narrative published in 1807, it is widely believed that the book was in fact written by one of his neighbors, and that Henry himself "was too illiterate to spell his own name correctly," as one critic put it.[22] This lack of formal learning would be confirmed by Henry himself, who claimed in his memoirs that, having spent so much of his time contributing to the family business, "no time had been allowed me to obtain knowledge, so that my education had been totally neglected, save the small pittance I had gleaned miscellaneously, by means of my own industry." Assuming that his contributions to the family business were as substantive as he claims, it is hard not to sympathize on some level with his belief that he was "entitled to some share of my father's estate" and "was injured by his ill-timed parsimony."[23] But rather than take his disappointment in stride, he decided to claim from his father what he felt he was entitled to. "I at last concluded," he wrote, "to take his horse." After stealing the horse, he rode it to Chester, New Hampshire, and sold it "for about thirty dollars."[24]

This enabled him to live relatively comfortably for a couple of months, but he concedes in his memoirs that he began to regret his actions, finding that he "had made a wrong estimate of human life," and decided to return home to apologize to his father. He hoped "to pacify my parent, by paying him what money I had left," and noted that when he arrived his father was "sorely displeased." Henry Tufts, Sr., "rebuked [him] sharply for [his] past bad conduct," predicting that such behavior would eventually lead to the gallows. But, as Henry explains, over time his father's "displeasure subsided by degrees," and the two reconciled.

* * *

Based on this anecdote, Henry Sr. appears to be a forgiving father, even if somewhat traditional. His indulgent nature would have been in keeping with the general trends of the era and possibly a reflection of the evolving attitudes towards parenting in the 18th century, which tended to lean towards leniency, at least in comparison to the previous century of harsh discipline to compel adherence to Puritan values. In contrast to the 1600s, when parents were expected to rigidly enforce religious norms and constrain youthful propensity towards immoral or sinful behavior,[25] by the 18th century, the climate of child rearing had changed dramatically and parents increasingly valued winning the sincere affection of their children, seeking to earn their devotion through kind and respectful treatment rather than just intimidating them into obedience. As part of the broader Enlightenment philosophies being developed in this period, there was a consistent loosening of the traditional patriarchal family structure that had been the norm for centuries. By the mid–18th century, few fathers dared to justify controlling their household dependents through an arbitrary and authoritarian approach, instead seeking to influence their family members through a combination of commanding respect and nurturing personal attachments.[26] Children, however, could often recognize their parents' limitations and hence fathers found that they no longer enjoyed the level of power and influence they once did.[27]

John Adams would later observe that these changes in familial relations and the move away from strict patriarchy in the 18th century would play a significant role in inspiring the revolutionary movement of the 1760s and '70s. "The source of revolution, democracy, Jacobinism," John Adams told his son Thomas in 1799, "has been a systematical dissolution of the true family authority." Adams observed that "there can never be any regular government of a nation without a marked subordination of mother and children to the father," which was undermined by patriarchy being in disarray. It was this fundamental challenge to the family structure that enabled the rise of republicanism, the rejection of monarchy, and the rebellious spirit that would ultimately result in the American Revolution, according to Adams.[28]

But of course, this rebelliousness would not manifest itself the same way among all Americans. While Henry Tufts would essentially become a rebel without a cause, some, such as Samuel Adams, externalized the "systematical dissolution of the true family authority" that was taking place in the 18th century and applied this questioning of authority not only to their fathers but also to King George III himself.

* * *

While most histories of the American Revolution start with the crisis that took hold in the 1760s with the adoption of new taxes and restrictions imposed on self-governance in the colonies, grievances against British rule date back much earlier than that. As one of the most influential of the Boston radicals who challenged royal authorities, Samuel Adams, in fact, was deeply affected by a decision in the early 1740s that would have a profound and lasting effect on his family. The issue in 1740s Massachusetts that ultimately set Adams on his course of revolutionary radicalism was a mortgage bank that had been established by his father and a number of his political allies in an attempt to counter the effects of a crushing economic depression that hit the colony in 1740. In response to rising inflation and the refusal of creditors to accept paper money as payment, Samuel Adams, Sr., and fellow members of Boston's Caucus Club created a system of floating currency backed by their own real estate, the result being the so-called Land Bank.[29]

The colony's wealthiest merchants complained that allowing debtors to pay creditors with paper currency would undermine the assets of creditors and further increase inflation, so the merchant class coordinated with Parliament to have the Land Bank declared illegal in 1741. Its directors were then charged with financial crimes, nearly leading to the prosecution of Samuel Adams, Sr.

Land Bank supporters won a healthy majority in the Massachusetts House and Samuel Adams, Sr., was sent to the colony's upper chamber, the Council, which appeared for a moment to be a triumph of colonial democracy. Governor Thomas Hutchinson, however, vetoed the appointment and threatened to strip the titles and offices of anyone who invested in the Land Bank, effectively destroying it and making shareholders liable for the bank's debts.[30] The bank's inability to continue granting paper money to farmers led to lawsuits that sliced Samuel Adams's potential inheritance to a sliver of its former value,[31] and when Samuel Adams, Sr., passed away in 1748, his estate was put up for sale at public auction to settle his debts. Intent to stop the sale, the younger Samuel Adams threatened to bring legal action against the sheriff or anyone who attempted to purchase the property. The tactic worked and the estate remained in his possession, while the debt to the Land Bank Company remained unresolved.[32]

This episode would shape Samuel Adams's views on issues such as the right to property and liberty. In the midst of the ordeal that his father endured at the whims of royal authorities issuing dictates from thousands of miles away, Adams was at Harvard College working on his master's thesis, titled "Whether it be lawful to resist the supreme magistrate if the commonwealth cannot otherwise be preserved," which denounced the colony's rich and powerful men for their greed and lack of piety.

Soon after finishing at Harvard, in 1748 he helped launch a newspaper, *The Independent Advertiser*, which aimed to "defend the rights and liberties of mankind, to advance useful knowledge and the cause of virtue, to improve the trade, the manufactures and the Husbandry of the country, whatever may tend to inspire its people with a just and proper sense of their own condition, to point out to them their true interest, and rouse them to pursue it."[33] He regularly contributed articles to the newspaper but unfortunately it lasted less than a year before being terminated. The newspaper would later be reconstituted as the *Boston Gazette*, where Adams would write dozens of articles under the pen names "Candidus" and "Vindex."

During the 1750s, Adams ran the malt business he inherited from his father into the ground. His lack of a business sense combined with his obsession with politics inhibited his ability to hold a steady job until he was elected to the position of tax collector in 1756, which also raised his profile locally. The following year, tragedy struck when his first wife, Elizabeth, passed away. At this point, "[h]e is all loose ends and blighted promise," biographer Stacy Schiff writes, and "appears to be shambling his way to obscurity."[34]

But then, on April 5, 1764, the British Parliament adopted the Sugar Act, prohibiting the importation of all foreign rum and cutting the duty on foreign molasses in an effort to curb smuggling. The law raised concerns among the colonists about the principle of taxation without representation, while also undermining the business model of merchants who relied on smuggling. Taking up the cause, Adams found his voice as an advocate for colonial rights. In May 1764 he drafted a report for the Massachusetts General Court, which denounced the Sugar Act as a subversion of "our Charter Right to govern & tax ourselves."

"If Taxes are laid upon us in any shape without our having a legal Representation where they are laid, are we not reduced from the Character of free Subjects to the miserable State of tributary Slaves?" Adams asked, imploring the Massachusetts assembly to "carefully to look into the Laws of Excise." He argued that "as the Preservation of Morals as well as Property & Right, so much depends upon the impartial Distribution of Justice, agreeable to good and wholesom Law … it is incumbent upon you at all times to give your voice for their honorable Maintenance." As elected representatives, Adams recalled, they should not forget that their mandate is to uphold "the Morals of this People, which is the basis for publick Happiness." Therefore, they should "joyn in any Proposals which may be made for the better cultivating the Lands & improving the Husbandry of the Province … [and] to support our Commerce in all its just Rights."[35]

Samuel Adams's instructions to the General Court represented a perspective of propertied colonists that linked ownership intrinsically with liberty. When infringements were made upon their wealth and status, or their ability to trade freely, they viewed it as an affront not only to their livelihoods, but also to their natural rights, as well as an impediment to the broader colonial project, which it was understood relied on land acquisition, industry, and commerce.

With property ownership relatively widespread in the colonies, many Americans shared the sense of independence and entitlement that prompted Adams into action. In addition, the desire for increasing this ownership provided an impetus for western settlement, which brought colonists into conflict with the Indians, and increased the financial cost to the British in administering the empire. Prior to the Revolutionary War, the westward movement of Americans had accelerated at a steady pace. Struggling farmers sought opportunities at the edges of the empire, setting out for distant places in northern New England, Nova Scotia, Maine, West Florida, and along the Susquehanna River in Pennsylvania and the lower Mississippi River. Some 20,000 moved from southern New England into New Hampshire and what would later become Vermont between 1760 and 1776, establishing a total of 264 new towns in northern New England.[36]

Lord Dunmore, the royal governor of Virginia, marveled that the colonists "acquire no attachment to place: but wandering about seems engrafted in their nature; and it is a weakness incident to it that they should forever imagine the lands further off are still better than those upon which they are already settled."[37] This attitude led to a growing land fever and a belief in both opportunity and class mobility among the colonists, or in the case of Henry Tufts, a rootless vagabond lifestyle existing on the edges of society. To the elite, however, it contributed to property and wealth acquisition, which were considered essential to the development of the colonies.

* * *

Following the French and Indian War in 1763, peace opened possibilities for expansion, but it turned out that this was at odds with British priorities—including the imperative of settling debts that had been incurred during the previous several years of fighting the French. It was due to this reality that London introduced the Royal Proclamation Act of 1763, which prohibited expansion west of the Appalachian Mountains, and began to enact a series of new taxes in the 1760s, which sparked the rebellion among dissidents who saw taxation as akin to slavery and land as the future.

Many colonists agreed with the worldview of George Washington, who considered land as essential for promoting both national growth and personal economic prosperity, and rejected the limitations placed on westward expansion. "Land is the most permanent estate and the most likely to increase in value," wrote Washington.[38] The colonists persistently sought cheap land to plant and develop, leading Washington to observe that "no Country ever was or ever will be settled without this Indulgence."[39]

Rejecting London's claim that continued settlement would spark costly conflicts with the Native American tribes and that it should fall on the colonists to pay the costs already incurred in the French and Indian War, Samuel Adams pointed out that the burdens placed on the colonists—particularly those of Massachusetts—were inherently unfair, as they were the ones who had personally fought the French, and it was their labor that had enriched the empire. "It is well known that the People of this Province have not only settled this Country, but enlargd & defended the British Dominion in America, with a vast Expence of Treasure & Blood," he wrote in 1765. "They have exerted themselves in the most distinguished Services for their King; by which they have often been reducd to the greatest Distress."[40] He also rejected the idea that the colonies should be made to pay for the Crown's expenses, or that it was even possible to do so. "By their surprizing Exertions, they have bro't upon themselves, a Debt almost insupportable," and the revenue that London sought to extract from the colonies "would have appeard greatly beyond our Proportion."[41]

With the colonists remaining adamant in their desire to accumulate land and refusing to pay excessive taxes, the stage was set for a growing state of friction with London, which was fueled by the intellectual freedom that came with economic prosperity and Enlightenment ideas disseminated by a vibrant printing press and thriving literary culture. With the population of the colonies doubling every couple decades in the 18th century, the urban centers of Charleston, Philadelphia, New York, Newport and Boston were growing—and changing—particularly fast. This led to the rise of the "tavern patriots," generally literate colonists who gathered in public houses to drink, read the news of the day, bring news from other colonies, and discuss the ideas of intellectuals like Thomas Paine, James Chalmers, and Thomas Jefferson. One of these ideas was that of the link between land, liberty and property. As historian Edmund S. Morgan has noted, "Ownership of property gave not only economic independence but also political independence to the average American."[42]

One can only wonder then whether Henry Tufts might have followed a different path had he been granted some land and property by his father, or had the chance to attend a university that might have introduced him to the political philosophies that shaped Samuel Adams. If the inheritance had been split more equitably between Henry and his siblings, and had he been given access to better education, might he have become a revolutionary leader rather than a common criminal?

When Henry ponders his choices that set him on a life of crime, he does at times cite his lack of opportunity and notes that when he tried to pursue honest endeavors, he was held back by an "inability to support self and family in the manner I desired."[43] But it's also clear from his memoirs that he suffered from an almost addictive compulsion to steal. Henry openly recognized this compulsion, noting that "the prevalency of habit … begets a mental alliance in its favor," and he quickly "became attached to favorite irregularities."[44] Rather than settling down, he travelled regularly up and down the mid–Atlantic from Canada to Virginia, taking what he needed or wanted, whether it was food, clothes, boots, or occasionally, a beehive. His specialty, though, was stealing horses, at which he was so adept that he would boast of some 50 successful thefts over his career. He developed particular techniques, such as selecting horses to steal by observing their way of eating hay, and could so effectively disguise the animals with paint that their owners could not recognize them.

Henry Tufts spent 19 days in this jail in or around the year 1770. As he told the story, the day after Thanksgiving, he and a fellow thief named Dennis were being transported to Old York Jail when they stopped at a tavern in Wells, Maine. Dennis managed to break out of his handcuffs and escape, and a few minutes later their captors asked Henry where Dennis had gone. "If he be the prudent man I think him," Henry said, "he's by this time, three miles ahead at the least." They proceeded to take Henry to the jail and to prevent him from getting into any mischief, he was "strongly handcuffed, and cast into the securest ward" (photograph published ca. 1901 by Detroit Publishing Company, Library of Congress, gift of the State Historical Society of Colorado, Library of Congress Prints and Photographs Division).

Henry also tried various attempts at honest labor, but even when he had some success in acquiring a few possessions and beginning to get ahead, it seemed that the universe conspired against him. In autumn 1778, for instance, his house caught fire and was burned to the ground, destroying all of his "household furniture, meat, corn, and indeed, every article I possessed." These items, Henry claims, had been obtained "by industry; yea, by the sweat of my brow," lamenting that "it was my all." Soon after that unfortunate incident he fell back into his old habits, stealing a young horse that belonged to a resident of Lee, New Hampshire, named James Davis.[45]

Henry was resourceful, though, and seemed to understand the value of having multiple revenue streams. Besides stealing, he tried his hand at various times as a day laborer, medicine man, fortune teller, and preacher. "I passed from place to place, appearing sometimes in the character of a physician, and sometimes of priest, as best suited my purposes," he explains.[46] But despite at times finding himself momentarily happy living a quiet family life, noting that when he was living with his first wife Lydia, "my vices lay listless and dormant,"[47] at other times he finds himself giving into "the indulgence of corrupt appetites."[48]

Meanwhile, Samuel Adams would increasingly devote himself to fighting such corrupt appetites.

2

Crime, Vice and Enlightenment

Provided the standard education on the founding of the republic, Americans might be forgiven for believing that the abuses that colonists endured at the hands of the British Crown were the only difficulties that they faced. While most schoolchildren are well-versed on the excessive taxes such as the Stamp Act and the growing tensions that led to the occupation of Boston, for example, few would be able to discuss social problems that existed in the colonies, or might believe that moral crimes such as adultery—as depicted in Nathaniel Hawthorne's *Scarlet Letter*, required reading for generations of sophomores and juniors in America's high schools—were the most serious offenses that took place in strait-laced Puritan society. Some might even assume that crime as we think of it today perhaps didn't exist.

But, of course, it would be a mistake to assume that colonial America was free from day-to-day problems such as poverty and economic want, or crime and vice. New Englanders prided themselves on their morality and work ethic, but naturally there were exceptions to the rule, and many individuals who breached the norms of society whether through crime, vice or idleness. Henry Tufts is a case in point, but he was far from the only one giving over to vice on a regular basis. In fact, there was such an extensive and developed criminal subculture that it even had its own language, a dialect known as "flash lingo." Described by Henry as "partly English and partly an arbitrary gibberish," which sounds to outsiders as an "unintelligible jargon," the dialect used alternative words such as a "nipping jig" to describe a gallows and "prad" for horse.[1]

Henry's memoirs, indeed, reveal a vast underworld that existed throughout the country during the revolutionary period, peeling back the curtain on a wide array of apolitical and antisocial elements consisting of thieves, reprobates and loose women. Wherever Henry went, from Canada to Virginia, he seemed to come across an old acquaintance or would easily make a new friend—never having any difficulty in identifying a fellow scoundrel or finding a willing mistress.

So, although many of Henry's critics have branded him as a uniquely villainous vagabond, a closer look uncovers that the lifestyle he embraced was not particularly rare. The historical record makes clear that petty crimes such as theft, as well as more serious crimes such as piracy and murder—along with moral and religious crimes such as sodomy, witchcraft and prostitution—were common even in Puritanical Massachusetts. Dating back to the earliest days of colonial settlement in America, authorities had to deal with antisocial behaviors that posed persistent challenges to the social order.

* * *

In 1621, John Billington—one of the original Pilgrims who signed the Mayflower Compact—became the first person to commit a crime in America when he refused to obey military orders, and nine years later became America's first known murderer when he shot and killed fellow colonist John Newcomen. Billington was subsequently convicted of murder and hanged.[2]

Following the Billington case, several other murders and robberies would result in capital punishment throughout the 1630s. In one infamous incident, in 1636, a young woman named Mary Sholy hired a guide named William Schooler to help her make the perilous 23-mile journey from Newbury to Pascataquack, in the Massachusetts Bay Colony. Sholy, however, never made it to Pascataquack, and an Agawam Indian later found her naked body lying in a thick swamp about three miles north of the Merrimack River, with her clothing in a pile nearby. Following an investigation in which it was discovered that he had blood on his hat and a scratch on his nose the "breadth of a small nail," Schooler was put on trial and found guilty of murder.[3] Continuing to profess his innocence, he was hanged September 28, 1637, along with John Williams, a thief who murdered a fellow criminal named John Hoddy after a falling out.[4]

Far from being an isolated incident, the Sholy case was one of many heinous crimes committed in the 17th century. A comprehensive account of legal matters from 1630 to 1692 in the Massachusetts Bay Colony contains a dozen references to murder, ten to rape, and about 85 references to theft.[5] Considering this record of crime, it was clearly an issue that required substantial attention of the Puritans as they attempted to build their "city upon a hill," based on what they believed was a holy covenant with God. For the Puritans, dealing swiftly and harshly with criminal activity was essential. As John Winthrop declared in his 1630 treatise, "the eyes of all people are upon us," warning that their sins and mistakes would be seen by all. "So that if we shall deal falsely with our God in this work we have undertaken and so cause him to withdraw his present help from us," Winthrop cautioned, "we shall be made a story and a byword through the world."[6]

In this spirit, when criminals were apprehended and convicted, they were executed publicly and with much fanfare—often with thousands of spectators in attendance. Ministers held sermons prior to the execution, which would then be reprinted and distributed widely. In one such sermon, from 1722, the Rev. Cotton Mather described "the TERROURS of HELL" and "the TERRIBLE MISERIES of the PUNISHMENTS" that awaited a convicted murderer after his sentence was carried out. Having been found guilty of bludgeoning his neighbor to death with an axe, Jeremiah Fenwick was described by Mather as a "miserable wretch" who was facing "a Destruction of Soul as well as of Body, in a dreadful HELL, after Death; A Destruction more dreadful than any Death."[7] Sermons such as these were intended to remind all colonists of the grave fate that awaited sinners and to reaffirm the divine purpose of the Puritan community that they were attempting to build in the New World.

In spite of the Puritans' best efforts to curtail it, crime was given a boost by a growing tendency of rootlessness that increasingly characterized colonial life in the mid- to late-18th century. While in early colonial history, the norm was for individuals to remain rooted in small communities in which everyone knew each other, in the 18th century, increasing movement of people enabled the anonymity that career thieves relied on to carry out their misdeeds. Fragmentation of communities also resulted in vagrancy and diminished the authority of churches and colonial governments, and particularly in the backcountry, lawlessness was on the rise.[8] In 1757, an American magazine fretted over this trend, noting that "a vagrant life is unfavourable to instruction; and without settlements and fixed habitations ... we cannot expect, in the present situation of affairs that their friendship will be steady and firm."[9]

To counter the increase in vagrancy and to address the related issue of poverty and economic want, laws were adopted throughout the colonies to control the movements of the poor, provide the destitute a minimal level of subsistence, and tackle the problem of idleness, which did not simply mean inactivity, but rather the wide spectrum of anti-social behavior associated with unemployment and indolence.[10] Idleness was criminalized to counter the unpredictable threat posed by those who were disinclined to perform traditional labor, particularly those, like Henry Tufts, who bounced from town to town. A South Carolina law of 1721, for example, forbade poor whites from freely migrating, identifying the threat to public order inherent in allowing too much mobility: "Whereas, notwithstanding the precautions taken for preventing the large credit given to the poorer sort of people, and more especially to loose, idle and disorderly persons, who, continually running in debt much beyond what they are able to pay, daily desert the Province."[11]

In spite of these legal efforts to contain vagrancy and provide social welfare benefits to the indigent, crime continued to impact the colonies all the way into the revolutionary era. A review of hangings conducted in Massachusetts from the onset of the revolutionary crisis in 1763 to the signing of the Treaty of Paris recognizing American independence in 1783 reveals that crimes of all sorts were prevalent even as patriots struggled for the cause of liberty. According to one tally, there were more than 20 executions that took place in this timeframe,[12] for crimes including burglary, rape and murder. Prostitution, too, was a common problem, particularly in port cities such as New York and Boston.

* * *

New York's redlight district was ironically dubbed "Holy Ground" because of the presence of numerous brothels in the shadow of Trinity Church's 172-foot steeple. By the 1760s, the area had become well-known for its "sinful and despicable" activity, and during the early stages of the Revolutionary War, Continental soldiers frequented the brothels for "intimate connections," as Lieutenant Isaac Bangs of Massachusetts described it. "When I visited them [prostitutes], at first I thought nothing could exceed them for impudence and immodesty, but I found the more I was acquainted with them, the more they excelled in their Brutality," he wrote in his diary. "To mention the Perticulars of their Behaviour would so pollute the Paper I write upon that I must excuse myself."[13] General George Washington's judge advocate William Tudor wrote to his fiancée that "every brutal gratification can be so easily indulged in this place that the army will be debauched here in a month more than in twelve at Cambridge."[14]

Although it couldn't hold a candle to New York, Boston's redlight district was somewhat notorious as well, and was actually identified on maps of the city as "Mount Whoredom" until 1823.[15] A British Lieutenant named Richard Williams was shocked that the historical epicenter of Puritanism would have such a toleration for the world's oldest profession, noting in his journal that "there's perhaps no town of its size [that] could turn out more whores than this could."[16]

While Lieutenant Williams claimed to be appalled by the prevalence of such vice in colonial America, perhaps as a Brit he should not have been too surprised. After all, in his native country, prostitution was widely accepted in the 18th century, as evidenced by the existence of directories that openly listed the locations of brothels.[17] It is estimated that Britain's sex industry was worth about £10.4 million at the end of the century, compared to its construction industry which was valued at £4.5 million. There were approximately 50,000 prostitutes working in London in the late 18th century, making sex work the second-largest employer of women, after domestic service.[18]

Indeed, crime of all sorts—ranging from homicide to highway robbery to property crime to smuggling and poaching—was pernicious in England, leading to the adoption of novel and innovative approaches to handle the challenge. Common punishments were floggings and brandings, but these sanctions did not suffice as a deterrent or to reduce recidivism. Popular opinion consequently grew in eighteenth-century England to deport "Malcontents in the State" who might disrupt the "body politick," and the American colonies were increasingly considered a suitable place for those of "lower conditions." In the early 18th century, King James I recommended deportation to America as a policy to both populate the New World and offer a form of reprieve to condemned convicts. So, starting with the adoption of the Transportation Act in 1718, the British began experimenting with convict transport, and for the next six decades—until the revolution broke out in the mid–1770s—more than 52,000 convicts were transported from the British Isles to America, to be sold as slaves to the highest bidder.[19]

So many were sent to the New World, in fact, that it led to growing consternation among the colonial elite, with Benjamin Franklin complaining in 1751 that England was forcing these convict transfers against their wishes. "The Government at home will not suffer our mistaken Assemblies to make any Law for preventing or discouraging the Importation of Convicts from Great Britain," Franklin wrote in the *Pennsylvania Gazette*, "for this kind Reason, 'That such Laws are against the Publick Utility, as they tend to prevent the Improvement and Well Peopling of the Colonies.'"[20]

In spite of these complaints, as late as 1773, even on the brink of war with troubles growing in the colony, a London police magistrate continued to advocate for transporting convicts to America as "the wisest, … most humane and effectual, punishment we have." Not only did the practice "remove the evil" from England, he reasoned, it "gives [the criminal] a fresh opportunity of being an useful member of society."[21] With America seen as an effective and appropriate place of penance due to its hardship and remoteness, the exiles were sent across the ocean with increasing frequency, and the use of convict labor became so popular that it essentially replaced indentured servitude.[22] By the time of the revolution, it is estimated that transported convicts made up a quarter of the British immigrants in America,[23] influencing London's perceptions of the colonies as a haven of unruly and undesirable elements.[24]

The history of criminals settling America is today not well-known since historical records of the transported convicts are scarce, and therefore it is difficult to judge the full impact it had on the development of the American character including its tendencies of degeneracy and rebelliousness. As Anthony Vaver explains in his study of the topic, *Bound with an Iron Chain: The Untold Story of How the British Transported 50,000 Convicts to Colonial America*, the felons who came to America were mostly illiterate and at any rate were generally not inclined to write about their experiences. "If anything, they wanted to hide their criminal past, not record it for posterity," Vaver points out.[25] Likewise, the merchants who engaged in the transport of convicts tended to keep their activities discreet, careful to shield their methods and profits from authorities, as well as from unscrupulous competitors.

But although this lack of documentation poses challenges for historians, many of the contemporaries of these convicts were well aware of their existence, as newspapers often reported on the exploits of notorious criminals such as Englishman Jack Sheppard who became a media sensation in both Britain and the colonies after he somehow broke out of prison despite being chained to the floor.[26] Sheppard, a career thief who was arrested and imprisoned five times in the 1720s but managed to escape four times—sometimes with the help of his prostitute lady friends—became something of a folk hero among the poor in England. After his final escape from the infamous Newgate Prison, he was later arrested and sentenced to hang. In order to hasten his execution and ensure a less painful death, his supporters pulled on his legs as he hanged from the gallows.[27] Following his demise, "Jack Sheppard" became such a household name that newspapers would casually drop it nearly a century later with the assumption being that readers would understand the reference. "As will might we fancy that a king of England would write a letter of compliment to Jack Sheppard in the condemned hole of Newgate," read an 1802 article in a Richmond newspaper about a slave rebellion in Haiti.[28]

Similarly, Henry Tufts would become something of a legend in New England for generations due to his crimes and jailbreaks. An 1892 book, *Landmarks in Ancient Dover, New Hampshire*, notes that his exploits "have made him proverbially infamous throughout New Hampshire," pointing out that a common colloquial expression to describe "superlative wickedness" was to say, "as big a liar (or thief, etc., etc., as the case might be) as old Hen Turf."[29] But while his iniquitous reputation endured into the 20th century, his autobiography also offered unique perspectives on criminal life, filling a gap in the literature on 18th-century criminality and providing insights into the motivations that may lead people into anti-social behavior.

At times, Henry would go to great lengths to explain why he chose to steal. As Henry tells it, he came from a relatively poor family, with a grandfather who was a clergyman. With no real schooling, he worked on the family farm and occasionally performed odd jobs, claiming that he was generally content as a child but that "lasting happiness was not in store for me." As a youth, he sometimes stole fruit and vegetables from his neighbors but there was no major criminality to speak of, nor were there "those characteristic marks of a depraved disposition, which were so fully developed in my riper manhood."[30] The big turning point seems to be the theft of his father's horse, which gave him a taste for the thrill of the heist. Soon afterwards, he also happened to meet a fellow thief named Dennis who introduced him to the art of breaking and entering.

Although Henry had many female companions, it wasn't until he met a young lady named Lydia Bickford, described as a "Cyprian goddess" and a "bewitching deity," that he fell in love. They settled in the town of Lee, New Hampshire, and had nine children together. There, Henry earned a reputation in the community as a rather brazen thief. According to one story passed down from generation to generation, following a daylight robbery, Henry was seen walking down the street with a large sack slung over his shoulder. The neighbor greeted him and made an off-hand remark about the weather. Apparently, it was an overcast day, so Henry used this as an opportunity to make a sly reference to the black sheep that he had in the sack. He said, "the wether is dark and heavy," which, it would later turn out, was a play on words. Pronounced the same way as "weather," a wether is a male sheep castrated before sexual maturity. Although the passerby didn't think much of his choice of words, the meaning became evident when it was discovered that a black male sheep had been stolen from someone in town.[31]

Henry got away with that offense, but was later arrested and jailed for robbing a store with Dennis. The partners in crime then came up with an ill-conceived idea to escape from jail by setting fire to it, "intending to burn a hole through sufficiently large for our exit," as Henry explained. Unfortunately, the fire spread "with surprising rapidity, and began blazing, inside and out, with much briskness," proving this method of escape "impracticable." He and his fellow inmate were forced to begin shouting for help to avoid perishing in the smoke and flames. Despite nearly destroying the jailhouse, Henry was offered a deal to avoid further punishment. The prosecutor told Henry that if he would serve three months on his brother's ship on a voyage to the West Indies, and pay his wages as a fine, he would be "liberated." The prosecutor, as an encouragement to good behavior, even furnished Tufts with two quintals of fish for the sea venture.[32]

Tufts readily agreed, but then on the way to the ship to serve out his sentence, he had a change of heart and decided to head to western New Hampshire instead. Now a fugitive from justice, he worked for a while as a driver at a fort on the Connecticut River, and then proceeded to Claremont, New Hampshire, where he was employed by a farmer named Enoch Judd. Tufts married one of Judd's daughters, the news of which would get back to Lydia, who was still his lawful wife. When he returned to Lydia, she gave him "an uncouth welcome," but they eventually worked it out and "cohabited … as formerly."[33]

Tufts then met a "kindred soul" named James Smith, with whom he would launch a partnership stealing "hens, turkies, sheep and the like." They would eventually graduate to robbing a store, stealing "cloths to the value of about one hundred dollars, two guineas in money, sundry pieces of silver, with a large quantity of other articles." But Tufts would be caught again and since he had by that time earned a reputation for breaking out of jail, the authorities took necessary precautions and placed him in a dungeon for 90 days, chained and shackled in solitary confinement as he awaited trial. He describes this three-month period of "sufferings" in some detail:

> My feet were shackled together with a large iron bolt, of two feet in length, which, at either end, was fastened with rivets to the irons surrounding my ancles; a strong chain, of two feet only, proceeded from the bolt to the floor, and was there secured with a huge iron staple. These iron appendages kept my feet at just such a distance asunder, and rendered my stepping one foot before the other upon the floor, altogether impossible. It was with extreme difficulty I could reach the place of office, or stretch my limbs on a miserable couch of straw. In such deplorable condition I continued ninety days and nights … sequestered from all intercourse with the rest of mankind, and accompanied only with pain, shame, remorse and darkness, in a mansion of darkness, with hardly sufficient food and clothing to prevent me from perishing.[34]

At long last, Henry was put on trial and found guilty. As punishment, he received 20 lashes and was confined again to the dungeon for another 31 days. This time, though, he was prepared with a plan to escape. "In a few days my friends supplied me with instruments, by which, with much toil, I drilled a hole through the wall, sufficiently capacious, when stript to the skin, for my corporal exit," he writes.[35]

He returned to his "thievish pursuits," and again, he would provide the reader ample justifications for his crimes. While his initial actions were explained by providing a litany of grievances against his father, Tufts offered rationales for later resuming his criminal career out of sheer necessity, claiming that he often stole simply to prevent from going hungry. "My farming business was wholly interrupted," Tufts explains, "and I durst not venture to hire out." Faced with the choice of hunger or crime, he chose crime. "To steal or starve, then, was the question," he writes. "I wisely preferred the former, and drove a brisk stroke at the dangerous pursuit."[36]

* * *

Despite the transgressions he recorded, Henry Tufts demonstrated through his writings that he was not just a one-dimensional, mindless criminal, but was actually something of an Enlightenment man, peppering his narrative with casual references to Cicero and Greco-Roman mythology. With epigraphs including quotations from Milton and Shakespeare, passages in his book allude to common themes of Enlightenment thinking, in particular an emphasis on finding genuine happiness and pursuing a life of ease, or "the good life" as Plato and Aristotle called it, as well as an appreciation for education and knowledge. And although he is best known as a criminal, he also had some artistic talent and poetic flair, with each chapter of his book ending with a small engraving and verses interspersed throughout the text. "Hail!" reads one of his brief poems, "heroes, patriots divine, On whom the rays of freedom shine With bright meridian blaze, Once more conven'd to celebrate Your rising empire's glorious date, And Freedom's column raise."[37]

While Tufts referred repeatedly in his book to themes of accentuating pleasure and contentment, Samuel Adams tended to emphasize instead the need for vigilance in defense of liberty and the dangers of complacency. "Among the Numbers of Men," Adams wrote, "are to be found not only those who have 'preferred ease, slumber, and good chear to liberty'; but others, who have eagerly sought after Thrones, and Sceptres, hereditary shares in Sovereignty Riches … and many other childish play things, at the expence of real Nobility, without one thought, or care for the liberty, and happiness of the rest of Mankind."[38] But although Tufts and Adams emphasized different aspects of what makes happiness possible, with Tufts focusing on how he might overcome his "sufferings" and Adams intent on overcoming "tyranny," both sought to establish a reality in which strife and adversity were replaced with wellbeing and comfort. This, ultimately, is what the Enlightenment was all about, and in turn, what inspired the American Revolution.

The political upheaval of the period was based largely on the development of new ideas questioning the legitimacy of monarchy and the divine right of kings. The Enlightenment, though, was not just concerned with spreading liberty and republican values—it sought to establish a civilization based on knowledge and reason. By developing humanity's

The end of each chapter of Henry Tufts's *Narrative* is punctuated with etchings presumably made by the author. Here is a small sample (Henry Tufts, *A Narrative of the Life, Adventures, Travels and Sufferings of Henry Tufts, Now Residing at Lemington, in the District of Maine In substance, as compiled from his own mouth*, Samuel Bragg, 1807).

intellectual capacity and reducing ignorance and superstition, a more universal happiness would naturally follow. As Samuel Adams described the Enlightenment Man: "The Man of good understanding who has been well educated, and improves these advantages as far as his circumstances will allow, in promoting the happiness of Mankind."[39]

New innovations were intended not just to produce more efficiency and productivity, but to increase the ease of living. These advancements could be seen everywhere, with eighteenth-century inventions including such marvels as the steam engine, the tuning fork, the piano, the thermometer, the threshing machine, and the spinning mule. Enlightenment thinkers believed that these novelties would not only make life better but might even help to vanquish evil. When a pump was invented to remove stagnant water from ships, for instance, Benjamin Rush wrote that "the machine may further tend to lessen the inconveniencies of long sea voyages," and in doing so "affords a fresh proof of the dominion of human reason over natural evil, and it may serve to nourish a hope that the time will come when, comparatively speaking, 'evil there shall be none' upon the surface of our globe."[40]

The inventions were all part of the development of a systematic approach to increasing pleasure and reducing pain, which was a recurring theme in the writings of Enlightenment philosophers. Sometimes, this systematic approach to pain reduction and pleasure maximization would reach rather absurd levels, with algebraic equations offered to help people along in their pursuit of happiness. "Suppose A, B, and C, three distinct Beings; A and B, animate, capable of Pleasure and Pain, C an inanimate Piece of Matter, insensible of either," wrote Benjamin Franklin in *A Dissertation on Liberty and Necessity, Pleasure and Pain*. "A receives ten Degrees of Pain, which are necessarily succeeded by ten Degrees of Pleasure: B receives fifteen of Pain, and the consequent equal Number of Pleasure: C all the while lies unconcern'd, and as he has not suffer'd the former, has no right to the latter." Franklin goes on to explain that nothing can be more equal and just than this, because "A has no Reason to complain that his Portion of Pleasure was five Degrees less than that of B, for his Portion of Pain was five Degrees less likewise." Ultimately, according to Franklin's calculations, "They are then both on the same Foot with C, that is, they are neither Gainers nor Losers."[41]

But of course, in the real world, there were gainers and losers, as well as significant impediments to true happiness, and many of these related to the failure to counter evil, both in society at large and within the individual. "There are some ends," wrote William Wollaston in his 1722 work *The Religion of Nature Delineated*, "by which the nature of things and truth require us to aim at, and at which therefore if we do not aim, nature and truth are denied." Wollaston explains that "if a man does not desire to prevent evils, and to be happy, he denies both his own nature and the nature and definition of happiness to be what they are."[42] Enlightenment, in this sense, was not just a matter of republican ideals, or material comfort and a reduction of pain, but one of personal and social morality. True happiness could only be achieved when one becomes enlightened enough to know how to properly treat other people. This is a lesson that Henry Tufts, through his life of adversity and habitually committing wrongs against others—whether his many love interests or the victims of his thefts—would come to learn all too well. In fact, as he tells it, this is what prompted him to share his life story.

As Henry explains, the value of writing the book was not simply to share a bunch of amusing anecdotes, but rather as a cautionary tale to others, intended to influence the younger generation to pursue moral endeavors. Henry refers to himself as a "slave to vice," who, due to his poor choices, experiences a lifetime of "rugged trials" and "bitter sufferings,"[43] expressing hope that his story will serve as a "caveat to others, to shun such pursuits as have involved me in complicated difficulties and rendered my life truly miserable."[44]

Laying bare all of his transgressions, Henry observes that while "history of the wise and benevolent is beneficial to society, by serving as a pattern or stimulous to deeds equally laudable; that of the vicious, affords, also, instruction, by shewing the effects of vice and immorality." In contrast to the many stories that are told celebrating the accomplishments and wisdom of national heroes, according to this view, the stories of scoundrels are equally important. "The one does good, positively, by alluring to virtue," Henry writes, "the other, negatively, by exhibiting guilt, infamy and punishment, as dissuasives from vice."[45] Ultimately, Henry observes that "both may lead to the same end, although the opposites of each other."

* * *

Henry's reflections are in keeping with Enlightenment ideas that sought to explain the underlying motivations for crime and dissuade criminal activity by addressing its root causes. Samuel Adams, Thomas Jefferson and others offered alternatives to the harsh penal codes of the colonial era, advocating for punishments that focused on compelling criminals to feel their internal guilt through extended periods of imprisonment, rather than relying on public shaming through flogging and mutilation.[46] Concepts popularized by Italian philosopher Cesare Beccaria offered alternatives to the traditional approach to criminal justice, with a focus on developing individual reason to inspire virtuous behavior rather than simply implementing draconian punishments as a disincentive to vice. His views were attractive to republican-minded Whigs and his seminal tract, titled *On Crimes and Punishments*, published in English in 1767, was widely read by the Founding Fathers. Beccaria's ideas inspired a number of state constitutions to prohibit "cruel and unusual punishments" in an effort to make them "less sanguinary."

"Pleasure and pain are the only springs of actions in beings endowed with sensibility," Beccaria wrote. "Even amongst the motives which incite men to acts of religion, the invisible legislator has ordained rewards and punishments." A man who has sufficiently developed reason will be more content, according to Beccaria, because he more fully understands the world and therefore may more aptly enjoy its pleasures and avoid its pains.

Beccaria argued that virtue is not a constant concept but is malleable "in proportion to the alteration of circumstances." Rather than being an eternal truth, he wrote that "the passions and vices of one age are the foundation of the morality of the following."[47]

Similarly, Henry Tufts, in his book, writes, "if fable and romance have long amused the world and attracted its notice, why shall not plain truth and real fact, though clad in plebeian habiliments, elicit subordinate attention?" He observes that "one property of truth is, whether it illustrate virtue or depict vice, to afford manner from which some inference may be drawn or moral extracted, conducive to the use and benefit of mankind."[48] Candidly offering his lessons and showing the destructiveness of his choices upon himself and others might help inspire moral behavior, Tufts claims.

Whether Tufts was aware of it or not, his *Narrative* followed a long line of criminal histories that were printed in colonial New England, beginning with Cotton Mather publishing a 1699 book called *Pillars of Salt: An History of Some Criminals Executed in This Land for Capital Crimes*. As Mather explained it, this collection of true crime anecdotes was intended to "correct and reform" people's propensities towards sinfulness and "to suppress growing vice." In the book, Mather explains that "crime itself was its own punishment [in that] a man could not be worse punished than by being Left unto such a Beastly Crime," adding, "Sin is its own plague."[49]

Other books would appear in subsequent years with titles such as *The American Bloody Register* and *The United States Criminal Calendar*. These collections provided details on the offenses of convicted criminals, sharing their pre-execution confessions and last words for all to read. In another book, titled *A narrative of the life and conversion of Alexander White*, a young sailor who was convicted of murder implores the reader to disavow crime and shares his mental anguish over the fate that he had created for himself:

> Oh wretched creature that I am, how can I think to face God Almighty, after abusing his holy law as I have done. O what an amazing thing it is to think of the mercy and patience of such a mighty power! O why does he not sink the world in a moment! Why does he not destroy ME without mercy![50]

Opposite: cover page for the 1699 publication *Pillars of Salt*, by Cotton Mather. This book was intended to "correct and reform" criminal behavior and "suppress growing vice" in the Massachusetts Bay Colony. Providing gratuitous tales of violence and declaring that "sin is its own plague," Mather hoped to terrify criminals into abandoning their wicked ways. The book also helped satisfy readers' fascination with crime, not unlike Henry Tufts's book that would come out a little more than a century later (Printed by B. Green, and J. Allen, for Samuel Phillips, 1699).

Pillars of Salt.

An HISTORY
OF SOME
CRIMINALS Executed in this Land,
FOR
Capital Crimes.
With some of their Dying
Speeches ;
Collected and Published,
For the WARNING of such as *Live* in
Destructive *Courses* of Ungodliness.

Whereto is added,
For the better Improvement of this History,
A Brief Discourse about the Dreadful
Justice of God, in Punishing of
S I N, with S I N.

By Cotton Mather.
Deut. 19. 20.
Those which remain shall hear & fear, and shall henceforth commit no more any such Evil among you.

BOSTON in New-England.
Printed by B. Green, and J. Allen, for Samuel Phillips at the Brick Shop near the Old Meeting-House. 1699.

In 1791, a criminal by the name of Stephen Burroughs was asked by an acquaintance to write his story and replied with a letter that offered some thoughts about what he had learned from a life of crime. "I have learned fortitude in the school of adversity," Burroughs wrote to his friend. "In draining the cup of bitterness to its dregs, I have been taught to despise the occurrences of misfortune." He explained that he had come to believe that happiness is found in the "ability of preventing that misery which is so common to unfortunate situations." Despite the fact that most people are "apt to be governed by the opinion of others," true happiness is simply a "state of mind" which is regulated by each individual, he explained.[51]

Burroughs ultimately decided to follow his friend's advice and write his memoirs, adding his to a well-established genre of books that were ostensibly intended to provide moral lessons and dissuade readers from criminality but the popularity of which may have been an indication that many Americans—then as now—enjoyed reading about criminal behavior for the vicarious thrill or to better understand the dark side of human nature. While earlier books were framed almost entirely as "final confessions" and "dying speeches," focusing on the criminal's end-of-life attempts to repent and redeem themselves, and affirmed the righteousness of the broader society, Burroughs's and Tufts's narratives represented a new trend—one that dramatized the criminal's defiance of authority and attempts to escape the limitations placed on the individual by law and societal norms. In this way, the book was in keeping with the broader currents taking place in society to resist the Crown's infringements on natural rights, serving as a reminder of the stark reality of human nature as the revolutionaries sought to replace monarchical rule with republican governance. Samuel Adams, in particular, was seen as an acute judge of his fellow man, described by loyalist Peter Oliver as someone who "understood human Nature, in low life, so well, that he could turn the Minds of the great Vulgar as well as the small into any Course that he might chuse."[52]

Adams, like many of the American revolutionaries, was informed in his views on human nature by European political philosophers such as Jean Jacques Rousseau, Baron de Montesquieu, John Locke, and Thomas Hobbes, who described life as "solitary, poor, nasty, brutish, and short" because individuals are in a "war of all against all."[53] Locke argued that government is morally obliged to protect life, liberty, and property, and that when government fails to live up to these obligations, people may legitimately rebel. "The state of nature has a law of nature to govern it, which obliges every one: and reason, which is that law, teaches all mankind, who will but consult it, that being all equal and independent, no one ought to harm another in his life, health, liberty, or possessions," Locke wrote in 1689.[54]

These arguments found a receptive audience among colonists who saw unmistakable parallels between what Locke described as the "state of nature" and their own struggle to build a life in the New World. Having achieved some material success, they saw it as fundamentally tyrannical for a faraway government to seize that hard-earned wealth through unfair taxes and to impose other restrictions on their "natural rights," including their right to move westward and settle new lands. Influenced by the ideas of Locke, Adams would develop his family's personal experiences into a coherent argument for resisting tyrannical authority, explained eloquently in *The Rights of the Colonists*, published in 1772. "Among the natural rights of the Colonists are these," Samuel Adams wrote:

> First, a right to life. Secondly, to liberty. Thirdly, to property; together with the right to support and defend them in the best manner they can. These are evident branches of, rather than deductions from, the duty of self-preservation, commonly called the first law of nature.[55]

Locke's and Adams's assertions of natural rights were tempered by the Hobbesian worldview, which focused on the natural inclination of people to dominate others. This conception of human nature, confirmed in some ways by the existence of incorrigible criminals like Henry Tufts, deeply influenced the founders' approach to grand principles related to "natural rights," as well as more mundane concerns about crime and public safety.

Even in a time of widespread lawlessness such as the 1760s and '70s, a time in which respectable merchants like John Hancock routinely violated customs duties, Henry Tufts was an example of someone who took unlawful behavior too far and committed it for the wrong reasons. If he had teamed up with the patriots and put his talents to work smuggling tea, he might have been seen as a revolutionary hero, but by stealing from the wrong people, he was deemed a common criminal—widely seen by his contemporaries, as Henry understood, as "a pest to society."

Although the reader of his autobiography would barely notice it from the narrative he provides, Henry Tufts's descent into a life of crime directly coincided with the colonies' descent into a bloody war that would ultimately lead to independence from England. Not unlike Tufts breaking away from his father, patriots were increasingly advocating for eliminating the bonds that held together monarchical rule—namely kinship, patriarchy and patronage.[56]

Seeking to replace these arbitrary and outdated modes of social relations with those based on merit, respect and consent, in the 1760s—about the time that Tufts was launching his career as a thief—Boston Whigs were launching increasingly bold acts of civil disobedience and sometimes violent resistance to British rule. Their goal was the establishment of a society based on virtue and disinterested public leadership that would be more resistant, if not immune, from the sort of corruption and tyranny that they increasingly identified in the king's dominion over the colonies. Like Tufts, they would justify their actions as necessary by citing a litany of abuses that they endured at the hands of the British, who, for their part, categorically rejected colonial grievances and responded to the growing unrest with further oppression.

3

Legitimate Lawlessness

About the time that Henry Tufts was complaining about his unfair treatment at the hands of his father and launching his life of crime in the 1760s, Samuel Adams and many of his fellow colonists were launching acts of resistance over unfair treatment by the British Parliament, King George III and local customs officials, in particular a series of laws passed intended to increase revenue from the colonies and clamp down on smuggling. Not unlike Henry Tufts, who responded to a perceived injustice by taking matters into his own hands, people throughout the colonies would engage in collective direct action to place a check on what they saw as overreaching by London. Although colonial authorities would attempt to dismiss the grievances of the colonists as the intemperate complaints of an irrational "rabble," as they were often called, through riots and other mob actions, the rabble would ensure that their concerns were taken seriously. Progressively brazen mob actions prevented customs officials from carrying out their duties and placed the colonists' grievances firmly in the political arena, making it impossible for the monarchy to dismiss them and ultimately upending British plans for reorganizing the empire.[1]

Driven by economic interests and by fervently held convictions of liberty rooted in their English identity, shaped by the history of the Magna Carta of 1215 institutionalizing legal protections of freedom against arbitrary authority and the British Bill of Rights of 1689 providing for jury trials and other civil rights, firebrands launched protest actions that served both to promote colonial unity and to clearly define the sides of the struggle. Descending from early waves of English emigration, these colonists zealously protected every right that they assumed as Englishmen and fiercely defended their prerogatives of self-government. Ever since the Massachusetts Body of Liberties was adopted in 1641, which codified the colonists' privileges deriving from the Magna Carta, the settlers of Massachusetts, as well as other colonies such as Maryland, Virginia, and Pennsylvania, assiduously asserted their rights to jury trials and a free press, as well as to petition lawmaking bodies and peaceably assemble.[2]

The revolutionary crisis that ensued in the mid-18th century may have been driven by the Enlightenment ideas given voice by English political thinkers such as Thomas Hobbes and John Locke but the fundamental impetus was the perceived disrespect the British showed to their subjects, targeting trade and threatening the profitability of colonists' businesses. Laws adopted by Parliament, in disregard of the objections expressed in the colonies, tended to be implemented arbitrarily and unevenly, which drove many merchants into opposition to the Crown. Customs officials were deeply entangled in local politics, which made evenhanded enforcement of the law impossible and led to an increasing sense of unfairness.[3]

This unfairness was rooted in the fact that for generations, the colonists enjoyed a high degree of self-government and did not pay direct taxes to the Crown. When drastic changes started to be made with the introduction of new laws adopted by Parliament without input from the colonies, some who were already primed for rebellion like Samuel Adams would begin fighting back. Although the British generally considered the colonies subservient to the Crown and viewed them primarily as useful tools for their broader global ambitions, by violating their natural rights, they increasingly raised the ire of uncompromising patriots. As colonists grew discontented over breaches of these rights and London attempted to assert more control through increasingly draconian measures, the revolutionary crisis escalated in an ongoing series of reciprocal hostilities.

In the early stages, much of this conflict would play out as a personal dispute between key figures such as Samuel Adams and lieutenant-governor and then-governor Thomas Hutchinson. Like Adams and Tufts, Hutchinson's ancestors were long-time residents of New England, and he became one of the most respected and influential figures in Massachusetts. One of Adams's main complaints against Hutchinson, in fact, was that as a Massachusetts native, he routinely betrayed the colonists by siding with London. Adams wrote that the colonists had the "most sanguine expectations [of Hutchinson] as being born and educated among us, and who we are told accepted the government with great reluctance,"[4] and therefore were baffled by Hutchinson's implementation of the Crown's policies. Adams turned Hutchinson into a scapegoat for British tyranny, over time essentially ruining his political reputation, while Hutchinson for his part considered Adams a character assassin and personally blamed him for inciting the mob and exploiting grievances for illegitimate ends.[5]

To the revolutionaries, however, resistance to unjust laws was legitimate and could not be equated with common crime. The existence of vagabonds like Henry Tufts drew a contrast between vice and virtue, as well as crime and justifiable rebellion. During the revolutionary period, lawbreaking was justified if it was directed at the appropriate targets—namely

King George III and his minions—but not if the victims were fellow colonists, unless of course they were deemed loyal to the Crown. In the case of attacking loyalists and enforcers of unpopular laws, riots and mob actions were considered acceptable tools of coercion and resistance.

In a society defined by stringently enforced hierarchical codes and mores, the upper class attempted to discredit the colonists' grievances by highlighting the lower class's lack of education and refinement, but they found it difficult to dismiss the moral urgency and effectiveness of a riot.[6] While these sorts of protest had taken place sporadically throughout the 18th century and would operate under various legal statuses—sometimes sanctioned by the authorities as a posse comitatus—as the 1760s got under way, they would take on a new and more openly lawless character, leading stamp agents and other colonial officials to recoil in terror. While the actions were wrapped in the rhetoric of liberty, ultimately they were inspired by a spirit of rebellion rooted in economic and geopolitical realities emerging from the turmoil following England's victory in the French and Indian War, as the North American theater of the Seven Years' War was known.[7]

* * *

Following the conclusion of this war in 1763, Britain had gained control of French Canada but in doing so nearly doubled its national debt. In order to manage the newly acquired land, the Crown sent additional troops to the continent and required the colonists to pay for the soldiers' expense of coming to and residing in British North America. From the British perspective, the colonies existed as a means of enriching the empire, and with the American colonies increasingly seen as a drain on the royal coffers, King George III viewed taxes on the colonists as a necessary measure to raise revenue and to administer newly acquired territory. The king's attempts to increase control over the colonies and ensure that they were contributing their fair share included the Royal Proclamation of 1763, the Sugar Act of 1764, the Quartering Act of 1765, the Stamp Act of 1765, the Declaratory Act of 1766, and the Townshend Acts of 1767.

The Sugar Act, a tax on molasses imported into the colonies from the West Indies, was a trade regulation intended to raise revenue while curtailing smuggling but was seen as disproportionately affecting Massachusetts and the other New England colonies that depended on the molasses for their rum distilling industries. It was during the protests surrounding the Sugar Act that Samuel Adams, as a member of the Town Meeting, began to emerge as a prominent voice in local politics. Soon finding himself involved with various resistance groups including the Sons of Liberty, the Monday Night Club and the North End Club,[8] Adams began advocating for all 13 colonies to unite in opposition to the Sugar Act and started to emphasize the issue of "taxation without representation." He warned that the Sugar Act was just the first salvo in what would surely be more unjust taxes imposed by Westminster and Whitehall, arguing that without principled resistance from the colonies, the Sugar Act would lead to a slippery slope of ever-increasing encroachments on the right to property. "For if our Trade may be taxed, why not our Lands?" Adams wrote. "Why not the Produce of our Lands & everything we possess or make use of?"[9]

Samuel Adams's fears would be realized the following year with the Stamp Act, which required that colonists use stamped paper produced in London, carrying an embossed revenue stamp, for the printing of legal documents, magazines, playing cards, newspapers, and other types of paper used throughout the colonies. Going beyond this comprehensive taxation on nearly all activities in the colonies that required paper, the Act also included a provision to replace jury trials with trials in Admiralty Court.

Adams expressed the views of many when he wrote that the law "annihilates the most valuable privileges of our Charter, deprives us of the most essential rights of Britons, and greatly weakens the best security of our Lives, Liberties and Estates."[10] He also personalized the issue, directing vitriol at local officials and Lieutenant Governor Hutchinson, despite the fact that Hutchinson, in his private correspondence at least, had made clear his opposition to the Stamp Act from the beginning, and earnestly tried to convey to London the Massachusetts colony's opposition to the law.

In October and November 1764, Hutchinson chaired a committee that attempted to revise a petition to Parliament prepared by the Massachusetts legislature, which was seen as too strident in its tone. The original draft stated the colony's objections to the stamp duties in theoretical terms, grounded in principles of natural rights, which Hutchinson's committee considered "informal and incautiously expressed," followed by two new versions, which were "both very exceptionable." Hutchinson, being perhaps better in tune with the proper way to express complaints to a king, attempted to explain the folly of expressing grandiose principles and urged instead the need for calm and compromise. Emphasizing the logic of supporting existing structures because they were the basis of civil order, Hutchinson tried to avoid shrill and counterproductive approaches that would only serve to widen the rift between London and the colonies. The result was a watered-down version, which appealed to London for allowing American control over taxation as "a matter of favor," rather than "a claim of right."[11]

In spite of this attempt at a diplomatic and conciliatory approach, the Stamp Act was adopted anyway, a development that many blamed on Hutchinson, thinking that his softening of the petition had emboldened London. Had it been more uncompromising, the malcontents believed, the king might have taken them more seriously. Plus, since the true focus of their ire—Parliament and King George III—were thousands of miles away, the local enforcers of the law would have to suffice as surrogate targets. The imposition of the law sparked outrage throughout the colonies, leading to riots breaking out from Portsmouth, New Hampshire, to Savannah, Georgia, with mobs at ports blocking British ships from landing with stamp papers. Street theater played a powerful role in the protests, with effigies put on "trial," hanged and thrown into bonfires, while others were buried, beaten with cudgels, or shot with pistols. Conscious of the power of public displays to rally the people, demonstrators constructed 12-foot tall Stamp Act monsters with illuminated heads and paraded them through town.[12] The demonstrations were complemented by an effective strategy of nonimportation that was coordinated by the small businessmen and principal merchants of Boston.[13]

* * *

Following the adoption of the law, a cousin of Samuel Adams named Henry Bass and several others formed the Loyal Nine resistance group. Gathering at what became known as the Liberty Tree, this group hung an effigy of the local stamp master, Andrew Oliver, and on August 14, 1765, a crowd carried it to his home and burned it. The mob then pulled down the fence that surrounded Oliver's house, smashed the windows, raided his wine cellar, and destroyed much of his furniture. The action targeting Oliver's property symbolized the general argument that colonists made about the British government failing to respect individuals' personal property without being represented in the taxing body.

Not satisfied that the message had been heard, two weeks later, on August 26, a mob attacked the home of Thomas Hutchinson. With thousands of onlookers, Hutchinson's brick mansion was thoroughly ransacked, with the interior walls torn down, furniture smashed to pieces, and the garden ripped up. During the eight hours of mayhem, the axe-wielding mob hacked beds to pieces, tore down curtains, and destroyed or scattered all of Hutchinson's books and papers, including many important historical documents covering Massachusetts's early colonial past. The rioters also carried off paintings, jewelry, clocks, china, silver, and even Hutchinson's microscope and telescope.[14]

The following day, the Boston Town Meeting convened in Faneuil Hall to express its "utter detestation" over the attack. Individual chapters of the Sons of Liberty, such as the Milford, Connecticut, group, declared their "greatest abhorrence" of the lawlessness. The Annapolis group declared its opposition to "all riots or unlawful assemblies tending to the disturbance of the public tranquility."[15] Among those who publicly expressed disapproval was Samuel Adams, speaking out both at Faneuil Hall and in a letter to a friend in London. He wrote that the August 26 attack was of a "truly mobbish nature" and expressed support to the magistrate "in preventing or suppressing any further disorder."[16]

Regarding the attack two weeks earlier on Oliver's home, however, Adams was exultant. Excusing the rioters' excesses, Adams argued that they only intended to sacrifice an effigy and Oliver's mansion just "fell in their way" and, furthermore, the damage had been modest.[17] With Oliver resigning his office, Adams celebrated it as a momentous occasion that should be recorded in the history books. In an article in the *Boston Gazette*, Adams hailed "the Sons of Liberty [who] on the 14th of August 1765, a Day which ought to be for ever remembered in America, animated with a zeal for their country then upon the brink of destruction, and resolved at once to save her." He spoke in biblical terms, comparing the mob with Samson and likening the target of their wrath with the Philistines. "The People shouted," Adams wrote, "and their shout was heard to the distant end of this Continent." He relished the terror that the ransacking of Oliver's home must have sent through the colonies, noting that "every Stampman trembled" when he heard the news, "and swore by his Maker, that he would never execute a commission which he had so infamously received."[18]

With no officer daring to apprehend the leaders of the riots, no attorney general willing to prosecute them, and no Bostonian willing to testify against them, a climate of impunity began to set in.[19] The rioters who trashed the

Left: **Published in newspapers throughout the colonies in late 1765, variations of a skull-and-crossbones "stamp" served as a warning against royal officials enforcing the Stamp Act. Under the law, anyone who purchased anything printed on paper was required to buy a revenue stamp for it, leading to protests, riots and mob actions throughout the colonies (*Pennsylvania Journal and Weekly Advertiser*, October 24, 1765, Library of Congress).**

homes of two prominent colonial officials walked the streets with de facto immunity from prosecution and word began to circulate that anyone who tried to sell the officially stamped paper would be killed. Newspapers carried menacing skull-and-crossbones cartoons as warnings to customs officials and the commander of the British forces in North America, Thomas Gage, alluded to the dread that ran rampant when he confided that "each individual feared he might be the next Victim to their Rapacity."[20] The Brits began to realize that it would be impossible to enforce the Stamp Act.[21]

In response to the growing threat against royal officials and in an effort to pacify the colonists' anger, Parliament repealed the law on March 18, 1766. On the very same day, however, it attempted to reassert the prerogative of Westminster and Whitehall to exercise "full power and authority" over the colonies by passing the Declaratory Act, which reaffirmed Parliament's power to tax the colonists.

* * *

Historians have long debated what direct role, if any, Samuel Adams may have played in whipping up mobs in the 1760s and specifically whether he had a hand in the attacks on Oliver's and Hutchinson's homes. Stanford professor of history John C. Miller, who published a biography of Adams in 1936, alleges that he "spirited up the mobs which terrorized Boston during the revolutionary period" and "inflamed the mob against the lieutenant governor by picturing him as the author of the Stamp Act."[22] Despite the fact that Hutchinson opposed the act and raised objections to London, Adams and others had spread the rumor that he had been personally involved in the planning and execution of the unpopular law. Historian William Fowler, Jr., concurs with Miller, noting in his 1997 biography of Adams that he clearly knew about the mob actions in advance, and provided "at the very least tacit consent."[23]

Some historians are also skeptical of Adams's protestations of shock and outrage over the trashing of Hutchinson's house, noting that he may well have been dismayed by the excess of the ransacking, but only because it was counterproductive. As Richard Brookhiser, author of *America's First Dynasty: The Adamses*, has explained, the attack served as a source of genuine shock in Boston and its "intensity conferred on its target, for a while at least, the aura of martyrdom." Brookhiser calls Samuel Adams's expressions of dismay over the attack a "sham," noting that "Adams had been defaming Thomas Hutchinson in print and in public meetings; it was his polemics more than anything else that had stirred the mob up."[24]

Others, however, note that as an adherent of John Locke, Adams would not have supported mob violence at this stage in the struggle.

Pointing out that lawful methods of seeking redress to grievances were still available in 1765, another Adams biographer—the University of Cincinnati's John Alexander—contends that followers of Locke would have rejected violence and instead supported civil action to ensure that the government lived up to its obligations to protect life, liberty, and property. Locke, after all, advocated a representative form of government, not rule by the mob. He argued for the justness of the rule of law and executive prerogative, stressing that legislative remedies preserve the political community. Protesting the Quartering Act of 1765, Adams quoted Locke who wrote, "Where Law ends, … TYRANNY begins, if the Law be transgress'd to anothers harm." Expanding on this principle, Adams observed that "it is always safe to ADHERE TO THE LAW, and to keep every man of every denomination and character WITHIN ITS BOUNDS." Arguing for using "legal and constitutional methods to prevent the incroachments of ANY KIND OF POWER," Adams insisted on upholding the law, which "is the collected and long digested sentiment OF THE WHOLE."[25]

Even while citing Locke's views on adhering to the law, however, Adams was so infuriated over the injustices endured by the colonies—and particularly the insidious Stamp Act—that he could easily find justification for the right of people to legitimately rebel. As Locke wrote in his *Second Treatise on Government*,

> whenever the Legislators endeavor to take away, and destroy the Property of the People, or to reduce them to Slavery under Arbitrary Power, they put themselves into a state of War with the People, who are thereupon absolved from any farther Obedience, and are left to the common Refuge, which God hath provided for all Men, against Force and Violence.[26]

This oblique justification of "force and violence" was on the forefront of the minds of disgruntled colonists such as Adams, who considered the Stamp Act to be unconstitutional and a blatant violation of the "rights and privileges of natural free born subjects of Great Britain." In his mind, Locke's reference to the legislators destroying the property of the people may have provided the rationale needed for the people to destroy the property of their oppressors. It is a contradictory view but one that is somewhat common among people who feel they have been treated unfairly. This discordant approach on property rights could also be seen in the mentality of Henry Tufts, who resented being denied the right to inherit his father's property but had a hard time respecting the property of others. When Tufts began his life of thievery, as he concedes in his memoirs, he failed to consider the ramifications of his actions on the victims. "Instead of considering the sanctity of individual property," Tufts admits, "my mind was principally employed in adjusting the degrees of impunity, which might,

3. Legitimate Lawlessness

or might not attend, the commission of such deeds in the future."[27] In other words, how he could make sure that he didn't get caught.

* * *

According to the timeline that Tufts provides in his autobiography, the theft of his father's horse would have been in about the year 1768—a heady time in the 13 colonies and particularly in New England. Kicking off with denunciations of the Townshend Acts and calls to boycott British goods, 1768 consisted of a string of escalatory actions and counter-actions that steadily widened the gap between colonists and the Crown, and is said to be the year that Samuel Adams decided that independence was the only way forward for America.[28] Adopted by the British Parliament to assert control over the colonies by suspending an insubordinate representative assembly and by strictly enforcing customs duties, the Townshend Acts were seen as unlawful infringements on colonial rights, further legitimizing law-breaking by colonists.

In February 1768, the Massachusetts House of Representatives issued a circular letter, written by Samuel Adams, that denounced the Townshend Acts. Royal official Lord Hillsborough demanded the letter be revoked, and when the House refused to do so, Governor Francis Bernard dissolved the Massachusetts assembly. The response from the colonists was intensified resistance. Regularly under attack, custom officials were unable to enforce navigation regulations and appealed to London for support. In response, the British sent a warship to Boston, arriving in June 1768, and authorities seized John Hancock's ship *Liberty* for violating the trade acts. This set off a fierce riot, with some 3,000 colonists attacking the customs house and forcing British sailors to retreat to Castle William.[29]

Tensions continued to rise following this incident, and the next year, four American sailors would be charged with killing a British naval officer who had boarded their ship to claim them for the British Navy. Impressment, essentially a legal form of kidnapping, entailed press gangs capturing merchant sailors and taking them by force onto their ship. The ship's officer would then inform the civilian that he was now a sailor in the Royal Navy and that he would be subject to execution if he attempted to desert. Although this practice was legal throughout much of the British Empire, a law passed in the early 1700s prohibited impressment of sailors in America. Regardless, press gangs from the Royal Navy—whether ignorant of the local law or just indifferent—continued the practice, which served as a source of growing tension with the colonists.

On April 22, 1769, British sailors demanded to board the Massachusetts brig *Pitt Packet* as it was approaching the port of Marblehead, Massachusetts. As the press gang attempted to extract several of the crew members for impressment, a scuffle broke out. The six-man crew resisted and in the ensuing fight, one of the sailors, a man named Michael Corbett, was shot in the face. He then took a harpoon and struck it into the throat of Lieutenant Henry Gibson Panton, who was in charge of the gang. Panton died within minutes, and all six crew members were subsequently arrested for murder. Ultimately, Corbett and three others would stand trial before a special 12-member Admiralty Court made up of various military and colonial government officials and would be represented by John Adams and James Otis. Despite being denied a jury of their peers, the men were acquitted on the grounds of justifiable homicide. While avoiding the question of whether any impressment in the colonies was legal, the court held that this particular attempt was illegal, and since there was no warrant presented, the sailors had a right to defend themselves against the illegal use of force.[30]

The acquittal helped quell tensions for a while, but a slew of other grievances continued to contribute to a general climate of lawlessness taking hold in the colonies and especially Massachusetts. London's attempts to collect taxes and enforce customs duties led to violent acts of street justice that grew in frequency and brutality. Anyone deemed to be cooperating with customs officials by reporting violations to authorities could find themselves with a new suit of tar and feathers.

The practice of tar-and-feathering, dating back to medieval times, entailed heating sap from pine trees to a temperature over 140 degrees Fahrenheit, at which point it becomes liquid. With both tar and feathers readily available and the tar-and-feathering punishment seen as an effective means of instilling terror, starting in 1766 it became the go-to tactic used against perceived enemies of the patriot cause. The targets would usually be stripped before being tarred, or—if they were lucky—would have the tar applied directly to their clothes. While the tar was still hot, the mob would dump a bag of feathers over him, or, alternatively, would roll him in a pile of feathers. Then, with the tar hardening and the feathers firmly affixed to their bodies, the victim would be paraded around town and subjected to ridicule. People would frequently jeer the victim, spit at him, and throw objects such as rocks and rotten eggs. In at least one instance, a tar-and-feathering resulted in death, with a suspected loyalist minister tarred, feathered, hanged, and burned in Charleston, South Carolina. According to a contemporary news report,

> This Morning John Roberts, a Dissenting Minister, was seized at this Place, on Suspicion of being an Enemy to the Rights of America, when he was tarred and feathered, after which the Populace, whose Fury could not be appeased, erected a Gibbet, on which they hanged him, and afterwards made a Bonfire, in which Roberts, together with the Gibbet, was consumed to Ashes.[31]

3. Legitimate Lawlessness 59

Boston held its first tar-and-feathering on October 28, 1769. Accused of informing on his own ship for smuggling, George Gailer was stripped, tarred and feathered, and then carried around town for about three hours. He was forced to hold a lantern and the mob also demanded that all residents place candles in their windows to show "support." Houses without candles were pelted with stones. Gailer would file a lawsuit against his tormentors three months later in January 1770, with one of the defendants, the Boston tailor David Bradlee, represented by John Adams. In Gailer's warrant, he alleged that he was

> tarred and feathered ... and with Clubbs, Staves, and a hand saw did then and there strike him the said George Gailer, sundry heavy and grievous Blows, upon the said George Gailers naked Body, and greatly bruise, and wound him and hit him the said George Gailer diverse grievous Blows, with Stones.

Despite this awful ordeal, the case was decided in the defendants' favor because their actions were not considered grievous enough to justify a legal judgment.[32] Notwithstanding his legal defense of Bradlee, John Adams deplored the tactic that was used against Gailer, writing that "these tarrings and featherings ... must be discountenanced."[33] Whether Samuel Adams approved of tar-and-featherings is a matter of debate, which in recent years has been given new life by portrayals in popular culture.

In the first episode of HBO's critically acclaimed *John Adams* miniseries, which first aired in 2008, a customs inspector challenges John Hancock, played by Justin Theroux, for avoiding British taxes, impertinently calling Hancock a "smuggler." To this, Hancock responds, "Teach him a lesson, tar the bastard!" which a mob quickly forms to do. The inspector is stripped of his clothes and his body applied with hot tar as Hancock looks on, along with John Adams, played by Paul Giamatti, and Samuel, played by Danny Huston. At the beginning of the ordeal, a sly grin could be seen on Samuel's face, indicating that he may have taken some pleasure in watching the mob carry out its action, but John cries out, "God, Sam, that's barbarism." He asks his cousin, "Do you approve of this?" to which Samuel declines to answer.

Samuel's silence might be interpreted by the audience as tacit approval of the tar-and-feathering punishment, but of course, the incident depicted does not appear to be based in historical reality—it was likely meant as a composite portrayal of a fictional tar-and-feathering for dramatic effect and as a hint of the brutality that radical Whigs such as Samuel Adams were willing to employ against their enemies. But despite HBO's portrayal, historian Alfred Young has found that "in Boston, Whig leaders," such as Samuel Adams, "invariably were hostile to tar-and-feathering" and even "tried to rescue the victims."[34] Adams's biographer Ira Stoll criticized HBO for "inaccurately, well, tarring the reputations of Hancock and Samuel Adams, and by conjuring a situation that there is no evidence existed."[35]

Be that as it may, the liberal use of tar-and-featherings in the pre-revolutionary period, as well as other acts of violent lawlessness, colored London's perceptions of the colonies, and in particular the people of Boston.

* * *

In England, as parliamentary debates raged over how to deal with the colonial crisis, one parliamentarian argued that "Americans were a strange sett of people, and that it was in vain to expect any degree of reasoning from them; that instead of making their claim by argument, they always chose to decide the matter by tarring and feathering."[36] With the colonists increasingly seen as irrational and dangerous, British soldiers were deployed to Boston in an attempt to restore order. Two regiments, constituting 4,000 troops, were dispatched to Boston in October 1768, which provided some protection to officials implementing customs duties but the contact between British soldiers and colonists also served to increase tensions.

The British troops' deployment was full of hardship, and with little food, bad water and no cooperation from the townspeople, discipline problems—and desertion—ran rampant. The redcoats were fond of cheap New England rum and their attitudes toward the colonists appeared at times to be a mix of envy and contempt, routinely disrespecting the locals by rudely demanding that they identify themselves on command. In his written accounts of the occupation, Samuel Adams tended to amplify every altercation between Bostonians and the occupiers, for example highlighting incidents in which the troops attempted to court the wives of the locals. While many of the sources of friction between the occupiers and occupied were real, in his writings, Adams frequently embellished episodes, with articles in the *Boston Evening Post*, for example, telling tawdry tales of girls brutalized after refusing advances of randy redcoats. Governor Hutchinson complained that nine-tenths of the paper's content was "either absolutely false or grossly misrepresented."[37]

With tensions rising in the town, a crowd gathered on February 22, 1770, outside the house of customs officer Ebenezer Richardson in the North End. The mob threw stones that shattered Richardson's windows, with one striking his wife. Fearful of the mob sacking his home, Richardson fired a gun into the crowd and fatally wounded an 11-year-old boy named Christopher Seider who had joined the protest. It was precisely the sort of incident needed to intensify the struggle. Samuel Adams arranged the funeral, which was attended by more than 2,000 people, and the boy's

3. *Legitimate Lawlessness* 61

This hand-colored engraving by Paul Revere was widely printed in the colonies following the violent confrontation between local residents and British troops on March 5, 1770. Together with the writings of Samuel Adams, Revere's depiction of the event helped solidify the popular perception of the "Boston Massacre" but was not enough to convince a jury to convict the British soldiers (*The Boston Massacre*, engraved, printed and sold by Paul Revere, Jr., 1770. Metropolitan Museum of Art, Gift of Mrs. Russell Sage, 1910).

casket that was inscribed with the slogan, "innocence itself is not safe." In the *Boston Gazette*, Seider was hailed as a "little Hero and first Martyr to the noble Cause."[38]

Following the killing of young Seider, one of the most well-known but also most highly disputed incidents took place in the pre-revolutionary period—the so-called Boston Massacre. On March 5, 1770, a crowd of some 300 Bostonians, still seething over Seider's death, confronted a group of nine troops on King Street, and began verbally abusing them and throwing various projectiles, including rocks, ice and snowballs. Some also took swings at the soldiers with clubs. Afraid for his life, one soldier fired, and others followed suit and began discharging their weapons, leading to the deaths of five colonists.

The next day, at a meeting at Faneuil Hall, Samuel Adams was selected to chair a 15-member committee to petition Lieutenant Governor Hutchinson for the immediate removal of the two regiments of troops from Boston. Backed by thousands of angry Bostonians and farmers who had arrived from the countryside, Adams presented the demand to Hutchinson, who responded that he would agree to removing one regiment but that he lacked the authority to order the removal of all troops. Adams replied that "if the Lieutenant Governor or Colonel Dalrymple, or both together, have the authority to remove one regiment, they have the authority to remove two," adding that nothing less "will satisfy the public mind or preserve the peace." Hutchinson relented and withdrew both regiments to Castle William.[39]

Although the withdrawal of the troops, known to posterity as "Sam Adams' two regiments," may have served to calm immediate tensions and stave off further violence, the ramifications of the incident on King Street were just beginning to be felt. Boston firebrands began to publicize the event as an unprovoked "massacre," using the press to spread their narrative and leverage the incident a rallying cry for revolution. Paul Revere produced an image that was widely published, depicting an unprovoked act of aggression, and Adams wrote articles in local newspapers calling the incident a senseless act of violence against innocent bystanders. "It is a glaring mistake to say, the Soldiers were in danger from the inhabitants," Adams wrote in one paper. "The reverse is true: the inhabitants were in danger from the Soldiers."[40]

The trial took place seven months after the incident with the soldiers represented by John Adams who touted the case as an important demonstration of the colonists' commitment to the rule of law and principles of liberty. "We talk of liberty and property," John Adams said in his defense of the accused, "but, if we cut up the law of self-defense, we cut up the foundation of both, and if we give up this, the rest is of very little value." He raised the prospect of the British soldiers being tarred and feathered by the mob, asserting that anyone facing that threat "would have a good right to have stood upon his defense, the defense of his liberty, and if he could not preserve that without hazard to his own life, he would be warranted, in depriving those of life, who were endeavouring to deprive him of his."[41]

John Adams's defense of the soldiers was perhaps a bit too robust for his cousin's taste. Although Samuel Adams desired the appearance of a fair trial to show that Boston was not run by a lawless mob, he very much wanted the soldiers to be convicted, which would have demonstrated that Bostonians were the victims of an unjust occupation.[42] The jury, however, was persuaded by John Adams's arguments and convinced by the evidence that the accused had indeed acted in self-defense. They acquitted Captain Thomas Preston of manslaughter, taking Preston's word that he had not ordered his soldiers to open fire on the angry mob, and also found that six of the eight soldiers were innocent. Even in the hotbed of revolutionary activity known as Boston, the jurors agreed with John Adams that the British soldiers had no choice but to open fire on the mob,[43] and ultimately, just two of the soldiers were found guilty of manslaughter. Although this was a capital offense, the two appealed to the "benefit of clergy," which was a common practice of the English legal system in which a first-time offender could read a biblical passage and receive a branding, usually on his thumb, and then be set free.

So, despite all of the noise made by patriots such as Samuel Adams about a bloody massacre carried out in the streets of Boston, only two soldiers would be punished, and rather than being executed would receive no more than a branding. Samuel Adams denounced the outcome as a miscarriage of justice, but although he was disappointed by the acquittals, he expressed confidence that the soldiers would someday be held accountable in the eyes of God. "In their day of trial, may God send them good deliverance," he wrote.[44]

Samuel Adams continued to publicly agitate on the issue of the Boston Massacre, and the following year, spearheaded the first of several March 5 "Massacre Day" remembrances. These days of mourning would keep the incident fresh in the minds of colonists, laying the groundwork for even more confrontational resistance against the British. John Adams would later claim that "the foundation of American independence was laid" on March 5, 1770, when five members of a mob were killed in Boston.[45]

Samuel Adams's task of public agitation and organizing resistance to the British, for what it's worth, was greatly enabled by the prevailing atmosphere in New England, where it was not particularly difficult to raise a mob for any purpose. While much of the focus of historians has naturally been on the role of street theater in advocating against unpopular taxes, unruly mobs could also be whipped up for more pedestrian reasons, such as to intimidate undesirable members of a community—as Henry Tufts would find out in 1770. Having moved to Lee, New Hampshire, after having some trouble with the law in Falmouth, Maine, Henry would discover that word travelled fast in New England. When he attempted to settle into his new community, he found that "the people of Lee were in full possession of my late misadventures," were "much embittered against me," and "had now a colourable pretext to treat me with indignity."[46]

A man named Elisha Thomas decided that Henry wasn't welcome in Lee and led a mob to his home with a "design of pulling my house in pieces," much as a mob had done to Thomas Hutchinson's house in Boston five years earlier. Henry observed that the assembled crowd was "highly stimulated, I believe, with drink," and was impervious to reason. Henry grabbed his musket to scare the mob off but Thomas just "repeated his determination of tearing my house in pieces," and proceeded to lead the attack. So, Henry aimed and pulled the trigger but nothing happened—it was a misfire. He tried once more, but again, the musket failed to discharge. Thomas, at this point, seemed to get the message and decided to retreat, "march[ing] off with his whole party."[47]

Elisha Thomas may have survived that altercation, but several years later his hot temper would get the better of him. After serving in the Revolutionary War, he got into a quarrel with a fellow veteran named Peter Drown, and under the influence of New England rum, stabbed him with a knife. Thomas was subsequently convicted for murder and hanged.[48]

4

Escalation

As the 1770s got underway, life in the colonies was characterized by increasingly audacious rebellion against royal authority. The widespread protest and militancy of the era is a demonstration of the power of collective action to achieve results, but also a reminder that respect for the rule of law, to put it mildly, was not the top priority of American colonists. Although the patriots were quick to point out "lawless" overreaching by King George and Parliament, they often were prone to disregard the law themselves in their pursuit of higher principles of "natural rights." Whether they were scheming to avoid taxes by smuggling goods into ports without declaring them to the Customs Boards or physically attacking the homes of customs officials or instilling terror in loyalists through tar-and-featherings, the rebels had clearly decided that they would not submit to what they considered unjust infringements on their liberty. Just as Henry Tufts found himself taking increasingly drastic measures in his accelerating life of crime, rebellious colonists—and the royal authorities attempting to govern them—saw escalation as the only way forward.

The escalatory actions and hardening of positions were based on the belief, expressed by radicals such as Samuel Adams, that passively accepting the injustices of British rule would only encourage additional abuses. Adams understood that London was exasperated with its colonists in Massachusetts and that the British Ministry would resort to any means at its disposal to enforce the supremacy of Parliament. What he may have exaggerated, however, is that their attempts to rein in smuggling and collect taxes amounted to a plot to enslave America.

Viewing the struggle as an all-or-nothing existential threat to liberty, Adams felt justified in escalating the rebels' tactics, with the understanding that they could provoke further drastic actions by the Crown. "The liberties of our country, the freedom of our civil constitution, are worth defending at all hazards; and it is our duty to defend them against all attacks," he wrote in 1771, adding: "If we suffer tamely a lawless attack upon our liberty, we encourage it, and involve others in our doom."[1] It was a testament to their fierce commitment to liberty that intensification of the struggle was seen as their only option, seeing compromise as nothing less than surrender.

In explaining his rejection of British authority and providing a rationale for civil disobedience, Adams objected pointedly to a decision in 1772 that provided for judges of the Massachusetts Superior Court being paid by the Crown rather than the legislature. "To what a state of infamy," Adams wrote, "wretchedness, and misery shall we be reduced if our judges shall be prevailed upon to be thus degraded to hirelings, and the Body of the People shall suffer their free Constitution to be overturned and ruined?" He called upon his fellow colonists to reject this power grab lest "the iron hand of tyranny ravish our laws and seize the badge of freedom … and the murderous rage of lawless power be ever seen on the sacred seat of justice!"[2]

As Adams conceived it, he and his compatriots were defending natural rights from liberty-hating tyrants. But although the patriots were perhaps its most vocal champions, liberty was not a concept entirely unique to the colonies and was in fact embraced by Englishmen everywhere, of all political persuasions.[3] Ever since the Magna Carta, Englishmen had celebrated their rights to habeas corpus, trial by jury, and freedom of speech, as well as to trade and travel freely. Even King George had embraced the concept. "The pride, the glory of Britain, and the direct end of its constitution," he said, "is political liberty."[4]

Although not unique to the colonists, the embrace of English concepts of liberty was more pronounced in the New World, perhaps even exaggerated to some extent. With vast numbers of colonial farmers owning their own land, as opposed to the norm of tenant farming in the old country, as well as the proliferation of various religious confessions, there was a distinct commitment to liberty, freedom and independence that was peculiar to the British ministers attempting to govern the colonies. To their chagrin, it seemed that every time the royal authorities attempted to assert more control, the efforts were foiled by militant mob actions that posed a direct threat to the rule of law, which classically was considered the bulwark protecting individual liberties. This paradox was not only felt by the Crown. Colonists who rejected overreaching by London but were nevertheless inclined to support the rule of law, such as Samuel's cousin John, could see the contradictions of mob rule and grappled with the morality of responding to "a lawless attack upon our liberty" with more lawlessness.

As John Adams wrote to his wife Abigail in 1774,

> Mobs are the.… Sources of all kinds of Evils, Vices, and Crimes, they say. They give Rise to Prophaneness, Intemperance, Thefts, Robberies, Murders, and Treason. Cursing, Swearing, Drunkenness, Gluttony, Leudness, Trespasses,

Maims, are necessarily involved in them and occasioned by them. Besides, they render the Populace, the Rabble, the scum of the Earth, insolent, and disorderly, impudent, and abusive. They give Rise to Lying, Hypocricy, Chicanery, and even Perjury among the People, who are driven to such Artifices, and Crimes, to conceal themselves and their Companions, from Prosecutions in Consequence of them.[5]

Despite that harsh assessment, John Adams would recognize that mobs played an important role in checking the abuses of power, and warned against submitting to tyranny simply in order to prevent the lawlessness of mob action. "Shall We submit to Parliamentary Taxation, to avoid Mobs?" John asked Abigail. "Will not Parliamentary Taxation if established, occasion Vices, Crimes and Follies, infinitely more numerous, dangerous, and fatal to the Community?" He warned that such taxes would only lead to "Corruption, among the public Officers, and Magistrates and Rulers, in the Community." This corruption, he cautioned, could "descend, and spread downwards among the People."

Ultimately, John Adams, like many other colonists, would conclude that riots served a useful purpose in checking abuse of power, viewing the violence committed by the British to be far more harmful. "Is not the Insolence of Officers and Soldiers, and Seamen, in the Army and Navy as mischievous as that of Porters, [or] Sailors in Merchant Service?" he asked. "Are not Riots raised and made by Armed Men, as bad as those by unarmed? Is not an Assault upon a civil officer, and a Rescue of a Prisoner from of lawfull Authority, made by Soldiers with Swords or Bayonets, as bad as if made [by] Tradesmen with Staves?" Taking this moral equivalence a step further, he pointed out that "pulling down a House" was nothing compared to "the Killing of a Child ... and the slaughter of half a Dozen Citizens by a Party of Soldiers ... even if both should be allowed to be unlawfull."[6]

Samuel Adams, of course, agreed with this distinction but would go even further in justifying lawless actions of the people, which he likened "to the raging of the sea." In a letter to Elbridge Gerry, dated March 25, 1774, Samuel Adams argued that "when the passions of a multitude become headstrong, they generally will have their course: a direct opposition only tends to increase them; and as to reasoning, one may as well expect that the foaming billows will hearken to a lecture of morality and be quiet." Since this is the natural course of events, it is up to a "skilful pilot [to] carefully keep the helm, and so steer the ship while the storm continues, as to prevent, if possible, her receiving injury."[7] The British, however, did not possess this common sense, in Adams's view.

"Our enemies," Samuel Adams wrote, seemed to believe that they require the military "to protect them from the fury of an ungoverned mob," which was based on their fundamental misunderstanding of the core issue at hand. "They seemed to me to be disposed to confound the distinction," Adams wrote, "between a lawless attack upon property in a case where if there had been right there was remedy, and the people's rising in the necessary defence of their liberties, and deliberately, and I may add rationally destroying property, after trying every method to preserve it." It was the British colonial authorities, Adams believed, that "had rendered the destruction of that property the only means of securing the property of ALL."[8] In other words, in order to uphold higher principles of natural law, some breaking of manmade law was required.

The Brits, for their part, grew increasingly exasperated by what they saw as ingratitude, intransigence and an insufferable devotion to liberty. Thomas Gage, a British Army officer and colonial official who was born to an aristocratic family in England, married an American-born woman, and served with George Washington in the French and Indian War, advised his superiors that a hard line needed to be taken.[9] Concerned that "lenient measures ... have only served to render them more daring and licentious,"[10] Gage advocated as early as 1770 for more stringent measures to coerce the rebels into submission, namely by rescinding the charter of Massachusetts and abolishing town meetings. But Parliament, exercising caution so as not to antagonize the colonists too much, balked. London wasn't ready to implement Gage's advice at that time, but following a series of events in the early part of the decade, the Crown came to believe that Gage was correct in his assessment that only through severe measures could the colonists be reined in.

* * *

On October 26, 1771, when the ship *Resolution* returned to Portsmouth, New Hampshire, from the Caribbean, Captain Richard Keating tried to sneak 100 barrels of molasses past the customs officials without paying duties on them. The Collector of His Majesty's Customs for the colony, George Meserve, discovered the smuggling attempt and had the vessel and its contents immediately seized. But the colonists were not about to meekly accept this attempt to enforce the law. Three days later, according to a contemporary press report, "between the hours of Eleven and Twelve O' Clock at night there entered on board of said Brigantine a Numerous Company of Men in disguise Armed with Clubs, and wrested said Vessel out of the hands of the proper Officers then on board, turned Some of them out of the Vessel and Confined others in the Cabbin, then proceeded to unload and Carry away the molasses."[11] This so-called "molasses party," while significant at the time, would largely be eclipsed by the Boston Tea Party, which took place two years later and ultimately had deeper political impact.

4. Escalation

In May 1773, Parliament passed the Tea Act, intended to bail out the floundering East India Company—Britain's second largest firm—by giving it a monopoly on the importation and sale of tea in the colonies. Initially there was some confusion over the provisions of the act, with some reports falsely claiming that Parliament had removed all duties, which would have been a great victory for the patriots. In fact, Parliament left the American import duties in place but granted the East India Company relief from duties on tea landing in Britain and headed to America. Essentially, the monopoly could pay a modest American import duty and deliver its product directly to colonists.

When in early September 1773 the Tea Act's full text was published in the colonies, making clear that duties would still apply to tea, merchants in Philadelphia, New York, and Boston, who had been making considerable profits smuggling Dutch tea into the colonies, could see that it posed a threat to their illicit business. Smuggling tea and other commodities from Holland and other European nations provided an economic impetus for rejecting the Tea Act, and once the patriots had a clear understanding of the law's political ramifications, there was also an ideological basis for rejecting it. Merchants and radicals alike opposed any revenue duties going to England,[12] and more fundamentally rejected the law on the principle of self-governance. The fundamental issue for the patriots was that by deciding how taxes were levied, Parliament was able to decide how to spend the money. Colonists insisted that they were more than capable of taxing and ruling themselves,[13] and spoke in a unified voice against the move by London. A resolution prepared by Samuel Adams and adopted unanimously at a Boston Town Meeting on November 5, declared "that it is the Duty of every American to oppose this attempt" and designated anyone who "aid[s] or abet[s] in unloading receiving or vending the Tea ... an Enemy to America."[14]

It was in this context that the ship *Dartmouth* arrived in Boston Harbor with 114 chests of East India Company tea aboard on Sunday November 28. As the first tea ship to reach America since the adoption of the Tea Act, patriots insisted that it be returned to England. But if returned, the government would confiscate the tea and the colonial merchants who were receiving the tea on consignment would be liable for the cost. As soon as the ship entered the harbor, the clock started ticking, with someone required to pay the duties on the tea within 20 days or officials would seize the tea, pay the duty, and sell it themselves. Two more ships would arrive in the harbor in the subsequent days and Adams and his allies were determined to prevent the tea from being landed.

Thousands gathered from Boston and surrounding towns to meet at Faneuil Hall. Under the leadership of Adams, they resolved on November

29 that "as the town of Boston, in a full legal meeting, has resolved to do the utmost in its power to prevent the landing of the tea." The November 29 meeting was the first of a series of gatherings that would culminate in a meeting of several thousand on December 16 at the Old South Meeting House. The patriots had a simple demand for Governor Hutchinson to order the tea ships out of Boston. When Hutchinson, determined to avoid bowing to what he called "a lawless and highly criminal assembly of men,"[15] responded at about 6:00 p.m. with a firm "no," Adams stood up and declared, "This meeting can do no more to save this country!" Following this statement, a group broke out of the larger meeting and marched toward the water to begin their task of destroying the ships' cargo, in what would become known as the Boston Tea Party.[16]

Between 30 and 60 men, many of them dressed as Mohawk Indians, boarded three ships docked at Griffin's Wharf, and dumped 340 chests of tea into harbor. With Adams communicating with the crew from the wharf, as informers later claimed,[17] for about three hours they went about their work. A crowd of several hundred watched from the pier, while the British Army and Navy, just a few hundred yards away, declined to intervene. Admiral John Montagu later claimed that he could have fired on the attackers, but worried that he would have also hit the bystanders watching the events, so made no attempt to stop them.[18]

The participants endeavored to ensure that no one stole any of the tea—that it all ended up in the harbor and not in anyone's pockets. According to an account by one of the participants, "the greatest care [was] taken to prevent the tea from being purloined by the populace." Those who were caught pocketing "a small quantity, were stripped of their acquisitions and very roughly handled."[19] One tea thief was beaten, stripped and forced to run home naked. Through this approach, the radicals hoped to demonstrate that they would not tolerate theft, and that by demonstrating their moral rectitude, they aspired to win the support of sympathetic colonists and rally them to the cause of the Boston patriots. The discipline that they showed would also distinguish them from common criminals like Henry Tufts.

Nevertheless, the Boston Tea Party was controversial among some American patriots for its disrespect toward the principle of property rights. Although the Tea Party participants were fastidious in demonstrating that they respected *legitimate* property rights—even taking the time to replace a broken lock on one of the ships[20]—and explicitly stated that their acts of violence were in defense of "Liberty and laws," these gestures were lost on many observers. The financial costs were immediately highlighted, with a Boston merchant named John Andrews writing to his brother-in-law in Philadelphia on December 18, 1773, that "ten thousand pounds sterling of the East India Company's tea was destroy'd," an amount working out to more than $1,700,000 in today's dollars, noting that "poor Boston will feel the whole weight of ministerial vengeance" for this act of sabotage.[21] George Washington was one of many who chided Bostonians for "their conduct in destroying tea," and Benjamin Franklin even argued that they should compensate the East India Company for its losses.[22]

Governor Hutchinson, of course, was furious, and initially insisted that the perpetrators be charged with high treason, a charge that was later reduced to burglary, but he found to his dismay that no justice of the peace or grand jury would assist with the prosecution.[23]

* * *

The Boston Tea Party resulted in a drastic escalation of the crisis with Parliament's adoption of the Coercive Acts in 1774, dubbed the Intolerable Acts in the colonies. These were a series of four laws that were intended to punish Massachusetts for the attack on the East India Company, as well as to restore some semblance of authority. The laws were drafted and enforced by General Thomas Gage, who was known to have a predisposition for fairness and prudence but came to increasingly view the Americans as exorbitant in their demands.[24] Following the Boston Tea Party, rumors swirled that the colonists were focused on reaching compromises and complying with Gage's dictates, as well as paying reparations for the tea they destroyed. Gage, however, was being deceived. These rumors were a farce, likely initiated by Samuel Adams to conceal the true intention of the meetings taking place in Massachusetts—which was to plot the next steps for what the radicals knew would be a harsh reaction to their actions in Boston harbor.[25]

In response to the colonists' growing rebelliousness, Gage offered suggestions for reining them in, which King George told his ministers that they should implement to compel Boston to "submit to whatever may be thought necessary." With an intimate knowledge of the colonies and what he believed was a good understanding of what was needed to bring them to heel, Gage was instrumental in crafting the Coercive Acts' most inflammatory provisions designed to compel the unruly colonists to submit to British authority and force those responsible to pay for the tea that had been destroyed.

The first of these measures was the Boston Port Act, which authorized the Royal Navy to blockade Boston Harbor because "the commerce of his Majesty's subjects cannot be safely carried on there."[26] This action was based on the principle of collective punishment, intended to cripple Boston's economy by cutting off its trade, and drew some criticism in Parliament. Parliamentarian Edmund Burke, who tended to be sympathetic to the colonists, suggested that rather than punishing the whole town, the authorities should instead target the ringleaders. "The persons guilty [were] Mr. Hancock, and Samuel Adams," he pointed out. "Punish Hancock, Adams, and others you know, but not all." He called the Port Act "the most dangerous unjust" measure "that ever was," but over his objection, the law passed on March 31, 1774.[27]

Next, the Government Act sought to reestablish "the peace and good order of the said province," based on the belief that Massachusetts had fallen to mob rule. The act provided the royal governor the authority to unilaterally choose judges and for appointed sheriffs to select jurors, severely restricting the independence of the judicial system. Under the terms of this law, Gage could personally nominate royal judges, but he soon found that juries refused to serve in these courts, and judges, fearing for their lives, sometimes declined to sit on the bench.[28] The Government Act also restricted town meetings to once a year and provided for the king's appointment of the Massachusetts Council, which had previously been constituted as an elected body with the governor's approval.[29]

The Act for the Impartial Administration of Justice further restricted the colony's judicial independence by empowering the royal governor to move trials to Britain if it was determined that a fair trial couldn't be held in Massachusetts. The idea was to protect royal officials from the jeopardy of facing hostile patriot juries, particularly in the case of the discharge of their duties in "the suppression of riots, or in the support of the laws of revenue."[30] Finally, the Quartering Act, adopted on June 2, 1774, allowed high-ranking military officials to demand better accommodations for troops, providing that soldiers were to be housed in "uninhabited houses, out-houses, barns, or other buildings" at the colonists' expense.[31] Although the Quartering Act was the only one of the four that applied to all of the American colonies, taken as a whole, the Coercive Acts effectively united the colonies against the British. George Washington, who had previously questioned the radical Boston Tea Party, fully rallied behind the Boston patriots following the aggressive response by London and called for a boycott of British imports.[32] Even royal officials came to realize that the punishment of Boston was counterproductive, with a Crown officer in Philadelphia lamenting in July 1774 that the Coercive Acts vastly overshadowed the vandalism that they were punishing and served to rally all the colonies behind the rebel cause.[33]

While the Coercive Acts themselves were considered "intolerable," drastically curtailing Massachusetts's right to self-government and commerce, their enforcement was even more problematic, leading to a further escalation of the crisis and setting the course for armed conflict. Gage,

4. Escalation

having been named royal governor of Massachusetts, took seriously his task of enforcing the laws, determined to counter any attempts by the patriots to circumvent royal authority. This led to more draconian measures and a "venal system of administration," as Mercy Warren described it, noting that "the faithless Gage will be marked with infamy for breach of promise, by the impartial historian."[34] With the Massachusetts Charter revoked and the General Assembly stripped of the right to elect the members of the Council, the upper chamber was replaced by 36 members appointed by Gage, known as the Mandamus Council. Just 25 accepted the appointments though, with the other 11 declining out of fear for the repercussions they might face from the patriots.[35]

Stripped of the freedom to elect their own representatives, Massachusetts residents began preparing for more encroachments on their liberty, predicting that the next target of the royal clampdown might be the confiscation of firearms. Stored in powder houses throughout the colony, these arsenals of weapons, ammunition and gunpowder had been under the control of the British authorities, but following the establishment of Massachusetts's provincial government, Gage worried that they could be used against British soldiers. The towns began removing them for transfer to more covert locations but Gage started to make his own arrangements to foil these efforts. Gage received a letter from William Brattle, the leader of the provincial militia, that the king's powder remained in a storehouse in Charlestown, so Gage decided to send a detachment to relocate it to a secure location.

On the morning on September 1, 1774, some 250 British troops descended on Charlestown, searching the town and finding two small field guns as well as some gunpowder. They took the weapons and gunpowder to Castle William in Boston Harbor, where they offloaded the contraband for storage. Although the operation went smoothly and without bloodshed, rumors started to spread that the British had killed six Bostonians and that the Royal Navy had opened fire on the town and destroyed the seaport. Brattle's letter to Gage had been intercepted by the patriots and leaked to the press, and when newspapers published the details, the people of Massachusetts were incensed. Suddenly, Whig leaders who for the previous decade had been working to arouse the people to the cause of liberty were striving to contain the people's fury from being unleashed, or as Joseph Warren put it, "to prevent the people from coming to immediate acts of violence."[36] Throughout the day, thousands of militiamen from the Massachusetts countryside descended upon Charlestown to protest the atrocities they believed the British had committed. Once they realized that the rumors were false, the situation calmed down somewhat but the mob then turned its attention to the royally appointed Mandamus Council, with several councilors forced to resign, including Lieutenant Governor Thomas Oliver.[37]

*　*　*

Elsewhere in America, patriots rallied to the cause—largely thanks to the Committees of Correspondence that Samuel Adams had helped to organize. All of the colonies, with the exception of Georgia, would unite behind Massachusetts and decided to convene the First Continental Congress on September 5, 1774, with men from 12 colonies, including Samuel and John Adams, gathering in Philadelphia to determine a response to the escalating crisis. The following day, news of the Powder Alarm reached the Congress, with John Adams calling it "a confused account, but an alarming one indeed." Cries of "War!" reverberated in the halls of the meeting at Philadelphia, with the rumor of a possible British attack on Boston motivating the delegates to coordinate a strong response, and representatives from the various colonies quickly assuring the New England delegates that they would stand behind Massachusetts.[38]

In an effort to ensure that this support continued, Samuel Adams beseeched his allies in Boston to avoid rash and violent actions that would cause moderate delegates to waver. Knowing that radicals had been talking of attacking the British garrison and pushing for independence,[39] Samuel Adams wrote to James Warren, asking him to "implore every Friend in Boston by every thing dear and sacred to Men of Sense and Virtue to avoid Blood and Tumult." Reminding Warren that "they will have time enough to dye," Adams urged the Boston radicals to give delegates from other colonies "opportunity to think and resolve," pointing out, "Rash Spirits that would by their Impetuosity involve us in unsurmountable Difficulties will be left to perish by themselves despisd by their Enemies, and almost detested by their Friends." He added: "Nothing can ruin us but our Violence."[40]

Following weeks of debate, the delegates to the First Continental Congress decided to boycott British goods and sent a petition to London calling for the Intolerable Acts to be repealed. Although they stopped short of declaring independence, prominent colonists were forced to confront the question of what terms they could remain in the empire, and pushed into a more confrontational position, many began preparing for open conflict. "The People began now to arm with Powder & Ball, and to discipline their Militia," Tory Peter Oliver later recalled. "The People were continually purchasing Muskets, Powder & Ball in the Town of Boston, & carrying them into the Country, under the Pretense that the Law of the Province obliged every Town & Person to be provided with each of those Articles."[41]

Samuel Adams, however, continued to urge calm, acting as mediator between the radicals and the more cautious leaders from other colonies and ultimately convincing Massachusetts insurgents to show restraint during the crucial period that the First Continental Congress met. Largely due to his influence, the people of Massachusetts had refrained from more violence, waiting instead for another British provocation.[42] They wouldn't have to wait long.

* * *

In London, King George III insisted that a tougher stand must be taken against this "most daring spirit of resistance and disobedience to the law," tasking General Gage to take further steps to quell the unrest. Regulars were deployed everywhere, and an increasingly visible and unpopular military occupation of Boston took shape.

In early 1775, Captain John Brown and Ensign Henry de Berniere were sent west through Suffolk and Worcester Counties to get a lay of the land, and in surveying Middlesex County, they discovered a cache of weapons and supplies in Concord, which also served as a meeting place of the illegal Provincial Congress. Gage decided to strike. The mission was to arrest Whig leaders, with the primary targets being John Hancock and Samuel Adams, and to confiscate the rebels' munitions. The rebels, however, were prepared. Benefiting from a clandestine network of spies and sympathizers, including Paul Revere and lesser-known figures such as Henry Tufts's kinsman Samuel Tufts, the minutemen were tipped off and by the time the regulars got to Lexington, the armed insurgents were waiting for them.

On the morning of April 19, 1775, just as the sun was rising, a shot was fired at Lexington. The question of who fired first has long been a subject of intense debate, and with both sides blaming the other and no conclusive evidence to settle the matter, it continues to be an open question. But whoever fired the Shot Heard Round the World, whether it was intentional or not, the British responded with a barrage of gunfire, starting with a slow popping sound, quickly erupting into a sharp crackle, and then followed by a "continual roar of musketry," as Paul Revere described it.[43] Soon after the fighting started, the militia decided to fall back. The regulars proceeded west to Concord, about a two-hour march. In Concord, the patriots were better prepared. Approximately 400 militiamen engaged 100 British troops at about 11:00 a.m., resulting in casualties on both sides. Repelled at North Bridge, the outnumbered regulars retreated and were pursued by a growing militia force. By the end of the day, the one-sided skirmish on Lexington Green had turned into the hours-long, running Battle of Lexington and Concord.[44] The militia chased General Gage's forces all the way back to Boston, and once there, 20,000 militiamen laid siege to the town to prevent Gage's troops from launching any more incursions into the countryside.

While Samuel Tufts played a role in the Midnight Ride at the early stages of the battle, another one of Henry's kinsmen, Cotton Tufts, would play a small part in the latter part of the battle. As the regulars proceeded to Boston, they passed through the town of Menotomy, where a 78-year-old Whig named Samuel Whittemore lived. As the redcoats approached, Whittemore took a position behind a stone wall, armed with a musket, two pistols and a saber, waiting for the British column to approach. Once they were in sight, Whittemore engaged. The regulars sent a detachment to assault his position, and Whittemore killed one of them with his musket and shot two more with his pistols. The regulars returned fire, blowing away part of his face, and thrust their bayonets into his body. He was later found barely alive, bleeding from more than a dozen wounds. He was taken to Dr. Cotton Tufts, who shook his head and offered a grim prognosis, saying he had little chance of making it. Miraculously, though, Whittemore survived and lived another 18 years, passing away in 1793 of natural causes.[45]

Samuel Adams, for his part, spent the battle in hiding, first at various houses of patriot sympathizers, and then in the woods of Woburn, a little less than five miles northeast of Lexington. As he and Hancock began their escape, they could hear the rattle of musketry in the distance. Adams turned to his fellow fugitive and said, "It is a fine day!" to which Hancock replied, "Very pleasant." Adams, realizing that Hancock thought he was talking about the weather, clarified by saying, "I mean, this is a glorious day for America!"[46]

* * *

With 250 redcoats and 95 patriots killed and wounded at the end of the day, both sides hurled accusations of a "bloody butchery" and the possibilities for rapprochement seemed to decisively disappear. Letters were dispatched with haste, first to Worcester and then beyond the borders of Massachusetts. British Canada, Connecticut, and New York received word by April 25, and over the next several days the news made its way farther south. By the end of the month, word had spread throughout the colonies, leading to solidified convictions that conflict was inevitable.[47] Thomas Paine would later claim that "no man was a warmer wisher for a reconciliation than myself before the fatal nineteenth of April 1775, but the moment the event of that day was made known, I rejected the hardened, sullen-tempered Pharaoh of England forever."[48]

The Brits, for their part, also hardened their views. While prior to April 19, there may have appeared to be some possibility of reconciliation, after the battle, the Brits' opinions of the colonists developed into a growing hatred. The regulars all felt the sting of defeat and rejected what they saw as the militia's cowardly fighting style, which seemed to borrow tactics from Indian "savages." As a wounded soldier wrote to his family in England, "They did not fight us like a regular army, only like savages behind trees and stone walls, and out of the woods and houses, where in the latter we killed numbers of them." One particular atrocity involving a regular being killed with a hatchet made a strong impression on the Brits, with one claiming that "these people ... are as bad as the Indians for scalping and cutting the dead men's ears and noses off."[49]

The patriots understood full well the ramifications of the battle and knew that continued escalation would only lead to all-out war, an outcome many seemed to resign themselves to, if not openly embrace. Joseph Warren, serving as president of the Provincial Congress in John Hancock's absence, said that "the barbarous murders committed on our innocent brethren, on Wednesday the 19th instant, have made it absolutely, necessary that we immediately raise an army to defend our wives and our children from the butchering hands of an inhuman soldiery."[50] London also prepared for battle, sending British generals William Howe, Henry Clinton, and John Burgoyne to Boston with reinforcements for General Gage, including a large fleet of warships.

* * *

"Now, alas! is made a garrison of mercenary troops, the strong hold of despotism," said clergyman Samuel Langdon in a sermon at the Provincial Congress in Watertown on May 31, 1775. "America is threatened with cruel oppression, and the arm of power is stretched out against New-England, and especially against this Colony, to compel us to submit to the arbitrary acts of legislators who are not our representatives, and who will not themselves bear the least part of the burdens which, without mercy, they are laying upon us."[51] Samuel Adams was not present for this sermon, as he had returned to Philadelphia for the Second Continental Congress, which focused its efforts on preparation for war. Adams and George Washington were appointed to a committee tasked with preparing the defense of New York, deciding how many troops would be needed and where they should be posted. Adams also helped prepare a letter to Canada appealing for solidarity against London, and joined Benjamin Franklin and Richard Henry Lee on a committee "to consider the best means of establishing posts for conveying letters and intelligence throughout this continent."[52]

On June 12, 1775, General Gage declared Massachusetts to be in a state of rebellion. In a Proclamation, he recounted the events of Lexington and Concord, recalling that "many thousands assembled on the 19th of April last, and from behind walls, and lurking holes, attacked a detachment of the King's troops, who not expecting so consummate an act of phrenzy, unprepared for vengeance, and willing to decline it, made use of their arms only in their own defence." Despite the treachery of these actions, as well as subsequent engagements in which "the rebels, deriving confidence from impunity, have added insult to outrage; have repeatedly fired upon the King's ships and subjects," Gage felt it prudent to grant a pardon to all those who had been involved in the resistance—with the exception of John Hancock and Samuel Adams. "I do hereby in his Majesty's name," Gage wrote,

> offer and promise, his most gracious pardon in all who shall forthwith lay down their arms, and return to the duties of peaceable subjects, excepting only from the benefit of such pardon, Samuel Adams and John Hancock, whose offences are of too flagitious a nature to admit of any other consideration about that of condign punishments.[53]

The rebels, however, were not particularly interested in a pardon. Five days after Gage's declaration, the first formal battle of the revolution took place at Bunker Hill, where the British would suffer heavy losses. As one soldier who survived the battle would later say, "Never had the British Army so ungenerous an enemy to oppose." Rather than fighting out in the open, the American riflemen "conceal[ed] themselves behind trees etc till an opportunity present[ed] itself of taking a shot at our advance sentries, which done they immediately retreat."[54] He complained that this was "an unfair method of carrying on a war," but to the Americans, it was considered good strategy to employ ambush tactics and use the terrain against a stronger force, employing techniques

Painted by John Singleton Copley and engraved by Charles Goodman and Robert Piggot, this likeness of Samuel Adams was originally produced to celebrate the moment that Adams confronted Thomas Hutchinson the day after the Boston Massacre to demand that he remove British troops from Massachusetts (Library of Congress).

they had learned from many years of being on the receiving end of Indian raids.⁵⁵

Following Bunker Hill, the Continental Congress resolved to launch preparations for military defense but also looked to avoid war with the "Olive Branch Petition." On July 5, 1775, the Congress adopted the petition, written by John Dickinson, a Quaker and one of the wealthiest men in the colonies, which appealed directly to King George III and expressed hope for reconciliation. The 1,400-word document addressed the king in gracious and humble terms, attempting to distinguish between his benevolent rule and the ministerial policies that were being implemented in his name. "Your Majesty's Ministers," the petition reads, "persevering in their measures, and proceeding to open hostilities for enforcing them, have compelled us to arm in our own defence, and have engaged us in a controversy so peculiarly abhorrent to the affections of your still faithful Colonists." The petition, which was signed by Samuel Adams and 48 others, ends with a statement of loyalty: "That your Majesty may enjoy long and prosperous reign, and that your descendants may govern your Dominions with honour to themselves and happiness to their subjects, is our sincere prayer."⁵⁶

When the petition was delivered to the king on November 12, 1775, he refused to receive it, leading to growing fury among the colonists. No one was more incensed than Abigail Adams, who wrote to her husband, "Let us separate, they are unworthy to be our Brethren. Let us renounce them and instead of supplications as formerly for their prosperity and happiness, Let us beseech the almighty to blast their councils and bring to Nought all their devices."⁵⁷

Meanwhile, Samuel Adams's stature continued to rise. He had made quite a name for himself at the Second Continental Congress, sitting on four of the six committees that had been formed to deal with various issues. Further enhancing his status was the election of John Hancock as president of the Congress, meaning that he had access to one of the most powerful men in the colonies when he needed it.⁵⁸ Often working behind the scenes, Adams earned a reputation for both uniting the colonies and ensuring that practical work got done, and was prudent enough to allow the Virginians to take the lead on some key matters, as they were seen as less fanatical than the New Englanders and would help keep the more moderate delegates on board. By nationalizing the struggle, Adams helped to create a national identity.

Of course, Adams's enemies saw it quite differently. While the patriots would readily cite Locke and principles of natural rights in justifying their actions, the Tories who bore the brunt of their wrath viewed the radicals as little more than common criminals. As Peter Oliver would describe

Samuel Adams, "he was so thorough a Machiavilian, that he divested himself of every worthy Principle, & would stick at no Crime to accomplish his Ends."[59]

Although his motives in life were quite different, the same could be said of Henry Tufts, having seemingly abandoned principles in his pursuit of self-advancement through theft, and increasingly brazen in his willingness to commit crime to accomplish his ends. Despite recognizing the pitfalls of his actions, the only path he could see for himself was "to plunge me more deeply, more irreversibly, into the abyss of depravity and woe," as he wrote in his memoirs. Samuel Adams might have found this propensity for escalation relatable, but while Adams always managed to position himself at the center of the key events leading inexorably to revolution, Tufts had an uncanny ability to ensure the opposite—always remaining on the periphery of society and generally removed from the historic activity unfolding around him.

5

Living with the Indians

Following an unfortunate accident Henry Tufts suffered in 1772 while playing with a jack knife—which ended up embedded in his thigh, causing a serious infection—he was advised by a "great Indian hunter" named Josiah Miles to seek medical attention from the Abenaki tribe of Sudbury, Canada (present-day Bethel, Maine). Henry was inclined to take his friend's advice, but as he explains in the book, his condition was poor and he knew that the journey would be "long and tedious." He was able to walk, he said, but just barely—in fact, he was so weak and pale that he "more resembled a ghost, than a living person." He decided to give himself one month to rest at home to recuperate his strength, and would then set out to find the tribe. If he was concerned about how the Abenakis would respond to a white man dropping in unannounced on their village, he kept those anxieties to himself, instead offering a stoic adage reflecting the direness of his situation: "I prefer a savage life, To gloomy cares or vexing strife."[1]

His journey, Henry wrote, was full of "difficulties and discouragements, arising from pain, sickness, want, and sometimes almost despair." He spent "several uncomfortable nights in the howling wilderness, where the frequent yellings of the wild beasts inspired ideas of horror and amazement."[2] It was very much unknown territory he was venturing into, with "Canada" itself a relatively vague concept, generally considered some ill-defined place beyond the furthest western settlements. One map, made by Samuel Langdon in 1756, revealed the lack of knowledge that whites had of the interior. Some sections of rivers were depicted fairly accurately on the map, but others were distorted or omitted altogether, and a large area in western Maine was simply marked "Wilderness Unknown."[3]

Heading into this unknown wilderness, Henry wrote, he "surmount[ed] many obstacles" and "pursued my course, 'till certain footsteps, and other vestiges, indicated my proximity to the frontiers of the Indian settlements." Climbing to the top of a great hill, he finally caught a glimpse of their wigwams. When he arrived at the encampments, he was taken aback by "the uncouth appearance of those wretched habitations" and, for the first time, he expressed concern about "what sort of reception" he would "find among the rude and uncultivated sons of nature." Henry was pleased, however, that they "expressed great willingness to receive" him and "treated [him] in a friendly and obliging manner." Apparently, he was not the first white man they had ever seen. It is unclear from his narrative how much experience Henry had previously had with Indians, but he didn't seem to know much about them other than that they were "extravagantly fond of rum."[4]

Despite his initial lack of knowledge about the Abenaki, he would become quite familiar with their ways over the next three years. Not only did he gain proficiency in their language but he would also find a new love interest and win the friendship of many others. "I acquired such competent skill in the Indian dialect," Henry writes, "as to be able to converse freely with the natives, and had moreover formed a personal acquaintance with most of them belonging to the vicinity, particularly so with Polly Susap, the niece of old king Tumkin Hagen." Polly "appeared more beautiful" in Henry's eyes "than any other female of her whole tribe," and he "presented her with many little tokens of my love and esteem, till, by such assiduities, I attracted her notice, and captivated her fondest affections."[5]

He insists, however, that he was not looking for a new wife, and concedes that his "principal and indeed sole inducement in cultivating the friendship of this young woman, or if you please, savage, was to remedy the want of a female companion, while in these rude regions." Polly, he writes, "rendered my abode, in this unpleasant wilderness, much more tolerable, furnishing me with many of the comforts and necessaries of life," and his "tedious hours at home were enlivened with her social company."[6]

Although he knew little about them before joining their camp, his initial introduction to the Abenakis spurred his curiosity. Prompted to learn as much about them as possible, Henry moved every day from one place to another until he had visited the whole band, and his observations would later serve as a valuable source of historical information for generations of scholars. In 1974, Gordon Day published an article in the journal *Ethnohistory* titled "Henry Tufts as a Source on the Eighteenth Century Abenakis," which lauded his autobiography as a substantial resource for information about the tribe.[7] In a 1990 book titled *The Western Abenakis of Vermont, 1600–1800: War, Migration, and the Survival of an Indian People*, Colin G. Calloway refers to Henry as "an ethnographic observer of some merit," noting that his observations provided substantial insight into the Abenaki way of life, for example their tendency to live in family band camps and forgo congregating into tribes.[8] A 1993 article by David Ghere in *American Indian Quarterly* also cites data from Henry's account to counter misconceptions about Abenaki population levels.[9]

5. Living with the Indians

* * *

The Abenaki (or as they refer themselves, Alnôbak, meaning human beings), were the original inhabitants of the current states of Vermont, New Hampshire, parts of western Maine, parts of northern Massachusetts, and parts of southern Quebec. Historically, the Abenaki Nation consisted of various villages including Androscoggin, Amoskeag, Coosuk, Kennebec, Missisquoi, Nashaway, Norridgewock, Ossipee, Pawtucket, Penacook, Pigwacket, Sokoki, Squakheag, Wawenoc, Winnipesaukee, and Winooski. As early as 1503, the Abenakis established relationships with whites who ventured into their waters. Along with the Passamaquoddy, Micmacs, Malacites, and Penobscots, the Abenakis traded food and furs for metal tools, kettles and cloth.[10] The Huron and Iroquois were also known as great traders, and from 1506 to 1518 established relationships with fishermen from France.[11]

Indians generally believed that whichever trading partner offered the best goods at the lowest prices represented the most favorable ally, and sometimes played Europeans off each other and used trade as a precondition for a diplomatic or military relationship.[12] When there was a decline in trade, therefore, it was often interpreted by the English as evidence that the Indians were allying with the French.[13] Knowing that the Indians' allegiances depended entirely on their own circumstances and their calculations of which partner would prove the most beneficial, whites had a high degree of distrust of their indigenous neighbors. The Indians, of course, also learned to be wary of the whites. Some fishermen were engaged in human trafficking and would kidnap Indians to sell as slaves, so the Abenakis kept the whites at arm's length and would often prevent them from landing. Eager to obtain European goods, however, they sometimes traded from boats off the shore,[14] and ultimately would find that their willingness to coexist with the whites eroded their independence and forced them to make difficult choices, namely whether to assimilate, to fight, or to migrate in order to maintain their way of life.

Soon after first contact with the whites, disease began to ravage indigenous communities that lacked the natural immunity to European viruses. From 1633–1635, smallpox, measles and other epidemics killed more than 10,000 Huron throughout the colonies of New England, New France and New Netherlands. Oral histories tell of missionaries informing Indians that baptizing their babies as Catholics would protect them from the disease, and then providing blankets from smallpox victims to those who refused the baptisms to ensure that the predictions came true.[15] These pressures also compelled Indians into alliances and their increasing dependence on trade and technologies such as firearms made it far more difficult to remain neutral in intra–European rivalries.

The two cultures, although drastically different from one other, strove to find common ground upon which to engage, the result being the emergence of new worlds that were not wholly European or Indian, but a hybrid of the two. The French were more adept at operating in the middle ground than the British, with French traders often marrying Indian women and finding ways to live that blended their distinct cultures. French colonial authorities often discouraged frontier mingling, believing that it was important to maintain the area's demographic composition to continue the trading relationships from which they obtained valuable animal pelts.[16]

While the French were perhaps more skilled in navigating the world of Indians, all colonists seemed to appreciate it on some level.[17] In the backcountries of colonies up and down the Atlantic, the cultural fusion between whites and Indians was remarkable, often blurring distinctions between settler and native lifestyles. The two peoples, for example, often lived in similarly constructed log cabins and drew their subsistence from the same mix of hunting, herding, farming, and trading.[18]

A fluid people, the Abenaki traveled and lived among many of different villages throughout their lifetimes. Most historians prior to the 1980s believed that the Abenakis in western Maine had permanently migrated to the Jesuit missions of St. Francis and Becancour in the 1720s, but scholarship since then (some of which utilizing Henry Tufts's memoirs) has shown that Abenakis remained in Maine.[19] During the wars and epidemics of the 17th and 18th centuries, some Abenakis did indeed retreat to St. Francis, but many others stayed south of the Canadian border, or subsequently returned.[20] As Gordon Day has demonstrated, for the first half of the 18th century, the main inhabitants of St. Francis were the Western Abenakis, particularly Sokokis from New Hampshire and Vermont, and it wasn't until mid-century that Eastern Abenakis from Maine migrated to St. Francis.[21]

Reeling from the losses they experienced from early contact, in the mid–1670s, the Abenaki joined the Wampanoag in King Philip's War, repelling white settlement in subsequent years, and in the 1740s fought with the French against the British and the Iroquois Confederacy in King George's War. After this conflict, there were five years of official peace, but tit-for-tat murders of Abenakis and retaliatory strikes against whites continued to sour relations and erode trust.[22] In the French and Indian War, the Abenaki would once again take up the hatchet against the British.

Following these conflicts, the Abenaki took in refugees from the Pocomtuc, Mahican and Nipmuc tribes, but while they demonstrated a humanitarian impulse towards their friends, they could be vicious toward their enemies. In one notorious incident in the late 17th century, an Abenaki war party encountered a band of Mohawks near an island on the Richelieu River that the Abenaki laid claim to. The Abenaki attacked and following their victory, decapitated the defeated Mohawk warriors, mounted their heads on stakes and placed them around the perimeter of the island to discourage further incursions into their territory. The Abenaki named the island Odepsék, meaning "place of the heads." In French, it is called Île aux Têtes, or Island of Heads.[23]

Henry Tufts would get a front row seat to witness this propensity for brutality against those seen as encroaching on Indian lands. His *Narrative* relates the story of a hunter named Abbot who was tracking animals in the wilderness north of Saratoga, an area "infested with hostile Indians, who kept the frontiers in consternation." Abbot was taken captive by six braves, who "formed the horrid conclusion of putting their prisoner to a painful and lingering death," Tufts explains, "and, in order to execute the infernal purpose, led him off to some distance, where having gagged and prostrated the wretched victim on his back, they cut holes through his wrists and heels, between the bones and tendons."[24]

The Indians then threaded the holes with rope, stretched his arms and legs "to a degree exquisitely painful" and then attached him to four small trees. Abbot was left hanging in that state while his tormentors withdrew to a cluster of bushes, "with intent to make merry, and enjoy, in idea, the excruciating tortures of the sufferer." Luckily, Abbot's hunting partners went searching for him and found him "stretched and bound" in his "horrible confinement." They broke him free and set out to take revenge on the "horrid hell-hounds" who had done this to him. Before long, they tracked down the Indians, and shot several of them dead. One ran away but the hunters let loose their dog, which "overtook the fugitive" and "destroyed his prey in a manner too shocking to relate." Henry expressed some satisfaction in this outcome, noting that "these savages reaped the reward of their cruelty." Abbot, Henry reports, ultimately survived the ordeal and settled in Maine.[25]

Despite the Indians' reputation for brutality and their history of being a thorn in the side of the colonists, Henry was apparently more concerned with overcoming his self-inflicted wound than he was with being decapitated or scalped. Although he had some complaints about the food and his first impression of them was less than positive, taking note of their "uncouth" and "uncultivated" nature, he soon found himself amazed by their hardiness, noting that they "seem[ed] to pay so little regard to the cold piercing blast, that one would have been tempted to consider them as insensible of feeling, as their native oaks and pine." He also expressed some admiration over the quality of the chief's wigwam, which he described as "a structure of some curiosity, being ornamented with many rude draughts and pictures of men, various other animals and implements of war."[26] While Henry might have been impressed by their "friendly behaviour" and grew enamored by their culture, he would continue throughout the pages of his *Narrative* to refer to them as "savages," a reminder that whites' interactions with Indians were often tinged with a certain amount of racism and contempt—even when paradoxically expressing admiration or appreciation for their culture.

* * *

Notwithstanding Henry's prejudices, these "savages" were quite effective in treating his ailment. He was competently cared for by a medicine woman known as Molly Ockett, which was an adapted version of the name that she was baptized with, Mary Agatha. Ockett had a well-known reputation as a skilled healer, and would be remembered in later years as the last living member of the Pigwacket Abenakis,[27] with her name attached to numerous locations in the Androscoggin River valley and surrounding territory, including a middle school in Fryeburg, Maine. As Henry describes it, she diligently tended to his wounded leg and provided him with medicines including "a large variety of roots, herbs, barks and other materials." He expressed "much faith in the skill of my physician," and consumed "every potion she prescribed," noting that the treatment "had a timely and beneficial effect" in healing him. In fact, he "gathered strength so rapidly, that in two months, I could visit about with comfort."[28]

It is a testament to the medical expertise of the Indians that Henry eschewed the more standard treatment that he might have been able to find from a white doctor closer to home without the difficulties of trekking through the wilderness. The apparent effectiveness of the Indians' traditional array of roots and barks recalls that despite their reputation as "savages," the native peoples of North America often had much wisdom and knowledge to impart upon the white colonists. While the stories of Indians teaching the early Plymouth Colony fishing and agricultural techniques (culminating in the first Thanksgiving) are fairly well-known to Americans, less appreciated are the many healing techniques that they shared with whites. Native herbalists offered common-sense remedies that could be found in any forest, and also bestowed a philosophy towards health that affirmed wellbeing as the body's natural state, leading to a belief among some whites that diseases and deformities could be eradicated by heeding the naturalistic example offered by the Indians.[29]

Historian Robert Jay observes that "the myriad Indian potions and remedies" became popular among white colonists based on "the assumption that the red man, in his unique communion with nature, possessed knowledge of its curative powers unrevealed to civilized man."[30] This led to increasing interest among physicians in colonial America in harnessing the knowledge of the Native Americans. As Jack Weatherford explains in *Indian Givers: How Native Americans Transformed the World*, "the Indians of America had refined a complex set of active drugs that ... became the basis for modern medicine and pharmacology."[31] Indeed, one of the earliest known patents for medicine, issued in 1711, was a cure for consumption known as "Tuscarora Rice,"[32] named after the Tuscarora tribe, one of the Six Nations of the Iroquois Confederacy.

Another remedy borrowed from the Indians was a bark known as quina, which prevented malaria and was effective in curing cramps, chills and heart-rhythm disorders. Brought to Europe from the New World around 1630, the bark was put to immediate use, making extensive European settlement of America possible. In the Virginia colony, one out of five settlers was dying of malaria before the introduction of quina, but following the incorporation of the treatment, not a single colonist was known to perish from the disease.[33]

Yet another ailment that whites learned to treat from Indians was scurvy. When the crew of the ships *Grande Hermyne*, the *Petite Hermyne* and the *Emerillon* came down with the ailment during a 1535 visit to the Huron town of Hochelaga (later site of Montreal), French explorer Jacques Cartier learned from the locals that it could be effectively treated by a tonic from the bark and needles of an evergreen that the Hurons called annedda (probably a hemlock or a pine). Containing a massive dose of scurvy-crushing vitamin C, the concoction cured the men's sickness within a week.[34]

Eager to learn the Abenakis' healing techniques, Henry Tufts came up with an idea to obtain their knowledge. He procured "ten gallons of rum," which he generously shared with his Indian friends to win "their good will and gratitude." He then expressed his "desire to learn the healing art," which they promptly agreed to teach him. The Indians provided him "every instruction in their power," and once he felt satisfied in his knowledge, he left the village and resolved to "mak[e] use of Indian medicines" by hawking "their methods of cure" to other whites. After three years with the Abenakis, he left the camp, bought a black suit and honed his salesman pitch using the theatrical incantation of a street peddler. He must have been rather convincing because he was soon amazed at "how easy to deceive is the unreflecting multitude" and to pass himself off as a genuine Indian doctor. "Indeed I found it was in no way difficult to cajole my ignorant followers into the belief of whatever idle tale I was pleased to fabricate," Henry explained.[35]

* * *

Standing in marked contrast to other encounters in the colonies during the 18th century, Henry's generally positive experience with the

Indians is a reminder of the complexity of the relationship and the possibility for cooperation between the two cultures. But the cultural exchanges also had a dark side. Alcohol introduced by whites, for instance, devastated some Indian tribes, and more subtly, the supplanting of traditional customs with new amenities and tools sometimes caused the forgetting of indigenous wisdom and resourcefulness, leading in some cases to the Indians' dependence on whites.[36]

John Stuart, Superintendent of Indian Affairs, explained the symbiotic nature of the inter-cultural links—as well as their pitfalls—in a report to London in 1764. "The original great tie between the Indians and Europeans was mutual conveniency," he explained. What prompted the indigenous peoples to tolerate and sometimes welcome the foreigners was that they brought useful technology and luxuries such as weapons, ammunition, tools, and rum. Over time, the Indians came to rely more heavily on their trade with the whites not just out of convenience but increasingly out of necessity. According to Stuart, the Indians of the late 18th century had lost some of their ancient skills and therefore needed the technological goods that the whites possessed. "A modern Indian cannot subsist without Europeans," Stuart wrote, "and would handle a flint ax or any other rude utensil used by his ancestors very awkwardly."[37]

Not only did their growing reliance on European goods lead to a diminished knowledge of their traditional skills, but increased trade also caused significant depletions of fur-bearing animals, spurring inter-tribal warfare in competition for hunting grounds. Raids to gain control of fur-bearing and fur-trading territories, known as "the beaver wars," proved devastating to Huron towns and villages in the Ohio Valley, causing by the end of the 17th century the dislocation and disappearances of some tribes.[38]

European geopolitical rivalries also compelled Indians into choosing sides, leading to deteriorating relations with white settlers in general. Supplied by the French, Abenaki war parties were known to strike the New England frontier primarily in the spring or the fall, with two or three raiding parties consisting of a dozen or so warriors each routinely attacking English villages. Primarily interested in targeting their livestock for food, the Abenakis would sometimes spare the lives of the settlers, but were also known to kill them or take them as captives.[39] "Apprehensions of attack or injury from the Indians," wrote William Durkee Williamson in a local history of Maine published in 1832, "were the sources of their greatest troubles; as a few garrisons and fortified habitations were, under the Divine protection, their principal, if not their only safeguard and shield."[40]

This, of course, was not a unique experience in New England, but indeed was the reality of life throughout the colonies. One of the biggest hotspots was the backcountry of Virginia and the Carolinas. In the early 1750s settlers and Indians increasingly engaged in hostilities in this region,[41] and a number of incidents served to sour colonial relations with tribes such as the Cherokee and Shawnee. In western Carolina, a white pregnant woman was murdered by a group of Cherokee in 1757 in a manner that shocked colonial authorities and precipitated an all-out war a couple years later. According to a contemporary account, a Cherokee known as Savannah Tom "executed his inhuman, cruel, and barbarous Will on her Body by stabbing her several times with a knife, scalping and opening her Belly, and taking out a poor infant Creature that she had in her body."[42] These sorts of incidents, which the Cherokees largely saw as retaliation for injustices visited upon themselves and as a warning against further encroachments, would continue to erode trust, leading to the Cherokee War of 1759–1761, marked by three separate campaigns that whites launched into Cherokee towns.

Similarly, the French and Indian War, which laid the foundation for the revolutionary crisis in the 1760s and the war for independence a decade later, was triggered by France's expansion into the Ohio River valley. With the French falling into frequent disputes with British colonists' claims, a series of skirmishes starting in 1754 led to an official British declaration of war in 1756, with English colonists joined by the Iroquois Confederacy, the Wyandot, Catawba, Mingo, and the Cherokee Nation. The war unleashed unprecedented violence in the American colonies with the worst of the fighting between colonists and Indians taking place in the backcountry of Pennsylvania, Maryland, and Virginia, where Ohio Valley tribes raided unmercifully for years[43] and communities were laid to waste by roving bands of both Indians and French soldiers.

Some battles between the belligerents amounted to lopsided massacres. British Army officers were unacquainted with the Indians' methods of war, including their frequent ambushes, and often did not know how to respond. A lieutenant in the Royal American Regiment named Rudolph Bentinck described a battle at the French Fort Duquesne, in which 400 British troops were attacked by "1500 French and Indians [who] sallied out upon us, with a Horrid Howling, like a wild Beast." The Brits lined up in traditional military formation but were completely surrounded. "All at once," Bentinck recalled, "we received a very hot fire, without seeing the Enemy, and within a few minutes, all the officers, and above half the men were killed or wounded, upon which the remainder retreated in the greatest confusion."[44] The British forces suffered 342 casualties in the battle.

The Brits were appalled by the Indians' customs in handling prisoners of war, forgoing traditional prisoner exchanges on the European model and instead preferring torture, execution, or enslavement of their enemies.

For instance, in the Battle of Fort Oswego in 1756, after the French and their allies captured the British fortifications, the Indians carried out a massacre of the captives. According to a French officer, "more than 100 persons who were included in the capitulation" were scalped at Fort Oswego.[45] Another notorious incident was the massacre at Fort William Henry in 1757, in which Indians attacked the British garrison after it had agreed to surrender. Following their victory, the Indians brutally killed and scalped about 185 British soldiers and took hundreds of others as prisoners.[46]

Recognizing the unprecedented challenges of frontier warfare and the importance of the war for Britain's imperial ambitions, a new British prime minister, William Pitt, determined to make a full national war effort, and invested considerable resources to gain advantage both on land and at sea. Pitt revived the militia and reorganized the Navy, borrowing heavily to finance the war. The mobilization began to pay off in 1758 when victories at Louisbourg, Fort Frontenac and the French-Canadian stronghold of Quebec helped turn the tide in the British favor.[47] During the war, George Washington emerged as an important figure, serving as a major in the militia of the British Province of Virginia. The war was a pivotal event in Washington's life and career, not only providing lessons about military command and diplomacy, but also coloring his perceptions of the nature of British colonial policies.[48]

The war also brought dramatic changes to the balance of power. Indians, who had established close relationships with the French, would find themselves bereft of their traditional benefactors when France ceded to Britain all of its land claims east of the Mississippi, while Spain gave up East Florida. For the Indians who had for more than half a century tactfully played one European power off another, and developed diplomatic protocols to resolve grievances, a very different situation took shape. Their ability to navigate between European powers disappeared and they were essentially placed at the mercy of the British, forcing them to reconsider their relations with the Crown.[49] Many colonists, for their part, after suffering bloody attacks by Indians in the backcountry for years, had grown to more deeply distrust their indigenous neighbors,[50] and when the war finally came to an end, they dearly hoped for a return to peace and normalcy. These dreams were shattered in early 1763, some two months after the end of the French and Indian War, when in the Great Lakes regions of Pennsylvania, Ohio, and New York, the Ottawa tribe, led by a warrior named Pontiac, launched a rebellion that would significantly impact the course of the revolution.

* * *

At the time of the signing of the Treaty of Paris by the kingdoms of Great Britain, France and Spain, which brought an end to the Seven Years'

War on February 10, 1763, there were perhaps 150,000 Indians still inhabiting the eastern woodlands,[51] and many of these were unsatisfied with the emerging status quo. Pontiac convinced a group of Indians near Detroit to join him in an assault on a British garrison in the spring of 1763, and by the autumn, every British fort in the west had been attacked. At least ten forts fell to the Indian warriors, while the garrisons at Detroit and Fort Pitt just barely held out against prolonged sieges.[52]

Pontiac's Rebellion, as the series of skirmishes came to be known, made clear the depth of hostility to British rule that prevailed among many tribes, and prompted colonial authorities to attempt to prevent such fighting in the future while also containing the financial burden of maintaining a far-flung empire. This led to the issuance of new taxes and efforts to contain settlement activity that would infuriate Boston radicals such as Samuel Adams over the next couple years. Effectively, Britain's policies spurred white settlers into revolutionary action.

Settlers in the backcountry, while perhaps not as concerned over issues such as trade and taxation that aroused fellow colonists in coastal towns, would instead be motivated by issues such as safety and security, particularly those related to land acquisition and Indian policy. Britain, convinced that further encroachments into Indian territory would only exacerbate tensions and recognizing that stirring up trouble in the complex web of tribal alliances and animosities would prove to be a drain on royal resources, decided that the best way to handle the issue was to restrict settlement. London wished not only to avoid additional Indian wars but also to use the western land as a means of generating revenue, which was undermined by providing grants to settlers.[53] But London's response to the troubles, the creation of a boundary between colonists and Natives with the Royal Proclamation issued in October 1763, only served to anger many whites on the frontier, who grew exasperated with both the king and the government in Philadelphia.[54]

Samuel Adams expressed the views of many colonists when he complained of the Crown's tone-deaf approach towards the interests of its subjects living in North America. Outlining the position of settlers who had duly acquired land through purchases from Indians and through much toil had made it arable for farming, Adams objected to a decision-making process that excluded the people most affected by the decisions. He explained the problems inherent in this process in *The Rights of the Colonists*, adopted by the town of Boston on November 20, 1772.

"Another Grievance under which we labour is the frequent alteration of the bounds of the Colonies by decisions before the King and Council, explanatory of former grants and Charters," Adams wrote. Not only does this subject men "to live under a constitution to which they have not consented," but also affects "the right of Soil." The rulings of "Governors, or Ministers, or both in conjunction, have pretended to Grant in consequence of a Mandamus many thousands of Acres of Lands appropriated near a Century past," Adams argued, "and rendered valuable by the labors of the present Cultivators and their Ancestors." He explained the inter-colony chaos and turmoil being introduced by the Crown's shortsighted decisions. "There are very notable instances of Setlers, who having first purchased the Soil of the Natives, have at considerable expence obtained confermation of title from this Province [of Massachusetts]." The complications posed by royal decrees "cannot here be recited," Adams wrote, "but so much may be said, that they have been most cruelly harassed, and even threatened with a military force, to dragoon them into a compliance, with the most unreasonable demands."[55]

* * *

As the colonists' relationship with the Crown deteriorated, warfare and adversity continued to play a big role in the relationship between Indians and whites. At the same time, the relationship continued to be characterized to a significant degree by trade and cultural exchange, which was carried out both formally and informally. Jacob Treadwell, for instance, was granted a license to trade with the Abenakis of New Hampshire in 1769,[56] while others like Henry Tufts simply showed up at a village with some rum. Trading furs and deerskins created a newfound prosperity in some indigenous communities, and novel technologies and conveniences such as firearms and European clothing led to new lifestyles being adopted that were considerably more comfortable than those they had previously been accustomed to. Even the most distrustful of the Indian tribes could see the benefits of trading with whites.[57]

Samuel Adams saw the potential in this situation for Indians to learn the benefits of civilization and possibly even come to participate in government. "Even Savages might, by the means of Education, be instructed to frame the best civil, and political Institutions with as much skill and ingenuity, as they now shape their Arrows," he wrote.[58] Benjamin Franklin, meanwhile, looked to the Iroquois Confederacy for inspiration and guidance on how the American colonies might be able to unite and form governing institutions across vast geographical areas. "It would be a very strange Thing, if six Nations of ignorant Savages should be capable of forming a Scheme for such an Union," Franklin wrote to James Parker, "and yet that a like Union should be impracticable for ten or a Dozen English Colonies, to whom it is more necessary, and must be more advantageous; and who cannot be supposed to want an equal Understanding of their Interests."[59] Having participated in the Albany Congress of 1754, in which seven colonies negotiated with approximately 150 Iroquois, Franklin had been impressed by the ability of the Six Nations to speak in a unified voice.

Franklin first proposed the idea of an intercolonial government, modelled to some extent on the Iroquois Confederacy, in 1751, which would take a quarter century to materialize with the Articles of Confederation in 1777. The extent to which the Iroquois Confederacy actually influenced the political union of the colonies and later the United States continues to be a subject of debate among historians, but it is clear that the strength of the Iroquois Confederacy impressed many colonists and at the very least served as inspiration. "In spite of different reasons for jealousy, [they] have always kept united, and to indicate their union they say that they form a single house which we call the Iroquois Longhouse,"[60] wrote Jesuit Father Joseph Lafitau, a missionary and naturalist who worked in Canada in the first half of the 18th century. However, it should also be noted that the unity of the Six Nations waxed and waned, and during the American Revolution, the tribes had competing loyalties and became embroiled in a brutal internecine conflict.[61]

In 1775, after the Battle of Lexington and Concord, the Six Nations met to discuss the brewing war, with many advocating neutrality. A Mohawk warrior named Joseph Brant, however, argued that American independence was a threat to all Native Americans and viewed the protection of the Crown as the best hope for his people to hold their lands and maintain their way of life. He argued that if the British were defeated, it would be a disaster for the Indians, convincing four of the Six Nations—the Mohawks, Onondagas, Cayugas, and the Senecas—to fight with the British. Working with a loyalist militia known as Butler's Rangers, Brant's fighters waged a brutal campaign on the New York frontier to force the rebels to cede the region. Aimed at destroying food and property, as well as capturing or killing patriots, these raids resulted in numerous massacres, including the Wyoming Valley Massacre—with some 300 patriot casualties—and the Cherry Valley Massacre, in which 30 non-combatants were slaughtered.[62]

Brant's army also participated in the Battle of Oriskany on August 6, 1777, which was one of the bloodiest battles in the Revolutionary War, notable not only for the heavy casualties the patriots suffered but also because it pitted some of the Six Nations against each other. With several hundred Indians from different tribes fighting with the loyalists, the patriots were backed up by Oneidas and allied Iroquois. The Battle of Oriskany marked the extinguishing of the Iroquois Confederacy's "Great Council Fire," and would become known to the Indians as "a place of great sadness," as it essentially meant the end of a system that had ruled the American Northeast for centuries.

With the Six Nations divided, they would generally act on their own during the Revolutionary War,[63] with some working with the British, some with the patriots and some attempting to stay neutral. As for the Iroquois who continued to fight with the British, they would suffer the wrath of Continental Army in 1779, when General George Washington launched a campaign to scatter them from their lands in western Pennsylvania and New York. No mercy was to be shown. "Parties should be detached to lay waste all the settlements around with instructions to do it in the most effectual manner," Washington ordered, "that the country may not be merely overrun but destroyed."[64]

The Abenaki Nation, for its part, also suffered from displacement and division. While many desired to remain neutral in the conflict between England and the colonies, 14 Pigwacket Abenakis from Fryeburg petitioned the Massachusetts legislature to enlist in the Continental Army, while the Androscoggin Abenakis fought for the British Army.[65] Abenakis from Penobscot and St. Francis guided Benedict Arnold through the New England wilderness and some 40 St. Francis Abenakis joined the patriots in the Quebec campaign. Other Abenakis from St. Francis, however, fought alongside British regulars in defense of Quebec and helped defeat Arnold's fleet at the Battle of Valcour Island in October 1776.[66] The shifting allegiances of the Abenakis were indicative not only of the challenges facing Native Americans but also the broader problems facing the patriot cause, in particular the challenge of finding reliable allies and fighters.

Washington came to believe that Indian allies were too fickle to be trusted,[67] but would also discover that the same problem could be found among whites. Henry Tufts was a case in point. After having learned from them medicine and hunting techniques, and having "already seen as much of [their] manners and customs" as he wished, Henry "formed a design of quitting the country sometime in the spring ensuing, or whenever the weather and travelling should permit."[68] This was now spring 1775, at which point the tensions between the colonists and the British had broken out into open violence.

Not unlike his old friends the Abenakis, Henry would have some divided loyalties of his own. Largely unconcerned with the political drama unfolding around him and seemingly indifferent to the outcome of the revolutionary struggle, his allegiances would depend on his own calculations of which attachments might be most advantageous to him personally. In this way, his actions reflected common approaches to the conflict—not only those on display among Native American nations but also among many white colonists.

Part II

Incongruities

"No man for any considerable period can wear one face to himself, and another to the multitude, without finally getting bewildered as to which may be the true."
—Nathaniel Hawthorne

"I have worn no masks, no disguises, but have appeared in my everyday dress."
—Henry Tufts

6

Patriots, Slaves and Loyalists

The Revolutionary War was a battle for hearts and minds as much as it was a military campaign, and with persuasive arguments made on both sides—and with the outcome of the conflict very much uncertain—common working people often declined to take a stand in the struggle, while others remained opposed to it. The patriot cause clearly had a broad base of support, drawing active backing from perhaps 40 to 45 percent of the white populace,[1] but so too did the loyalist cause, with an estimated 15–20 percent of the adult white male population remaining actively loyal to the Crown—and as many as 100,000 loyalists seeking refuge in England, Canada, Bermuda and Jamaica.[2]

Motivated by economic interests as well as ideology, there were hundreds of loyalist regiments that would fight on the side of the British during the war. Some, such as the New Jersey Volunteers, the King's Royal Regiment of New York, the South Carolina Royalists, and the King's American Dragoons, were integrated into the royal armed forces, but many others were self-organized and informal networks of farmers who simply opposed the revolutionary cause. Loyalists generally supported monarchism and opposed any form of rebellion, advocating instead for the use of legally organized bodies to implement reforms, and rejected the patriots' claims of a tyrannical king.[3] More than 15,000 loyalists fought at one time or another in the war, with the bulk of those residing in New York. The British believed that there were 7,000–10,000 loyalist militiamen in the city, but it seems they may have overestimated their strength by a few thousand.[4] Nevertheless, Tory sentiment was so strong in New York that General Washington openly worried about the threat from "internal foes."[5]

Some of these "internal foes," as well as fence-sitters who declined to take a side, objected both to the rebels' ferocity and to their perceived hypocrisy—particularly as it related to slavery, or as it was euphemistically called, "the African trade." The patriots, it was observed, seemed singularly concerned with their own liberties but were callously indifferent to the rights of others. As one loyalist named Theophilus Lillie wrote in 1770, "it always seemed strange to me that people who contend so much for civil and religious liberty should be so ready to deprive others of their natural liberty."[6] In his 1775 tract *Taxation No Tyranny* the Tory essayist Samuel Johnson refuted the colonists' grievances over their lack of liberty, which some complained amounted to being shackled in chains. Johnson retorted that "chains need not be put upon those who will be restrained without them" and highlighted the obvious double standards of the rebels, noting that "the loudest yelps for liberty [are heard] among the drivers of negroes."[7]

With this hypocrisy in mind, it isn't surprising that most blacks who fought in the war chose the side of the Tories rather than the Whigs, with an estimated 20,000 fighting for the British Army in the hopes of winning freedom from bondage. Slaves, naturally, had a different view on concepts such as liberty and natural rights, a perspective rooted in their personal life experiences. When slaves spoke of liberty, such as in the Stono Rebellion of 1739, what they generally meant was freedom from bondage. In this slave revolt, which took place in Stono, South Carolina, three decades before the American Revolution, about 80 enslaved Africans rose up in violent resistance, killing 20 whites, stealing guns and ammunition, and setting buildings on fire. They marched down a roadway with a banner that read "Liberty!" and according to a contemporary newspaper account, "they called out Liberty, marched on with Colours displayed, and two Drums beating."[8]

Understanding that slaves held this more personalized view of liberty, the Brits sought to woo them to their side, and in Lord Dunmore's Proclamation of 1775, freedom was offered to "Negroes [who] join[ed] his Majesty's troops" during the Revolutionary War. This led to hundreds of enslaved Africans forming the Ethiopian Regiment to fight for the Crown.[9] Still though, some 9,000 blacks fought on the side of the Continental Army, often out of the same convictions that motivated whites.[10] Charles Bowles, for example, joined the army at the age of 16 "to risk his life in defence of the holy cause of liberty," according to his biographer John Lewis.[11] More often, though, they fought because they hoped for a better life, with some states, especially in New England, promising freedom in return for military service.[12] In the 1855 study *The Colored Patriots of the American Revolution*, William Cooper Nell writes that slaves "were induced to enter the service in consequence of a law of Congress, by which, on condition of their serving in the ranks during the war, they were made freemen." It was "this hope of liberty [that] inspired them with fresh courage to oppose their breasts to the Hessian bayonet at Red Bank, and enabled them to endure with fortitude the cold and famine of Valley Forge."[13]

Regardless of which side they fought on, the participation of slaves in the conflict underlined the inherent contradictions of a war for liberty being fought in the midst of human bondage, but the reality is that prior to the Revolutionary War, there was scant debate over the question of slavery's morality. Even in the hotbed of revolutionary activity known as New England, slavery was not particularly controversial, with most people generally not giving much thought to the injustice of the system, or finding it particularly unusual.

* * *

The nonchalant attitude toward slavery is illuminated by the way it was described in Henry Tufts's memoirs. It turns out that Henry was briefly a participant in what later became known as the Peculiar Institution, albeit as a slave driver rather than an owner, and the casual nature he uses to describe his experience is a reminder of how commonly accepted slavery was as a fact of life.

According to his autobiography, Henry worked for a while as an overseer in Virginia, a job he claims he performed not for the money or because he had a particular interest in dominating other humans, but because he was interested in the slave-owner's daughter. "To tell the truth," Henry writes, "the personal charms of the young lady, rather than the old don's money, were my principal temptations in courting an alliance with the family." So, in order to pursue this love interest and ingratiate himself with the woman's father, Henry took on the task of "superintendence of the negroes," which he called "irksome" because the slaves were prone to "tardiness" and exhibited a "disinclination to labour." Henry, however, performed his job "much to the satisfaction of my employer, who could not but observe with what rapidity his business progressed under my strenuous management."[14] (One can only wonder what sort of "strenuous management" Henry might have used to motivate the slaves to overcome their "disinclination to labour." Common punishments for insubordination included flogging, pillorying, stocking, branding, hanging, gibbeting, quartering, and disfigurement such as boring tongues or cropping ears,[15] but hopefully he didn't resort to such harsh measures.)

Although Henry never expressed any sense of superiority or hostility to black people, who make appearances in his narrative on a number of occasions, the contradictions inherent in managing slaves led many others in the slave-owning class to develop a heightened racial consciousness and an inflated sense of their own importance. Paradoxically, this tended to deepen their commitment to protecting their own freedoms and liberties. As British parliamentarian and slavery opponent Edmund Burke observed, "Where there is a vast multitude of slaves as in Virginia and Carolina, those who are free, are by far the most proud and jealous of their freedom." He argued that because of the arrogance that comes with their status as slave-owners and due to the cruelty inflicted on slaves that they perpetrated, slave-owning founders developed a unique perspective on human nature and jealously guarded their liberty against those they suspected of attempting to enslave *them*. "To the masters of slaves, the haughtiness of domination combines with the spirit of freedom, fortifies it, and renders it invincible," Burke remarked.[16]

For his part, Samuel Adams found chattel slavery objectionable, but didn't place much focus on it or treat it as the exigency that he considered the British oppression of the white colonists. He supported anti-slavery measures in Massachusetts, advocating as early as 1766 for the prohibition of buying and selling slaves in the colony, and urged ending the transatlantic slave trade. But these efforts were half-hearted at best (at least when compared to his spirited anti–British agitation), and with slavery still legal in Massachusetts on the eve of revolution in 1773, a group of slaves in the colony petitioned the House of Representatives for their freedom. Adams was appointed to the committee that would consider the petition and tentatively urged for a decision to be made granting their freedom. He wrote to fellow committee member John Pickering, Jr., that the slaves "earnestly wish that you would compleat a plan for their reliefe," and appealed to Pickering to put his plans into writing, "if it be not too much trouble."[17]

While Adams chose his words carefully and avoided overly emotional language, the slaves he advocated for were less reserved in their rhetoric. Their petition to the House appealed to Christian values in demanding their freedom from bondage, noting that they had been "held in a state of Slavery within the bowels of a free and Christian Country." Their "deplorable situation" prevented them from "shewing [their] obedience to Almighty God," the slaves wrote.[18]

It does not appear, however, that the leaders of Massachusetts shared their sense of urgency and were clearly far more concerned with the liberty of white people than the freedom of black people. In contrast to the cautious language that Samuel Adams used in politely advocating for the group of slaves petitioning for their freedom, he would forcefully denounce taxes placed on the colonies by London as akin to human bondage. In this way, it's clear that what concerned him was not so much the institution of slavery or universal principles of liberty that would extend to all people regardless of race, color or creed—what bothered him was being *treated* like slaves. "Let the Colonies still convince their implacable Enemies, that they are united in constitutional Principles, and are resolvd they WILL NOT be Slaves," he wrote in 1770.[19]

Adams repeatedly returned to this metaphor over the years, habitually and rather hyperbolically comparing British despotism to enslavement. As he stated on June 29, 1771, in the Massachusetts House of Representatives, "taxing their property without their consent, and thus appropriating it to the purposes of their slavery and destruction, is justly considered, as contrary to and subversive of their original social compact."[20] In early 1772, Adams continued to rail against slavery—not the chattel slavery as practiced in the American colonies but the metaphorical slavery allegedly being imposed on the colonists by King George. Arguing against taxation without representation, Adams wrote on January 20 that laws made in the British Parliament, "especially such laws as tend to render precarious their property," make the colonists "slaves and not free men."[21] He added that "perfect political slavery consists in their being bound to obey any laws for taxing them, to which they cannot consent."[22] Such unfair taxation "strikes at our British privileges," Adams said, noting that if "taxes are laid upon us in any shape without our having a legal Representation where they are laid, are we not reduced from the Character of free Subjects to the miserable State of tributary Slaves?"[23]

With so much focus on the evils of "slavery," i.e., the metaphorical kind, one might expect that abolishing human bondage would have been a priority for Adams and other patriots, but in fact, the practice of *actual* slavery continued in Massachusetts through the revolutionary period and was not even outlawed by the Massachusetts Constitution adopted in 1780. It was only abolished incrementally through case law, specifically by three related legal challenges considered by the Supreme Judicial Court from 1781 to 1783, which finally freed the slaves in Massachusetts.

As their approach to slavery makes clear, the patriots were rebelling against a system of monarchical and hereditary power that increasingly encroached on their rights—not clamoring for universal equality and the rights of all mankind, but for republicanism and self-government. They were resisting infringements on their liberty and in doing so hoped to topple a system in which rank and position were bestowed artificially from above, not necessarily based on merit or competence but from hereditary or personal connections that originated, ultimately, from the Crown. The position or rank of an individual in a republican society, in contrast, would come naturally from talent and ability.

But in many cases, it was precisely because of the gratitude felt for the favors that had been bestowed upon them by the Crown that some in the colonies found it difficult to break completely from the monarchical system to which they owed their status, rank, and wealth. Others genuinely felt that King George and his ministers were magnanimous benefactors acting in good faith, and were being treated unfairly by intransigent zealots such as the Loyal Nine and Sons of Liberty. They resented the rebels for bringing on the revolutionary crisis through their uncompromising stance, their fanatical rhetoric, and their escalatory violence, essentially blaming the patriots—not King George—for the ensuing war.

* * *

The loyalist ideology reflected values of tradition, law, civility, and British identity, and their views, far from being an aberration, were actually rather mainstream at one time—indeed, what the question really came down to was not *whether* someone was a loyalist or a rebel, but *at what point in time* one decided to break with the Crown. As late as 1765, Samuel Adams himself would express loyalty to Britain, stressing the colonists' "duty to the King; who holds the rights of all his subjects sacred as his own prerogative." Adams declared that the people of Massachusetts had "a warm sense of honor, freedom and independence of the subjects of a patriot King" and held "the strongest affection for his Majesty, under whose happy government they have felt all the blessings of liberty."[24] It was only by the end of the 1760s that the term "patriot" began being associated with those rebelling against the Crown rather than those who were loyal to the British Empire.[25]

Even in the early stages of the conflict in 1775, rebels largely considered themselves loyal Englishmen who were defending their rights as colonists, not necessarily challenging the legitimacy of the monarchy. In the Massachusetts Bay Colony's document explaining the events of Lexington and Concord, titled *The Narrative, of the Excursion and Ravages of the King's Troops Under the Command of General Gage, on the Nineteenth of April 1775*, the combatants were referred to as "the loyal American subjects of the British King" who were attacked by "a detachment of the forces under the command of General Gage, stationed at Boston."[26] The language describing "loyal American subjects" is a reminder that even following the Battle of Lexington and Concord and after American blood was shed on American soil, loyalty to the Crown was the norm rather than the exception.

Following the battles of Lexington, Concord, and Bunker Hill, the Second Continental Congress still hoped to avoid an all-out conflagration and appealed for peace in the Olive Branch Petition of July 5, 1775. In this document, addressed to "the King's Most Excellent Majesty," the representatives of the 13 colonies referred to themselves as "your Majesty's faithful subjects," imploring him to "entreat [his] gracious attention to this our humble petition." The colonists "assure[d] your Majesty that notwithstanding the sufferings of your loyal colonists during the course of the present controversy, our breasts retain too tender a regard for the kingdom from which we derive our origin to request such a reconciliation as might in any manner be inconsistent with her dignity or her welfare."²⁷

It was only after King George declared that the colonies were in a state of rebellion that positions would harden irrevocably and those like Adams who had previously expressed loyalty would decidedly change their tone. Following the king's August 23, 1775, declaration, the colonists realized that there was no turning back and that they were moving inexorably towards a break with England. Samuel Adams was one of the early advocates in the Continental Congress for independence. Together with John Adams and Richard Henry Lee of Virginia, Samuel Adams devised plans to dissolve royal charters and establish new state governments.²⁸ Many conceived of the struggle as something unprecedented in human history, believing that their cause was to not only defend their own liberty, but to bring freedom to the world. The revolution would open "a new prospect in human affairs," beginning "a new era in the history of mankind" and "may prove the most important step in the progressive course of human improvement," a Welsh political philosopher named Richard Price observed.²⁹

Henry Tufts, of course, remained blissfully unaware of the events unfolding. When the Shot Heard Round the World was fired in Lexington, incidentally, Henry was living comfortably with the "slothful Indians" in Canada, "contract[ing]," as he put it, "a habit of indolence, that unfitted [him] for laborious employments."³⁰ He was also ambivalent to the cause of liberty championed by Samuel Adams, holding a decidedly different perspective on this concept than the Whigs.

Much like enslaved Africans who viewed "liberty" as meaning personal freedom and emancipation from bondage rather than some abstract ideal related to the rights bestowed by the Magna Carta, Henry had a personal view of liberty that was informed by his many experiences being jailed for his crimes. In one passage of his autobiography, for example, he discusses the pain of imprisonment and confides that he "incessantly pined after that liberty, of which, by folly and indiscretion, I saw myself so totally divested."³¹ With this personal perspective, the broader version of "liberty" that the patriots clamored for held little relevance to him and he remained apathetic about the cause. Henry discovered, however, that during his three years in Indian country, his wife "had been reduced to many difficulties to sustain herself and children," and saw the unfolding war as a financial opportunity. With the enticing prospect of collecting a bounty, the cash-strapped Henry ultimately decided to enlist.³²

Other colonists, meanwhile, continued to favor a moderate path of reform and reconciliation, rejecting both the radicalism of Boston patriots and the unquestioning obedience of some supporters of King George.

But by the end of 1775 the space for a middle ground was shrinking rapidly, with a turning point being the publication of *Common Sense*, a 47-page pamphlet written by Thomas Paine advocating independence from Britain. Paine's clear and persuasive prose in *Common Sense*, published anonymously on January 10, 1776, provided moral and political arguments to encourage common people to fight against British rule. Not only did it explicitly advocate independence from England, it called into question the very foundation of monarchy, appealing to reason in the rejection of the divine right of kings to rule—especially from 3,000 miles away.

"There is something exceedingly ridiculous in the composition of Monarchy," Paine observed.

> It first excludes a man from the means of information, yet empowers him to act in cases where the highest judgment is required. The state of a king shuts him from the World, yet the business of a king requires him to know it thoroughly; wherefore the different parts, by unnaturally opposing and destroying each other, prove the whole character to be absurd and useless.

By presenting the arguments against monarchy and for self-rule so clearly, Paine inspired many colonists to join the struggle not just for their rights as Englishmen, but for a new system of government—a republic. "We have it in our power to begin the world over again," Paine wrote. "The birthday of a new world is at hand, and a race of men, perhaps as numerous as all Europe contains, are to receive their portion of freedom from the events of a few months."[33]

The pamphlet was distributed widely and read aloud at taverns and meeting places, becoming a widespread sensation and a rallying cry for the patriot cause. Buoyed by the intellectual arguments against monarchy and for independence (and with blood being shed on the battlefield), it became increasingly difficult for Americans to maintain neutrality. *Common Sense* more clearly defined what was at stake in the struggle and all colonists were expected to choose sides.

Many Americans, however, continued to find themselves personally conflicted. Peter Oliver, for example, was a Boston native who graduated from Harvard College in 1730 and went on to run an importing business and an iron works before being appointed Justice of the Peace in 1744. During the revolutionary crisis he came down on the side of reconciliation with London and was harassed by Sons of Liberty for his oblique defense of British imperial power. He was forced from his judgeship in 1774 due to public outrage over his acceptance of a pay raise paid for by the Crown and would become a vocal critic of the armed revolution.

On January 11, 1776—the day after *Common Sense* was first published—Oliver described the mental anguish that he felt over the situation facing the colonies. "Many a tear of pity have I dropped for you and for the fate of my country, and many more tears I fear that I shall be forced to shed for that wrath which awaits you from an offended Heaven and an injured government," Oliver wrote in *The Massachusetts Gazette & Boston Weekly News-Letter*. He appealed to the conscience of those who had taken up arms to come to their senses, noting that "many of your associates have already quitted the field of battle to appear before that solemn tribunal where the plea of the united force of all the colonies will be of no avail to bribe the judgment or avert the sentence of an offended Deity."[34]

Oliver's lamentations provide a window into the difficulties that many people who would be lumped into the "loyalist" camp were experiencing—conflicted over love of their country with an intimate understanding of the horrors of war, and deeply concerned about God's judgment for the violence being committed in the name of liberty. But these distinctions were unwelcome to many in the patriot camp, who increasingly viewed those like Oliver, despite their nuanced or even somewhat sympathetic views, as incorrigible enemies. Lukewarm support for the patriot cause was viewed by many rebels as insufficient; nothing less than complete devotion to the revolution was acceptable.

* * *

Just as in the Civil War that would be fought nearly a century later, the Revolutionary War deeply divided families. These familial divisions impacted those who fought on the battlefield and those who exercised the power of the pen rather than the sword. Gouverneur Morris, for example, who would later be one of the principal authors of the United States Constitution, was a backer of the patriot cause, which would align him with one half-brother—Lewis Morris, a signer of the Declaration of Independence—but would alienate him from another half-brother who served as a general in the British Army. His mother would remain a committed loyalist throughout the war, and two of his sisters married loyalists.[35]

Another prominent family of early America divided by loyalties was the Clintons. George Clinton served as the royal governor of New York from 1743 to 1753 and was an admiral in the British Navy. His son, Sir Henry Clinton, succeeded General Howe as commander of the British forces in 1778, and led a number of important military campaigns.[36] He fought the patriots at the Battle of Bunker Hill and remained active in the British service throughout the war, resigning finally in June 1782. Meanwhile, another branch of the Clinton family was active in the patriot cause, with James Clinton one of the most successful generals in the war. American General James Clinton participated in a triumphant effort to prevent British General Henry Clinton from assisting General John Burgoyne at Saratoga, but failed to hold Forts Clinton and Montgomery. Meanwhile, his brother George Clinton, a signer of the Declaration of Independence, served as the first governor of the state of New York, and then eight years as the nation's fourth vice-president in the administrations of Thomas Jefferson and James Madison.[37]

Benjamin Franklin's family would also be divided by the war, with his son William taking the side of the king. And then of course, there is America's most infamous turncoat, Benedict Arnold, who appeared to be motivated by a number of factors in his fateful decision to switch sides in 1780, including his bitterness over perceived slights by the Continental Army, a malicious prosecution, his personal ambitions and debts, and the loyalist sympathies of his wife, Peggy Shippen Arnold.

The Tufts family also had divided loyalties, with some choosing personal relationships over ideology. Henry's great-uncle Simon Tufts, for example, testified on behalf of suspected loyalist Isaac Royall, from Medford, Massachusetts, who was facing the prospect of having his property confiscated in 1778. The state of Massachusetts had decided that it would begin seizing the property of absentees who supported the British Crown, and as Royall had sailed to England, he granted power of attorney to Simon Tufts to defend him. Simon was respected and fairly well-connected, often appearing in the diary of John Adams as an associate with whom he would have tea, and Royall hoped that his support would carry enough weight to convince the state to return his property. Simon Tufts testified that Royall was "a friend of the American cause," but that out of fear and confusion, decided to flee revolutionary Massachusetts, a claim that the selectmen of Medford rejected. Dismissing Tufts's arguments, they ruled that Royall had chosen the side of the Crown, which made his property liable to confiscate. Simon Tufts and Isaac Royall remained in contact, however, and as of 1779, Royall was writing to Tufts to insist that he hoped "to return home as soon as my health will admit of."[38]

Simon Tufts's son, Simon Tufts, Jr., was also branded a Tory and essentially exiled from his American homeland. A Boston storeowner, Simon Tufts, Jr., left for Halifax with the British Army in 1776 and later made his way to London. The Massachusetts Act of October 16, 1778, banished him as a loyalist but years later he sought to return. Cotton Tufts wrote to Abigail Adams in 1786, while she was living in London, asking whether she might be able to inquire about his status. "Do you know whether my Brors Son Simon is in England," Cotton wrote. "If in London information may be had of them, should it lay in your Way, I wish you to enquire him out." Cotton informed Abigail that Simon Jr. wished to return home, "but conscious to himself of the inoffensive part which he has acted, that he does not incline to return untill the way is fully open." Despite the best efforts of Cotton Tufts, Simon Tufts, Jr., never returned to the United States.[39]

For his part, despite enlisting in the army, Henry Tufts did not appear to be particularly enamored with the patriot cause, dismissively describing in his memoirs "the horrors of a civil war [that] had burst forth between England and her colonies in America."[40] He continued to apply his trade as a thief while in the army, stealing from officers when his rations were too low, and rather than touting the glory of the cause, he eventually expressed regret for enlisting. He became one of many thousands who would desert from the Continental Army once the harsh realities of war hit home.

Many other Tuftses, however, would serve honorably in Continental Army, with the number of patriot soldiers numbering 15 according to one tally. Among the Tuftses who fought on the patriot side were Henry's brother Eliphalet, who appears to have served from 1777 until the end of the war in 1781. He fought in the Battle of Saratoga, a major turning point in the war, and was discharged on November 11, 1781, less than a month after the British surrendered following the Battle of Yorktown.[41] The Tufts clan can also boast one African American member of the Continental Army. Although nothing is known of his early life, Cato Tufts appears to be a former slave who took the surname of his owner, and appears on various lists of black soldiers in the war. In *Massachusetts Soldiers and Sailors of the Revolutionary War*, published in 1896, it notes that he joined the eight month's service on May 15, 1775, in the company of Capt. Oliver Parker.[42] The 1903 study *Medford in the Revolution* claims that he fought at the Battle of Bunker Hill.[43]

Another Tufts, or rather a William *Tuffs*, possibly a relative of Henry Tufts, also claims to have fought in the Battle of Bunker Hill, as well as having taken part in the Boston Tea Party.[44] Although the genealogy is not entirely clear, it appears that William was the son of John Tufts, a mariner who raised a family in Medford, Massachusetts, then moved to North Yarmouth, Maine, and appears to have settled in Halifax, New Brunswick. John, apparently, was suspected at one time of being a loyalist, with his name appearing on a blacklist in revolutionary New England, which would have made for tumultuous times in his household if his son was a radical who dumped British tea in the Boston harbor. Family researcher Tom Tufts notes that simply judging by geographical clues, it is reasonable to conclude that John Tufts was in fact a loyalist. As a mariner based in Halifax, he would have been engaged in transport and commerce for the British and it would have been hard to resist England which ran a naval port there. The area has also been described as settled by loyalists.[45]

While it is not clear how strong John Tufts's loyalist sympathies may have been—or even whether he harbored any at all—it appears that at least in his case, the loyalty that he may have had for the Crown would have had economic motives rather than political ones. This sense of pragmatic opportunism was also what motivated Henry Tufts to first join the revolutionary cause in order to receive the bounty and later to become an unwitting agent for the British as a counterfeiter.

* * *

The Revolutionary War was an economic conflict as well as a military confrontation, and London employed various methods to damage the economy and undermine the cause. Limiting American trade with foreign nations and counterfeiting Congressional currency were two of the most effective means.[46] To diminish the value of authentic money, the British distributed counterfeit currency, calculating that if the economy was in tatters, it would be impossible for the Continental Congress to pay for the men and material needed to continue the war, and few soldiers or officers would be inclined to serve in a military that could only pay them in nearly worthless paper currency. The counterfeiting scheme contributed to persistent depreciation of Continental currency, leading to the popular expression "not worth a Continental." Prices climbed to eight times what they had been at the beginning of the conflict and merchants began to refuse doing business with the paper currency.[47]

In May 1780, King George III expressed confidence that America's financial distress would force the Continentals to surrender, and hoped to hasten the process by circulating counterfeit bills. Congress was well aware of this practice and publicized how to identify the fake money, noting, for example that "in the Border at the Top of the Bill over the Words 'United States,' the two L's in the Word 'Dollars' are more irregular and more from a straight Line than in the true Bills."[48]

According to his autobiography, Henry Tufts would become a participant in this British scheme, which had nothing to do with any desire to undermine the cause of independence but simply because it was profitable. As Henry describes it, while he was in a tavern one day in 1780, "a stranger, a genteel, well looking man, who, on committing his steed to the hoostler, assumed a seat near mine." Striking up a conversation, Tufts describes the man as "affable and engaging," and the two became fast friends. The man, named Whiting, identified himself as an agent for the British, who had employed him as an emissary to circulate counterfeit money.

He offered Henry $1000 to help him distribute, an offer which Henry claims that he initially hesitated to accept—not because of any moral scruples over the crime of counterfeiting or undermining the revolutionary cause, but simply because he worried that it was too much money to accept from a stranger. Whiting, however, assured him that he could "spare it very well," as he had $50,000 in his pocket, and in fact he "should esteem it a great favour" if Henry would assist him in "discharg[ing] bills, at particular places."

Henry understood full well the purpose of the counterfeit money. As he describes it,

> Congress had issued a paper medium to raise armies, and pay off their troops, it imported their adversaries to discredit the currency as effectually as possible. And, as such large quantities of paper, had been emitted already, the speediest way to effect the entire dissolution of that system was to inundate the country with counterfeit bills.[49]

Henry also had personally experienced the effects of inflation, as he explained in an earlier passage of the book. At one point he had attempted to buy a farm, he explained, only to discover that his paper money had "depreciated, at such a rate, that I eventually lost the major part of" it.[50] But although he knew firsthand the effects of inflation and understood that the counterfeit currency was intended to further cripple the American economy and undermine the war effort, Henry had no qualms about participating in the scheme. The only real concern that he seemed to have about accepting the money from Whiting was whether the counterfeit bills would be detected. As soon as he began distributing them, however, he realized that the British were quite adept at counterfeiting American money. "I found not the slightest difficulty in passing them," Henry writes. "Indeed my bills were such an exact imitation of the genuine ones, that a man must have had more penetration than ordinary, to had discerned the slightest difference." He put the fake money to use right away, purchasing for himself "a good horse, a new suit of clothes, and materials for a complete suit of female apparel." The "female apparel" he gave to his lady friend Sally, to whom he also presented 50 counterfeit dollars to atone for "the damage her character had sustained through my means."[51]

Henry was lucky that his passing of counterfeit money was never detected, as the Continental Army naturally took this offense quite seriously. A fellow deserter by the name of David Gambell was found with counterfeit money in his possession and was sentenced to death by order of General George Washington.[52]

* * *

Flooding the country with counterfeit currency was just one of the perfidious acts employed by the wily British to undermine the American war effort. Bribery of American patriots also proved to be an effective method of divide-and-conquer, and one that would even be attempted against Samuel Adams. When royal officials suggested to Governor Thomas Hutchinson that an attempt be made to allure Adams to the British side with offers of lucrative offices, the governor replied that "such is the obstinacy and inflexible disposition of the man, that he never can be conciliated by any office or gift whatever."[53] Nevertheless, the Brits tried to bribe him anyway.

According to an 1865 biography of Adams by his great-grandson, William V. Wells, Governor Thomas Gage tried to win Adams over in the summer of 1774 after Adams had fallen on hard times financially and had difficulty feeding his family. Through an emissary named John Fenton, an army captain, Governor Gage "sent a confidential and verbal message," Wells recounts. "He said that ... he had been empowered to confer upon him such benefits as would be satisfactory, upon the condition that he would engage to cease in his opposition to the measures of government." Gage's offer of riches was also accompanied by a veiled threat of punishment if Adams persisted in his rebellious activities. Adams was warned that "his conduct had been such as made him liable to the penalties ... by which persons could be sent to England for trial." By affirming his loyalty and cooperating with the Crown, Adams "would not only receive great personal advantages, but would thereby make his peace with the King."[54]

After listening politely, Adams reportedly replied:

> Sir, I trust I have long since made my peace with the King of kings. No personal consideration shall induce me to abandon the righteous cause of my country. Tell Governor Gage it is the advice of Samuel Adams to him no longer to insult the feelings of an exasperated people.

The exchange between Adams and Fenton is credited to an oral history by Hannah Wells, who was the revolutionary's last surviving child, and although it has been widely cited in subsequent works on Samuel Adams, the bribery attempt has not been corroborated by British documents or New England sources. The anecdote, however, would be in keeping with what is known about Adams's uncompromising integrity and the scorn that he had for those who failed to get behind the cause of liberty. He called loyalists and fence-sitters "contemptible enemies," noting that they suffer from a "spirit which can render them patient of slavery."[55]

* * *

This, however, may not have been a fair representation of all the fence-sitters, as some had just come to believe during the fighting that war, perhaps, was simply not the answer to the grievances that colonists had about their treatment at the hands of King George III and the unfair taxation imposed by Parliament. Towards the end of 1776, following a series of defeats suffered by the Continental Army, London continued to make peace overtures and offers of a negotiated settlement. Admiral Lord Howe, in November 1776, appealed for conciliation with the rebels, offering an amnesty to patriot fighters who would take an oath of allegiance to the king and pledge their "peaceable obedience." According to this proclamation, dated November 30, anyone who accepted the offer would "reap the benefit of his Majesty's paternal goodness, in the preservation of their property, the restoration of their commerce, and the security of their most valuable rights." This led to thousands of rebels flocking to British camps to declare their loyalty.[56]

For rebels who declined this carrot offered by the king, the Brits also had plenty of sticks. Patriots captured in battle could expect to endure hellish conditions as prisoners of war, and sometimes faced summary execution. With some 20,000 Americans taken prisoner during the conflict, at least 8,000 and as many as 11,000 died in captivity.[57] Particularly following Washington's defeat at the Battle of Long Island in 1776, the numbers of American POWs swelled, with multitudes crowded into warehouses and prison ships anchored offshore, the most notorious of which was the *Jersey*. Philip Freneau was among the prisoners on this cramped and vermin-infested ship, and immortalized his ordeal in a widely read poem about his experiences, titled *The British Prison Ship*:

> The various horrors of these hulks to tell,
> These Prison Ships where pain and horror dwell,
> Where death in tenfold vengeance holds his reign,
> And injur'd ghosts, yet unaveng'd, complain;
> This be my task—ungenerous Britons, you
> Conspire to murder those you can't subdue.[58]

The horrendous treatment that prisoners endured, combined with frustration over battlefield defeats and the continued resistance to the revolution from loyalists, led rebels to increase their demands for public endorsements of independence and denunciations of the British. In the 1770s, the American colonies passed laws demanding oaths of allegiance and instituted the death penalty for those who expressed loyalty to King George. Suspected Tories were put on trial and if found guilty, typically received 39 lashes as punishment (39 being the upper limit of what was considered allowed under Christian principles, as this was the number of lashes that Jesus purportedly received before being crucified[59]). Those who refused to shout "Liberty Forever" would be suspended by their thumbs until they did so,[60] and suspected loyalists could also face the mob justice of tar-and-feathering, scalping, or burning.[61] One loyalist woman in Connecticut was threatened by the patriots with a tar-and-feathering simply for naming her baby "Thomas Gage," after the British general.[62]

The rigid enforcement of the patriotic hive mind even extended to religious worship. During the spring of 1776, the rector of New York City's Trinity Church, Charles Inglis, continued to lead prayers for King George and the royal family despite growing threats from the patriots.

6. Patriots, Slaves and Loyalists

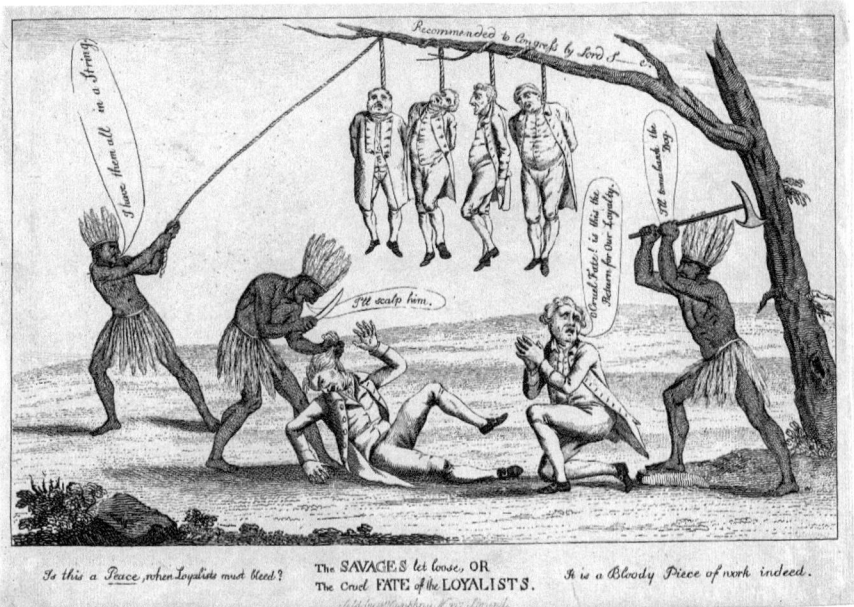

This cartoon by William Humphrey, "Savages Let Loose, or the Cruel Fate of the Loyalists," reflects the British perspective on Americans exacting revenge on loyalists following the conclusion of the Revolutionary War. With the Indians symbolizing Americans, loyalists are shown being scalped and hanged. During the war, the British often criticized American fighting tactics such as ambushes and raids, which in some cases were borrowed from Native Americans (*The Savages Let Loose, or the Cruel Fate of the Loyalists*, William Humphrey, London, 1783. Metropolitan Museum of Art, Gift of William H. Huntington, 1883).

One Sunday an angry mob of more than 150 men stormed the church carrying muskets and bayonets, threatening to shoot anyone who prayed for the king. Undeterred, Inglis prayed anyway. The mob held its fire but due to continued threats, the congregation decided by mid–July to close the Anglican churches and Inglis fled to upstate New York. A few months later, on September 21, 1776, Trinity Church would be burned to the ground in a huge fire that the British blamed on rebel arsonists.[63]

In this climate, many colonists who harbored sympathies with the British cause kept it a closely guarded secret, while others fled the cities and sought refuge in the countryside. Some remained loyal to the king in their hearts but would outwardly display support for the patriot cause to avoid reprisals. Others—like Henry Tufts—joined the Continental Army only out of expediency and not necessarily out of a deep commitment to the revolution, and even those inspired to take up arms after reading

Painted by Archibald Willard for the 100th anniversary of the Declaration of Independence, *The Spirit of '76* (originally known as *Yankee Doodle*) was initially derided by art critics but grew in popularity over time. Displayed at Philadelphia's Centennial Exhibition in 1876, the painting was reproduced as a lithograph that was purchased by thousands across the country. The original painting is displayed at Abbot Hall in Marblehead, Massachusetts, which also happens to be the site of Henry Tufts's final arrest for stealing six silver spoons in 1794 (courtesy Abbot Hall in Marblehead, Massachusetts).

Common Sense may have come to regret their choice once the realities of military life came more closely into focus. But regardless how many identified as patriots, loyalists, or neutral bystanders, one thing that is clear is that the conflict was anything but a simple, one-dimensional struggle of right and wrong, or "patriots vs. redcoats." It was in fact a morally ambiguous and complicated affair in which financial interests played a sizable role, and one that deeply divided the country, compelling many to rethink their views on concepts such as loyalty and patriotism.

The hardships imposed by the revolution also led some to question the very utility of war itself, with women, in particular, increasingly voicing dissent and dissatisfaction. A widely read poem authored by "A Daughter of Liberty, Living in Marblehead," called for peace and urged those responsible for launching the revolution to repent. "If we forsake our heinous sins," the poem read, "For sin is all the cause of this, We must not take it then amiss."

Assuming an increasingly strident tone, the poem challenged the basis for the revolutionary struggle and seemed to question the wisdom of the patriots' uncompromising stance:

> Wan't it for our polluted tongues
> This cruel war would ne'er begun.
> We should hear no fife nor drum,
> Nor training bands would never come:
> Should we go on our sinful course,
> Times will grow on us worse and worse.
> Then gracious GOD now cause to cease,
> This bloody war and give us peace![64]

One can only wonder if Samuel Adams read this poem and whether he took the reference to the "polluted tongues" to heart. After all, it was his tongue—and pen—that was more responsible than anyone's for setting the colonies on this "sinful course," and ensuring that times would grow "worse and worse." But as someone who was known as steadfast in the cause and thoroughly convinced of its righteousness, if he ever had doubts about the course he had set, he kept them to himself.

7

Spirit of '76?

Marblehead, Massachusetts, has more than one claim to fame. Not only is it the location of one of the defining moments during the build-up to the Revolutionary War—the rebellion against a British impressment gang in 1769—it also played a key role in the war itself, contributing hundreds of able-bodied men who proved indispensable at the Battle of Trenton in late 1776. The town is also the host of one of America's most famous paintings, "The Spirit of '76," which was produced in 1876 for America's first centennial and originally titled "Yankee Doodle." Marblehead, for what it's worth, also has the dubious distinction of being the location of Henry Tufts's final arrest in 1794.

Being the site of Tufts's last run-in with the law and the home of one of the best-known paintings celebrating the American Revolution, Marblehead perfectly embodies the contradictory currents that helped to characterize an era that is best known for the lofty rhetoric in the Declaration of Independence and the founding of the republic, but was also characterized by petty crime and widespread political indifference among colonists scraping to get by. Even the name of the painting, "The Spirit of '76," implies that a certain level of zeal was widely shared during this period of upheaval. To be alive in the year 1776 when America declared its independence must mean, it is assumed, that you were a patriot who fully embraced the revolutionary cause. In contrast to the painting that symbolized the spirit of the American Revolution, depicting three generations of Continental soldiers marching fearlessly into battle beating a drum and blowing a fife, Tufts's arrest for stealing six silver spoons offered a reminder that not all shared the revolutionary spirit.

Henry Tufts was one of many Americans at the lower end of the social hierarchy more interested in trying to get ahead than defending liberty. He saw military service not as a chance to valiantly take on the British, but as an opportunity for personal gain. While this might not have been the motivation that Samuel Adams had in mind when he helped set America on course for a bloody revolution, facing shortages of men, the

Continental Army could not be too picky. At the beginning of the celebrated year of 1776, General Washington would worry that the contest would be lost not on the battlefield but simply because of personnel problems, with thousands of soldiers abandoning the cause before it even had a chance to succeed. Popular support for the war appeared to peak at the high point of enthusiasm in spring and summer 1775, and as winter set in and 1775 came to an end, people grew increasingly weary of worthless money, supply shortages, harassment by local committees of safety, and seemingly endless fighting.[1]

Out of a colonial population of 2.5 million, the Continental Army had managed to recruit a little more than 22,000 soldiers, but with enlistment contracts expiring on January 1, 1776, entire regiments were leaving the battlefield and heading for home, with more than half of the enlisted men calling it quits. Congress hadn't paid the army for two months in a row, and many dissatisfied soldiers believed their commitments were over. Washington wrote that "few people know the predicament we are in,"[2] pulling no punches about the army's dire circumstances. "Search the volumes of history through," Washington wrote, "and I much question whether a case similar to ours is to be found ... to have one army disbanded, and another to raise, within the same distance of a reinforced enemy; it is too much to attempt—what may be the final issue of the last manouvre, time can only tell."[3] In an effort to salvage what it could of the Continental Army, Congress changed the standard enlistment from one to three years, or the duration of the war, and authorized the "Eighty-eight Battalion Resolve," which would be the largest reorganization of the war.[4]

Washington found that many soldiers were not only fickle but often unruly and difficult to control. The army consisted of hardy, independent folk who were accustomed to difficult conditions and hard work, but not particularly used to taking orders. In some cases, the material that Washington had to work with consisted of the dregs of society, but more often they were simple laborers and farmers. The vast majority were not lawyers such as John Adams or merchants such as John Hancock or politicians such as Samuel Adams, but shoemakers, carpenters, blacksmiths, coopers, ship chandlers, sailors, fishermen, and tailors.[5]

The story of Henry Tufts serves as a reminder that while many of these people may have joined the Continental Army at one time or another during the seven-year Revolutionary War, their commitment to the cause was often lukewarm at best and depended very much on their personal circumstances—a reality that Samuel Adams came to realize in 1776. Towards the end of the year, he wrote to James Warren expressing hope that an "increase of Pay will ... induce them to continue in the Army till a full Inlistment of our Quota for a new Army shall be compleated."[6] This was a tacit recognition that while revolutionary ideals may have been a motivating factor among some patriots, the enticement of increasing pay was a more realistic way to ensure the survival of the cause. Likewise, Tufts describes his decision to join the Continental Army as "the best method of supporting self and family, in a way consistent with my beloved ease, and at the same time, as, certainly more honorable than thievish pursuits, though a soldier in fact, may be a thief."[7]

Indeed, although some soldiers, especially early on in the conflict, were undoubtedly motivated by patriotism and a sense of duty, quite a few of them, like Henry, were criminals, and even when they took up arms, they were not quite ready to give up their "thievish pursuits." Whether out of necessity or iniquity, soldiers often engaged in theft, stealing from each other, from the officers, and from the civilians. As Henry told it, when he joined the army and was stationed at Winter Hill in Boston, "our troops fared, at times, so slenderly, that we had to atone for the dearth of allowance, by stealing pigs, poultry, and other such like articles."[8]

Disobedience and theft, in fact, were widespread in the Continental Army and a growing cause for concern among the military leadership. Joseph Reed, one of George Washington's aides-de-camp early in the war who would eventually hold the ranks of colonel and adjutant-general, wrote in 1776 that "a spirit of desertion, cowardice, plunder, and shirking from duty when attended with fatigue or danger, prevailed but too generally."[9] With civilians routinely victimized, many looked with disdain at the soldiery as the riffraff of society, often viewing them as both foolish for having enlisted and as a potential threat that might steal their fowl, fruits and vegetables.[10]

Even General Washington was known to lament that the people who made up his fighting force were not always of the highest quality, and worried that their disrespect for the private property of civilians might push neutrals into the loyalist camp. Following some unfortunate incidents in the summer of 1776, Washington wrote to John Hancock expressing dismay over "the infamous practice of Plundering," which he described as "Instances of People being frieghtned out of their Houses under pretence of those Houses being ordered to be burnt, & this is done with a view of siezing the Goods." In other words, Washington's soldiers threatened civilians with burning their houses down in order to steal the contents of the homes. In some instances, Washington regretted that "houses have actually been burnt to cover the theft."[11]

In order to deal with these war crimes, Washington ordered Major General Israel Putnam to ensure that "the Officers also, are to exert themselves to the utmost to prevent every kind of abuse to private property, or to bring every offender, to the punishment he deserves." Noting how shameful it was to see "men, who have come hither, in defense of the rights of mankind, should turn invaders of it by destroying the substance of their friends," Washington forbade "the burning of houses ... & the pillaging of them." He expressed hope that "men who have property of their own, & a reguard for the rights of others, will shudder at the thought of rendering any man's situation, to whose protection he had come, more insufferable than his open and avowed Enemy would make it."[12]

As a southern aristocratic gentleman, Washington had little tolerance for the low breeding and ill manners of the men under his command, particularly those from New England. He called the yankees "exceeding[ly] dirty and nasty," observing an "unaccountable kind of stupidity in the lower class," which was not limited to the rank and file but also could be found in the officers.[13] "These people," he wrote, had "such a dearth of public spirit and want of virtue." Washington could not comprehend the "dirty, mercenary spirit [that] pervades the whole," and at times, he regretted taking on the responsibility of leading such an army of rabble. "Could I have foreseen what I have and am like to experience, no consideration upon earth should have induced me to accept this command," he admitted.[14] Washington recognized that this army of rabble lacked both discipline and motivation.

"The distinction between a well regulated army, & a mob, is the good order & discipline of the first, & the licentious & disorderly behaviour of the latter," Washington wrote to Putnam. "Men, therefore, who are not employed, as mere hirelings, but have step'd forth in defence of every thing that is dear & valuable, not only to themselves but to posterity, should take uncommon pains to conduct themselves with uncommon propriety & good order; as their honor reputation &c. call loudly upon them for it."[15] This reflected General Washington's belief in the need for proper leadership, impressing upon his colleagues in the military command that they must show "perseverance and spirit" in commanding their troops and remind them of "the goodness of our cause."[16]

But the hardships were considerable and in some cases soldiers found them intolerable. One soldier under Washington's command described the "sufferings" his company endured in the autumn of 1776, during a torrential rain storm in Newark, there was "no tent to cover us at night—exposed to cold and rains day and night."[17] Soldiers also had to grapple with their fear of combat, homesickness, and family problems, all of which contributed to a sense of desperation among many who saw fleeing the army as their only hope, despite the risk of hanging or death by firing squad that desertion entailed.

Many soldiers were also less concerned with the cause than with the financial compensation for fighting, and a good number, Henry Tufts among them, would desert once the realities of war became clear or once they had collected their first payment. John Adams had observed that more men were dying of "dirty frying pans," meaning dysentery, than from musket fire, but desertions would prove to be an even bigger challenge than disease. Following a series of British victories in New York during the summer of 1776, American soldiers began leaving in droves, with many defecting to the enemy.[18] One or two men were deserting at a time, and sometimes entire companies would walk off *en masse*, leaving fewer and fewer troops to face the British.[19] The effects of this are difficult to overstate.

At the beginning of the New York campaign, in August 1776, Washington had an army of about 20,000. By November, following defeats at Brooklyn, Kips Bay, and White Plains, his band of soldiers would dwindle to under 10,000.[20] Then, in an army that was already desperately hemorrhaging men, the American surrender of Fort Washington on November 16, 1776, would prove to be an utter catastrophe for the patriot cause. In the final devastating chapter of Washington's disastrous New York campaign, thousands were taken as prisoners of war by the British,[21] and following this defeat, Washington's army would number just 3,500.[22]

The shortage of men was such a chronic problem that Congress decided in 1776 to provide soldiers bounties of 20 dollars and 100 acres of land,[23] which individual states would increase to bonuses of 400 dollars and 300 acres to those who would commit for the duration. This led at times to men enlisting to receive the bonus, then deserting and re-enlisting in another unit, in order to receive another bounty. One soldier was convicted in 1778 of deserting seven times.[24] Henry Tufts himself enlisted and deserted twice, it seems, and much of his narrative focuses on the difficulties he faced being constantly hunted as a deserter. After taking his leave from the army, he was relentlessly pursued wherever he went. Trying to blend in proved difficult, as he would discover in Litchfield, Vermont, where a rumor spread that he was a deserter, which "caused sundry people to concert schemes of seizing me by surprise." Chased by "several men on horseback," he took refuge with his brother Thomas Tufts, but eventually had to flee to the woods. "At this era of the revolution," Henry observed, "there existed the greatest exigency for men to recruit the army, which was the main reason, I presume, of my being hunted with such obstinate pertinacity."[25] He was ultimately captured and put in Exeter jail for desertion but subsequently escaped.

Late in the war, he was taken by surprise by a group of citizens in Lee, New Hampshire, who held an "an inveterate grudge" against him for his "former misdemeanors." They captured Henry and handed him over to the army. Locked up in prison in Newbury with two fellow deserters,

Mark White and James Atkins, who Henry points out "had deserted from the army, sundry times before," the three eventually managed to escape together.[26]

* * *

All in all, it is estimated that the average desertion rate in the Continental Army was 20 to 25 percent, with some estimates as high as one-third. The rate in the state militias was even higher, with the New Jersey regiment suffering from a 42 percent desertion rate in 1777[27] and a conservative estimate putting the rate of desertion from the Virginia militia at half.[28] While many of these were bona fide desertions, quite a few would more properly be defined in today's terms as soldiers going absent without leave, or AWOL. Historian David McCullough points out that "for every full-fledged deserter there were half a dozen others inclined to stroll off on almost any pretext, to do a little clam digging perhaps, or who might vanish for several weeks to see wives and children, help with the harvest at home, or ply their trades for some much needed 'hard money.'"[29]

Although the desertion rate declined toward the end of the war, the revolutionary cause was plagued throughout the conflict by a chronic shortage of men, with one of the main problems being the resistance to harsh military discipline administered for minor violations, which was naturally a turnoff to many soldiers. The Continental officers, often quite unfamiliar with military life and having little idea what they were supposed to do,[30] were notorious for their arrogance and severity, with as many as 500 lashes being meted out over a period of several weeks for trivial offenses. Stories such as a soldier receiving 50 lashes for cutting up a blanket were not uncommon, and more serious offenses, such as striking an officer, inciting a mutiny, and cowardice in the face of the enemy could all be punished by death.[31] The harsh discipline increased the level of resentment in the ranks. As one enlisted man from Maryland, revealing a certain level of animosity towards the command structure of military life, declared in 1776, "it was better for the poor people to lay down their arms and pay the duties and taxes laid upon them by King and Parliament than to be brought into slavery and ordered about as they were."[32]

Drinking was a common problem, and New England soldiers, in particular, were known for their fondness of rum, but would also imbibe in grog, gin, wine and brandy. According to a British ship's surgeon who visited some rebel camps and observed the provisions being offered to the troops, the average consumption of rum consisted of one bottle a day per man.[33] In his autobiography, Henry Tufts alludes to the prevalence of drinking in the camp with an anecdote of pilfering a gallon of rum with a fake four-dollar bill. Henry and his friends drank the liquor with meat stolen from the commissary and "regaled ourselves like lords upon these goodly things, which we devoured with as keen avidity, as though they had been acquired ever so honestly, while I received the applause of every guest, as well for my zeal, as ingenious contrivance."[34]

The Continental Army was notorious for its harsh conditions, with common hardships being poor or non-existent food and clothing, crowded and unsanitary camps, and rampant disease, realities which were compounded by infrequent paydays and rampant monetary inflation.[35] Even when soldiers did receive pay, they often had to use it in order to purchase their own provisions, a reality that Henry explains in his memoirs. Early in the war, he describes being encamped at Cambridge, where "we were forced to submit to much hardship, and were extremely exposed to the fire of the enemy the whole time." With provisions being scarce, the soldiers were "obliged to spend part of our wages to prevent absolute starvation," Henry recalled.[36] Not satisfied with this situation, Henry resorted to theft to supplement his meager rations. "Having enlisted," Henry writes, "I had orders to repair to Andover by a certain day, there to pass muster, and receive bounty and accoutrements, which, indeed, had been my only inducement to the transaction." But after receiving "some money and other articles" upon enlistment, Tufts was disappointed that it was "not … the quantity stipulated."[37]

* * *

While desertion, discipline and enlistment shortfalls were widespread problems, they were only symptomatic of a more fundamental issue facing the revolutionary cause, which was popular ambivalence over the rebellion, as well as a lack of clarity about the rebellion's aims. Many of the enlistees simply didn't share the sense of zeal for the revolutionary cause that people such as Samuel Adams held. Even among those who joined the army, at least at the beginning of the conflict, democratic ideals and independence from Britain were not at the forefront of their thoughts. A few weeks after the Battle of Lexington and Concord, Richard Henry Lee had introduced in the Congress "proposals for raising an Army," but was met with questions from fellow delegates about what the purpose of such an army might be. John Rutledge, a delegate from South Carolina, emphasized that "some other points must be settled, such as do We aim at independency? or do We only ask for a Restoration of Rights and putting of Us on Our old footing."[38] These questions were generally avoided, with even General Washington skirting the subject of independence, instead calling the rebellion "a defense of all that is dear and valuable in life."[39]

Those who fought at Lexington and Concord or at Bunker Hill were not at that time calling for independence, and most in the army in early

1776 would have said that what they were fighting for was defense of their country and their rightful liberties as Englishmen, not necessarily to break away from the mother country. Nathanael Greene, who was a major general of the Continental Army and earned a reputation as one of General Washington's most indispensable officers, considered the British redcoats as "invaders" who had to be repelled and told his wife that the objective of the war was to "defend our common rights."[40] It wasn't until later in 1776 that talk of declaring independence became more prominent.

Samuel Adams, who as early as 1774 had stated that "the country shall be independent, and we will be satisfied with nothing short of it,"[41] was among the most vocal advocates for a Declaration of Independence, arguing that America was for all intents and purposes already independent. As he asked in a letter to the Rev. Samuel Cooper on April 3, 1776, "Can Nations at War be said to be dependent either upon the other?" Rejecting the notion that formally declaring independence would "forever shut the Door of Reconciliation," Adams pointed out that any reconciliation with Britain would be based on "our abjectly submitting to tyranny."[42]

On June 7, Richard Henry Lee, possibly at the prodding of Adams who was one of the most influential delegates in the Continental Congress, offered a resolution which stated "that these United Colonies are, and of right ought to be, free and independent States, that they are absolved from all allegiance to the British Crown, and that all political connection between them and the State of Great Britain is, and to be, totally dissolved." Two committees were then formed in Congress—one to draft the Declaration of Independence, with Thomas Jefferson to be the chief author, and another committee to develop the Articles of Confederation. Adams was appointed to the latter committee.[43]

The Declaration of Independence was adopted on July 4, 1776, with nearly one-half of the 1,300-word Declaration of Independence devoted to complaints about the colonists' perceived mistreatment at the hands of King George III. The Declaration of Independence would highlight, among many other grievances, of the king's "cutting off our Trade with all Parts of the World, ... imposing Taxes on us without our Consent, ... [and] depriving us, in many Cases, of the Benefits of Trial by Jury."

Some of its language echoed points made in Samuel Adams's *The Rights of the Colonists*, which was submitted as a Report of the Committee of Correspondence to the Boston Town Meeting in November 1772. Whereas Adams in 1772 had expressed "the natural rights of the Colonists" as "a right to life ... liberty ... [and] property,"[44] Jefferson in the Declaration of Independence wrote that "all men ... are endowed by their Creator with certain unalienable Rights, that among these are Life, Liberty and the pursuit of Happiness." While Adams emphasized "the first law of nature," which entitled men "to remain in a state of nature as long as they please; and in case of intolerable oppression, civil or religious, to leave the society they belong to, and enter into another," Jefferson wrote that "it becomes necessary for one people to dissolve the political bands which have connected them with another, and to assume among the powers of the earth, the separate and equal station to which the Laws of Nature and of Nature's God entitle them." And, similar to Adams's objection that "the Colonists have been branded with the odious names of traitors and rebels only for complaining of their grievances," Jefferson wrote that "in every stage of these Oppressions we have Petitioned for Redress in the most humble Terms: Our repeated Petitions have been answered only by repeated Injury."

The similarities may have been intentional. As Jefferson explained it, the Declaration of Independence was meant to synthesize commonly held views and its authority "rest[ed] on the harmonizing sentiments of the day, whether expressed in conversation, letters, printed essays, or in the elementary books of public right, as Aristotle, Cicero, Locke, Sidney & c."[45] In other words, he was simply trying to encapsulate the thinking of many who came before him, summarize the grievances and attitudes that were prevalent in colonial America, and present them "in terms so plain and firm as to command their assent."

Jefferson acknowledged that although the ideas he articulated were not new, they needed to be expressed in a way that made the "common sense of the subject" axiomatic and inarguable. This was done both through righteous, declaratory language about the rights of man and through a catalogue of complaints about how those rights had been violated. While the Declaration of Independence is remembered most fondly for its opening, with powerful lines such as, "We hold these Truths to be self-evident, that all Men are created equal, that they are endowed by their Creator with certain unalienable Rights," its list of grievances against the King were perhaps more politically significant in the context of 1776—as a way to both rally people to the cause and counter arguments from loyalists and pacifists that the patriots were rash and unreasonable.

In this way, it served a similar function as Henry Tufts's litany of grievances against his father justifying the theft of his horse. The similarities, while coincidental, reflect the reality that the colonies' break with the Crown was very much like a child breaking with a parent, which is a theme that the revolution's protagonists sometimes alluded to explicitly. Samuel Adams referred to England as a "parent state"[46] and Thomas Paine wrote in *Common Sense* that King George had assumed "the pretended title of FATHER OF HIS PEOPLE." Following the outbreak of violence in the colonies, however, the king "can unfeelingly hear of their slaughter, and composedly sleep with their blood upon his soul," Paine wrote.[47]

* * *

The Declaration could also be seen as a way to more clearly define the struggle against the British, to unite the 13 rebel colonies together as a political unit and to expand the recruiting base beyond New England. It offered revolutionaries the opportunity to publicly identify as a distinct group and to "educate" those who were neutral, as well as identify and isolate enemies.[48] It was meant, as Jefferson would say, "to be an expression of the American mind, and to give that expression the proper tone and spirit called for by the occasion." John Hancock, in a letter to General Washington, also expressed hopes that the Declaration would help turn the tide of the war, which hadn't been going well in recent months:

> fully convinced, that our Affairs may take a more favourable Turn, the Congress have judged it necessary to dissolve the Connection between Great Britain and the American Colonies, and to declare them free & independent States; as you will perceive by the enclosed Declaration, which I am directed to transmit to you, and to request you will have it proclaimed at the Head of the Army in the Way, you shall think most proper.

In the same letter, Hancock went on to express his "great Pleasure" to inform the general "that the Militia of this Colony, of Delaware Government, and Maryland, are, and will be every Day in Motion to form the flying Camp; and that all the Militia of this Colony will soon be in the Jersey, ready to receive such Orders as you shall please to give them."[49] It is clear from Hancock's letter that the Declaration was closely related to the issue of replenishing the ranks in order to provide Washington with the soldiers he needed to continue the war effort. According to historian Pauline Maier, "By raising the spirit of the people, the Declaration might also encourage men to join the army."[50]

And indeed, the Declaration proved to be a powerful recruitment tool. It was first celebrated publicly at an event in Philadelphia on July 8, 1776, and throughout the summer would be marked in communities across the colonies by massive celebrations at which the document was read aloud to assembled crowds.[51] In New York City on July 9, Washington's troops were told that "the General hopes this important Event will serve as a free incentive to every officer, and soldier, to act with Fidelity and Courage, as knowing that now the peace and safety of his Country depends (under God) solely on the success of our arms." Upon hearing of the Declaration, men as old as 70 gathered on July 16 in Watertown, Massachusetts, to form themselves into "an independent company ... and determined, at the risk of their lives to defend the Free and Independent States of America." At a celebration in Bridgetown, New Jersey, on August 7, the Chairman of Inspection for the County of Cumberland denounced anyone who failed to join the cause as a coward.[52]

Samuel Adams also gave a speech celebrating the adoption of the Declaration, telling his countrymen: "Be yourselves, O Americans, the authors of those laws on which your happiness depends." His address was a rallying cry that thoroughly demonized the enemy and served to reassure Americans that they could win the war:

> You have now in the field armies sufficient to repel the whole force of your enemies, and their base and mercenary auxiliaries. The hearts of your soldiers beat high with the spirit of freedom—they are animated with the justice of their cause, and while they grasp their swords, can look up to heaven for assistance. Your adversaries are composed of wretches who laugh at the rights of humanity, who turn religion into derision, and would, for higher wages, direct their swords against their leaders or their country.[53]

* * *

By forcing Americans to take sides in the conflict, the Declaration more clearly identified those who remained loyal to the Crown as irredeemable foes of the American cause. The excitement stirred up by the Declaration led to reprisals against loyalists, who "were hunted after & shot at in the Woods & Swamps, to which they had fled for these four months to avoid the savage Fury of the Rebels," according to British Under-Secretary of State for the Colonies Ambrose Serle.[54] It also had dire consequences for loyalist prisoners, who were no longer seen as worthy of the humane conventions of Enlightenment warfare that they had previously enjoyed, and were subjected to punitive treatment and acts of violence and humiliation.[55] Serle concluded that the Declaration of Independence confirmed the "Villainy & the Madness of these deluded People."[56]

But despite the patriotic fervor that was stirred up by the Declaration, it is not entirely clear whether it was effective in substantially increasing recruitment into the Continental Army. In an article at the *Journal of the American Revolution*, Marvin L. Simner writes that "although there are no data that bear directly on this question, a tentative answer can be found in recommendations from the Board of War." Simner notes that just one month after the final celebrations of the Declaration were held, "Congress received for its consideration recommendations from the board which stemmed from Washington's long-held beliefs." In this document, Congress endorsed a system of granting enlistment bonuses which were considered essential to ensure the necessary number of recruits. It was agreed that land would be granted "to the officers and soldiers who shall so engage in the service, and continue therein to the close of the war, or until discharged by Congress and to the representatives of such officers and soldiers as shall be slain by the enemy."[57]

In some isolated cases, it is clear that the Declaration would contribute to a spike in recruitment, but the patriotic sentiment inspired by the document would quickly wane. More than 2,000 South Carolinians enlisted in 1776, for example, but by 1778 only a handful remained in service. With a quota to meet, the South Carolina General Assembly decreed that volunteers would receive a bonus of 100 acres in the lands ceded by the Cherokee, but with few signing up, in 1779, the legislature added $500 cash to the land bonus. The following year, still suffering from a recruitment shortfall, the legislature adopted "An Act to Procure Recruits and Prevent Deserters," which authorized a bonus of one slave for each year of service to volunteers, but the offer still did not produce the desired results.[58]

These incentives are powerful clues that the Declaration, despite its fiery rhetoric, ultimately failed to generate enough anti–British sentiment to meet enlistment needs.[59] Apathy would continue to plague the revolutionary effort, leading Alexander Hamilton to bitterly complain that "our countrymen have all the folly of the ass and all the passiveness of the sheep in their compositions. They are determined not to be free and they can neither be frightened, discouraged nor persuaded to change their resolution."[60]

* * *

As 1776 dragged on, the situation for the Continental Army would grow more dire, leading Thomas Paine to write *The American Crisis* on December 23, 1776. Using a battle drum for a writing desk, in the freezing cold, Paine penned the immortal opening lines, "These are the times that try men's souls," and like Samuel Adams, compared the British oppression of white Americans to slavery. "Britain, with an army to enforce her tyranny," Paine wrote, "has declared that she has a right (not only to TAX) but 'to BIND us in ALL CASES WHATSOEVER' and if being bound in that manner, is not slavery, then is there not such a thing as slavery upon earth." Paine observed that "tyranny, like hell, is not easily conquered; yet we have this consolation with us that the harder the conflict, the more glorious the triumph." Looking forward to the posterity of future American generations, Paine pleaded with his fellow patriots to keep the fight alive:

> Let it be told to the future world, that in the depth of winter, when nothing but hope and virtue could survive, that the city and the country, alarmed at one common danger, came forth to meet and to repulse it. Say not that thousands are gone, turn out your tens of thousands; throw not the burden of the day upon Providence, but "show your faith by your works," that God may bless you. It matters not where you live, or what rank of life you hold, the evil or the blessing will reach you all. The far and the near, the home counties and the back, the rich and the poor, will suffer or rejoice alike.

General Washington was reportedly so moved by these words that he ordered the text to be read out loud to his troops.

With his fighting force increasingly in dire straits, Washington focused on leading by example, earning respect from his men, and by demonstrating that even he—one of the richest men in America—was willing to risk his life for the cause of liberty, which served as an inspiration to others to do the same.[61] He also grew increasingly reluctant to grant furloughs to officers because of the message that it sent to enlisted men, preferring to let officers resign than granting them the privilege of leaving camp whenever they wanted.[62] Rather than forcing them to stay, Washington would use shame and appeals to honor and patriotism to disgrace officers who quit.[63]

But despite his considerable leadership skills and the example he personally set, the troops under Washington's command grew increasingly tired of the hardships of military life and eagerly looked forward to the end of their enlistments at the end of the year. Most of them were New England men who had served longer than anyone else in the Continental Army and were ready to go home. At the end of 1776, during the decisive battles of Trenton and Princeton, Washington would resort essentially to begging and pleading with his battered band of soldiers to continue to fight—even overstepping his authority by offering bounties of ten dollars to anyone who would commit to another six months. The soldiers, however, had seen enough of combat and were less than enticed by the financial incentive; not a single one would step forward to reenlist and collect the bounty. Washington then utilized his oratory skills and appealed to the conscience of the troops, reminding them, once again, of the righteousness of their cause.

"My brave fellows," Washington said on December 31, 1776,

> you have done all I asked you to do, and more than could be reasonably expected, but your country is at stake, your wives, your houses, and all that you hold dear. You have worn yourselves out with fatigues and hardships, but we know not how to spare you. If you will consent to stay one month longer, you will render that service to the cause of liberty, and to your country, which you can probably never do under any other circumstances.[64]

Following this appeal, to Washington's great relief, his men began stepping forward to reenlist. The fight would go on.

* * *

Considering all the difficulties that the patriot cause faced in recruiting and retaining committed soldiers, not only in the year 1776, but throughout the conflict, it is ironic that the image that is conjured up when thinking of "the Spirit of '76" is of the scrappy, fearless Continental soldier heading off to face the British oppressors. For those who lived through it, 1776 would actually not be remembered fondly. Robert Morris, a delegate to the Second Continental Congress and signer of the Declaration of Independence, would write to Washington at the end of the year expressing relief that 1777 was just around the corner. "The year 1776 is over," he wrote. "I am heartily glad for it and I hope you nor America will ever be plagued with such another."[65]

While 1775 was defined by the heroic, exciting battles of Bunker Hill, Lexington and Concord, and Fort Ticonderoga, 1776 was defined by a series of defeats of the Americans, ever-growing hardships for soldiers, and an ever-dwindling army. Henry Tufts's second thoughts about his enlistment, which he conceded "turned out greatly to my disadvantage, and became, for a long while, a source of continual persecution and embarrassment," were more common than many would care to admit and might be closer to capturing the reality of 1776 than the famous painting hanging in Marblehead.

Underlining the climate of adversity and hopelessness, even the Continental Congress's first chaplain, the Rev. Jacob Duché, would abandon ship following the disastrous year of 1776. Although he was only elected to the position in July, just after the Declaration of Independence was adopted, Duché defected to the British the next year. In October 1777, he wrote a letter to General Washington while he was camped at Valley Forge, Pennsylvania. Calling the war an "unhappy contest," Duché told Washington that he could "follow my Countrymen as far only as virtue & the righteousness of their cause would permit me."[66] He implored Washington to lay down arms and negotiate with the British, rejecting the view that total victory was the only acceptable outcome:

> Perhaps it may be said, that it is "better to die than to be Slaves." This indeed is a splendid Maxim in theory: And perhaps in some instances may be found experimentally true. But where there is the least Probability of an happy Accommodation, surely wisdom & Humanity call for some Sacrifices to be made, to prevent inevitable Destruction. You well know, that there is but one invincible Bar to such an Accommodation. Could this be removed, other Obstacles might readily be overcome. 'Tis to you, and you alone your bleeding Country looks, & calls aloud for this Sacrifice. Your Arm alone has Strength sufficient to remove this Bar. May Heaven inspire you with the glorious Resolution of exerting this Strength at so interesting a Crisis, and thus immortalizing yourself as Friend & Guardian of your Country!

Samuel Adams, on the other hand, continued to believe in the necessity for decisive victory. As 1776 came to an end, the congressional delegate would write to his wife citing Scripture in his certainty that despite the setbacks in New York, the patriots would prevail in the struggle that he was so instrumental in launching as a Boston radical a decade earlier. "The Name of the Lord," Adams wrote, "is a strong Tower, thither the Righteous flee and are safe. Let us secure his Favor, and he will lead us through the Journey of this Life and at length receive us to a better." He concluded with a reaffirmation of the righteousness of the cause, noting that "if we defend it as it becomes us, we may expect the Blessings of Heaven."[67]

8

Class Divisions in the Revolution

With no real possessions to speak of, Henry Tufts would most properly be classified as a member of the landless poor—a category that one historian described as "for the most part men and women of low grade, lazy, unambitious, ignorant, prone to small crimes and petty evasions, an unsavory and sometimes a dangerous class."[1] But for someone with little of his own property who made a living by stealing from those better off, Henry appeared to harbor remarkably little class resentment. His memoirs offer no indication that he held any particular grudges against the wealthy, and in fact at times he provides sage advice on finding contentment regardless of one's financial standing. The trick, he suggested, was not to covet other people's wealth but to be satisfied with what one had. "Content with fortune's lot," Henry wrote in one of his poems, "I sought no more, Nor courted the rich miser's ample store."[2]

If anything bothered Henry about the well-to-do, it was only that they tended to be miserly. As he explained, when he was flush with money, he always spent it freely and frequently helped "the indigent and the distressed … to the utmost of my power," claiming that he "received no less satisfaction in the disbursement of property, than in its acquirement."[3] He observed, however, that "others, in better circumstances, have refused" to share their wealth, which it seemed was his only real gripe with the rich. This is despite occasionally complaining about "abject poverty treading snugly on the heels of my late misfortunes," and claiming that he sometimes "saw no other method than theft, however horrid the name, by which to obtain a possible livelihood."[4]

At times though he hinted at grander ambitions and seemed to think that crime would enable him to live in the lap of luxury, indicating that he wasn't completely uninterested in class advancement. As he described his first major heist—the theft of his father's horse—he imagined that it would set him on a course of "future riches and prosperity," noting that the 30 dollars he acquired upon selling the animal "appeared, in my enraptured view, as a plentiful fund." He confided that he was "much swollen in imagination, as though I had been proprietor of the mines of Potosi or Peru, and enjoyed imaginary happiness, in long perspective, as my indubitable destiny."[5]

Of course, his career as a criminal didn't work out precisely as he had imagined at the outset. Rather than living in perpetual happiness and abundance, his life consisted of an endless series of ups and downs, one moment on top of the world with wads of cash and new prospects and promises, and the next moment manacled and chained, subsisting on maggoty bread in a dank, rat-infested dungeon. Throughout his narrative, he describes the unglamorous realities of life on the run, and while at times he would come into possession of relatively substantial sums of money, he seemed to spend the money as soon as he obtained it. He also tended to take it in stride when he lost his possessions, for example when a gambler "stripped me of both watch and money," recalling the old adage, "light come, light go,"[6] an eighteenth-century version of the expression "easy come, easy go."

In keeping with this spirit, his propensity to steal seemed to be less motivated by greed, malice or jealousy than it was by a compulsion that drove him to continue his life of rambling, even at moments when his circumstances were relatively stable and prosperous. Describing his life with the slave-owner's daughter in Virginia, for example, he noted that on the plantation he "had found, at last the horn of plenty," and that "the cup of pleasure and prosperity was fondly presented to my lips." Henry could have lived comfortably if he had stayed with this woman, who was poised to inherit a fortune from her ailing father, but he appeared to be pushed by some innate personality trait that compelled him to squander opportunities and act against his own best interests. Consequently, Henry writes, his "horn and cup vanished as a phantasma, … leaving nought but regret behind."[7]

While occasionally regretting his life decisions that left him more or less destitute, his unselfish approach toward personal property and congenial outlook toward the more well-off reflected a popular attitude that was relatively free of the class animosities that marked life in the Old World. While class divisions clearly existed in early America, there was also a general acceptance of the social order, as well as appreciation for possibilities of class advancement that the system provided. Some Americans, such as Henry, may have found difficulty in getting ahead, but a relatively high standard of living meant that colonists were not, on the whole, motivated to rebel by hunger or bitterness over inequality, and in real ways, America was a land of upward mobility for those who sought economic advancement and applied themselves toward that end.

These sorts of ambitions, however, were anathema to Samuel Adams, who was singularly focused on the cause of liberty and generally ambivalent—if not hostile—toward the acquisition of material wealth. Described by 19th-century historian George Bancroft as "poor, and so contented with poverty that men censured him as wanting wisdom to estimate riches at their just value,"[8] Adams maintained that acquiescence to tyranny—not poverty—was the lowest state of human existence, and mocked those who prioritized financial gain over liberty. "I glory in being what the world calls a poor man," he once wrote to his wife. "If my mind has ever been tinctured with envy, the rich and the great have not been its objects." Having squandered a fortune and incurred massive debts, Adams relied at times on the charity of his friends, and at one point his wife supported the household. "Alone among our founders," writes Adams biographer Stacy Schiff, "his is a riches-to-rags story."[9]

Fittingly, the rebellion that Adams led against England was motivated less by class resentments than by anger over infringements on natural rights. This, however, is not to say that class divisions played no role in the revolution, which upended social norms in a number of ways. In eighteenth-century colonial America, there was an expectation that those at the lower end of the economic order would always address those higher in social rank with deference and humility, and class dynamics played out at all levels of society, including within the family unit, in the local community, and on the national and international levels.[10] Just as in a family where the father was the undisputed authority, with all other family members expected to meekly obey his commands, the colonists were subjects of a king—represented by ministers and royal governors—whose dictates were expected to be unquestioningly followed. This system of subservience was turned on its head during the revolutionary struggle, which at times took on a uniquely class-conscious nature.

Linked to the laborers through networks that included taverns and fire companies, Adams and his associates such as James Otis ensured that mechanics and artisans played a central role in the revolutionary movement. This reflected a view that not only challenged the Crown's right to rule the colonies, but the hierarchy that enforced the system. "I am forced to get my living by the labor of my hand," Otis said in 1762, "and ... earned under the frowns of some who have no natural or divine right to be above me."[11] Much of the resistance against British rule had been coordinated not by the colonial assemblies, but by ad hoc committees in which artisans, farmers and fishermen were active, and at times these individuals highlighted the unjust nature of the class system in which they lived. A contributor to the *Boston Gazette* wrote in 1763, for instance, that "a few persons in power" were working to keep "the poor people poor in order to make them humble."[12] These varying perspectives were rooted in the different experiences that colonists had, with the population consisting of a mixture of long-established families who made up the core of the revolutionary movement, and more recent arrivals more focused on their next meal than natural rights.

There were also divisions between large landholders and small farmers, which often took an openly violent and class-based character. From 1766 to 1771, a militant and highly organized movement of white farmers—known as the Regulators—mobilized against wealthy officials in North Carolina. Following a population boom in the 1760s, which created a migration of colonists arriving in western North Carolina from eastern cities, the arrival of merchants and lawyers upset the social and political structure of the colony. Many farmers had come to rely on the goods offered by newly arrived merchants, but due to economic hardship, farmers often fell into debt.[13]

The merchants used courts to settle disputes, which led to widespread foreclosures and financial ruin among farmers, exacerbated by a class imbalance that existed in the colony's courthouses. Magistrates were men of property, so when cases were brought before them, they tended to rule in favor of their friends in the upper classes. Wealthy officials and well-educated lawyers used their superior knowledge of the law to claim more land and property, leading to the emergence of a so-called "courthouse ring." In response, an uprising of poor farmers took hold, which came to be known as the War of the Regulation, or the Regulator War. Comprised of mostly lower-class citizens who made up the majority of the backcountry population, the Regulators sought to establish an honest government and reduce taxes. Referring to themselves as "the wretched poor" who were oppressed by "rich and powerful ... designing Monsters," their aim was to counter endemic corruption and democratize local governments.[14] The conflict ended in defeat for the Regulators, who were forced to sign loyalty oaths to the government, but largely based on this experience they questioned the motives of the patriot cause and would largely remain neutral during the Revolutionary War.[15]

These sorts of socioeconomic divisions led to direct appeals for cross-class unity in the revolutionary struggle. For example, around the time of the Stamp Act being adopted, a Virginian implored the poor to join forces with the rich. "Are not the gentlemen made of the same materials as the lowest and poorest among you?" he asked. "Listen to no doctrines which may tend to divide us, but let us go hand in hand, as brothers."[16]

But while appeals were made for colonial unity, the class divisions continued to impact the movement against the Crown. In early 1774, a Virginian wrote that "the lower Class of People here are in tumult on account of Reports from Boston, many of them expect to be press'd & compell'd to go and fight the Britains!"[17] As the upper classes railed against being taxed by a faraway government and having their grievances dismissed by an out-of-touch king, many in the lower classes simply objected to taxes because of economic hardship, which of course was exacerbated by the war itself. While many people suffered due to hyperinflation, others got richer—adeptly leveraging their assets and profiting off of wartime economic chaos.

Those in the upper classes, while appreciative of the role that the underclasses had played in the movement for colonial rights (and later independence), worried about the newfound power of the mob, and not entirely without reason. At times, the mob carried out actions that scared not only the British and loyalists, but also patriots and members of the American elite.

Demands for unconditional support for the patriot cause through acts of public humiliation and torture, while perhaps effective in some respects, often had the effect of frightening the upper echelons of society and causing them to second-guess the wisdom of whipping up radical sentiments by the likes of Samuel Adams. Following a number of patriot assaults on Tories in Philadelphia in 1775, James Allen, a wealthy Philadelphian with Whig sympathies, expressed alarm over the power of the people. "I love the cause of liberty [but] the madness of the multitude is but one degree better than submission to the Tea Act," he fretted.[18]

* * *

While the colonies grappled with internal class divisions, the British also resented the opulence that they saw among those who claimed to be oppressed. When redcoats arrived in Flatbush as part of a campaign to regain control of New York City in mid–August 1776, for example, they marveled at the magnificence of the colonists' homes and wondered how such financially successful people could ever rebel against a system that had made them so wealthy. An officer described scenes of roads lined with dead cattle, burned-out houses and fields in ashes, as well as "chests of drawers, chairs, mirrors with gold-gilded frames, porcelain, and all sorts of items of the best and most expensive manufacture" scattered across the landscape. Astonished to see firsthand how blessed the Americans were with such luxuries, the Brits viewed the affluence as evidence that the colonies had grown rich at the expense of the motherland.[19]

The British troops were mostly young farmers and unskilled laborers, as well as some tradesmen such as blacksmiths, carpenters and weavers.[20] Although they were better equipped and cared for than their American counterparts, with new uniforms and healthier food, their class origins were similar to most of the soldiers who made up the core of the

Continental Army. While the officers of the British Army were generally very well-to-do, the enlisted men came from the peasantry, disproportionately from oppressed regions such as Ireland and Scotland. Many of them had entered the ranks after being convicted of a crime in order to avoid a death sentence, while others had been tricked into enlisting by unscrupulous recruiters. In some cases, the soldiers had been compelled into service by press gangs who would simply kidnap young men and force them into terms that ranged from 21 years to life.

Once they arrived in America, they saw more economic abundance than they had ever imagined. America in the 1770s had a far greater standard of living than any country in the world,[21] with many living on their own land and enjoying material wealth that others could only dream of. Although there were substantial differences in the quality of life on a plantation and a subsistence farm, as well as between an urban dwelling and a homestead on the frontier, on the whole, the average American was far better off than the average Brit.[22]

There was inequality in the colonies, however, with the top 20 percent of colonists in 1774 holding 47 percent of the wealth, and the bottom 40 percent holding just 12 percent. The colonial middle class was sizeable, with the mid–40 percent range of households holding just over 40 percent of the colonies' wealth, but certain regions were more stratified than others. The middle colonies were the most egalitarian, followed by the northern colonies, and lagging behind in terms of income equality were the southern colonies. The poor in the South were poorer than the poor in the North, with the bottom 40 percent of households in the southern colonies holding just about 11 percent of the wealth.[23]

But while inequality certainly existed, so too did opportunity. Abundant land both provided the means for prosperity to anyone willing to work and effectively capped the accumulation of wealth among the upper classes. Because land was so cheap, white Americans typically would not work for others except for brief periods, which tended to keep wages high.[24] Therefore, the prosperity of economic growth was spread relatively evenly and the view of a typical farmer was that of gratitude for their blessings, not of envy. As Henry Tufts described his appreciation upon coming into some money after working for a while on a farm, he "fared like a prince" and was "supplied ... with every gratification that imagination could suggest or heart desire."[25] Similarly, as J. Hector St. John de Crèvecoeur explained in a collection of essays published in London in the early 1780s, American life was one of equal opportunity and self-determination, where ingenuity, hard work and grit paid off with economic success. With plentiful land and opportunity, there was no reason to covet the wealth of others, according to Crèvecoeur:

8. Class Divisions in the Revolution

I bless God for all the good He has given me; I envy no man's prosperity, and with no other portion of happiness than that I may live to teach the same philosophy to my children and give each of them a farm, show them how to cultivate it, and be like their father, good, substantial, independent American farmers—an appellation which will be the most fortunate one a man of my class can possess so long as our civil government continues to shed blessings on our husbandry.[26]

He contrasted the American experience with that of Ireland, where "lands possessed by a few are leased down ad infinitum" and the "poor are worse lodged there than anywhere else in Europe."[27]

* * *

Essentially, the colonists lived exceptional lives that enabled them to develop a unique outlook that seemed strange to their counterparts from across the pond. To the British soldiers who arrived in 1776, in fact, the idea that these privileged people would take up arms in rebellion was probably incomprehensible, but the reality was that, paradoxically, it was due to their high standing that American colonists would rebel. The reasons for this are varied, but one of them is because of the ideology of republicanism that found fertile ground in the New World, which was made possible by high literacy rates and the widespread availability of cheap land, particularly on the frontier.

Thomas Gage observed that "democracy is too prevalent in America," noting that the ability of colonists to develop their own institutions far away from the centers of power in coastal towns had eroded royal authority. "The people themselves have gradually retired from the Coast," Gage explained to London, which made them harder to control and provided the independence to develop republican ideas. The colonists in the backcountry, he said in 1770, "are, already, almost out of the reach of Law and Government."[28] He urged his superiors to "confine the Colonists" closer to the coast, believing that this would undermine the material base of democratic ideas—namely the political and economic independence that colonists enjoyed on the frontier.

Those friendlier to the American cause could also see the link between the colonists' land ownership, economic independence and their devotion to liberty that inspired the rebellion. A young French officer named Viscount de Mauroy who travelled to America in 1777 to help fight the Brits explained his views on Americans by chalking up their motives to "fanaticism, insatiable greed, and poverty." These, he said, are "the three causes that incessantly drive to these shores masses of immigrants, who come to slay the natives and destroy in a wasteful spirit, forests as old as the world itself." Once these fanatical and greedy immigrants set root and established themselves in America, according to de Mauroy's view, they let loose "the vices and prejudices of their respective mother countries."[29] De Mauroy's colleague Marquis de Lafayette, who travelled with him to America and would go on to play a major role in the revolution, had a generally more positive view.

"Simplicity of manner, kindness of heart, love of country and of liberty, and a delightful state of equality, are met with universally," Lafayette wrote to his wife, Adrienne, on June 19, 1777. "The richest and the poorest man," Lafayette marveled, "are completely on a level; and although there are some immense fortunes in this country, I may challenge any one to point out the slightest difference in their respective manner toward each other."[30]

Lafayette may have had a bit of an overly rosy perception of the country that he had come to fight for, but his observations on the spirit of equality in America were probably not too far removed from reality. There was indeed a strong egalitarian streak and sense of independence that Americans enjoyed, which some members of the European elite may have mistaken for weakness.

Upper-class Brits were pointedly unimpressed by the American elite. A visiting Englishman in the 1770s noted that Washington—although one of the richest men in the colonies—was "in point of rank only equal to the better sort of yeoman in England."[31] Washington tended to eschew the appearances of opulence and preferred the "simplicity of dress, and every thing which can tend to support propriety of character without partaking of the follies of luxury and ostentation," as he wrote in a letter to an English historian named Catharine Macaulay.[32]

But this is not to say that the colonial elite lacked class consciousness. They were well aware of their own social standing and even alluded to their financial wealth, land holdings and other assets in the closing line of the Declaration of Independence, in which the signatories "mutually pledge[d] to each other our Lives, our Fortunes and our sacred Honor." By highlighting their fortunes, they were attempting to drive home the fact that they had much to lose in committing what was legally an act of treason by rebelling against the Crown. They knew that if their revolutionary cause failed, they would most likely lose everything they had—if not their lives—so they wanted to make clear that they were not desperados who had nothing to fear, but men of wealth and privilege who were willing to risk it all in order to challenge the status quo and fight for their ideals.

In contrast, those patriots of limited fortunes—men such as Samuel Adams—were regarded by the wealthier and more aristocratic members as agitators who could afford to be rash since they had nothing to lose and everything to gain. It was also understood that true desperados such as Henry Tufts, while perhaps never fully trusted or embraced by the elite, would have to be recruited to actually fight the war. Although the elite leadership of the patriot cause distrusted the mobs of poor, they knew that they would be needed to succeed in the revolution. One way that they were wooed was the allure of land, with a major general promised more than 1,000 acres and privates receiving 100 acres.[33] The promises would be fulfilled with bounty-land warrants, typically granted for 160 acres, which were issued to military veterans starting in the 1770s and continuing into the mid–19th century.[34]

* * *

Land speculation was the preferred get-rich-quick scheme of people of means in colonial America, and since land was plentiful and cheap, becoming a landholder was not prohibitively difficult. Speculators often undervalued the price of land, particularly wild land, and the better land could be obtained on credit.[35] This meant that a poor person could become not only a relatively prosperous farmer, but also a fully enfranchised citizen, with up to 75 percent of the adult males in some American colonies qualifying as voters.[36] In most of the colonies, however, this voting group fell far short of a majority of the people, with around half being women and many others falling into various other non-voting categories.

Land ownership and speculation, however, also had a downside. "From what I have Seen, heard," Washington confided in 1778, "speculation—peculation—& an insatiable thirst for riches seems to have got the better of every other consideration and almost of every order of Men." He lamented that "personal quarrels are the great business of the day" while challenges such as "accumulated debt—ruined finances—depreciated money—& want of credit … are but secondary considerations & postponed from day to day."[37] When these concerns were considered, the response was generally to raise taxes, ultimately creating heavier tax burdens than the British had attempted to impose. This led, increasingly, to violent resistance among hard-pressed taxpayers.[38]

During the Revolutionary War, indeed, tax resistance would prove a major challenge to the Continental elite, with evidence indicating that citizens throughout the states defied contributing their share. Tax collectors met violent resistance that occasionally escalated into riots. When a two percent tax increase was ordered in Virginia in 1781, for instance, the result was a "dangerous insurrection," which local officials struggled for months to get under control.[39] In Norwich, Connecticut, rioters broke open the town jail to free those who had been incarcerated for tax delinquency.[40]

More often, tax collectors avoided violence by declining to collect.

Locally elected selectmen routinely abated the taxes of those in need of relief, increasing from a rate of about five percent abatement in Connecticut to heights of 25 percent in later years. Elsewhere, elected representatives would endeavor to ensure that the tax burden fell disproportionately on the rich. In New York, the legislature adopted the Confiscation Act in 1779, the first of many harsh laws that would strike at the wealthy by allowing tax assessors to rate them according to "circumstances and other abilities to pay taxes, collectively considered." Alexander Hamilton denounced this progressive taxation scheme as "radically vicious," but it proved popular among the lower classes of New York who wanted the rich to pay their fair share.[41]

Class conflict persisted, though, and facing war-related deprivations in 1775 and 1776, farmers in Virginia and Maryland united to attack the plantations of prominent patriots who were suspected of hoarding supplies. Even George Washington's Mount Vernon estate would be affected by this rebellion, and narrowly avoided being raided by a mob demanding salt.[42] Some members of the Continental elite viewed these riots as an act of treachery inspired by loyalism, with one denouncing the Maryland rioters as Tories who "by their declarations against the present measures of the country and in favour of the King shew themselves intirely disaffected to our cause."[43] Others, however, recognized the grievances of the lower classes as similar to the issues that prompted the Revolutionary War. Prominent Virginian George Mason expressed concern over the power of the mob rectifying what it saw as an injustice, in this case rich people's hoarding of badly needed supplies, and drew parallels with the broader struggle against the Crown. "The same Principles which first induced us to draw the Sword will again dictate Resistance to Injustice & Oppression, in whatever Shape, or under whatever Pretence, it may be offered," Mason observed.[44]

* * *

Throughout the war, the reluctance of the lower classes to fight for what they saw, in many cases, as a rich man's cause would prove to be an enduring challenge for the revolutionary leaders. These "neutrals" are often overlooked because their voices at the time were muted and generally lost in the cacophony of vocal advocates of revolution or loyalism, but their defiance would arguably pose as great a challenge to revolution as armed loyalist resistance. As historian Michael McDonnell has explained, "resistance to *the* Revolution was not always a function of loyalism, but was often a manifestation of adherence to a *different* kind of revolution—or at the very least to a different conception of social, economic, and political relations than that envisioned by the Revolution's leadership."[45]

While populist firebrands such as Samuel Adams tended to speak and write on behalf of all colonists and the Declaration of Independence

8. Class Divisions in the Revolution

employed broad, inclusive language about the "Right of the People" to abolish tyrannical government, the reality was that not all residents of the 13 colonies shared the same interests. As Henry Tufts's autobiography makes clear, there was clearly a large swath of the country in which a disadvantaged and criminal underclass held more or less free rein. These mavericks—much like the various Indian tribes that allied with whichever side was more favorable to their interests—would become something of a wild card for the revolution, with both sides coveting their services but neither able to fully rely on them.

Meanwhile, many remained bounded in slavery or in a labor system that was not too far removed from slavery—namely indentured servitude. Indentured servants were seen as a dangerous group by the elites, and efforts would be made by both the revolutionaries and the British to win their loyalty. Lord Dunmore specifically mentioned indentured servants in his proclamation of November 25, 1775, which threatened to seize the land of rebels in Virginia and hinted that those who fought for the Crown might receive those spoils of war upon British victory. Dunmore also demonstrated a nuanced understanding of the social dynamics of the colony, highlighting the reality that servants represented useful leverage over the rebels. Since most servants had little chance of owning land due to their unfree status, the threat of seizing the land of traitors to the Crown forced them to confront questions of which side would better serve their personal interests.[46] Should they fight for their masters who routinely abused them, or for the king, who was subtly offering them not just freedom but also land for their loyalty? The Revolutionary War pushed these questions of class divisions to the forefront.

And indeed, many servants, along with plenty of black slaves, opted to leave their masters and fight for the Crown. Less than a week after Lord Dunmore's Proclamation was issued, a servant belonging to Andrew Leitch abandoned his master to go find Dunmore, and once the proclamation was more widely disseminated, others would follow suit. In August 1776, Andrew Kelly, "an Irish servant man ... by trade a brick maker," left his master in Alexandria "to enlist in the land or sea service or attempt again to go to the British troops," as his master James Parsons recalled.[47]

Another indentured servant who answered Dunmore's call was Baker Fullam, who ran away from his master Thomas Blackburn of Prince William County. After robbing his master of clothes, Fullam fled to "offer his services to lord Dunmore," likely in the belief that fighting for the British offered his best chance for freedom and land.[48]

* * *

In addition to those who fought on the side of the loyalists or resisted the war effort through the most common act of subterfuge—desertion—there were many thousands of Americans who defied the revolution through underhanded, passive modes of resistance. These included farmers refusing to sell supplies to the army, laborers declining to cooperate with conscription efforts, soldiers who demanded higher bounties for their service, and locals repudiating the new states' oaths of allegiance.[49] One individual, upon refusing to swear a loyalty oath, argued that the Revolutionary War was a rich man's war. Fighting Britain, he said, was not "for the defence of American liberty of property, but for the purpose of enslaving the poor people thereof."[50]

Some of those who enlisted in the Continental Army, like Henry Tufts, would make plain the lower class's insistence for fairness by stealing rations from the officers. Camped in Boston in the early stages of the war, Henry noted that with "provisions being also scarce, we were reduced to half allowance," so, "with the connivance of several of the subaltern officers," he pilfered half a hog, "lugg[ing] it off very triumphantly, thus easing the unsuspecting commissary of the incumbrance in a trice."[51] While these subtle sorts of resistance may not have posed a major threat to the revolutionary cause, at other times, resistance would take the form of open rebellion in the ranks and pose a serious challenge to military leadership.

Constant shortages of supplies, unequal rations and difficult living conditions led to discontent among the soldiery, and sometimes, mutiny resulted. According to a comprehensive study by John A. Nagy, there were at least 56 mutinies between 1775 and 1783, such as one rebellion in the Connecticut brigade in 1778 due to anger over being paid in rapidly depreciating currency.[52] The most famous, though, was the Pennsylvania Line Mutiny of 1781. This rebellion was several years in the making, with shortages leading to widespread discontent in the unit as early as 1777. That year, General Anthony Wayne, the commander of the Pennsylvania Line, exhorted his superiors to address the lack of supplies for his men. He wrote to Washington in December 1777, describing the "Distressed and Naked Situation of your Troops," and Washington duly conveyed these concerns to the Continental Congress. While the Pennsylvanians endured the bitter cold of Valley Forge during the winter of 1777–1778, Washington desperately implored the political leaders in Philadelphia to ameliorate the army's wretched condition.

"I am now convinced beyond a doubt," Washington wrote from Valley Forge on December 23, 1777, "that, unless some great and capital change suddenly takes place in that line, this army must inevitably be reduced to one or other of these three things; starve, dissolve, or disperse in order to obtain subsistence in the best manner they can."[53] He noted that he hadn't received any assistance from the quartermaster-general for the past several months. This was likely the result of graft, and Washington knew it. In writing Congress, Washington accused the quartermaster-general of corruption and pressed for his removal, while General Wayne made similar accusations in letters to the Pennsylvania executive council.

Eventually, with their grievances not satisfactorily resolved, the soldiers revolted.[54] On New Year's Day, 1781, "a number of men in the 11th Regiment began to huzza and continued for some time," Captain Joseph McClellan recalled in his diary. "A number of the officers collected in order to quiet the men, which was done in a great measure. But in a short time a disturbance began on the right of the division, by the men parading with their arms, and firing some scattering shots, which soon became general through the division." He noted that "Captain [Adam] Bitting was shot through the body and soon died" and "Captain [Samuel] Tolbert was badly wounded."[55] The soldiers then began to march to Princeton.

A few days later, the mutineers issued their demands, which included "that all and such men as were enlisted in the year '76 or '77 and received the bounty of 20 dollars, shall be without any delay discharged; and all arrears and depreciation of pay be paid to the said men, without any fraud, clothing included." As for those who enlisted after the year 1777, they "shall be entitled to their discharge at the expiration of three years from the said enlistment, and their full depreciation of pay, and all arrears of clothing."[56]

Although their stated concerns were mostly related to conditions and pay, they were also dissatisfied with the leadership of the regimental officers in the Pennsylvania Line. Joseph Reed, president of Pennsylvania's Supreme Executive Council, reported to the Committee of Congress that the men "utterly reject[ed] their former officers, except a very few," but offered assurances that they were uninterested in "British gold," and held "a good disposition against the enemy."[57] The Committee of Congress also noted that the soldiers' anger was "chiefly against some of their own officers and complained of fine deception in their enlistments."[58]

Yet, although they were clearly dissatisfied with America's political leadership, they refused to defect to the British when British Army General Henry Clinton tried to entice them with an offer.[59] At the end of January, the Supreme Executive Council of Pennsylvania opened negotiations with the leaders of the mutiny and the rebellion ended, with many of the mutineers returning to fight for the Continental Army and serving honorably in future campaigns.

* * *

A review of mutinies during the Revolutionary War makes clear that the unrest was rarely due to disloyalty to the revolutionary cause, but was generally the result of soldiers exasperated over lack of pay, substandard clothing and deplorable living conditions.[60] The soldiers' disaffection was also aggravated by resentment over the privileges of the officers, who, for their part, at times were clearly motivated more by class advancement than by deeply held convictions for the revolution.

Indeed, to some, the military was seen mainly as an opportunity to advance in social status, as well as attain land and property. For instance, in John Shy's study *A People Numerous and Armed*, he tells the story of William Scott, a lieutenant at Bunker Hill. Scott was captured by the British and under questioning explained why he joined the rebel forces:

> I was a Shoemaker, & got my living by my Labor. When this Rebellion came on, I saw some of my Neighbors got into Commission, who were no better than myself. I was very ambitious, & did not like to see those Men above me.... I offered to enlist upon having a Lieutenants Commission; which was granted. I imagined my self now in a way of Promotion: if I was killed in Battle, there would be an end of me, but if any Captain was killed, I should rise in Rank, & should still have a Chance to rise higher. These Sir! were the only Motives of my entering into the Service; for as to the Dispute between Great Britain & the Colonies, I know nothing of it.[61]

Lieutenant Scott's sentiments of ambivalence to the patriot cause were perhaps more common than is typically acknowledged. At the time, he would have likely been designated as one of the many "disaffected" officers and enlisted men, those who adversely affected the Revolutionary War not through open acts of treachery or armed opposition to the patriot cause, but simply because of their opportunistic and cynical attitudes.[62] Many officers were elected to lead militias who were openly malcontent and held an indifference if not an outright antipathy towards service, which significantly hampered recruitment and conscription efforts.[63] But when examined more closely, much of the resistance that was attributed to the actions of the "disaffected," or those harboring loyalist sentiments, appear instead to be the rational actions of those simply who either disagreed with the revolutionary agenda, were dissatisfied with the means of pursuing the cause, or were more interested in their own economic advancement. These nuances, however, were largely lost on the Continental elite, who, as a general rule, accused their disaffected compatriots of being pro–British.

Fears of disaffection leading to defection to the British were ever-present among the revolutionary leadership, a view that appears to have been generally shared by their British counterparts. The king's ministers and generals seemed to believe that only a minority of rebellious Americans, although well-organized, desired independence from the mother country, which led to a distorted view that consistently underestimated the commitment and capability of the patriots, and inflated the strength of the loyalists. Both times British armies ventured into the

8. Class Divisions in the Revolution

interior, it was on the assumption there were large numbers of loyalists there who would support the Crown.[64]

* * *

The leaders of the revolution, however, were increasingly cognizant of the dilemma that they faced and understood that in order to broaden the appeal of the patriot cause, it would have to be more egalitarian. As John Adams wrote to Patrick Henry on June 3, 1776, "The Decree is gone forth, and it cannot be recalled, that a more equal Liberty, than has prevail'd in other Parts of the Earth, must be established in America."[65]

Samuel Adams, for his part, would continue to develop his ideas on class and property that had initially influenced his rebellion against the British. In 1779, he wrote to James Warren, who at the time was serving on the naval board of the Continental Navy, touting the benefits of patriotism to counter greed and avarice. "The vigilant Eye of so consistent a Patriot, may be formidable to a Combination of political & Commercial Men, who may be aiming to get the Trade, the Wealth, the Power and the Government of America into their own Hands," Adams wrote. "He must therefore be hunted down; and the young as well as the old Hounds are all ready for the Game."[66]

In other words, what Adams was saying, essentially, was that patriots needed to remain vigilant not only against the British, but also against domestic opportunists who seek wealth and power. This vigilance would only be partially successful, with the broader society growing more economically stratified but at the same time more egalitarian. After the revolution, for example, the primogeniture laws that disadvantaged younger family members like Henry Tufts would be abolished, and many states passed inheritance laws that equalized the rights of all children, including both for sons and daughters.[67] On the whole, wealth would become more unequally distributed throughout the country, but paradoxically there was a greater sense of social equality, with lower-class Americans displaying less overt demonstrations of deference to superiors, and a more informal manner of social relations taking hold. As Gordon Wood put it, "living in a free country meant never having to tip one's cap to anyone."[68]

9

Alcohol in the Revolution

Like Henry Tufts, Samuel Adams was something of a Jack of all trades—a tax collector, journalist, politician, and a brewer. In this respect, he followed in the footsteps of his father, Samuel Adams, Sr., who, in addition to serving as a minister, justice of the peace, selectman, and member of the General Court, also made malted barley and supplied it to brewers as an ingredient for beer. When Deacon Adams died in 1748, the younger Adams inherited his estate, including his malting business. The work was difficult, messy and labor-intensive, consisting of steeping, drying, sweating, and kilning barley. Although Adams men had thrived in the business since the 1650s,[1] Samuel evidently had more of a head for politics than business, and his career as a brewer was short-lived.

Within a few years after Samuel the Elder's death, the family business was bankrupt and the malt house began to crumble. But even after he had moved on from the brewing business, "Sam the Maltster" (as his political opponents mockingly called him) maintained a close relationship with alcohol, meeting at the taverns of Boston to collaborate with Paul Revere, John Hancock, Joseph Warren and other Whigs and Sons of Liberty. As John C. Miller wrote in a rather unsympathetic biography published in 1936, *Sam Adams: Pioneer in Propaganda*, taverns were attractive to Adams in pursuing his task of radical organizing and rabble rousing. "Sam Adams discovered these taverns with their 'tippling, nasty, vicious crew' excellent recruiting grounds for the mobs he later raised against the Tories and Crown officers," according to Miller. "Under Sam Adams, Boston taverns became nurseries of revolution."[2]

Miller claimed that Adams was a "familiar figure in Boston taverns," portraying him as a propagandist who whipped up drunk mobs to riot and ransack the homes of royal officials. More recently, historians have pushed back on this portrayal, which followed a trend in the early 20th century to depict Adams as a calculating and unscrupulous agitator rather than the earnest and pious political leader that earlier biographies had favored. "The new portrayal played down Adams's devout faith, his education (an

M.A. from Harvard), and his solidly genteel social status," writes J.L. Bell at *Journal of the American Revolution*. Noting that the only evidence Miller presented for his claim that Adams was a familiar figure at taverns was his nickname, "Samuel the Publican," Bell points out that the term "publican" could mean either someone who keeps a tavern, or a tax collector. Since Adams had worked as a Boston tax collector from 1756 to early 1765 and never owned a tavern, Bell suggests that the nickname the Tories gave Adams was more than likely a reference to his role collecting taxes rather than selling beer.[3]

But even if Adams never owned a tavern, he was certainly quite familiar with them. Taverns were of utmost importance to the movement that he led, a place not only to indulge in drink and socialize but also to share news and organize. In 1772, as he focused on establishing a committee of correspondence system in Massachusetts, Adams assembled with his colleagues once a week at a tavern where they drank beer and discussed the work at hand.[4] The Green Dragon Tavern in Boston's North End was probably the most famous of the patriots' stomping grounds, coming to be known as the "Headquarters of the American Revolution" because several secret groups met there, including the Sons of Liberty, the Boston Committee of Correspondence, and the Boston Caucus. Other important taverns in the revolutionary period included the Wayside Inn in Sudbury, Massachusetts; the Buckman Tavern in Lexington, Massachusetts; the Fraunces Tavern in Manhattan; the City Tavern in Philadelphia; the Reynolds Tavern in Annapolis, Maryland; and the Raleigh Tavern in Williamsburg, Virginia.[5] There was also a Tufts Tavern owned by one of Henry's kinsmen in Menotomy, Massachusetts.[6]

Henry, naturally, was also a regular tavern-goer, with some two dozen references to taverns in his book. His experience, however, was quite different than that of Samuel Adams and his associates. Whereas the Sons of Liberty would gather at taverns to read, discuss ideas, and share intelligence on the movement of British troops around Boston, Tufts would primarily utilize the tavern as a place to drink, sleep, and meet fellow outlaws or pick up women. In one anecdote, he recalled meeting a "beautiful young and debonair widow" at a tavern, and finding her approachable, he "made immediate love to her cheek, as delays are dangerous, boasted of [his] great riches, and, to speak all in a word, obtained her favor to the utmost latitude of [his] wishes." He spent two nights with her and then took "leave with assurances of a speedy return, and straightway revisited my [wife] Abigail."[7]

For the patriots, though, the tavern served as an indispensable organizing tool. With newspapers plastering the walls and revolutionary pamphlets readily available, literate tavern-goers would read broadsides aloud to the illiterate ones, and some taverns, such as James Pitson's Boston King Street Tavern—with its 88 books and 31 pamphlets on the bookshelf—more resembled libraries than bars.[8] Besides debating and sharing news, the tavern was where rebels met to plan their next moves, organize boycotts and recruit volunteers for high-risk actions. Patriots met in taverns before some of the key moments of the revolution, and indeed the "liquid courage" on tap may have helped enable some of the more audacious activities.

When Virginia's royal governor Lord Dunmore dissolved the colony's House of Burgesses, in May 1774, they reconvened in a nearby tavern to organize a "non-importation" agreement, to propose the First Continental Congress, and to schedule the first Virginia Convention.[9] The Boston Tea Party was said to have been planned at the Green Dragon, near Faneuil Hall, and when England responded to the destruction of the tea by closing the port of Boston, shipmasters and merchants in New York met at the Fraunces Tavern "in order to consult on measures proper to be pursued on the present critical and important situation," according to a posted advertisement for the meeting.[10] As tensions rose in Boston during late 1774 and early 1775, Paul Revere and his committee of about 30 spies and informers met regularly at the Green Dragon "for the purpose of watching the movements of the British soldiers, and gaining every intelligence of the movements of the Tories," as Revere recalled.[11]

Before the skirmish at Lexington kicked off the shooting war between the patriots and the redcoats, militiamen wet their whistles at the local tavern. "Many armed men had been in the Buckman Tavern that night," writes David Hackett Fischer in *Paul Revere's Ride*, "and more than a few had partaken liberally of the landlord's hospitality." Fischer notes that the alcohol they likely consumed may have contributed to the first shot being fired, perhaps inadvertently, pointing out that "firearms and alcohol made a highly explosive mixture."[12]

In Philadelphia, before convening the First Continental Congress, delegates met at the City Tavern. John Adams and George Washington visited the tavern upon their arrivals in Philadelphia, and other congressional delegates used it as an informal clubhouse.[13] Delegates would meet there before and after sessions of the First Continental Congress during the autumn of 1774, which convened at nearby Carpenters' Hall.[14] Once the war got underway, both Continental and British troops used the tavern to house prisoners of war, and to hold military courts-martial. General Washington and his aides-de-camp even set up a command center at the City Tavern twice in the summer of 1777, making it the official headquarters of the Continental Army for several days in late July[15] and again in early August.[16]

"When it wasn't being fought on the battlefields," says Lauren Clark, author of *Crafty Bastards: Beer in New England from the Mayflower to Modern Day*, "the American Revolution played out in taverns."[17]

* * *

The tavern, though, was just one iteration of alcohol featuring prominently in the American Revolution. In numerous ways, alcohol played a direct role—and sometimes an indirect role—in the two decades of revolutionary upheaval in the late 18th century. From John Hancock celebrating the repeal of the Stamp Act in 1766 by "treat[ing] the Populace with a Pipe of Madeira Wine," as one newspaper reported,[18] to General George Washington ordering "an extra ration of liquor to be issued to every man tomorrow, to drink Perpetual Peace, Independence & Happiness to the United States of America,"[19] in celebration of the war coming to an end with Britain's recognition of America's independence in 1783, alcohol made regular appearances at key moments of the revolution. This was a reflection of the fact that, for better or worse, drinking was an integral part of daily life in early America among all classes and regions. By all accounts, colonists drank a staggering amount.

Americans of the 18th century routinely consumed alcohol with every meal, with many beginning their day with an "eye opener" and closing it with a nightcap. Typically, beer and cider were consumed with breakfast and lunch, and rum and wine were served for dinner. Following dinner, the evenings were punctuated with claret, ratafias, creams, punches, and other cocktails. As a visitor in pre-revolutionary Philadelphia recorded in his diary, he was "given cider and punch for lunch; rum and brandy before dinner; punch, Madeira [wine], port and sherry at dinner; punch and liqueurs with the ladies; and wine, spirit and punch till bedtime, all in punchbowls big enough for a goose to swim in."[20]

Rum was the most popular spirit, and according to one estimate, at the time of the Revolutionary War, each person was consuming nearly four gallons of it per year.[21] Drinking wasn't limited to adults, either. Children and toddlers would get a taste of alcohol by getting to finish the sugary portion at the bottom of mom or dad's mug of rum toddy.[22] December, in particular, was known as a time to freely indulge in alcohol, with people typically beginning their daily intake at breakfast, with "egg-nog, punch and toddy ... freely served to the children," according to one contemporary observer.[23]

The roots of alcohol consumption in America run deep, with one popular story holding that the *Mayflower* docked at Plymouth rather than going farther south because the ship had run out of beer. Apparently, the *Mayflower* was forced to stop because the passengers were dangerously low on ale, which was considered safer to drink than water, so the captain decided to land at Plymouth Rock and winter there. Although some have dismissed it as a myth, it seems there is at least some truth to the story. As passenger and future governor of Plymouth Colony William Bradford wrote in his journal, "We could not now take time for further search or consideration, our victuals being much spent, especially our Beere."[24] He explained that he and other passengers "were hastened ashore and made to drink water, that the seamen might have the more beer." In order to meet the demands of the passengers and crew of the *Mayflower*, a brew house was among the first structures built at Plymouth in the winter of 1620–1621.[25]

Puritans called alcohol the "Good Creature of God," considering it a holy substance to be consumed piously and with respect. New England ministers warned against its excessive use, declaring public drunkenness a sin that contributed to idleness and crime. In *Pillars of Salt: An History of Some Criminals Executed in This Land for Capital Crimes*, Cotton Mather referred repeatedly to the pernicious effects of alcohol in the Massachusetts Bay Colony, noting that one criminal, prior to being executed, blamed his woes on drunkenness. "And one of them sadly Cryed out," Mather wrote, "Oh! 'Tis my Drunkenness, 'Tis my Drunkenness, that hath brought me to this Lamentable End!"[26] Another passage shares the last words of James Morgan, hanged for murder in Boston in 1686. "There are especially two Sins whereby I have offended the Great God; one is that Sin of Drunkenness, which has caused me to commit many other Sins; for when in Drink, I have been often guilty of Cursing and Swearing, and quarrelling, and striking others," he said. His other sin was that he rejected "the Word of God, and many a time refused to hear it preached."[27]

* * *

With waves of European migration bringing robust drinking habits to North America throughout the 1600s and 1700s, colonists began experimenting with brewing beer, fermenting peach juice, distilling rum, and making hard apple cider. Samuel Adams, despite his lack of success as a brewer, advocated the vigorous development of domestic beer production and urged a boycott of English imports in the mid–18th century. He and other patriots resented the profiteering that English merchants made by selling a product to America that colonists could produce themselves, so Adams spearheaded an early version of a "buy American" campaign. "It is to be hoped," he wrote in 1750, "that the Gentlemen of the Town will endeavour to bring our own OCTOBER BEER into Fashion again, by that most prevailing Motive, EXAMPLE, so that we may no longer be beholden to Foreigners for a Credible Liquor, which may be as successfully manufactured in this Country."[28]

Meanwhile, the rum distillery industry flourished, made possible by cheap imports of molasses from the West Indies, which eventually spawned one of the most important enterprises in New England. By one count, there were more than 150 rum distilleries in New England by 1770, and throughout the colonies some five million gallons of rum were being produced.[29] One reason that Massachusetts residents reacted so strongly to the Sugar Act of 1764, in fact, was that it increased the price of manufacturing rum and negatively affected the exporting capacity of New England distillers. It also targeted wine from Madeira, Portugal, which was popular throughout the colonies, as well as other commodities such as coffee. Although the tax was designed to cause little impact on the general consumer by including the duty in the cost of goods, the law sent shockwaves through the merchant class whose profits were directly threatened. In addition to extending the Molasses Act of 1733, which was initially passed for the benefit of the owners of sugar cane plantations in the British West Indies, the Sugar Act intended to crack down on smuggling.[30]

Samuel Adams led the charge against the Sugar Act, finding an ally in lawyer James Otis, who was an ardent opponent of the writs of assistance imposed by England in the early 1760s to allow royal officials to search property without cause. In May 1764 Adams drafted a report on the Sugar Act for the Massachusetts General Court, in which he denounced the measure as an infringement of the rights of the colonists, as well as a threat to commerce. "Our trade," Adams wrote, "centers in Great Britain, and in return for manufactures affords her more ready cash, beyond any comparison, than can possibly be expected by the most sanguine promoters of these extraordinary methods." He noted that Massachusetts is "ultimately yielding large supplies to the revenues of the mother country, while we are labouring for a very moderate subsistence for ourselves," highlighting the negative impact the Sugar Act would have on this commerce. "But if our trade is to be curtail'd in its most profitable branches, and burthens beyond all possible bearing, laid upon that which is suffer'd to remain, we shall be so far from being able to take off the manufactures of Great Britain, that it will be scarce possible for us to earn our bread," Adams wrote.[31]

One of the primary ways that the colonists earned their bread was the importation of wine, the smuggling of which often leading to friction with royal authorities. Several years before the Boston Tea Party, the so-called Liberty Affair of 1768 would help spark the coming war between America and Britain. On this occasion, John Hancock's sloop *Liberty* arrived in Boston from Madeira on May 9 with a cargo full of wine. Hancock boasted that he would unload his wine without paying duties, as he often did, and to do so the ship's captain illegally detained a royal official below decks while they unloaded most of the wine, only to declare a small fraction to the customs officials. When the authorities later learned of the incident, they attempted to seize the ship, which led to what John Adams later referred to as "a great Uproar [being] raised in Boston, on Account of the Unlading in the Night of a Cargo of Wines from the Sloop Liberty from Madeira."[32] A mob assaulted Customs Collector Joseph Harrison and Benjamin Hallowell, Comptroller of the Port of Boston. The patriots tore off the men's clothes and bludgeoned them with clubs and stones. They also attacked another customs inspector, Thomas Irwin, who was not involved with the seizure, but was just at the wrong place at the wrong time.[33] The mob smashed the windows of the customs officials' houses, and Harrison's pleasure boat was burned on Boston Common.[34] Some accounts say that as many as 2,000–3,000 rioters took part in the melee, while others say it was several hundred.

Samuel Adams downplayed the Liberty Affair, describing it as "something that had rather more of the appearance of riot, but it was only of a few hours existence, and with very little mischief," noting that "the people soon dispers'd after having broke a few panes of glass, not to the value of five pounds."[35] Naturally, he laid the blame for the disturbance with "the haughty behavior of the commissioners of the customs," rather than the attempt to smuggle wine without paying dues.

But while Adams vociferously defended the rights of colonists to profit from commerce including the lucrative wine importation and rum distilling industry and advocated vigorous production of domestic beer, he was not known to personally imbibe. Providing a clue to his temperate habits, he was described by Mercy Otis Warren as "placid, yet severe; sober and indefatiguable; calm in seasons of difficulty, tranquil and unruffled in the vortex of political altercation."[36] A Philadelphia colleague observed that "he eats little, drinks little, sleeps little, thinks much, and is most decisive and indefatigable in the pursuit of his objects."[37] In this way, Adams reflected colonial America's complex and nuanced relationship with booze, which some moralists warned about but many others had a rather open attitude toward.

* * *

Alcohol was held in great esteem by many of the Founding Fathers and intoxication was widely celebrated, which is attested to by the many quaint names used for being drunk, including "top'd," "tann'd," "tipium grove," "buskey," "bowz'd," and "seen a flock of moons."[38] According to Benjamin Franklin's count, which he tallied from his personal observations in Philadelphia taverns, there were some 200 synonyms for "drunk" in circulation in the mid–18th century, pointing out that "no one who has not much frequented Taverns would imagine the number of them so great as it really is."[39]

As Franklin explained, the euphemisms for being drunk were important because the term "drunkenness ... bears no kind of Similitude with any sort of Virtue." In order to help present intoxication in the least stigmatizing way, Franklin published "The Drinker's Dictionary" in 1737, which plainly expressed a sympathy with tavern culture. Despite his reputation for discipline, frugality and clean living, Franklin clearly appreciated the enjoyment that could be found by imbibing in drink, noting that he was reluctant to depict "drunkenness as a beastly Vice, since, 'tis well-known, that the Brutes are in general a very sober sort of People."[40] Franklin had a particular fondness for wine, which he considered a gift from God. As he wrote to his friend André Morellet while living in France, "Behold the rain which descends from heaven upon our vineyards, and which incorporates itself with the grapes to be changed into wine; a constant proof that God loves us, and loves to see us happy!"[41] He also seemed to advise against moderation in drinking, or at least not to dilute wine too much. Explaining that God "made wine to gladden the heart of man," he insisted that one should not "mingle water with it." After all, Franklin asked, "Why would you drown *truth*?"[42]

Virginians also had a rather liberal attitude toward drinking. It was a central part of the culture there, with jugs or bowls of liquor freely passed around on market days and for elections. Candidates running for office were expected to give away free drinks and those who were stingy saw their electoral prospects suffer.[43]

* * *

In addition to being a social lubricant and widely enjoyed intoxicant, alcohol was also utilized by criminals like Henry Tufts to win the trust of those being targeted for a robbery, or to simply knock them out. References to rum appear in the pages of Henry's autobiography on numerous occasions, including one anecdote in which he plied a new acquaintance with the beverage, supplemented with a dose of opium, in order to steal a horse. "Meantime I expressed a desire to purchase a little rum to cheer my spirits that cold evening," Henry recalled. So, he "took out [a] bottle, and tasting of the contents, offered it to [his] new acquaintance, who received the gratuity with cordiality." After "making a quick dispatch of the liquid," Henry "could but admire at its sudden effects, which were such, that immediately" his companions were passed out. "By searching their pockets," he wrote, "I found the key of the stable, which I unlocked and directly had the pleasure of fixing myself on the back of a very fine horse."[44]

Henry also used rum to win some new friends in the Abenaki tribe, which, of course, was a common technique in the 18th century. Whites often used rum to ingratiate themselves with their indigenous neighbors and sometimes won land concessions by convincing just two or three Indians, often with aid of a bit of liquor, to place their mark upon a deed. This practice often led to resentment and conflict, with other Indians rejecting the deals struck and claiming they had no validity.

The use of alcohol by "land jobbers" to manipulate Native Americans was so well-known, in fact, that it led to a prohibition in the Royal Proclamation of 1763 on defrauding Indian tribes through the use of gifts such as rum or firearms.[45] Specifically, the Crown proclaimed that "no private Person do presume to make any purchase from the said Indians of any Lands reserved to the said Indians." Since much of the conflict with the Indians was the result of anger over being cheated out of land, the Royal Proclamation tried to ensure that any land cessions were done through proper channels and not by land jobbers with a bottle of rum. "Whereas great Frauds and Abuses have been committed in purchasing Lands of the Indians, to the great Prejudice of our Interests and to the great Dissatisfaction of the said Indians," the Crown declared that lands "shall be Purchased only for Us, in our Name, at some public Meeting or Assembly of the said Indians."[46]

Besides souring relations due to land jobbers cheating Native Americans, alcohol also had a negative impact on white–Indian co-existence by fueling violence, theft and other anti-social activity. For instance, the Susquehannock, an Iroquoian-speaking people also called the Conestoga by some English settlers, were known as relatively peaceful but once introduced to alcohol, conflict and strife soon followed. In the backcountry of Pennsylvania, settlers complained that the Conestogas had become "rum debauched and Trader corrupted Thieves and vagabonds," with alcohol turning them into an "indisputably unfaithful and perfidious" people.[47] Pennsylvania had been "flourishing in Prosperity and Plenty" until, according to a 1757 article in the *Pennsylvania Gazette*, these "Savage Neighbors" attacked, in which "Great Numbers of the back Settlers were murdered, scalped and butchered, in the most shocking Manner."[48] Incidents such as these led to the rise of the Paxton Boys vigilante group, known as Pennsylvania's most aggressive colonists. On December 14, 1763, some 60 drunken Paxton Boys slaughtered 20 Susquehannock Indians, who had been suspected of pillaging, near the Conestoga River.[49]

There were also alcohol-fueled conflicts along the Ohio River in the backcountry of Virginia. One notorious event occurred in the spring of 1774, which shocked even hardened frontier folk for its brutality. Tensions had been rising in the region for months, and an Indian woman had warned the wife of a tavern owner named Joshua Baker, who often sold grog to both Indians and whites, that some Mingos were preparing to murder him and his family.[50] Baker got word out that he needed help and a settler named Daniel Greathouse came to his aid. On April 30, 1774, a group of Mingos from a town by the junction of Yellow Creek and the Ohio crossed the river to visit Baker's tavern and Baker sold alcohol to them, as he had done many times before. Leading a group of 21 men, Greathouse reached Baker's place and hid nearby.

Then, according to an eyewitness,

> The whites gave them rum, which three of them drank, and in a short time they became very drunk. The other two men and the woman refused to drink. The sober Indians were challenged to shoot at a mark, to which they agreed: and as soon as they had emptied their guns, the whites shot them down. ... The whites had a man in the cabin, prepared with a tomahawk for the purpose of killing the three drunken Indians, which was immediately done.[51]

Greathouse's men then opened fire on a group of Indian men who were coming across the river armed for war.

The incident became known as the Yellow Creek Massacre and was the final break in relations between the white settlers and the Indians in the Virginia backcountry, leading directly to Lord Dunmore's War of 1774, so named because it was the royal governor of Virginia, the Earl of Dunmore, who was blamed for inciting Indians on the frontier to wreak terrible acts of vengeance on the white settlers. His calculation seemed to be that by embroiling Virginians in the west, they would be unable to focus on participating in the federation of the colonies that was taking place in the east. Some historians consider this 10-month conflict, which was sparked by an alcohol-related massacre, as the opening of the American Revolution.[52] Of course, though, it was somewhat overshadowed by the events taking place in Boston—also largely related to alcohol. Indeed, the tensions that arose between occupying British soldiers and local Bostonians were sometimes attributed to the redcoats treating the town as a garrison post where they felt they had license to drink freely, leading to occasional assaults on women and other incidents.

* * *

Several key moments both during the pre-revolutionary phase and the fighting itself also appear to involve drinking. When anger over plans to implement the Stamp Act boiled over in 1765, for example, and a mob decided to ransack the home of Lieutenant Governor Thomas Hutchinson, the rioters made sure to target his exorbitant wine and sherry collection. According to Hutchinson, he lost ten pipes (each with a capacity of 126 gallons) and four quarter casks of "very good western Island wine," and four casks of sherry. Hutchinson also had a good amount of claret and white wine in bottles, none of which the rioters spared.[53]

A decade later, alcohol turns up again in a key moment leading up to the Revolutionary War, when, on April 18, 1775, Paul Revere began his famous ride to Lexington. As he hit the road to raise the alarm, he first stopped in Medford, where he visited the home of Captain Isaac Hall, commander of the town's minutemen. Hall dutifully triggered the alarm system, with "repeated gunshots, the beating of drums and the ringing of bells fill[ing] the air," as a townsman recalled.[54] In addition to warning of the approaching regulars, it has been widely speculated, Revere also may have enjoyed some of Hall's famous rum before continuing on his journey into the Massachusetts countryside.

Medford was known as a hub of the New England distillery industry, and Hall produced some of the best rum around, strong enough to make "a rabbit bite a bulldog," it was said.[55] Although there is no solid proof that Revere downed some of his rum before galloping off, the possibility has been raised in a number of books and a 1944 *New Yorker* article, which stated as fact that "Paul Revere had a stiff snort before starting his midnight ride."[56] The story gained more traction in 1968, when on Patriots' Day, a holiday in Massachusetts and Maine commemorating the Midnight Ride, the *Boston Globe* asserted that Captain Hall "gave Paul a little something to warm his bones," namely "a little rum poured on top of patriotic fervor." Wayne Curtis, author of *And a Bottle of Rum: A History of the New World in Ten Cocktails*, investigated the claim in 2006 and although he couldn't find any real evidence, he was assured by a local Medford historian named Thomas Convery, "If you're going to stop by the house of the distiller, you're going to get rum."[57]

David Hackett Fischer, however, doesn't buy it. In the historiography section of *Paul Revere's Ride*, Fischer notes that there has been no evidence ever produced for this claim and its only possible foundation is simply that Hall owned a distillery. Fischer also stresses that it flies in the face of what is known about Revere, who by all accounts was a man of temperate habits. Revere scholar Jayne Triber concurs, chalking up to popular cynicism the belief that "Revere was drunk when he made the ride."[58] The reality is that Revere was deadly serious about his mission to raise the alarm over the march of the regulars and likely wouldn't have spent too much time at Hall's downing copious amounts of rum. This doesn't preclude the possibility, however, that he may have taken a shot or two before continuing on his journey.

Whether or not Hall gifted Revere some of his top-shelf product, he most certainly did supply it to the Continental Army once the war got underway. In 1775 and 1776 he acted as commissary for the troops who were quartered at Dorchester Heights, and apparently, he lost quite a bit money because of it. He and his brothers generously contributed large amounts of rum, medical equipment and military supplies, and receiving payment in a consistently depreciating currency, they saw their assets steadily dwindle. In 1787 he sold his distillery to his brother Ebenr.[59]

* * *

Shortly after Revere's ride and the Battle of Lexington and Concord, alcohol turns up again when a small force led by Ethan Allen and Colonel Benedict Arnold captured Fort Ticonderoga. On May 10, 1775, Allen, Arnold and the unruly Green Mountain Boys descended on the fort's British garrison to seize the armaments and send them to Boston for the siege underway. As many as 400 men arrived at the fort, which they took over without a fight, and before setting about in their important mission of plundering the weapons, they first helped themselves to the provisions of liquor. Allen justified the seizure for "the refreshment of the fatigued soldiery," and his Green Mountain Boys proceeded to drink all 90 gallons of rum.[60]

While few historians take issue with the role of alcohol in the attack on Fort Ticonderoga, more contentious are the claims of an alcohol-soaked Battle of Trenton, a key turning point in the Revolutionary War. According to some accounts, the pivotal battle in the winter of 1776 may have been influenced by the Christmas night overindulgence of the German Hessian troops, but many historians have forcefully pushed back on this claim.

What is known is that in late 1776, following a disastrous series of defeats in the New York campaign, General Washington desperately needed a battlefield victory, and he looked to the garrison of 1,500 Hessian mercenaries at Trenton as an attractive target for a surprise attack. His calculation was that a victory against the elite brigade of professional soldiers would lift the spirits of his beleaguered army. His staff was convinced that the Germans would be heavily imbibing for their Christmas celebrations, and that the garrison would likely be drunk, hungover and unprepared for combat. The early morning hours of December 26, therefore, seemed to be the perfect moment for a surprise attack. "They make a great deal of Christmas in Germany, and no doubt the Hessians will drink a great deal of beer and have a dance to-night," wrote an unknown officer in his diary. "They will be sleepy to-morrow morning. Washington will set the tune for them about daybreak."[61]

After a difficult march to the Delaware River and an even more difficult crossing, which had been complicated by a strong storm that brought freezing rain and winds, Washington's 2,400 troops attacked the Hessian troops quartered at Trenton. The Continental soldiers quickly overpowered the German mercenaries, capturing more than 1,000 enemy troops in the brief skirmish. The victory proved to be a major boost to the fledgling cause of independence.[62]

Whether the Hessians were actually drunk though is another question. It seems that the legend of inebriated Hessians originates from the time period, when British officers began circulating the story to excuse the embarrassing defeat, denigrate the Hessian soldiers, and deny the Americans some of the glory of their victory. Anecdotal evidence, however, suggests that it might be unfounded. Contrary to the notion of the Hessians being heavily impaired, Washington told Congress that the Hessians "behaved very well" and maintained "a constant retreating fire from behind houses."[63] Continental soldiers who participated in the battle also rebutted the claims, noting that they did not see any inebriated Hessians. "I am willing to go upon oath that I did not see even a solitary drunken soldier belonging to the enemy," wrote John Greenwood.[64]

Of course, though, just as the Brits may have exaggerated the possibility of drunken Hessians to deny the Americans their glory of victory, the Continentals also may have downplayed this story for the opposite reason, and whether or not all or even some of the Hessians were "top'd," it seems that their commander may have been. Colonel Johann Rall apparently didn't take seriously some warnings that he had received from informers of an imminent attack and was famously playing cards on the night of the attack. "Rhall seeing so little precaution taken by the general, looked upon the intelligence as false, and got drunk as usual," reads an account from 1780.[65]

So, in spite of the doubts raised by historians about the Hessians being impaired during the fighting, it seems that alcohol may have played a role before the battle and could have impacted the outcome. And whether it affected the actual fighting, alcohol certainly featured prominently *following* the defeat of the Hessians, with some Americans, after taking over the garrison, breaking into the rum supply and heartily celebrating their victory.[66] This made the return trip after the battle in some ways more difficult than the first crossing of the Delaware. Due to the large number of intoxicated soldiers, the second crossing was slowed down considerably by the frequent stops to rescue troops who fell overboard into the icy waters.[67]

Incidentally, the looting of the Hessians' rum supply was in direct contravention of Washington's explicit orders for its destruction.[68] It was probably seen by the troops though as their right after putting their lives on the line and fighting hard—with alcohol widely seen as one of the spoils of war. Looting of alcohol was a common practice following battles, and at times, the Americans even looted their own rum. A month before the Battle of Trenton, for instance, the Brits and Hessians planned to attack Fort Lee. Many of the soldiers, however, having heard in advance of the pending attack, thought it was a good opportunity to break into the fort's stores and begin drinking the rum. The British arrived to find the fort

9. Alcohol in the Revolution

In this depiction of the preparations for the Battle of Trenton, General George Washington is seated on his horse observing troops loading into boats to cross the Delaware River. Washington very much needed a victory at the close of the disastrous year of 1776, and the Christmas Day routing of the Hessians in Trenton proved to be a major morale booster for his beleaguered troops (*Washington Crossing the Delaware–Evening Previous to the Battle of Trenton, December 25th, 1776*, lithographed and published by Nathaniel Currier, 1847. Metropolitan Museum of Art, Bequest of Adele S. Colgate).

nearly empty, with most hiding in the forest nearby, some passed out from drunkenness, and those who remained in the fort also mostly drunk.[69] The British took the fort easily.

Drunkenness, indeed, was a persistent problem in the Continental Army, and at times it was treated as a more serious offense than desertion. In Washington's General Orders of July 25, 1776, for instance, a soldier named Henry Davis, who had been tried for desertion, was to receive 20 lashes, while Patrick Lyons, who was accused of "Drunkenness and sleeping on his post," was to receive 30 lashes.[70] But even as the Continental Army harshly punished drunkenness, it also considered rum as an important part of the soldiers' daily provisions, and sometimes it was used as an incentive to recruit men to perform difficult tasks. During the New York campaign in summer 1776, for example, General Nathanael Greene enticed men to help fortify Cobble Hill in Brooklyn by promising extra rum. "The works on Cobble Hill being greatly retarded for want of men to lay turf," Greene wrote, "all those in Colonel Hitchcock's and Colonel Little's regiments, that understand that business, are desired to voluntarily turn out every day, and they shall be excused from all other duty, and allowed one half a pint of rum a day."[71]

It was also understood, however, that excessive drinking adversely impacted the revolutionary cause and on occasion it was blamed for patriot defeats on the battlefield, for instance at the Battle of Germantown on October 4, 1777. Despite fighting fiercely for five hours, the Americans failed to capture the camp and the British pushed the patriots back to their original positions, with Washington's casualties numbering 152 killed, 521 wounded, and approximately 400 captured. The Brits fared much better, with 70 lost lives and 451 wounded. Adam Stephen, who had just been promoted to the rank of Major General earlier that year, would bear the brunt of criticism for losing the battle, with alcohol seen as having impaired his decision-making abilities. Stephen was known for his intemperance and apparently was quite drunk during the fighting. He was subsequently court-martialed and found guilty of "unofficerlike behavior, in the retreat from Germantown, owing to inattention, or want of judgement." The court martial also found that "he has been frequently intoxicated since in the service,"[72] and for these transgressions he was stripped of his command and dismissed, making him the only general discharged from the Continental Army during the course of the war.[73]

The delicate balance that the army tried to find in its approach toward alcohol—on one hand tolerating and even encouraging limited alcohol use, but also punishing excessive drinking—was reflective more broadly of the equilibrium that society at large tried to establish with booze. It often seemed, however, that this was a losing battle, and following the revolution, America was destined to become a "nation of drunkards," as a temperance group called the Greene and Delaware Moral Society warned in the early 19th century. Other temperance groups sprouted up in the early republic including the Woman's Christian Temperance Union and the Anti-Saloon League, warning that excessive drinking in America was "too obvious not to be noticed" and that it was spreading "wider and wider" in the new nation, "like the plague." George Washington decried intemperance as "the ruin of half the workmen in this Country," while John Adams asked, "is it not mortifying ... that we, Americans, should exceed all other ... people in the world in this degrading, beastly vice?"[74]

John Adams, sadly, knew the pernicious effects of alcohol all too well. While serving as the second president of the United States in 1800, his son Charles died at the age of 30. While the official cause of death was "dropsy of the chest," which refers to a condition now known as pleurisy, it has been widely speculated that Charles in fact drank himself to death.

Charles struggled with alcohol all of his adult life and was never able to make a decent living in his chosen profession as a lawyer.[75] Following his untimely death, Abigail Adams wrote to John Quincy Adams with the sad news about his brother. "When I reflect, that he was cutt down in the bloom of Life," Abigail wrote, "in the midst of his days, he is numberd with the Dead; it becomes me in Silence to mourn; Mourn over him living, I have for a long time, and now he is gone." Her deep remorse is clear as she expresses "tender remembrance of what he once was," but also admitting her "wish to forget" what he became and conveying a hope that "he may have obtaind forgiveness."[76]

Another well-known public figure who may have suffered from alcoholism, particularly later in his life, was Thomas Paine. Although he was instrumental in launching the revolution with his radical pamphlet *Common Sense* and helped salvage the revolutionary cause at its most dire moment during the winter of 1776, Paine would become something of an outcast in his later years. This was partly due to the fact that he had publicly criticized George Washington for failing to help get him out of jail while he was imprisoned in France following the revolution in that country, as well as his reputation as an atheist after writing the anti-church screed *The Age of Reason*.

After Paine returned from France to the United States and was shunned by his former friends, he began drinking more heavily, it is believed. As an acquaintance wrote, Paine had "a mind, though strong enough to bear him up and to rise elastic under the heaviest hand of oppression, yet unable to endure the contempt of his former friends … and unhappily seeks refuge in low company, or looks for consolation in the sordid, solitary bottle."[77] Stories endure of him being pulled out of taverns with his beard showing a two weeks' old growth and his body giving off a "most disagreeable odor." The drinking gave him a noticeable proboscis of the nose, but it is unclear whether it also affected his longevity. He died in 1809 at age 72 from the effects of an earlier stroke.[78]

Like other alcohol-related stories from the revolutionary period such as the allegedly tipsy Paul Revere riding to warn of the redcoats advancing to Lexington or the possibly drunk and hungover Hessian troops being easily defeated at Trenton, the stories of Paine spending his twilight years perpetually inebriated have been vehemently disputed over the years. Supporters of Paine insist that the allegations stem from his political enemies who sought to disparage and discredit him with rumors and slander, but judging from most available evidence, there does appear to be some truth to the claims. Regardless of the ultimate reality, though, the enduring allegations are a clear indication that alcohol was a significant issue in the revolutionary period and early republic. The pushback from some historians who dispute the claims, likewise, points to a persistent effort to maintain an upright and honorable reputation for those involved in the American Revolution.

This honorable reputation, however, was undermined by subsequent events. Despite efforts to downplay the role of booze in the revolutionary era, its central importance would become impossible to ignore when an alcohol-related insurrection took hold in the early republic during the presidency of George Washington. The heavily indebted federal government decided in 1791 to impose an excise tax on domestically produced distilled spirits, disproportionately impacting farmers of the western frontier who manufactured whiskey and often used it as currency in an informal barter economy in the backcountry. Angered by what they saw as an unfair tax imposed by coastal elites, these farmers launched an insurrection that employed many of the violent tactics that had been used decades earlier in resisting taxes imposed by England, including tar-and-featherings.

Reaching a crescendo in 1794, the Whiskey Rebellion underlined the inescapable reality that alcohol and vice would continue to play an important role in shaping the new nation and served as a reminder of the unruliness of certain sectors of the newly formed nation. It also raised questions of the limits of government authority, as well as what sorts of protest would be considered legitimate in a democratic republic—questions that first came to the fore several years earlier in Shays's Rebellion of 1786–1787. In this affair, Samuel Adams would play a central—and somewhat controversial—role.

10

Framers vs. Farmers

"It is well known," political philosopher Hannah Arendt once observed, "that the most radical revolutionary will become a conservative on the day after the revolution."[1] Never would this truism be more on display than in the years following the American victory over the British, when Samuel Adams's transformation from revolutionary to statesman meant that he would have to defend those at the top against challenges to authority from below. After a long career as a radical rabble rouser who railed against unfair taxes and an unaccountable, faraway government, Adams would become—in the eyes of debt-ridden farmers and Revolutionary War veterans facing foreclosure and debtors prison—an embodiment of unfair taxes and unaccountable, faraway government. To Adams, of course, there was nothing hypocritical in doing so. As he saw it, to challenge a tyranny such as the British monarchy was not only legitimate but divine. On the other hand, to challenge a democratic government—such as the one that he helped establish—was unconscionable.

To the Massachusetts insurgents who took up arms in what became known as Shays's Rebellion, however, their cause was largely a continuation of the struggle that they had been fighting in the years prior to the signing of the Treaty of Paris in September 1783. Although the elite leadership of the fledgling republic may have thought that this treaty, which recognized American independence and established borders for the new nation, had effectively ended the war, to struggling farmers in the grips of an economic depression and saddled with debt, the underlying grievances that had led them to fight the British still existed. Meanwhile, many members of the new ruling elite remained understandably concerned that London would continue to meddle in American affairs, and suspected that the rebel leaders were agents of the Crown. This was false, of course, but in a roundabout way, there was some truth that London had a hand in the rebellion. The British, still smarting from their defeat on the battlefield, had sought to punish the former colony for its rebellion and implemented trade sanctions intended to cripple the American economy. Just four months after the Treaty of Paris, in January 1784, Parliament adopted the Navigation Acts, closing American access to British ports.[2] This led to a major loss of revenue for Boston merchants, who decided to call in debts from farmers in western Massachusetts, resulting in substantial hardship among the populace, which, in turn, led to an armed insurrection. So, in that way, perhaps the suspicions of a British hand in the rebellion were not completely baseless.

This time, rather than seeing their nemesis as British ministers or a king thousands of miles away, Massachusetts farmers identified the source of their troubles as being closer to home—namely the system of government that was established by the revolution that they had just fought. Torn between their anger over economic injustice that they endured, the harsh reality of foreclosures and imprisonment that they experienced, and the hopes that they had in the new government that they had fought to establish, the agitated farmers petitioned their elected representatives in Boston. As the crisis deepened, however, the shortcomings of representative democracy would become increasingly clear.

Indeed, in the eyes of some Regulators (as they called themselves), or Shaysites (as their adversaries called them), the government that was established after the revolution was actually a step backward in terms of ensuring democratic rights and economic justice, and would prove to be utterly unresponsive to their legitimate grievances. Much of their ire would be focused on the Massachusetts Constitution, which they considered elitist and undemocratic. But having had experience in the previous decades with exercising the power of direct action—including by taking up arms and seizing government offices—these farmers were well aware that militant tactics could be an effective means of achieving results. If the government was unable or unwilling to heed their concerns, they knew that popular revolt was always an option.

* * *

Massachusetts, despite being the leading force for the revolution, did not manage to adopt its constitution until four years after independence. The state had tried to enact one in 1778, but the people rejected it, largely due to the fact that it lacked a bill of rights.[3] By that time, five other state constitutions already contained bills of rights, and a motion was made to name a committee of 31 prominent citizens from across the state to draft a declaration of rights as well as a framework of government. Samuel Adams, John Adams and James Bowdoin were appointed to a three-man subcommittee to do the preliminary work. John Adams took the lead in preparing the committee's report, with the other two making few changes.[4]

The new version of the Constitution provided for a separation of powers and direct elections, but also contained some reactionary and aristocratic elements, such as raising property requirements for holding office. Much language was borrowed from the rejected 1778 constitution, including provisions on payment of monies and the phrasing on impeachment, while the powers bestowed on the General Court largely derived from the charter of 1691. But the convention made a number of significant alterations, with some of the most consequential relating to the powers given to the governor. While popular sentiment tended to be skeptical of strong executives, John Adams's view on the balance of power required that the governor should act nearly as a third branch of the legislature.

The Massachusetts Constitution therefore established a powerful executive and fortified the powers of the other branches of government, creating a Senate that would check potential overreaching by the more democratic lower House. It delineated a veto system, establishing that "no bill or resolve of the senate or house of representatives shall become a law, and have force as such, until it shall have been laid before the governor for his revisal." If the governor declined to sign it, the Constitution explained how the House and Senate could override the veto with a two-thirds supermajority. The Massachusetts Constitution also included "A Declaration of the Rights of the Inhabitants of the Commonwealth of Massachusetts," which affirmed that "all men are born free and equal, and have certain natural, essential, and unalienable rights; among which may be reckoned the right of enjoying and defending their lives and liberties; that of acquiring, possessing, and protecting property; in fine, that of seeking and obtaining their safety and happiness."[5]

Following its adoption, Samuel Adams wrote to his cousin John:

> The People of Massachusetts have at length agreed to the Form of a civil Constitution.... This great Business was carried through with much good Humour among the People, and even in Berkshire, where some Persons led us to expect it would meet with many Obstructions. Never was a good Constitution more wanted than at this juncture.[6]

In April 1781, Samuel Adams was elected to both the Massachusetts House of Representatives and to the Senate, but understanding that taking both jobs would undermine the system of checks and balances that the Constitution provided for, he declined the House position and became a state senator instead, subsequently chosen by his colleagues to serve as president of the Senate.

As Adams was settling into his new role, the first major challenge to the new constitutional and economic order would erupt when, in 1782, a Revolutionary War veteran and radical organizer named Samuel Ely led a crowd to the Hampshire County court to keep it closed in order to prevent legal proceedings against debtors. Leading the mob, Ely reportedly picked up a stick and shouted, "Come on, my brave boys, we'll go to the woodpiles and get clubs enough to knock their grey wigs off!" He claimed to have a replacement constitution in his pocket, which, he said, "even the Angel Gabriel could not find fault with." Ely was arrested, but a crowd of about 130 men broke him out of the Northampton jail.[7]

An associate of Samuel Adams named Joseph Hawley speculated that Ely's rebellion and jailbreak may have been the result of "British Emissaries, with British money," attempting to stir up sedition to undermine the new republic. This, of course, was less than a year after the Brits had surrendered at Yorktown, and Hawley suggested that the General Court appoint a committee to investigate. This committee was led by Adams and Artemas Ward, who traveled to Hampshire County in the summer of 1782 and met with delegates from 44 towns. The most common grievances that the committee heard related to high taxes, and Adams returned to the capital motivated to provide some relief to the farmers of western Massachusetts. He moved to defer debt repayment, and urged leniency for the rebels. None of the men who helped Ely break out of jail was punished and Ely only served six months in prison before his sentence was commuted by a legislative act.[8]

These measures, however, failed to resolve the underlying issues. During the war, Massachusetts had incurred a large debt, and in order to pay it, the government had increased taxes. This was done at a time of an economic downturn which was compounded by a lack of cash in circulation, and in order to obtain the cash needed to pay taxes, creditors called in their private debts. Poor farmers—many of whom were veterans of the revolution who never received the payments promised to them for their service—were often unable to pay, leading to a wave of foreclosures, which many blamed on the legal system just established by the new Massachusetts Constitution.

Through the 1780s, debt collection continued to lead to ruin for poor farmers, many of whom felt betrayed by a government that they had helped to establish by fighting a long and difficult war against the British. As an indication of how common it was for farmers to be imprisoned due to unpayable debts, Henry Tufts mentions in his memoirs coming across "prisoners for debt" while he was jailed in Newbury, Massachusetts, noting that they "invariably betrayed my counsel" when he attempted to hatch escape plans with them.[9] While Tufts doesn't offer details on how or why these prisoners rejected his overtures, perhaps, as patriotic and honest farmers and veterans, they did not want to associate with a known criminal.

From 1782 to 1786, western towns tried repeatedly to get state legislators in Boston to help alleviate the depressed backcountry economy, sending petitions and adopting resolutions at town meetings with calls to reduce taxes, issue paper money, reduce court and lawyers' fees, reduce salaries for state officials, and move the state capital from Boston to a more central location.[10]

* * *

Many also felt betrayed in the pivotal 1785 gubernatorial election, which pitted John Hancock's protege Thomas Cushing, who had championed Hancock's policies on tax leniency and depreciation of debts, against James Bowdoin, who allied with the merchant class and took a hard line on the commonwealth's financial policies. The 1785 election was highly political and divisive, with farmers worried that if elected, Bowdoin would implement policies that would lead to their financial ruin, and the elites casting Cushing as fiscally irresponsible. When the votes were certified, neither candidate had won a majority of the popular vote, so the election went to the General Court. There, the House voted for Cushing 134–89, but the Senate overrode the lower chamber. Bowdoin was ultimately elected by a vote of 18–10 in the General Court's aristocratic upper chamber. Bowdoin's term would be dominated by the economic crisis, with farmers growing increasingly exasperated by the government's inaction.[11]

Although attempts were made by the General Court to consider some of the farmers' demands, legislators and Bowdoin ultimately made matters worse when they enacted direct taxes that were enforced through the court system. With so many debtors lacking the money to meet the creditors' demands, "an amazing flood of lawsuits" followed, as a County Convention held at Worcester in September 1786 put it,[12] leading to a wave of defaults and arrests. Creditors demanded that obligations were satisfied "one way or the other," and with farmers unable to pay, farms were confiscated by the state and sold for a fraction of their true value. Meanwhile, the numbers of people imprisoned for non-payment of debts increased exponentially. Those with unpayable debts often found themselves in dark and filthy county jails. In the Worcester County debtors' prison, more than 20 inmates were crowded into a cramped and cold attic in December 1785, and plaintively petitioned for relief from conditions "by no means fit for any of the Human Race."[13] The debtors' crisis led to substantial overcrowding, with records showing that in the Worcester County jail in 1786, there were 80 inmates imprisoned for debt, compared to just eight who were incarcerated for other offenses.[14] Borrowing a page from the Henry Tufts playbook, many of these imprisoned debtors would manage to break out of jail, sometimes with the help of sympathetic mobs.[15]

The General Court was inundated with pleas asking for the legislature to pass laws making real and personal estate as well as gold and silver a legal tender. This proposal was not unlike the Land Bank that had been established by Samuel Adams's father some four decades earlier in response to the economic depression that hit Massachusetts in 1740, so one might think that he would have supported it, but Adams had changed since then. While the Land Bank crisis of the 1740s—and the resulting financial ruin of his father—had led a young Samuel Adams to argue for the legitimacy of popular resistance, four decades later he took a hard line against rebellion and had little sympathy for the western Massachusetts farmers.

As revolutionary veterans, however, the debtors could see the plain unfairness of their predicament. Many of these men had served the patriot cause during the most difficult periods of the war, and some of them for the duration of the fighting. Tax revenues were being allocated to pay the large foreign debt accumulated during the war and to speculators who had bought up state securities at depreciated rates. Now, many veterans had been forced by circumstance to sell these same securities for a slice of their value. While these winter soldiers had sacrificed everything for the cause of independence, those who had sat out the war found themselves in a much better financial situation, leading to resentment and bitterness from the indebted veterans. As "An Old Soldier" asked in a letter published in the *Hampshire Herald*,

> Shall the man, who has sauntered at home during the war, enjoying the smiles of fortune: wallowing in affluence, and fattening in the sunshine of ease and prosperity:- and shall I be taxed with my little farm to make them good in the hands of the present holders, who are mostly men of this description: forbid it humanity: forbid it gratitude and justice.[16]

* * *

After the General Court failed to enact debt relief, debtors decided to take action to stop the foreclosures and recruited Daniel Shays, a former Revolutionary War Captain, to lead them.[17] On August 29, 1786, some 1,500 Massachusetts Regulators closed the Northampton Court of Common Pleas, and from September 5 to 13, hundreds rose up in Worcester, Concord, Taunton, and Great Barrington. There was also an outbreak in Newbury, Vermont, in which Henry Tufts apparently took part. A local history published in 1902 claims that Tufts, brandishing a gun, "made an inflammatory speech" at the Newbury courthouse "and called on the people to ... turn out the judge, lawyers and jury." Tufts was immediately disarmed, jailed, and placed in the stocks, subsequently deciding to leave the town.[18]

Despite being disparaged as lawless insurrectionists, the rebels maintained a high degree of discipline. Inspired by the North Carolina Regulators, who fought corruption in the War of Regulation in Provincial North Carolina two decades earlier, they refrained from wanton destruction and focused their ire on the legal system that they saw as stacked against them. As one of the rebels, Adam Wheeler, wrote in a letter to a Springfield newspaper, there was "no intention to destroy the public government." Instead, he explained, the farmers were intent on ensuring a "redress of grievances in a constitutional way."[19]

The people of the region largely sympathized with their cause, with many supporters opening their homes to the rebels and providing them needed supplies, and the militia, called up to help quell the rebellion, instead taking the side of the protestors. In Great Barrington, Justice William Whiting asked the militia to show their loyalties, and 800 out of 1,000 militiamen publicly sided with the Regulators. They also had the support of many common people in other states who stood in solidarity with the Massachusetts farmers, encouraged that resistance in defense of liberty and property was alive and well in post-revolution America.[20] All states except for Virginia refused to contribute funds to support the deployment of federal soldiers to suppress the revolt.[21] With the official state militiamen unwilling to turn their muskets on their own people and the commonwealth unable to obtain help from other states, the Massachusetts elite tapped former Continental Army General Benjamin Lincoln to fight the rebels. Lincoln's private militia of some 3,000 mercenaries hailed almost entirely from eastern Massachusetts, and were funded by 125 merchants who contributed £6,000 to help put down the rebellion.[22]

Rather than implement meaningful changes to economic policy or make serious attempts to pursue dialogue with the farmers, the Massachusetts legislature declared them traitors and doubled down in its harsh response. Deeply concerned by the refusal of militiamen to protect the courts against farmers, legislators passed a law that threatened consequences against anyone who refused to muster. By virtue of the authority vested in it by the new Constitution, the legislature "solemnly pronounce[d] and declare[d], that a horrid and unnatural Rebellion and War, has been openly and traitorously raised and levied against this Commonwealth." The objective of the rebellion, according to the legislature, was to "to subvert and overthrow the Constitution and Form of Government thereof which has been most solemnly agreed to, and established by the Citizens of this Commonwealth." In order to uphold this nascent government, it would be necessary to "exert and bring forth, all the powers of the Commonwealth for the Suppression thereof; and all the horrors and evils that may follow in the consequence of this Rebellion." Despite the fact that most of them were Revolutionary War veterans, the men who had acted as "Fomenters, Abetters, and Supporters" of the rebellion were deemed traitors and villains.[23]

Although he was a revolutionary firebrand in his younger years, advocating back in the 1760s and '70s for drastic action against British customs agents and leading the Boston Tea Party, Adams's radical sentiments would not carry over into the post-revolutionary period. Adams insisted that the farmers' rebellion was misguided at best and a threat to the fledgling republic at worst. "A commonwealth or state is a body politic, or civil society of men, united together to promote their mutual safety and prosperity by means of their union," said Adams, recommending that the leaders of the insurgents be immediately executed. "In monarchies the crime of treason and rebellion may admit of being pardoned or lightly punished, but the man who dares rebel against the laws of a republic ought to suffer death," Adams argued.[24]

The views of Adams on this matter carried substantial weight, and when they were published in 1786, they caused as much dismay among the Regulators as they did celebrations among Boston's wealthy merchants. Speaking at an emergency meeting convened by Governor Bowdoin at Faneuil Hall, Adams's denunciation of the rebels in western Massachusetts was endorsed by thunderous applause from hundreds of assembled politicians and merchants.[25] Everyone knew that Adams had been instrumental in organizing the rebellion against the British, and therefore by distancing himself from the Regulators, he instantly diminished their credibility. But his words carried more than just symbolic weight. Since he served as one of Bowdoin's key advisers, his views mattered in a very real sense—directly shaping the response of the Massachusetts government.

While other public figures in Massachusetts, such as Great Barrington's Justice William Whiting, had expressed sympathy with the Shaysites and condemned the politicians and financiers in Boston as "overgrown Plunderers" who were "tyrannizing over the people," Adams, in contrast, found little merit in the protestors' grievances.[26] Whereas Whiting cited the Declaration of Independence in arguing that the people had an "indispensable duty" to combat "baneful injustice,"[27] in Adams's view, the contrast between the rebellion that he led two decades earlier and the protests of 1786 could not be clearer. While his band of rebels had been resisting the tyranny of a monarchical power, the Shaysites were undermining the very system of government that had been fought for and forged in the revolution—an unforgivable sin in his eyes. Not only did he therefore advocate for the execution of the rebellion's leaders, but also insisted that no leniency be shown to any of the rank and file who participated. He called for jailing every single one of them, in fact, but as

General Lincoln pointed out, all the jails of New England could not hold that many people. (And even if there was space for all these rebel farmers, where would the jailors then put common criminals such as Henry Tufts?)

Besides advocating the most draconian punishments imaginable for the leaders of the revolt, Adams proposed the Riot Act, which criminalized gatherings of more than 12 armed persons. In addition to pre-emptively absolving legal authorities who "shall be indemnified and held guiltless" for killing or wounding rioters during efforts to suppress a crowd after "the reading of" the Riot Act, the law also provided for the arrest of those who failed to disperse, and subsequent punishment of 39 lashes "on the naked back, at the public whipping post," as well as imprisonment for a period of six to 12 months. Following this law's adoption, the General Court passed the Militia Act, which provided for the execution of militia officers and soldiers who had taken up arms against the state. This law was in response to the trend of militiamen declining to muster and refusing orders to suppress the rebel farmers, and was intended to counter the Articles of Confederation's forbidding of each state's army from crossing state lines.

* * *

The rebellion deeply alarmed the nation's ruling elite, who, like many of the common people of various states who stood in solidarity with the Massachusetts farmers, saw it not as a regional issue but as a national one. Henry Lee of Virginia, a member of Congress, expressed the shock of many of his class when he said: "We are all in dire apprehension that a beginning of anarchy with all its calamitys has approached, and have no means to stop the dreadful work."[28] Abigail Adams denounced the Regulators as "ignorant, restless desperadoes, without conscience or principals, [who] have led a deluded multitude to follow their standard, under pretence of grievances which have no existence but in their own imaginations."[29] Many in the political class worried that the rebellion might spread throughout the country, and understood that the republic's legal framework was insufficient in dealing with such crises.

Newspapers also joined in by whipping up hysteria and painting the rebellion in the worst possible light. The *Hampshire Gazette*, for example, warned that Shays could overthrow the government and "declare himself dictator of the whole union." Fears that London continued to meddle in American affairs shaped many people's outlook on the crisis, with warnings circulating in the press that the Shaysites were being "excited, supported and encouraged by the emissaries of that nation to which we were formerly subject."[30]

The sense of crisis in news reports and direct pleas from the Massachusetts elite fueled fears about the rebellion and ultimately had wide-ranging effects, prompting, for example, George Washington to come out of retirement from politics. With Massachusetts militiamen refusing to turn their muskets on their own people, Henry Knox had written to Washington to warn him that the farmers' tax revolt could be part of a design to exploit the weakness of the federal government and redistribute property. He argued that the Articles of Confederation were woefully inadequate in dealing with these threats, pointing out that "thirteen independent sovereignties have been perpetually operating against each other and against the federal Head" ever since the end of the war. Congress, Knox said, lacked the authority to oblige states "to do those things which are essential for their own welfare & for the general good."[31]

Although he had been looking forward to some well-earned post-war leisure time on his Virginia estate, Washington agreed with Knox, stating that "commotions of this sort, like snow-balls, gather strength as they roll, if there is no opposition in the way to divide and crumble them."[32] After the rebellion had been quelled, he expressed his hopes "that good may result from the cloud of evils which threatened, not only the hemisphere of Massachusetts but by spreading its baneful influence, the tranquility of the Union."[33] The rebellion had called into question not only the state of the country's finances and the viability of the weak national government, but also raised doubts about the ability of state militias to quell possible future rebellions—a particular concern for slave-owners in the South.

Thus, although the insurgents would ultimately fail to achieve their objectives, the insurrection would have a profound and an enduring impact on the course of American history, mainly by reinforcing and amplifying the arguments for a strong central government (and the replacement of the sorely inadequate Articles of Confederation that had served as a sort of provisional constitution during the revolutionary period). It is for this reason that Shays's Rebellion is often called "the final battle of the American Revolution," as it represented the last true test of the ideological nature of the revolution. Precisely how democratic would the new republic be? Whose interests would be at the forefront of the new nation's agenda? Which classes would be represented in state capitals and in the national government? How would individual rights and liberties be balanced with the need for internal security?

The newly established American oligarchy—the merchants, land speculators, plantation owners, and bankers—had substantial differences of opinion on precisely what form the government should take, with some advocating a centralized republic, others a confederation of states, and still others a constitutional monarchy, but what they all seemed to agree on was that the revolutionary rhetoric about liberty was mainly meant to apply to free men who owned property.

Clearly, America's new ruling class did not take Shays's Rebellion lightly, and although most of the insurgents would escape the gallows, the insurrection would prove decisive in determining the course of the new nation.

PART III

Republican Values

"If men were angels, no government would be necessary."
—Federalist Paper No. 51

"All men would be tyrants if they could."
—Abigail Adams

11

We the Rabble

Shays's Rebellion revealed a certain level of popular discontent with the emerging post-war order, but perhaps more importantly to the political class, it exposed the central government's inability to govern effectively, especially in a nation of rabble whose respect for authority left a lot to be desired. Having tasted the power of direct action, which had been so effectively employed in recent years, Americans retained a rebellious spirit that would have to be reined in if the new nation were to succeed, the new republic's leadership believed. Insurgencies, much like the unchecked criminality of vagabonds such as Henry Tufts, exhibited a distortion of republican equality in which too many ordinary people were defying legitimate authority and destroying the public spirit that should be at the heart of republicanism. Everywhere one looked, it seemed, self-interest and individualism were eroding the qualities of virtue and sacrifice that were needed in a self-governing republic.[1]

The ruling class's concerns during this period manifested most pointedly in criticism of the governing document in place during the 1780s. Throughout the decade, the weaknesses of the Articles of Confederation would become more apparent, with Congress commanding little respect from the states and proving unable to govern effectively, to regulate trade or conduct foreign policy. Under the Articles of Confederation, there was no centralized executive to enforce the laws and no general judiciary. The national government consisted only of a unicameral legislature in which states had equal voting power, and despite the fact that the new nation had a large debt, Congress could not raise revenue. The various branches of the government were rendered impotent.

Ever since the Articles of Confederation were ratified in 1781, reformers led by Alexander Hamilton and James Madison had been clamoring to remedy their shortcomings. Federalists argued throughout the 1780s that the document that Samuel Adams had helped to write was insufficient in establishing the authority to issue taxes and regulate commerce, but Shays's Rebellion revealed another weakness—the challenges posed by strict state sovereignty in dealing with internal revolts. These concerns were not limited to just insurrections, and indeed could just as easily be applied to the need for law enforcement more generally—whether in dealing with an insurgent like Daniel Shays or a common criminal like Henry Tufts. "If government shrinks, or is unable to enforce its laws," Washington wrote, "anarchy & confusion must prevail—and every thing will be turned topsy turvey in that State; where it is not probable the mischiefs will terminate."[2] Essentially, the legal system was not ideal for the stability needed for social order and commerce, and it was to remedy this situation that the framers sought to devise a new centralized government.[3]

With anxieties over the survival of self-rule dominating the thoughts of the country's leaders, preparations started to be made for an overhaul of America's governing system. While Massachusetts was still busy suppressing its rebellion, nine other states were sending delegates to a Meeting of Commissioners to Remedy Defects of the Federal Government in Annapolis, Maryland, to discuss the need for reform, eventually resulting in the Philadelphia Convention of May 1787.[4] At the prodding of several prominent individuals who convinced him that his presence was needed at the Constitutional Convention, Washington went to Philadelphia to help facilitate the process, and his unanimous election as president of the Convention was one of the few things that 55 state delegates could agree on.

Although Washington was prompted to action by Shays's Rebellion, he also appeared to be motivated by concern over what sort of government might emerge from the Convention. "What astonishing changes a few years are capable of producing," he fretted to John Jay. "I am told that even respectable characters speak of a monarchical form of government without horror. ... What a triumph for the advocates of despotism to find that we are incapable of governing ourselves, and that systems founded on the basis of equal liberty are merely ideal & falacious!"[5]

* * *

While there may have been some in America who were sympathetic to a monarchical form of government, the framers of the Constitution mainly fell into two camps: the federalists and the anti-federalists. Broadly speaking, the federalists supported a strong union and argued that the central government formed under the Articles of Confederation was too weak. The anti-federalist camp, which boasted many Massachusetts men, including Samuel Adams, opposed a strong federal government and worried that the position of president, especially, was too close to a monarchy. Aptly expressing the anti-federalist position, Adams argued that "the private & personal Rights of the Citizens depend" on the sovereignty of individual states, noting that "without such Distinction there will be Danger of the Constitution issuing imperceptibly and gradually into a consolidated Government." Adams was convinced that because Americans live "in different Climates, of different Education and Manners, and possest of different Habits & feelings," they cannot remain free "under one consolidated Gove[rnment]."[6]

One of the key issues that highlighted Americans' "different Habits & feelings" was chattel slavery. The Constitutional Convention deftly sidestepped this issue, avoiding its moral implications and relegating it to a political problem that would be simpler to manage and reach compromises on. The document eschewed addressing slavery straightforwardly and declared that, for the purposes of representation in the House of Representatives, any person who was not free would be counted as three-fifths of a free individual. The delegates also decided to block ending the slave trade for a period of 20 years, a concession to the southern states that many abolitionists found repugnant.[7] John Dickinson, for example, wondered what "the World" would say "of this new principle of founding a Right to govern Freemen on a power derived from Slaves," observing that the three-fifths rule meant that each state's "Importation of Slaves will increase the power of the state over others."[8]

Samuel Adams, however, chose to look at the glass as half-full. As an opponent of slavery, he welcomed the clause blocking the prohibition of importing slaves because it opened the door to abolition at a future date. At the Massachusetts ratifying convention in early 1788, according to the record of the debates, some of his colleagues lamented that the "Constitution provided for the continuation of the slave trade for twenty years," but Adams "rejoiced that a door was now to be opened for the annihilation of this odious, abhorrent practice, in a certain time."[9]

Taxes were also central to the debate over the Constitution, along with broader questions of how wealth should be distributed. Richard Henry Lee of Virginia wrote in Antifederalist No. 36 that taxes are pernicious because they "fix themselves on every person and species of property in the community; they may be carried to any lengths, and in proportion as they are extended, numerous officers must be employed to assess them, and to enforce the collection of them." This is especially important to consider in a country as vast as the United States, "as many assessors and collectors of federal taxes will be above three hundred miles from the seat of the federal government." Lee pointed out that this would require "a great number of congressional ordinances" that would "continually interfere with the state laws, and thereby produce disorder and general dissatisfaction." Furthermore, there were significant regional and class differences to take into account, and Lee expressed doubts "that the interests, feelings, and opinions of three or four millions of people, especially touching internal taxation, can be collected in such a house."[10]

Hamilton countered that "a government ought to contain in itself every power requisite to the full accomplishment of the objects committed to its care, and to the complete execution of the trusts for which it is responsible," and therefore the "federal government must of necessity be invested with an unqualified power of taxation in the ordinary modes." Dismissing concerns about the practicalities of collecting taxes in a country as large as America, Hamilton focused instead on "the duties of superintending the national defence and of securing the public peace against foreign or domestic violence." He also touted the benefits of concentrated wealth that internal taxation could help facilitate, arguing that too widely distributed, money was merely money, but by consolidating it in just a few hands, it is turned into capital, which could be invested and used for building the nation.[11]

* * *

From May to September 1787, federalists and anti-federalists debated these issues and addressed other fundamental problems of the weak central government that existed under the Articles of Confederation. In doing so, the delegates were not only establishing a new government but also forging a national identity, expressed eloquently in the opening line of the Constitution's preamble, "We the People." Today this is considered practically a national motto but initially there was little thought given to whether the Constitution should even have a preamble, much less whether it should begin with such a powerful populist declaration. While prefatory texts were common for many legal documents of the time, no one at the Constitutional Convention proposed such an introduction to the Constitution until late July 1787, some two months after the Convention was established.[12]

Edmund Randolph of Virginia, a member of the Convention's Committee of Detail, suggested a brief preamble, urging it to avoid philosophical declarations and instead focus on explaining the shortcomings of the Articles of Confederation. "A Preamble seems proper," Randolph said, but "not for the purpose of designating the ends of government and human polities." Rather than a "display of theory," the preamble should succinctly explain why it was necessary to establish a supreme legislative, executive, and judiciary, in Randolph's view.[13]

The first draft of the preamble was concise and sidestepped delineating the Constitution's objectives. It did, however, delineate the 13 states that would initially comprise the United States. As issued by the Committee of Detail, it read: "We the People of the States of New-Hampshire, Massachusetts, Rhode-Island and Providence Plantations, Connecticut, New-York, New-Jersey, Pennsylvania, Delaware, Maryland, Virginia,

North-Carolina, South-Carolina, and Georgia, do ordain, declare and establish the following Constitution for the Government of Ourselves and our Posterity." The text was approved unanimously by the delegates, but it underwent significant changes after the draft Constitution was referred to the Committee of Style, chaired by Gouverneur Morris of Pennsylvania. It was Morris's idea to eliminate the listing of states, and identify instead the underlying power of the new federal government as, simply, "We, the People of the United States."[14]

Although it was intended as an informal introduction and not to officially outline the authorities of the federal government, the preamble's enduring power resides in the symbolism and elegant simplicity in identifying the ultimate source of the new nation's sovereignty—not the states themselves but the *people* of the *United* States. This confirmed more clearly that the government existed to serve the citizens of the nation and it also defined the nation more clearly as a political unit, rather than a loose confederation of individual states. As Morris's biographer Richard Brookhiser put it, "When Gouverneur Morris changed 'We the people of the states' into 'We the people,' he created a phrase that would ring throughout American history, defining every American as part of a single whole."[15]

The change in language had been done not just as a matter of style and concision but as an expression of nationalism, as a way to unite the country in the post-revolutionary period. This is a point that some opponents of the Constitution seized on, in fact, to argue that it went too far in usurping the powers of the states. As Patrick Henry insisted in a speech on June 5, 1788, "the question turns ... on that poor little thing—the expression, We, the people, instead of the States, of America." The anti-federalist Virginian noted that this phrase was "extremely pernicious, impolitic, and dangerous," warning that it threatened to establish a government more like a monarchy than a republic. America "is not a democracy," Henry said, "wherein the people retain all their rights securely." He regretted that by identifying the sovereign as "the people," we have "been brought to this alarming transition, from a Confederacy to a consolidated Government."[16]

Though supportive of the anti-federalist position, Samuel Adams disagreed with Patrick Henry's take on this point. In a letter to John Adams, Samuel welcomed the populist language of the preamble, noting that the phrase "we the people" delegates "the exercise of the powers of government to particular persons, who, after short intervals, resign their powers to the people." He takes it as a given that "the whole sovereignty" is "essentially in the people," and asks, "Is not government designed for the welfare and happiness of all the people?" The fact that the sovereignty resides in the people is so self-evident, Samuel Adams pointed out, that it "is a political doctrine which I have never heard an American politician seriously deny."[17] But although the Constitution's primary purpose is to "establish Justice, insure domestic Tranquility, provide for the common defence, promote the general Welfare, and secure the Blessings of Liberty to ourselves and our Posterity," the reality was that many of the individuals involved in framing it actually looked with disdain on those who collectively comprised "We the People."

* * *

Criminals like Henry Tufts were a bit of a conundrum, for instance. How would such outlaws fit into the framework of the national body politic? Revolutionary rhetoric was replete with appeals to those of low moral character to change their ways, imploring them to live virtuously, with Samuel Adams reminding people that "a Citizen owes everything to the Commonwealth." Republicanism emphasized the need for social cohesion through moral behavior and virtuous devotion to the common welfare, requiring citizens to be patriots who place the good of the country over their own personal ambitions.[18]

But the revolutionary leaders were not naive and some had significant reservations about entrusting the people blindly, or placing too much hope that they would all learn to behave as virtuous patriots. Naturally, for those unwilling to surrender their personal desires, and particularly those who insisted on breaking the law in pursuit of them, there would need to be coercion and punishment. In a republic, however, this should be done in a way consistent with Enlightenment values and therefore the new Constitution would have to reflect this. In grappling with issues of how to deal with crime, the framers universally touted the principle of trial by jury as fundamental.

Prominent federalists James Madison and Alexander Hamilton called jury trials "essential to secure the liberty of the people" and John Adams stated that "representative government and trial by jury are the heart and lungs of liberty." Jefferson agreed, insisting that trial by jury is "the only anchor yet imagined by man, by which a government can be held to the principles of its constitution." Although anti-federalists held fundamentally different views from federalists on most issues pertaining to the role and scope of government, they agreed that "trial by jury is the best appendage of freedom," as Patrick Henry put it. Indeed, upholding the rights of those accused of crimes was one of the few issues that virtually all founders agreed on at the Constitutional Convention. Essential to this was providing for due process and streamlining criminal justice.

With most delegates having served roles in debating and drafting constitutions for their own states, they had much experience and inspiration to draw from in this regard. Documents such as the Declaration of Rights, written by George Mason and adopted by the Virginia Constitutional Convention on June 12, 1776, provided a foundation for the United States Constitution and Bill of Rights, including principles related to crime, public safety and the right to property. In Virginia's Declaration, "the enjoyment of life and liberty" was closely tied with "the means of acquiring and possessing property," as well as "obtaining happiness and safety." This document maintained that "no free government, or the blessings of liberty, can be preserved to any people but by a firm adherence to justice." It provided for fair trials and principles of due process, declaring that "in all capital or criminal prosecutions a man hath a right to demand the cause and nature of his accusation to be confronted with the accusers and witnesses, to call for evidence in his favor, and to a speedy trial by an impartial jury." Additionally, it established that "no man be deprived of his liberty except by the law of the land or the judgement of his peers," nor that "excessive fines imposed; nor cruel and unusual punishments inflicted."[19]

But while state constitutions and other documents provided some basis for establishing a rights-based legal system, the status quo under the Articles of Confederation posed a number of significant challenges in this regard. In April 1787, James Madison published a criticism of the prevailing system of justice under the Articles of Confederation, providing a litany of its failures, including the states' "multiplicity and mutability of laws" that undermine fundamental principles of republican government. In "Vices of the Political System of the United States," Madison argued that "the multiplicity of laws" is "a nuisance of the most pestilent kind." He noted that since independence, the states had adopted a plethora of statutes that would fill "as many pages as the century which preceded it," and that every year "adds a new volume." Most of these laws were unnecessary and redundant, Madison argued, and some violated the rights of individuals and minority groups. Many statutes were "repealed or superseded, before any trial can have been made of their merits," and with 13 states all operating independently and little national cohesion provided under the Articles, the result was chaos.[20]

This chaos was compounded by the Articles of Confederation's complex system of jurisdiction and disputes between states. Running nearly 500 words and providing for a convoluted system of arbitration, this section of the Articles was, simply put, a mess. In disputes between states on jurisdiction, "or any other cause whatever," a specific procedure was prescribed that would be overwhelmingly cumbersome. "Whenever the legislative or executive authority, or lawful agent of any state in controversy with another," the Articles read, "a petition" shall state "the matter in question … and a day assigned for the appearance of the parties by their lawful agents, who shall then be directed to appoint, by joint consent, commissioners or judges to constitute a court for hearing and determining the matter in question." However, if they could not agree, "congress shall name three persons out of each of the united states, and from the list of such persons each party shall alternately strike out one, the petitioners beginning, until the number shall be reduced to thirteen," and so on and so forth. Finally, a panel of "commissioners or judges" would "determine the controversy, so always as a major part of the judges, who shall hear the cause, shall agree in the determination." If, however, they "shall refuse to submit to the authority of such court, or to appear or defend their claim or cause, the court shall nevertheless proceed to pronounce sentence, or judgment."[21]

Clearly, this verbose and unwieldy language would prove to be unworkable in the real world, and needed to be cleaned up by the Constitutional Convention. The alternative text on crime, jurisdiction, extradition and legal process was far simpler and easier to implement. Article III, Section 2 deals with the right to trial by jury, stipulating that "the Trial of all Crimes, except in Cases of Impeachment, shall be by Jury; and such Trial shall be held in the State where the said Crimes shall have been committed," while Article IV, Section 2 provides for the extradition of criminals from one state to another. "A Person charged in any State with Treason, Felony, or other Crime," the text reads, "who shall flee from Justice, and be found in another State, shall on Demand of the executive Authority of the State from which he fled, be delivered up, to be removed to the State having Jurisdiction of the Crime."

Having dealt with the impracticable Articles of Confederation for more than a decade, which had clearly suffered from the effects of having "too many cooks in the kitchen" who placed little value on brevity and clarity, the framers of the Constitution would go in the opposite direction. They strove for the most concise and simplest language possible, and on this front they clearly succeeded. Coming in at 4,543 words, it is among the shortest constitutions in the world.

* * *

Besides issues of crime and punishment, broader questions of republicanism—and indeed human nature itself—were grappled with at the Constitutional Convention, including how much democracy was the appropriate level, with some framers worried that expanding the franchise too broadly would lead to turmoil. Members of the Massachusetts delegation were among the most vocal opponents of electing members of Congress directly, arguing instead that state legislatures should appoint representatives to the national legislature. Debating the clause "that the members of the first branch of the National Legislature ought to be elected by the people of the several States" in May 1787, Massachusetts delegate Roger Sherman insisted that because they are generally intemperate and ignorant, the people should have as little to do as possible in the affairs of government. "They want information and are constantly liable to be misled," Sherman said. Elbridge Gerry concurred, noting that "the evils we experience flow from the excess of democracy."[22] He pointed out that in Massachusetts, common people are "daily misled into the most baneful measures and opinions by the false reports circulated by designing men, and which no one on the spot can refute."

Bolstering Sherman's and Gerry's cynical views of an overly credulous populace, Henry Tufts relates in his memoirs his experiences as a charlatan priest and fortune teller, marveling over the ease with which it was possible to fool people. "In the business of fortune telling, I prophecied with the acumen of a sybil; obtaining, thereby, the appellation of a Salem wizard," Henry explained. "That the rabble should believe this, was much to my advantage, as every craft exists on the strength of public opinion."[23]

With the people so easily duped, some founders warned that the result of empowering the masses could be a popular demand for reducing salaries of public servants. Gouverneur Morris generally agreed with Gerry's jaded view of the people's fickleness, but added his own twist—noting that their credulity would enable the rich to dominate the poor. "The people never act from reason alone," Morris said. "The rich will take advantage of their passions and make these the instrument for oppressing them. Give the votes to people who have no property, and they will sell them to the rich."[24]

George Mason heartily disagreed, arguing that it was essential for public servants to "know and sympathise with every part of the community," in order to understand the "different interests and views arising from difference of produce." Mason acknowledged that there were dangers of democratic excess but cautioned against going too far in curtailing democracy. "We ought to attend to the rights of every class of the people," Mason said. "Every selfish motive therefore, every family attachment, ought to recommend such a system of policy as would provide no less carefully for the rights and happiness of the lowest than of the highest orders of Citizens."[25] Fellow Virginian James Madison also argued for more direct democracy, insisting that the popular election of one branch of the national legislature was essential to the plan of free government. If there are too many indirect elections by state legislatures and executive appointments, "the people would be lost sight of altogether; and the necessary sympathy between them and their rulers and officers, too little felt."[26]

Alexander Hamilton believed that providing representation to all Americans in the new system of government was both unrealistic and foolish. "The idea of an actual representation of all classes of the people by persons of each class is altogether visionary," he wrote.[27] Hamilton insisted that instead of trying to include the interests of every group and subgroup within the United States, the government should represent three primary classes in society: the commercial, the landed, and the learned professions. His reasoning was that the merchant, being the natural representative of the mechanics and manufacturers, and the large landholder, being the natural representative of the small landholder, and educated classes—particularly lawyers—would consequently have the confidence of the broader society.

This argument was rejected by anti-federalists and populists who questioned whether all Americans could properly be represented under such a system, or whether various classes could possibly live in such harmony at all. At the Massachusetts convention, for example, Amos Singletary said that "these lawyers, and men of learning, and moneyed men, that talk so finely ... to make us poor illiterate people swallow down the pill ... will swallow up all us little folks, like the great Leviathan."[28] The federalists and elitists, for their part, dismissed the idea that the rabble could be entrusted with self-government. "Look through the rich and poor of the community, the learned and the ignorant," Hamilton pointed out. "Where does virtue predominate?" Suggesting that the upper classes were naturally more virtuous and moral, Hamilton observed that "vices are incident to various classes; and here the advantage of character belongs to the wealthy." People of wealth and prosperity, Hamilton argued, "partake less of moral depravity," and therefore these are the citizens who should be represented in a republican form of government.[29]

* * *

Although he may have welcomed the preamble, Samuel Adams had serious concerns about the broader developments in the Constitutional Convention, leading the anti-federalist attack from Massachusetts and railing against those who sought to scrap the old government. As one of the authors of the Articles of Confederation, Adams and his fellow anti-federalists feared that the Constitution would create an overly centralized government and erode individual liberties. His friend Elbridge Gerry was one of the most vocal delegates at the Constitutional Convention, aggravating everyone with his inconsistency and combativeness. One colleague stated that he "objected to everything he did not propose," and although he chaired the committee that produced the Great Compromise, Gerry ultimately rejected the final product because he deemed it a threat to republicanism and refused to sign the Constitution because it lacked a bill of rights.[30]

Washington, who had been so instrumental in leading the American Revolution, played a key role in bridging the differences between the various factions. Although he said little during the debates, his presence during the Constitutional Convention helped to promote consensus and encouraged an amiable atmosphere that allowed delegates to reach necessary compromises. On September 17, 1787, Washington signed a letter written by Gouverneur Morris, which was attached to the Constitution whenever it was printed. The letter explained that "it is obviously impracticable in the federal government of these states, to secure all rights of independent sovereignty to each, and yet provide for the interest and safety of all." After leading a revolution that was fought on the basis of defending liberty, Washington was now conceding that a perfect state of liberty might not be possible after all. "Individuals entering into society," Washington's letter read, "must give up a share of liberty to preserve the rest."[31]

The letter conveyed the difficulty with which the Constitution had been negotiated, explaining that the resulting compromise was reached with "the greatest interest of every true American" in mind, as well as "the consolidation of our Union, in which is involved our prosperity, felicity, safety, perhaps our national existence." The resulting Constitution, Washington explained, "is the result of a spirit of amity, and of that mutual deference and concession which the peculiarity of our political situation rendered indispensable."[32]

Washington's expressed support for the Constitution made the anti-federalist position increasingly untenable, yet Adams and Hancock continued to agitate against ratifying the Constitution in Massachusetts, demanding that it be amended before they would consider it or that amendments be a condition of ratification. With the federalists insisting that the document had to be accepted or rejected as it was, Adams and Hancock helped negotiate the Massachusetts Compromise, in which the delegates would put forth recommendations for amendments to be considered by the new Congress, should the document go into effect. The federalists agreed to support the proposed amendments, which set in motion the process by which the Bill of Rights would later be added to the Constitution.

With these assurances, Massachusetts ultimately voted to ratify the Constitution on February 6, 1788, although it was clear from the vote that the state was still very much divided between east and west. Many in Massachusetts's backcountry worried that the Constitution would subject them not only to the wealthy elite of their own state, but that of other states as well, and did not want their taxes going toward the suppression of slave revolts in the South or to redeem the war bonds held by rich speculators.[33] Consequently, of the 97 towns that had contributed men to Shays's Rebellion, only seven instructed their delegates to vote for ratification. Despite this overwhelming rejection of the document from western Massachusetts, support for the Constitution was strong in eastern towns, which counterbalanced the opposition of the commonwealth's anti-federalists. Ultimately, the decision came down to John Hancock, who tepidly voted to ratify on the condition of a Bill of Rights being subsequently added to protect individual liberties.[34]

Several more states then followed suit, voting for ratification on the condition of amendments being required. This induced the hold-out states to ultimately relent. New Hampshire became the critical ninth state to ratify the Constitution on June 21, 1788, and the new government would officially begin operating on March 4, 1789. George Washington took the oath of office as the first president of the United States on April 30, 1789.

In his First Inaugural Address, with the country still reeling from the contentious ratification process, Washington warned against "local prejudices or attachments" undermining the new government, as well as "party animosities," that could "misdirect the comprehensive and equal eye which ought to watch over this great assemblage of communities and interests." He stressed that "the foundation of our national policy will be laid in the pure and immutable principles of private morality," and highlighted "the preeminence of free government" that "can win the affections of its citizens and command the respect of the world."[35]

Recalling the event that prompted him to come out of retirement, three years after his inauguration, Washington would sign the federal Militia Act of May 2, 1792, based largely on the Massachusetts Riot Act. This law, intended to prevent another Shays's Rebellion, gave the president power to issue a proclamation to "command the insurgents to disperse, and retire peaceably to their respective abodes, within a limited time," authorizing him to use the militia if they failed to do so.[36]

* * *

The focus of the new government on containing the impetus of popular rebellion in the fledgling republic reflected the widespread concern—expressed so passionately during the Constitutional Convention—over the excesses of democracy that might result from a Constitution that derives its power from "We the People" rather than political or economic elites. Some continued to wonder who precisely was meant to be covered under this umbrella term. Does "the people" mean "all the people," or, perhaps, are there certain assumptions about who is included and who is not? A decade earlier in the Declaration of Independence, the signatories actually clarified that they were representing "the *good* People of these States" in their collective renunciation of British rule, but in the Constitution, there was no such qualifier. Does that mean that all the people—good and bad— are represented by the new government? The principal author of the Declaration, Thomas Jefferson, seemed to think so, as he adamantly embraced the people and considered the attitudes toward them the defining feature of an individual's character. "The sickly, weakly, timid man fears the people, and is a Tory by nature," Jefferson once wrote. "The healthy, strong and bold cherishes them, and is formed a Whig by nature."[37]

Samuel Adams sympathized with this perspective, and pushed back against the views of his cousin John, who wrote in 1790 that a republic is a government in which "the People have an essential share in the Sovereignty." Samuel insisted, conversely, that "the whole sovereignty" resides "in the People." As he rhetorically asked his cousin, "Is not Government designed for the Welfare, and happiness of all the People?"[38]

At the same time, though, Samuel Adams distinguished between people of virtue and those of vice. He fretted that "the Minds of many of our Countrymen have been inured to a cringing Obsequiousness," which he worried was "too deeply wrought into Habit to be easily eradicated." To counter this unfortunate reality, Adams looked to the nation's leaders to serve as a virtuous example to the citizens. If the "present Rulers" are blessed "with Wisdom & sound Understanding," Adams wrote to Gerry, "they will stamp the Character of the People." In a republic, Adams believed, the relationship between the people and the government was symbiotic—a moral people would elect moral leaders, and the leaders, through their words and deeds, would also have a profound influence over the people. "If we look into the History of Governors," Adams observed, "we shall find that their Principles & Manners have always had a mighty Influence on the People."[39]

In this respect, Adams, like Jefferson, had a firmly held faith in the people and believed that they would naturally thrive as citizens of a republic. Other founders, however, did not identify quite as strongly as populists, and some clearly viewed their fellow citizens with suspicion or even scorn. Washington likened them to livestock, referring to the common people as "the grazing multitude,"[40] and Hamilton spoke disparagingly of the "unthinking populace." Gerry observed that "the people do not want virtue, but are the dupes of pretended patriots."[41] John Adams once referred to "the people" as "the vile populace or rabble of the country," which he distinguished from "the greater and more judicious part of the subjects of all ranks."[42]

*　*　*

Readers of Henry Tufts's memoirs would have to concede that perhaps these Founding Fathers had a point. While the nation's elite were gathered in Philadelphia debating the virtues of the people and deciding how much "the vile populace" should be empowered in the new republic, Tufts was running around breaking laws—not to mention young ladies' hearts—and recklessly pursuing his own self-interest.

Henry tells the story, for example, of a widow named Abigail Kennison, who was "both young and beautiful." Her manners were "soft and engaging, and her personal charms uncommonly attractive." Henry found her "disposition amiable," so he "did not hesitate to pay her my devoirs, as a lover." Since he was already married and because he had a notorious reputation, Henry thought that it would be wise to employ an alias, so he used the "fictitious name of Gideon Garland." He visited Abigail once a week for three months, "at the end of which term she unfortunately proved to be pregnant." Henry grew "timorous of consequences," and decided to discontinue his visits. This was despite the fact that she had "riveted my affection, in a manner, which no other woman had hitherto been able."[43]

As Henry dithered, Abigail learned his real name and discovered that he was already married with a family. "Upon this unpleasing discovery," Henry writes, "she went before a magistrate, and legally charged me, on oath, with being the father of the child of which she was then pregnant." Further, she sent him a letter asking him to meet her at her former residence to settle the affair "in almost any manner, I might choose." When Henry showed up, he found that there was an officer waiting "who seized me, the moment I entered the house." Henry was taken before a magistrate and then to Exeter jail where his "mind was busily exercised in trying to devise ways and means to avoid paying for a child." Henry writes that he was torn by the "passion" that he felt for "the poor girl" whom he impregnated but also angry over the "rough treatment" he had received "at her instigation."[44]

Although Henry may have hoped to remedy the situation without involving the law, it seems that Abigail was simply doing what was necessary to protect herself from possible legal consequences. With the laws on bastardy established in the early colonial period, a child born out of wedlock automatically resulted in a trial to determine who the father was. The law provided for equal responsibility for men and women in the case of a child being conceived out of wedlock, with women typically pleading to the court that they would marry the man to prevent the birth of a bastard child.[45] In the case of Henry and Abigail, however, this was clearly unfeasible since he was already married, so another solution would have to be found. While sometimes women attempted to keep the pregnancy secret, Abigail would have also been aware of the penalty for concealing the birth of an illegitimate child—death. A well-known story from the era was the tragic case of Ruth Blay, a 31-year-old woman from Haverhill,

Massachusetts, who was convicted of "private burial and concealment of her bastard child," and hanged on December 30, 1768, in Portsmouth, New Hampshire.[46]

With this in mind, it is more than understandable that Abigail would have gone immediately to the authorities to attempt to resolve the situation before Henry skipped town. While in the Exeter jail, he was offered a way to settle the matter and be released from imprisonment. "Knowing I had a horse in Exeter, and supposing, perhaps, I might own other property," Henry writes, "they offered to discharge me on my giving an obligation for forty pounds, lawful money." Henry agreed to this and was released.

Although his immediate legal troubles were remedied, he still had the personal matter to settle with the woman he had wronged, which in some ways appeared more difficult. Abigail was devastated by the affair, and as Henry recalls in his memoirs, did not hold back from strongly rebuking him for his conduct. "Why, to compass my ruin," Henry recalls her saying, "did you conceal your present marriage, your real situation in life? Why betray me with false promises, not in your power to perform?"[47]

In tears, Abigail assured him that had she been aware of his "conjugal connections, nothing could have bribed my consent to the lewd intercourse we have been guilty of, nor should temptations have allured me from the path of virtue and decency!" Abigail agonized over her situation, lamenting that her "wretchedness is complete and remediless" and her "reputation blasted forever, and destitute am I left of all earthly comfort." Her friends and family had forsaken her, she said, but that was not the worst part. Apparently deeply in love with Henry, she lamented that she would now be losing him. She "might perhaps have borne" the pain of alienating friends and relatives, "but for the cruel disappointment I meet with in losing you, forever," she told Henry. "How cruel, how bitter has been my disappointment, and how insupportable are my afflictions!" she said. "The only remaining consolation, is, that my calamities will be of short continuance on this side of the grave."[48]

"Unfeeling man," she scolded Henry, "your cruelty has undone me; my peace and happiness are destroyed, forever!"[49]

Henry appeared to deeply empathize with her, writing that "the sight of her misery gave my heart a sympathetic pang, and sighs of compassion escaped from my swollen bosom." He reassured her that he would not abandon her and "at all times" would remain her "devoted friend," insisting that his love for her remained strong and that he would "relinquish both family and friends, and seek with you, alone, some distant retreat, in which we might live together in love and happiness, unnoticed and unknown."

So, Henry returned home, "full of the thoughts of my novel resolution, but anxious, at the same time, to keep the whole affair a profound secret, till I could carry it into complete execution." Meanwhile he continued to pay his mistress regular visits, and eventually the two eloped to the town of Fairfield, because "land was cheap in that quarter," as Henry explained.[50] He and Abigail, or Nabby as he fondly called her, would make a family and remain close until his ordeal with the spoons.

* * *

Judging him solely from stories like these, Henry's apparent lack of virtue might confirm the elitists' dim view of the lower classes in the deliberations that had played out in Philadelphia over how much democracy was the appropriate level. Not only was Henry utterly oblivious to the historic debates taking place during this period, but his decidedly apathetic and self-centered approach to citizenship seemingly validated the perspective of George Washington, who suggested that true patriotism is not possible without religion and morality, which he called the "great pillars of human happiness, these firmest props of the duties of Men and Citizens."[51]

But despite his vagabond ways, even Henry shared some of the spirit of patriotism that infused the revolutionary generation, and when Washington passed away on December 14, 1799, he was devastated. As Henry relates in his memoirs, "I received the distressing intelligence of the decease of the illustrious Gen. Washington, that truly magnanimous patriot, who had been the political saviour of his country, and founder of the American empire." He maintained that Washington was more worthy of the title of "great" than "any of the Alexanders, Pompeys, or Charlses who ever swayed a sceptre." His death, he writes, "was universally lamented, though the land of his preservation, by all ranks and orders of men ... for the matchless services he has rendered his country and the world."[52]

Despite having earlier expressed ambivalence over the cause of American independence and having deserted more than once from Washington's army, Henry was so distraught by his death that he commemorated the occasion by writing a poem, which he referred to as "a faint eulogy on his virtues, as a small tribute of praise to his sacred memory." The following lines were "written on the table of my heart," Henry explains:

> What dismal sounds invade the ear! What gloom o'erspreads the sky; What solemn tidings do we hear! What piercing, heartfelt cry!
> Hark! 'tis the mournful trump of fate, "Great Washington's no more"; Freed from this fleeting, mortal state, He seeks the heav'nly shore.
> His glorious race on earth is run, Immortal lives his fame; Admiring worlds, O, Washington! Shall still exalt thy name.
> With liberty, to bless mankind, To fight for freedom's cause;
> For these were form'd thy godlike mind, By fate's unerring laws.

When heav'n in wisdom plac'd thee here, She thus address'd her son; Go! save America, thice dear, Nor fear, brave Washington.

There found an empire, far and wide, On Freedom's sacred shore, Where lawless tyranny and pride Shall vex her realm no more.

Immortal Washington obey'd Th' empyreal decree, And well atchiev'd the glorious deed, And founded liberty.

This done, celestial anthems rise On harps of purest gold, Angels invite him to the skies, The heav'nly gates unfold.

Columbia, mourn, in wees of woe, Your chief, your patriot gone, Let ceaseless tears in concert flow, For Freedom's fav'rite son.

Yet, while our fond affections glow, With mingled grief and love, While still we mourn his death below, O, sing his birth above.

It is an enduring testament to Washington's leadership that even Henry Tufts, who had not only deserted from the Continental Army but also had actually participated in a British counterfeiting scheme to undermine the American war effort, would be so moved as to write such a touching poem. If even an incorrigible criminal could be transformed into a poet by the death of Washington, surely there was hope for the development of a virtuous citizenry that Samuel Adams pined for.

12

Crime and Capital Punishment

In the spring of 1787, as the founders gathered in Philadelphia to overhaul the nation's constitutional system, the free men of Massachusetts who held at least £60 in assets went to the polls and cast votes for governor, lieutenant governor, senators and representatives. John Hancock won the governor's race in a landslide election that surprised Samuel Adams for how one-sided the results were, writing to his wife Betsy that he "did not foresee that Boston would have been so united as I find they were, when two such Competitors as he & M' Bowdoin were set up."[1] Defeating James Bowdoin by a vote of 75.8 percent to 22.1 percent, Hancock's election was seen as a triumph for the little guy as well as a referendum on the government's handling of Shays's Rebellion. Voters also elected representatives to the General Court who were sympathetic to the Regulators,[2] proving to be a godsend to those who had participated in the rebellion.

Over the next several months, a series of reprieves were granted for all the six men who had been condemned to death for treason[3] and the General Court passed a resolution on June 15, 1787, that pardoned all citizens who had participated in the uprising, with the exception of nine. Adams, however, proved to be an obstacle. As president of the Senate, he continued to insist that rebel leaders Jason Parmenter (who had killed a militiaman) and Henry McCulloch be executed in order to uphold the authority and legitimacy of the state. Parmenter's and McCulloch's execution dates were postponed a number of times and then, finally, in September 1787, Hancock came to the conclusion that the executions "should be avoided for the public good." He granted McCulloch and Parmenter "a full, free and ample Pardon of all the Pains and penelties they were liabable to suffer and undergo by Virtue of the Sentences and Judgement."[4]

In March 1788, Shays, Luke Day, Eli Parsons, and a few others who had been exempted from previous reprieves were also pardoned. All in all, the only ones who suffered the death penalty for the rebellion were Charles

Rose and John Bly, who had been convicted of burglary related to a Shaysite raid on the home of a Lanesborough resident. Because these two had been convicted of robbery and were not accused of treason, they could not qualify for a pardon—demonstrating that while murder and rebellion were excusable, theft was not.[5]

Cotton Tufts, for one, bitterly complained that the instigators of the rebellion did not receive their due punishment. In a letter to John Adams on June 30, 1787, he claimed that in the General Court were "Enemies to the late Revolution," who took "Advantage of Discontents and encouraged every Kind of Faction—Disappointed Whigs, Convention Men & Debtors not a few." The debtors, he said, had joined forces "hoping for an Annihilation of public & private Debts, among these are some whose Characters once shone with Lustre—But are now meanly courting the Populace and practising the Arts of Corruption." He lamented that of all those who were "capitally convicted and sentenced to Death, not one as yet has been executed." Regrettably, Tufts wrote, "these Gallows deserving Fellows will be set at Liberty."[6]

* * *

A few years later, when Lieutenant Governor Samuel Adams assumed the governorship of Massachusetts following Governor Hancock's death in 1793, he was faced again with fundamental issues of crime and punishment. Adams would find that despite the most difficult questions of founding the United States being settled—with the Constitution ratified, the federal government established, the first president elected, the revenue system implemented, state powers defined, and the Bill of Rights adopted—more mundane problems remained to be tackled, including a growing crime wave in New England. One of his first acts as governor, in fact, was to appeal to Arthur Fenner, governor of the neighboring state of Rhode Island, to extradite a group of men charged with theft by a grand jury in Worcester County. Citing the separation of powers delineated in the recently adopted United States Constitution, he asked Governor Fenner to assist in apprehending the criminals and handing them over to the attorney general of Massachusetts for trial.[7]

The matter of the Rhode Island fugitives was just one indication of the challenges facing Adams's administration. Burglary was a growing problem in his state and had reached such a critical point that a pastor suggested in 1795 that guards be hired to protect the homes and property of churchgoers during Sunday services.[8] In these challenging times, new ideas would emerge to counter the difficulties posed by the criminal element. Samuel's cousin John hailed the effectiveness of burning the oil of sperm whales in streetlamps, which not only "gives the clearest and most

12. Crime and Capital Punishment

beautifull Flame, of any Substance that is known in Nature," but also helps prevent "Robberies, Burglaries and Murders." Lighting streets with oil lamps, John Adams wrote to John Jay, helps to "chase away before the Watchmen all the Villains, and save you the Trouble and Danger of introducing a new Police into the City."[9]

Samuel Adams, too, felt compelled to offer new ideas to address the growing crime wave. In his January 17, 1794, inaugural address to the General Court, after waxing eloquently about the "laws of the Creator," which dictate that "thou shall do no injury to thy neighbour" and that "every man hath an equal right by honest means to acquire property," the new governor emphasized the need for a strong social compact to protect the citizens of Massachusetts. Without one, he said, "the weak cannot always be protected from the violence of the strong, nor the honest and unsuspecting from the arts and intrigues of the selfish and cunning."[10]

It was with these thoughts on his mind that Governor Adams began to be inundated with appeals to grant reprieve to a hapless prisoner

The concluding section of the death warrant condemning Henry Tufts to hang, signed by Governor Samuel Adams. The document ends with the line, "Witness Samuel Adams Esq., our Governor and Commander in Chief at Boston this twenty-seventh day of June, in the year of our Lord, one thousand, seven hundred and ninety-four, and in the Eighteenth year of the Independence of the United States of America." Less than a month later, after being inundated with appeals for leniency, Adams would issue a reprieve.

named Henry Tufts. Convicted in Ipswich for stealing six silver spoons and scheduled to hang on August 14, 1794, Tufts appealed not only directly to Adams, but also to friends and contacts to increase the pressure on the governor. Although he most certainly was guilty of many transgressions throughout his life, he insisted that he was innocent of the crime that got him sentenced to death. As Tufts tells it in his memoirs, even remembering "those disastrous scenes" of his final arrest were "painful in the extreme," but "a just regard to truth" compelled him to tell his story in detail:

> I bought of a John Stewart, one silver table spoon, and five teaspoons of the same metal (would to God I had never set eyes on them or him!). He told me he found them in clearing out a cellar, as he came from Philadelphia. ... My little family made daily use of the spoons; but one morning, while I was eating breakfast, a young woman entered my apartment, who happened to espy and know them. Leaving the house, away she posted to the former owner, Daniel Jacobs, of Danvers, and informed him of the circumstance. My apprehension was the immediate consequence of this. I was presently convened before Esq. Sewall, and questioned, as to the manner of my acquiring the articles; my answer to the court, was, that I had bought them of one John Stewart. ... But a certain sheriff (who was, as was generally the case, no friend of mine), being present, and fearing, I conclude, that Stewart would confess all, to his own detriment without doubt, called him aside, to sift, as I then thought, something more from the witness. ... By the above and other proceedings, it was plain, that my adversaries were contriving to fasten upon me the crime of burglary, in respect to Jacobs' house, of which enormity, God knows, I was then, as I am now, entirely innocent.[11]

Henry then went on to describe the trial, noting that his attorneys argued in court that he ought to be acquitted not only due to the facts of the case and the lack of credibility of the witnesses against him, but also because of the severity of the punishment, citing "the extreme hardship of my being convicted and condemned to death."[12]

The jury was initially split on the decision to convict, returning from deliberations four times with a lack of unanimity, with a juror identified as Mr. Thurstin "not coinciding with his brethren to bring in the verdict, guilty," as Henry explains. After the fourth deliberation, the judge told Thurstin "that sufficient time for consideration had been taken, and that it was necessary to agree upon something." Following this admonition, "an unqualified verdict, declaring me guilty of the burglary was returned into

Opposite: **In this hand-written petition to Governor Adams, Henry Tufts asks that he may "live a little longer for repentance." Claiming that he was "not the contriver of the Burglay" for which he was convicted, Tufts implicated John Simpson as the one who "went himself and did the Crime," insisting that "Shore as i am a live this is true."**

12. Crime and Capital Punishment 195

ye most wrechd youenes of Boston this
world gives great torments now and I
am not the contemner of the Revelar
for john Simeson went him self and did
the Crime hea bored my shoos and said
hea wanted to goe a little way and woulds
hee paye next morning and soe hea did
come to me in murtherhead and said hea
have got som things as good to yea as the
money, and you must soll me your
Cote and this things is as good as money
to you and I sold him one Cote and tow
pare of stockings as shore as I am alien
this is true and the shawill that i
sent after my Candene was my
Snowey and said hea would doe me hurt
if hea told what i bege is the pawer of
your over to doe all you lan for me now
and the lounslers to doe ther me pray doe
for me if you noed as god you never
wold lonkene for me to die i ame pore
and distut of frends and nobody but god
for me to help me now as tedar in the
hands of god i hope that god will lefter
me to live a little longer to repent
of my sins and trangrasions that i hae
Cornit in the Bodey may god in liten
your anews of my afair now at this
time and set me line a little longer
for my renenewl   Henry Gyles

court and recorded by the same."[13] An hour later, Henry received his sentence: to be hanged by the neck until dead.

What Henry left out was that at the same court session at which he was convicted of stealing the spoons, he was also tried for three other incidents for which he pleaded guilty. One of those was a robbery that he committed on April 19, 1794, the 19th anniversary of the Battle of Lexington and Concord. On this day of solemn observance and celebration, Henry broke into the shop of Isaac Lane and stole nine raccoon skins, six hats, and two cat skins. Then he broke into two shoe-making shops, where he purloined shoes and some leather. Not quite satisfied, he then broke into the shop of John Dodge at Wehnam and swiped two pairs of boot-legs, two calfskins, and some more leather.[14]

Despite all this, it was for the spoons—not the raccoon skins, shoes or leather—that Henry was given a death sentence. After being convicted, he tried and failed to escape, at times betrayed by other prisoners or found out by diligent guards. Tormented by the thought of passing worlds with so many sins for which he needed to repent, Henry was not about to resign himself to the gallows and decided to take his case to the same governor who had signed his death warrant. "I prepared a petition, couched in becoming terms, and sent it to the governor," Henry wrote, "beseeching that my punishment of death might be remitted, or exchanged for confinement to the castle during life."[15] (By "castle," Tufts was referring to the Castle Island prison in Boston Harbor, which had been previously used as a military barracks for the British but was converted in 1785 by the Massachusetts state legislature as "a place of confinement for thieves, and other convicts to hard labor.")

In his petition to the governor, which was clearly written in his own hand and without the help of the ghost writer who assisted with his memoirs, Tufts implored Adams, whom he referred to as "the most oneribel gouerner of Boston," to "let me live a little longer for repentence." As for stealing the spoons, Tufts insisted that he was "not the contriver of the Burglay." With no mention of John Stewart, Tufts said it was actually John Simpson who "went himself and did the Crime he bored my shoos and said he wanted to goe a little way and he wold bee back next morning and soo he did come to me in marblehead and said he have got som things as good to you as the money and you must sall me your cote and thes things is as god as money to you and i sold him one cote and too pare of Stockings as Shore as i am a live this is true."[16]

Governor Adams, perhaps trying to decipher all the misspellings or just attending to other matters, did not immediately reply to this request for clemency, so Henry then contacted students at Harvard, asking them to intercede on his behalf. "This they had the humanity to do," Tufts wrote, "for which they have my sincere thanks." His wife Nabby, who years earlier had Henry locked up in Exeter after he impregnated her out of wedlock, appealed in person to the governor and his Executive Council, pleading for the life of her husband. In addition, according to Tufts, "many ladies" of the town of Ipswich reached out to Governor Adams, "stating the peculiar austerity of my doom, and recommending me to consideration and clemency."[17] Thurstin, the dissenting juror, had come to regret his decision to consent to the guilty verdict, and told the governor and the council "how uneasy he had been" in voting to convict. As Henry writes, "with much zeal, he represented me (and that more than once, I believe) as deserving the particular notice and compassion of his excellency."[18]

The appeals on behalf of Henry were surely heartfelt but unfortunately the communication was rather one-sided. With no word from the governor, Henry's sense of doom over his fate increased by the day. He could only "consider [Adams's] taciturnity as an inauspicious omen," he wrote, and the "dark and dubious complexion of things filled me with horrible prognostics." Henry dreaded his sentence, he claimed, not because of the momentary physical pain that a hanging would entail, but because he felt woefully unprepared for death. "The awful thoughts of exchanging worlds, in my present unprepared state, smote me with horror of mind, and with a dismay the most exquisitely painful," Henry confided.[19]

Describing in detail the passing moments as his execution approached, he related the horror he felt watching a "sexton passing by with his pick axe, hoe and shovel, to dig my grave beneath the gallows." A schoolmistress came to his window, he claimed, to tell him that she had seen his coffin and grave awaiting him. "The last hour of my surviving time drew near," Henry wrote, and "I shuddered at the sound of every footstep, as it had been the approach of the angel of death!"

As the clock ticked and "the wheel of unremitting time was rolling on Toward th' important hour of four," the prescribed time for his hanging, Henry appeared to grow resigned to his fate. To his surprise, however, and to the disappointment of the approximately 3,000 individuals who he claimed had gathered to watch the hanging, the deputies arrived at his cell to assure him that his "execution was respited," although they did not know for how long. "Thus by the goodness of God, did I at this time, very contrary to my fears and expectations, escape the bitterness of death," Henry wrote, "and although I knew not the length of my reprieve, yet the present deliverance exonerated my feelings of a vast load of inquietude."[20]

* * *

As thrilling as Henry's account reads in his memoirs, it seems that this portrayal of the reprieve may have been embellished. Although he describes in vivid detail how thousands of people had gathered to watch the hanging only to be denied the spectacle by a last-minute reprieve, the reality was probably less suspense-filled. As opposed to Henry's version of the execution being halted at the last moment, in reality, Governor Adams and his Executive Council stayed the execution nearly a month before it was scheduled to take place—Henry's execution date was August 14, 1794, and the reprieve was issued July 17, valid until September 25. During this period, the governor and his Council were investigating the question of a commutation, which eventually came down on September 2.[21]

So, with the reprieve being decided weeks before the execution date, it is highly unlikely that the jailers would have proceeded with planning for the execution, that the sexton would have dug his grave, and that thousands of people would have come to watch the event. As a 1984 article by Daniel E. Williams in *Early American Literature* puts it, "The sexton digging the grave, the three thousand spectators gathering at the scaffold, and the distraught schoolmistress informing Tufts his coffin and grave awaited him, no matter how pleasing to the imagination, are all fictions."[22]

While the precise details and timing of Henry's reprieve and commutation may have been exaggerated, however, the basic facts are clear—Governor Adams did indeed step in to halt Henry's execution. As *Dunlap and Claypoole's American Daily Advertiser* reported on September 23, 1794, "We have it from authority, that his Excellency the Governor, by advice of Council, has commuted the punishment of Henry Tufts, who was to have been executed at Ipswich, for burglary, on the 25th of September current, to hard labour on Castle Island, during his natural life."[23]

* * *

Little is known about the precise rationale behind the commutation, but the decision raises a number of questions about Adams's views on capital punishment and broader issues of the state of criminal justice in the early American republic. The first question that might come to mind is how someone could be sentenced to hang for six measly spoons in the first place. This harsh sentence is particularly mystifying when considering how haphazardly the death penalty could be applied in those days—sometimes handed down for seemingly trivial offenses, but withheld for more serious crimes like murder, or in the case of the Shaysites, for treason.

Burglary was indeed a capital offense, but only dyed-in-the-wool, repeat offenders like Tufts were typically eligible for the death penalty. Massachusetts law provided that a first-time burglar was to be branded with the letter B, while a second offense would entail a whipping. Only after a third offense would an offender be considered "incorrigible," and be eligible for the death penalty,[24] but even then, this punishment was rarely meted out.

12. Crime and Capital Punishment 199

Capital punishment seemed to be used relatively sparingly in Essex County, Massachusetts, where Tufts was convicted, with only three public executions from 1781 to 1821, and in each case the crime was murder. The *Newburyport Herald* recalled that "the individuals executed were Isaac Coombs, an Indian, for the murder of his wife—Henry Blackburn, an Englishman, for the murder of a sailor,—and a black, by the name of Pomp, for the murder of his master." The same article notes that "Henry Tufts was convicted of burglary, and sentenced to suffer capitally, but his punishment was commuted to imprisonment for life at castle William, in Boston harbor, from which he afterwards escaped."[25] (This, of course, was not precisely accurate. Henry did not escape from Castle William, but from a jail in Salem.)

A number of other cases from the era demonstrate that despite the harsh sentence given to Tufts, it was just as common in those days to be branded than to be hanged, regardless of the crime's severity. Israel Wilkins, for instance, was convicted on September 17, 1773, for killing his father but was spared the gallows and instead sentenced to be "burned with a hot Iron in the form of a letter T on the brawny part of the Thumb of his left hand, and it is further considered that the said Israel Wilkins forfeit all his Goods and Chattels to the King."[26] John Patten cut Thomas Shirley on the head with a scythe blade on Christmas Day 1775, a mortal wound that would lead to Shirley's death on February 1, 1776, and was convicted of manslaughter in September 1776. Patten was spared the gallows though and branded at the Superior Court of Hillsborough County. In September 1769 in Portsmouth, New Hampshire, Morris Cavenaugh beat George Henderson to death and was convicted of manslaughter, but despite the shocking nature of the crime, he got off with a branding instead of a hanging.[27]

The differences in how punishments could be handed out, with many murderers walking free but those convicted of petty crimes sentenced to death, largely has to do with a practice called the "benefit of clergy." This was essentially a legal loophole that granted first-time convicts a one-off chance for leniency even for serious crimes. Dating back to the Middle Ages, it was originally applied solely to clerics, but its practice was eventually expanded beyond the Church to cover civil affairs as well. Typically, a condemned prisoner was expected to read the third verse of Psalm 51, "O God, have mercy upon me, according to thine heartfelt mercifulness," which became known as the "neck verse," because it was so often used to save the neck of a convicted criminal.[28]

Largely due to this practice, capital punishment was often administered somewhat arbitrarily. Courts would typically only hand this sentence down for offenders who frequently found themselves in the dock, when prosecutors and judges became convinced that they were beyond redemption.[29] So, while Henry's death sentence for stealing spoons may seem excessive, what he was really being executed for was being a career criminal. Although he clearly had many supporters, Henry was also widely despised throughout New England, and was hunted for much of his adult life for being a deserter from the Continental Army. As even Henry would concede, although he insisted that he was innocent of this particular crime, he was most certainly guilty of many others, and it was for those—as well as likely future crimes—that he was really being punished.

As he had little compunction about "robbing friends and foes indiscriminately," Henry was well aware that many of his peers considered him "a pest to society," whose "nefarious misdeeds" made him "altogether insufferable."[30] The challenge that communities grappled with was how to deal with such people, especially those, like Henry, who not only compulsively stole from others, but were adept at escape. Henry found himself in jails so often throughout New England during the late 18th century that he developed a habit of concealing tools such as pickaxes, saws and "corrosive ingredients, to soften or eat away iron,"[31] so that, in case he was arrested, he would have the means of escape readily available. Often employing the help of a "connected string" of "confidential friends," stretching from New York to Canada, Henry managed to break out of jail a number of times in the 1770s and '80s and did so as recently as August 25, 1793, when he escaped from confinement in Dover, New Hampshire.[32] On this occasion, the resourceful Tufts claims he used a piece of pork and some soap to lubricate the passage, and after much effort was able "to gain ground, inch by inch," and finally "succeeded in forcing myself, feet foremost, into the street," falling about 12 feet to the ground.[33]

With such a long history of escape and a predilection for crime, following Henry's conviction for stealing the spoons, the authorities appeared intent on ridding society of this "pest." While his ostensible crime was the theft of the spoons, of which he may very well have been innocent, it appears that his true offense was being a public nuisance for much of his life. Henry, who had previously been falsely charged with a robbery in Exeter and was only released when the true culprit was discovered with "sundry of the articles in his possession,"[34] and had once prevailed in court when his lawyer proved that a witness was lying,[35] seemed to understand the nature of being prosecuted not for the actual crime at hand but rather for one's notorious reputation. Demonstrating his rather low opinion of the American legal system, in his memoirs, he dubbed deputies and magistrates "ministers of vengeance,"[36] rather than ministers of justice.

Despite signing his death warrant, Governor Adams may have come to agree with Tufts that his sentence amounted to vengeance and not

12. Crime and Capital Punishment

justice. While we don't know the exact rationale for Adams's decision to commute Tufts's punishment, and there is a chance that it was motivated—at least in part—due to the fact that the Adamses and Tuftses shared family ties (through Samuel's cousin John's marriage to Abigail Adams, a cousin to Cotton Tufts), or that he was influenced by the appeals of members of the community, Governor Adams's thinking might be better understood by reading a communication to the Massachusetts state legislature, dated June 4, 1794. In this text, Adams alludes to the use of alternatives to the death penalty such as life imprisonment. He notes that "a great number of persons have been sentenced to confinement and hard labor" at Castle Island in Boston Harbor, pointing out that "this mode of punishment has been found by experience to be of great utility in the preservation of good order, and the producing of safety in the Commonwealth, and has a manifest tendency to render unnecessary those sanguinary punishments which are too frequently inflicted in other Governments."[37]

In other words, Adams was arguing that alternative options such as life sentences might be more effective in promoting public safety than the use of capital punishment, which he considered representative of tyrannies. There was also some doubt about the appropriateness of hanging a man for burglary, with even the lawyer who prosecuted Henry conceding that although "burglary was a capital offence, by the laws of man, it was not so by the laws of God," as Henry related.[38] While Adams did not explicitly question the morality of taking a life as punishment, his reference to "sanguinary punishments ... inflicted in other Governments" indicates that the governor had a distaste for the gory and bloody sentences—such as torture and execution—that some judicial systems handed out for relatively minor offenses in those days. He may have specifically had in mind Britain, where the so-called Bloody Code laws included more than 200 crimes that were punishable by death. These were primarily concerned with defending property and included offenses such as stealing, cutting down a tree, and robbing a rabbit warren, with a disproportionate impact—naturally—on the poor and the destitute.[39] The overriding principle behind these harsh laws was deterrence, as expressed succinctly by George Savile, member of the British House of Commons in the late 17th century: "Men are not hanged for stealing horses, but that horses may not be stolen."[40]

With these dubious arguments offered for the death penalty, Adams had long pondered the punishment's efficacy, recognizing, perhaps, that its overly liberal use was counterproductive, as it led in some cases to juries refusing to convict. Long before he became governor, he delivered a speech to the Massachusetts House of Representatives in January 1773 that sought clarification on the death penalty. Addressing Governor

Thomas Hutchinson, Adams asked whether colonies are "vested with the power of ... enacting and determining what crimes shall be capital?" He insisted that colonies were empowered with "constituting courts of common law," and therefore were capable of "hearing, trying and punishing capital offenders with death."[41]

Although Adams was not averse to the death penalty per se—he did advocate for the execution of the insurrectionists who took part in Shays's Rebellion—he appeared to have something of a humanitarian impulse and was clearly preoccupied during his tenure as governor with concerns about how he might be judged by God. As Adams wrote to the General Court in 1796,

> I ought not to forget that there are other important duties constitutionally attached to the Supreme Executive—I hope I shall be enabled within my department, with the continued advice of a wise and faithful Council, so to act my part, as that a future retrospect of my conduct may afford me consoling reflections; and that my administration may be satisfactory to reasonable and candid men, and finally meet with the approbation of God, the Judge of all.[42]

Adams may have also been aware of calls for the abolition of the death penalty on moral grounds, with one of the strongest arguments from a religious perspective being that capital punishment denied criminals the chance at redemption. Proportionality was also a principal concern, with Benjamin Franklin suggesting in 1785 that disproportionate penalties such as hanging a man for theft was tantamount to murder. "To put a Man to Death for an Offence which does not deserve Death, is it not Murder?" Franklin asked. "Founded on the Eternal Principle of Justice and Equity, the Punishments should be proportioned to the Offences."[43]

Many of the American Founding Fathers had been influenced by Italian philosopher Cesare Beccaria's views on the death penalty as expressed in his treatise *On Crimes and Punishments*. A member of the Italian aristocracy, Beccaria developed a reputation as a humanist with his writings becoming widely influential in the late 18th century, and his ideas helping to shape American thoughts on criminal justice.[44] With a view towards deterrence as opposed to simply retribution, Beccaria argued for a humane legal system based on prompt and fair trials and proportional punishments. While traditionally, the purpose of punishment had been based in principles of morality and sought simply to provide redress for the crime, the reformers argued that punishment should also be geared towards prevention.[45] Beccaria took both a utilitarian and philosophical approach toward the question of criminal justice, arguing that "if there were an exact and universal scale of crimes and punishments, we should there have a common measure of the degree of liberty and slavery, humanity and cruelty of different nations." A "system of morality" that subjects "the best men to the severest punishments, render[s] the ideas of vice and virtue vague and fluctuating and even their existence doubtful."

For a generation of American radicals such as Samuel Adams, whose revolutionary ideas were considered treasonous one day and then written into the Constitution the next, Beccaria's relativist approach to questions of crime, vice and virtue made a good deal of sense. Although it is a matter of historical debate precisely how much influence he may have had over the founders, it is clear that Beccaria's views were well-known among them, with John Adams even quoting him in his defense of the British soldiers in the 1770 murder trial relating to the Boston Massacre.[46] A lengthy passage of Beccaria's views also appears in Thomas Jefferson's *Legal Commonplace Book*, a collection of notes from his readings that he considered worth preserving in professionally bound volumes. A "legislator [who] has false ideas of utility who considers particular more than general conveniencies," Jefferson quotes Beccaria in his book, "would deprive men of the use of fire for fear of their being burnt, and of water for fear of their being drowned; and who knows of no means of preventing evil but by destroying it."[47]

With these ideas in mind, from the 1770s on, alternatives were being explored for improving prisons and penal systems. Leading the way by experimenting with the confinement of criminals in penitentiaries intended to be schools of reformation, in 1794—the year that Tufts was sentenced to die for stealing spoons—Pennsylvania repealed the death penalty for all offenses except first-degree murder.[48] Other states followed suit by introducing new kinds of prisons and a number of Founding Fathers proposed liberalizing the harsh penal codes of the colonial period. Jefferson even introduced a bill to limit the use of the death penalty in Virginia to the crimes of murder and treason, a bill that was defeated by just one vote. American penal reforms were more comprehensive and progressive than anywhere else in the Western world.[49]

Adams's own state of Massachusetts would be the first to establish a state-wide program for criminal incarceration following independence, which marked a turning point in criminal justice and the transformation from brandings and hangings as go-to punishments to the alternative of long-term incarceration. Adams would also appeal to the Massachusetts General Court to improve the state's legal system and establish a "compleat, perfect and permanent system of jurisprudence," which he called "one of the greatest blessings which our country can possess." Adams hailed "Uncorrupted Juries" as "an effectual guard against the violations of our rights and property."[50] Mindful of the cost to the public, Adams noted that "the administration of justice should indeed be without oppressive or unnecessary expences on the people."[51] In the ensuing years,

This drawing depicts Castle William, which served during the colonial period as a British fortification, then converted to a prison, and was later used as a seacoast fortification by the United States. The day after the Boston Massacre, Samuel Adams led a crowd of thousands to the office of Lieutenant Governor Thomas Hutchinson, demanding that British troops be removed from Boston. Hutchinson relented and withdrew the troops to Castle William. Also known as Castle Island, Henry Tufts spent several years here after his death sentence was commuted. He described the prison as "a little hell" (created 1773. Medium: ink and watercolor. Library of Congress Prints and Photographs Division).

Massachusetts would focus heavily on criminal justice reform and by 1797 the sanction of hard labor, which Adams had championed, would become the preferred method of punishment. In 1805, Massachusetts established its first State Prison, in Charlestown.[52]

* * *

So, clearly there was a growing sentiment at the time against the use of capital punishment and although it is possible that Henry Tufts benefited from the public debate taking place, ultimately it is not known whether Adams was motivated by moral or personal considerations when he took mercy on Henry and commuted his death sentence to a lifetime of hard labor at Castle Island. While relieved to be spared his life, however, Henry was not thrilled with the prospect of spending the rest of his days living with hardened criminals. He became acutely aware that "life's best days were wasting away in bondage," and after some time, came to see the prison as a "little hell." This was especially the case when Henry got to know his cellmates a bit better, confiding that he "heartily despised my viler associates." It seemed that as Henry was growing older and wiser, his fellow convicts insisted on remaining immature degenerates. "To complete my wretchedness," Henry wrote, "the blasphemies, buffooneries and brutal manners of the convicts grew more and more repugnant to my feelings." He complained that he had many altercations and quarrels "with those worthless villains."[53]

Although making nails on an island in Boston Harbor surrounded by "worthless villains" might appear to be a rather dubious improvement in circumstances, Tufts's good fortunes were only just beginning. He had the luck to be sent to Castle Island at a time when the United States, in reaction to a growing threat of war with European powers, was attempting to build a navy and strengthen its coastal security. In 1794 Congress allocated funds to establish the first system of American seacoast fortifications.[54]

As Adams wrote to the General Court that year, although the Castle Island prison had been an effective tool of criminal justice, "the situation of our country now calls for fortifications on our seacoasts," appealing for the conversion of the prison to a fort. He pointed out that "the President of the United States [George Washington] has communicated the Act of Congress for erecting forts in the harbor of Boston, which now lies before you," and since the Castle Island prison was established by an act of the legislature, it was up to the legislature to deliver control of the island over to the federal government. This would mean that "the convicts under sentence, must be discharged, or another place of confinement be provided for them."[55]

Although it would take several years for the legislature to approve the plans, Castle Island would eventually be converted from a penal colony to a seacoast fortification, with the prisoners being transferred to other jails in the state. So, without having to beg for leniency once again or enlist the help of supporters to petition the governor, Henry Tufts would for a second time benefit from an intervention by Samuel Adams. After years imprisoned on the highly secure prison on Castle Island, he would be transferred to a jail in Salem, which he "had no intention of abiding long."[56]

As the *Salem Gazette* reported on Tuesday, November 20, 1798, the following individuals had broken out of jail together: James Hallywell, Miles Riley, William Brown, and Henry Tufts. The newspaper listed descriptions and ages of four fugitives, with Tufts, at 53, being the oldest by far. "A reward of Five Dollars will be paid," the newspaper noted, "for each of any of the above named criminals, whom any person may secure in either of the jails in this Commonwealth."[57] At least in the case of Tufts, no one would ever collect those five dollars.

13

Unleashing Genius and Dismantling Patriarchy

In reflecting upon his life choices that led ultimately to his brush with the gallows, Henry Tufts considered his lack of schooling to be one of the main factors influencing his poor decisions. Citing Scripture, he pointed to education as among the most fundamental requirements for living a virtuous life: "It is written (as 'tis said) in the Hebrew annals, that the man, who gave his son, neither property, education nor trade, brought him up to be a thief. The truth of this was verified in me." As Henry explains, rather than attending proper school, he was educated at "the school of adversity," which taught him only "the salutary doctrine of repentance." His lack of education produced in him "a disinclination for every laudable pursuit," and his "despondency had ... operated, as a deadly weight, to clog the wheels of useful enterprise."[1]

In the writings and speeches of Samuel Adams, it is clear that he, too, considered education essential to unlock human potential. "The Cottager may beget a wise Son; the Noble, a Fool," Adams wrote in 1790. "The one is capable of great Improvement—the other not." It is only through education, Adams believed, that people's natural abilities and virtues would flourish, hereditary privilege would cease to exist, and society would overcome class divisions.[2] "Wise, and judicious Modes of Education ... will draw together the Sons of the rich, and the poor, among whom it makes no distinction; it will cultivate the natural Genius, elevate the Soul, excite laudable Emulation to excel in Knowledge, Piety, and Benevolence, and finally it will reward its Patrons, and Benefactors by shedding its benign Influence on the Public Mind," he wrote.[3]

While Tufts's emphasis on the importance of learning came from his experience in being deprived of an education, the importance that Adams placed on academic pursuits came from his experience having had access to it. As a graduate of Harvard and a member of America's founding generation, Adams was a scholar who took seriously the power of the pen to effect change. His days at Harvard consisted of getting up at 5:00 a.m. for morning prayers, reading Euclid, memorizing passages of Homer, studying Hebrew, and learning to compose a syllogism. Both classical philosophers and Enlightenment thinkers were well-represented in the curriculum, and Adams grew intimately acquainted with Plutarch, Locke, Cicero, Sallust, Livy, Harrington, Pufendorf, Montesquieu, and Hume.[4]

For his master's thesis, he was provided several topics that he could argue, including such staples as the justness of slavery or the fairness of capital punishment. He eschewed those choices, and picked a theme that was closer to his heart, arguing in the affirmative for the question of "Whether it be lawful to resist the supreme magistrate, if the commonwealth cannot be otherwise saved." At Harvard, Adams honed his skills in rhetoric, holding debates and demonstrating "an uncanny ability to understand his opponents' views and remain one step ahead," as his biographer Mark Puls put it.[5]

Adams's studies at Harvard were heavy on ancient history,[6] and familiar with the failings that led to the collapse of the Greek and Roman republics, he and other founders believed that democracy was only possible with an informed citizenry. They did not take the success of the American republic for granted and believed that for it to survive, it had to remain strong, which required the development of human potential and the suppression of artificial aristocracy.[7] Samuel Adams, in particular, envisioned a "Christian Sparta" in America,[8] a reference to the ancient Greek city-state renowned for its social system and constitution, as well as its military prowess.

* * *

Along with his cousin John and associates such as Thomas Jefferson, John Jay, James Otis, James Madison, Benjamin Rush, James Wilson, and Elbridge Gerry, Samuel Adams was a first-generation gentleman, the first of his family to attend college and acquire a liberal arts education. Among such refined scholars, those founders who lacked formal education, such as George Washington, exhibited a certain degree of embarrassment. Washington was noticeably self-conscious about his lack of schooling, repeatedly expressing his "consciousness of a defective education," and was known to remain reticent in conversations with individuals who were more worldly than he. Chronically embarrassed that he never learned any foreign languages, Washington declined invitations to France because he thought it would be humiliating to have to communicate through an interpreter.[9]

Those who did have the advantage of enjoying the benefits of a formal education rather consciously cultivated a culture of leisure that came to define the lifestyle of an aristocratic gentleman. The revolutionary leaders immersed themselves in republican ideas, and armed with this knowledge, they sought to distance themselves from their fathers' generation and build a new world based on science and reason.[10] As Governor Francis Fauquier of Virginia declared, "the principal difference between one people and another proceeds only from the differing opportunities of improvement."[11]

In line with this thinking, an emerging middle class in America sought to take advantage of educational opportunities to improve their station. John Hector St. John, a French-American farmer who had been imprisoned by the British during the revolution as a suspected spy, wrote in the early 1780s that he wished his children "no literary accomplishments," but simply that they become "expert scholars in husbandry." As farming had "made our continent to flourish more rapidly than any other," he considered agricultural studies to be the most valuable education available.[12]

When the founders talked about education, however, they didn't just mean learning the skills needed to advance financially, or even simply the development of new knowledge and technologies for enhancing agriculture and industry. By building upon the republican ideals of Greece and Rome, they also meant that they would develop their own Homers and Virgils, and unleash the people's potential for genius and artistic talent. They believed that they were facilitating the flourishing of civilization, which was moving inexorably westward, from the Middle East to Greece to Rome to western Europe to America, and that they were the inheritors of the classical world's philosophies and fine arts.

But at the same time, the revolutionaries saw the potential of America as something entirely new, representing a break from the Old World and a novel experiment in republicanism and democracy. "No more of Memphis and her mighty kings," read a 1771 poem called "The Rising Glory of America" by Hugh Henry Brackenridge. "No more of Greece / Where learning next her early visit paid," the poem continued, and certainly "No more of Britain, and her kings renown'd." The popular poem proclaimed, "The rising glory of this western world, Where now the dawning light of science spreads," and celebrated "America's own sons," promising that "we too shall boast Our Alexanders, Pompeys, heroes, kings."[13]

While they looked to the ancient world for inspiration and considered America to be the natural heir to the republics of Greece and Rome, the founders hoped that the new nation would not fall victim to the corruption and social decay that plagued those earlier experiments in democracy. Tyranny, it was believed, was founded on ignorance, and to prevent it from taking hold in America, education was essential. According to Adams, education leads the youth to "the Study of human nature, society, and universal History," thereby inspiring "Men to thinking and reflection, to reasoning and demonstration." This, in turn, would create more informed citizens who would choose better leaders to represent them, thereby curbing corruption and contributing to the public good. Education also makes individuals better Christians, Adams believed, as it "discovers to them the moral and religious duties they owe to God, their Country and to all Mankind."[14]

Underscoring the importance of making education accessible to all, it was even highlighted in the Massachusetts Constitution of 1780 as an essential duty of the state government. Written by John Adams with an assist from Samuel, the document states forthrightly, "Wisdom and knowledge ... [are] necessary for the preservation of their rights and liberties." Legislatures must therefore "cherish the interests of literature and the sciences, and all seminaries of them; especially the university at Cambridge, public schools and grammar schools in the towns," the Constitution declared.[15] In line with this mandate and the general conviction among the founders that education helped promote republican values, educational institutions were widely established throughout the country following the revolution.

* * *

In 1776 there were just nine colleges in America, but that number more than doubled over the next quarter-century, with some 25 colleges in existence by 1800. The founders drew up plans for establishing comprehensive public school systems, leading to a proliferation of schools in the early 19th century,[16] as well as increasing access to books, newspapers and magazines. From 1786 to 1795, 28 new magazines were launched, compared to just 22 that had been established in the previous colonial period. Three-quarters of America's books and pamphlets that were published between 1637 and 1800 appeared following the onset of the revolutionary crisis in the 1760s, and while newspapers were relatively scarce before the revolution, they were soon being widely printed, making the American people the most avid newspaper readers in the world. Americans built libraries at an unprecedented rate, spawning reading clubs, lectures and debating societies.[17] The new republic prided itself on its literacy, with Americans voraciously reading Enlightenment philosophy and histories of the ancient world, with a particular interest in the republics of antiquity. One American of the time, in fact, complained that the names of these ancient republics had "grown trite by repetition."[18]

With this newfound knowledge, popular theories spread about such diverse topics as animal magnetism, the workings of electricity, and the lost tribes of Israel.[19] Also growing in popularity were new ideas about the efficacy of folk medicine, which provided the context for Henry Tufts to ply his trade as an Indian-trained yarb doctor. As he writes in his memoirs, for some time his "chief earnings had been derived from medical channels, and I may here say, with propriety, that my experience in medicine, however small, afforded me frequent relief, when destitute of all other resources."[20] Opening up the accessibility of information, Henry found, had created a market for self-taught herbalists to earn a decent living by hawking folk medicine cures for various ailments.

While skeptics might dismiss this as "quack doctoring," in some cases, these treatments proved effective, and Henry expressed some pride in his medical skills. "I restored to health," he wrote, "one woman, affected with an odious disease that she contracted by her familiar intercourse with a certain trader." For this service, Henry notes, he "was richly rewarded."[21]

Henry also tapped into Americans' newfound interest in various strands of evangelical Christianity that began sweeping the country in the 18th century and particularly in the wake of the American Revolution. New educational opportunities brought novel religious ideas and soon the Puritans in New England and the Anglicans in the South were being supplanted by denominations that were defined by their egalitarianism and accessibility to average people.[22] Revivalist Baptists, Methodists and New Light Presbyterians were moving to the center of American society, and evangelism was becoming the "grand absorbing theme" of American life, with revivals "becoming too numerous in our country" to be able to count, according to a contemporary journal.[23] In contrast to harsh Puritanism and Calvinism, the new evangelical denominations had roots in Enlightenment thinking, with some of these Christians rejecting the inhumane treatment of the marginalized, embracing a more inclusive view of human agency, and challenging ideas such as the widespread notion that Native Americans and enslaved Africans lacked the capacity to respond to the Gospel.[24] Evangelicals believed that human suffering could be alleviated through faith in God, education, and personal enlightenment.[25] Above all, they emphasized the importance of conversion and the need for an active life of personal piety.[26]

Although Henry denounced some religious leaders as "hypocrites, impostors, and wholly unworthy the name they feloniously usurp," he found that the Shaker community was welcoming, generous, and kind. He appreciated the warmness they showed him, which stood in contrast to the "zeal and sanctified hypocrisy" of other denominations, and expressed his "veneration for the sincerely pious, whom I esteem as the salt of the earth."[27] While Henry considered "Godly piety … the first, best source of human felicity," he also somewhat cynically saw the rise of evangelism in New England as an opportunity to make some money. "A set of religionists," Henry wrote, "who pretended to far greater sanctity than their neighbors, had arisen of late in divers places, especially in the town of Lee." These were the New Light Presbyterians, whose "enthusiastic meetings" Henry regularly attended and painstakingly observed "their manner of praying and exhorting." Emulating these "zealots," Henry began to make a steady living as a charlatan minister, preaching his version of the Gospel and collecting handsome donations from the unsuspecting multitudes.[28]

Samuel Adams, although he took issue with some Christian denominations such as the Quakers, whom he called "a sly artful People" and criticized for their "barefaced Falshood," generally welcomed the proliferation of evangelical confessions.[29] "Any person may worship in the manner he thinks most agreeable to the Deity," Adams wrote, "and if he behaves as a good citizen, no one concerns himself as to his faith or adorations, neither have we the least solicitude to exalt any one sect or profession above another."[30]

But with its vulnerabilities to unscrupulous opportunists like Henry Tufts, the rise of evangelism in the new America was not embraced by all Founding Fathers, with Thomas Jefferson, for one, criticizing New England for spawning this religious movement which seemed to be overwhelming the spirit of republicanism that he believed should be at the heart of the revolution. More comfortable with Unitarianism and theistic rationalism, which emphasized the importance of rational thought to balance the conflicts and contradictions of religious fundamentalism, Jefferson saw the rise of evangelism along with other troubling trends in the early 19th century as evidence that ordinary people might not be capable of being entrusted with the republic's future after all.[31] While certainly not opposed to religion per se, Jefferson worried about the Bible being misused, and placed more emphasis on the importance of education in promoting responsible citizenship.[32]

* * *

In addition to protecting Americans's rights and liberties, education was considered essential to prevent the rise of a hereditary aristocracy. Jefferson's famous line in the Declaration of Independence, "all men are created equal," was an adage that expressed not only a belief in equality but also implied that through education and self-improvement, everyone could advance. To be enlightened was to believe in both the natural equality of people, and that through education, individuals could unleash their human potential. Since this would not be possible with an entrenched hereditary aristocracy enjoying all the benefits and making all the decisions, Jefferson wanted to nurture "a natural aristocracy among men," based on "virtue and talents" that would bloom with instruction.

Jefferson lauded education as a means to ensure freedom, writing in 1816 that "if a nation expects to be ignorant & free, in a state of civilisation, it expects what never was & never will be." Literacy is the bare minimum required to prevent tyranny, according to Jefferson, who observed that "where the press is free and every man able to read, all is safe."[33] To ensure the highest level of education possible, he pressed for legislative initiatives that would support a "general diffusion of learning" with a network of district schools for teaching reading, writing, and arithmetic. From these schools, a certain number of the most promising subjects would be selected to complete at a university, "where all the useful sciences should be taught." In this way, "Worth and genius would thus have been sought out from every condition of life, and completely prepared by education for defeating the competition and birth for public trusts."[34]

Like Jefferson, Samuel Adams considered education not just a privilege for the elite but something that was so necessary for the republic's future that it must be made accessible to all Americans regardless of class or status. He pointed to the efforts of Virginia as a model for the rest of the nation, and even in the midst of the Revolutionary War he insisted that education receive its proper place. As Adams lamented in 1779, it "gives me the greatest Concern to hear that some of our Gentlemen in the Country begin to think the Maintenance of Schools too great a Burden." He added, "If Virtue & Knowledge are diffusd among the People, they will never be enslavd. This will be their great Security."[35]

Not only did Adams consider education essential to building a nation and nourishing republican values, but also as a way to curtail criminal activity. In his 1794 inaugural address, Adams spoke about the importance of improving education to combat crime—a theme that Henry Tufts would have surely identified with. "Human laws excite fears and apprehensions, least crimes committed may be detected and punished," Adams said. "But a virtuous education is calculated to reach and influence the heart, and to prevent crimes." Such an education, he stressed, will teach the youth "universal benevolence, and a warm attachment and affection towards their country," as well as "inspire them with a sense of true honor, which consists in conforming as much as possible, their principles, habits, and manners to that original character."[36]

As a champion of education, Adams pushed back on trends in the 1790s to close the school doors to those without means. "If we continue to be a happy people," Adams said in a January 1795 address to the state legislature, "that happiness must be assured by the enacting and executing of reasonable and wise laws, expressed in the plainest language, and by establishing such modes of education as tend to inculcate in the minds of youth, the feelings and habits of 'piety, religion and morality.'"[37]

Returning to the subject six months later in an address to the legislature, Adams criticized the trend of private schools such as Philips Academy and Lawrence Academy. The Harvard-educated Adams regretted that establishing these elite institutions had the effect of eroding the egalitarian nature of the town-based grammar schools, which imparted "useful learning, instruction and social feelings in the early part of life," worrying that a class-based education system "may cease to be so equally and universally disseminated, as it has heretofore been." The private academies, Adams said, "have a tendency to injure the ancient and beneficial mode of Education in Town Grammar Schools" where "the poor and the rich may derive equal benefit." At the private academies, on the other hand, "none excepting the more wealthy, generally speaking, can avail themselves of the benefits."[38]

While this attitude was surely held sincerely by Adams, it was also in keeping with popular opinion of the time, and as a politician he may have understood the need to meet the people's demands, including those of the lower classes, to have the same opportunities as the upper classes. Notably, women were beginning to speak up and demand education, as well as other rights. Prior to the revolution, in keeping with the patriarchal view that the center of the woman's world should properly be considered the home rather than the public sphere, formal and informal education offered to girls and young women was limited to preparing them for their roles as wives, mothers, and homemakers. They had few opportunities for higher learning, which was considered beyond their mental capacity and unnecessary since they had few prospects for professional employment besides school teaching.[39] During the revolution, however, the commitment and contribution of women to the patriot cause won them widespread respect from men, and changed the general perception of what a woman should be.

Samuel Adams's wife Betsy, for example, was a well-read woman who enjoyed engaging in political discussions with the wives of her husband's colleagues, and could "converse upon any subject and give a solid and sensible opinion on most," a relative recalled. Adams often read correspondence from other patriots aloud to her and solicited her views, and also relied on her to relay messages to associates.[40] In the mid–19th century, historian George Bancroft described Adams as "a tender husband" and his wife as "prudent and industrious," noting she was "endowed with the best qualities of a New England woman." She "knew how to work with her own hands, so that the small resources, which men of the least opulent class would have deemed a very imperfect support, were sufficient for his simple wants."[41]

Betsy Adams was one of many women who actively engaged in the debates that drove the movement for independence, often in the confines of the home or in letters with their husbands, but sometimes also more publicly. Women published plays and poems proclaiming their patriotic views, and a good number took to the streets during riots in the lead-up to the revolution. During the war, they supported the cause by managing farms and businesses and otherwise assuming the burdens of absent husbands. In addition, women went door to door in cities across the colonies collecting money for the Continental Army,[42] and some even participated in combat. During the Battle of Fort Washington, for instance, on November 16, 1776, husband and wife John and Margaret Corbin of Virginia both participated in the fighting on the patriot side. When John was killed, Margaret took over his cannon, loading and firing the gun several times until she too was badly wounded. She survived the battle, but lost the use of her left arm.[43]

This sort of direct participation in combat by women, however, was rare. When women did bear arms to defend a fort or participate in other military engagements, they often had to pose as males.[44] More frequently, women participated in the revolution as "camp followers" who played a critical role in the daily functions of the revolutionary cause, marching with the troops and working as seamstresses, nurses, and cooks at their camps. There were thousands of women who served in this function, many of whom were widows, runaway servants, or the destitute. A British intelligence report estimated in 1778 that of the 20,000 rebels who mustered at White Plains, "near the half" were comprised of "Women and Waggoners."[45] Farther away from the battlefield, there were also groups of women who strongarmed Tories or shopkeepers who hoarded scarce supplies.[46]

* * *

Having served the revolution in these functions, after independence many women sought a more expansive role for themselves, and men who had welcomed their support for the war effort continued to seek their guidance and help. The "ideal" republican woman was no longer just a submissive homemaker who lived to obey her husband, but a competent conversationalist who could engage with men in serious discussions on complex political and social issues. There was a widespread recognition, however, that women's general lack of knowledge had left them ill-prepared for their new roles, and that they would have to be suitably educated if they were to live up to such high expectations.

A watershed moment was the publication of the essay "On the Equality of the Sexes" by Judith Sargent Murray in 1790. Originally published in *The Massachusetts Magazine*, Murray's essay argued for improved educational opportunities for women, insisting that the success of the new nation required intelligent and virtuous citizens—both men and women. Since the education of children largely rested with mothers, Murray pointed out, women should be properly educated in order to raise virtuous republican citizens. She challenged pseudoscientific notions that the female brain was somehow inferior, arguing that women were not held back by biological limitations but by lack of access to schooling.[47] The widely read essay helped lay the foundation for the figure of the "Republican Mother" in the new republic.[48]

Even more influential, perhaps, was the publication in 1792 of *A Vindication of the Rights of Woman: with Strictures on Political and Moral Subjects*, written by British philosopher Mary Wollstonecraft. Published first in Britain and appearing in American periodicals shortly thereafter, *A Vindication* was the strongest statement of women's rights to date. Wollstonecraft directly addressed the issue, challenging the gendered assumptions of language that had the effect of marginalizing women, such as Thomas Paine's 1791 publication *Rights of Man*, arguing that natural rights apply to women as well as men. Wollstonecraft identified lack of education as the primary culprit in keeping women in a child-like state of innocence.

"Men, indeed, seem to me to act in a very unphilosophical manner when they try to secure the good conduct of women by keeping them always in a state of childhood," she wrote. "Children, I agree, should be innocent; but when 'innocent' is applied to men or women it is merely a polite word for 'weak.'"[49] A "male aristocracy" had oppressed women, in Wollstonecraft's view, and to overcome this oppression, women would need to receive a rational education. "Contending for the rights of woman," she wrote, "my main argument is built on this simple principle, that if she be not prepared by education to become the companion of man, she will stop the progress of knowledge and virtue."[50] With many Americans coming to agree with this view, schools and academies were founded throughout the newly independent United States that began accepting female students.[51]

Women's increased access to education had instant effects, with literacy rising rapidly throughout the country. Between 1784 and 1860, more than 100 periodicals geared toward women appeared, and in the same time frame, white women achieved parity in literacy with men.[52] Historian Gordon Wood, in fact, considers the revolution's impact on women, including the increased access to education that it afforded them, as one of its greatest accomplishments. "The Revolution made possible the ... women's rights movements of the nineteenth century and in fact all our current egalitarian thinking," Wood writes. Not only did it change "the personal and social relationships of people including the position of women, but also destroyed aristocracy as it had been understood in the Western world for at least two millennia."[53]

Women also started pushing back on more subtle forms of domination by their male counterparts, rejecting language in marriage vows that compelled them to "obey" their husbands, for instance. Considered before the revolution as completely dependent on their husbands or fathers, with documents referring to them as "wife of" or "daughter of" some male, women were not allowed to enter into contracts or exercise legal rights. They could not sue or be sued, make contracts or buy and sell property,[54] much less expect to have equal opportunity in educational institutions or professional careers.

The revolution made people more aware of these forms of oppression and under growing pressure for equality, patriarchy would be steadily eroded in the 19th century and greater parity would eventually prevail between the two genders. Abigail Adams spoke for many when she wrote to her husband while he was serving at the Continental Congress in 1776, urging him to "Remember the Ladies, and be more generous and favourable to them than your ancestors." She warned John Adams that if "perticuliar care and attention is not paid to the Laidies we are determined to foment a Rebelion, and will not hold ourselves bound by any Laws in which we have no voice, or Representation."[55]

* * *

More subtly, Henry Tufts's biography also highlights the growing independence and personal strength of women in the late 18th century. Although women tend to play a role in his story that often elicits pity, as he is constantly deceiving and abandoning them, there is also a strong sense of self-confidence that shines through from his lady companions. Shattering the stereotype of the meek and submissive colonial woman, they often keep him in check by giving him a stern lecture, never shying away from speaking their minds or even turning him over to the magistrate when needed. Indeed, Henry confides that at times he grew weary of listening to "the multiplicity of curtain lectures, that were constantly chiming in my stunned ears" from his chafed lovers. He observes that as women age, their "eyes grow dim [and] their teeth decay," but unfortunately for him, "their tongue should never fail."[56]

Women, however, are far from one-dimensional characters in his memoirs. Despite his often lustful intentions, Henry respectfully refers to them as "kind and charitable" with "manners soft and engaging," and highlights their "personal charms." Henry does come across as a bit of a womanizer, conceding that he "engaged in a variety of amours with sundry females, to whom I paid my addresses alternately, as best suited my

13. Unleashing Genius and Dismantling Patriarchy 217

inclination or convenience,"[57] but his female companions rarely seem to play the hapless victim. Indeed, on one occasion his wife Nabby fearlessly rescued Henry from some "remorseless knaves" who had robbed and kidnapped him at gunpoint. In a riveting account of the incident, Henry relates that "my faithful female, indignant at such treatment, like a true amazon, mustered seven or eight men, and placing herself at their head, sallied out for my rescue." When the rescue team approached, his abductor "drew out a pistol" and threatened to kill Henry, but he managed to knock the gun from his hand. "The heroic Nabby seized the pistol," Henry writes, and threatened to "shoot him with his own weapon, if he did not instantly set me free." Another one of the rescuers that Nabby had mobilized then hit the bandit with a musket, which "put an end to the contest."[58]

Henry also shares stories of drinking, playing cards and gambling with women, and the impression is that they could generally hold their own. In one instance, however, a woman got so drunk that she gave Henry nearly 200 dollars by mistake. Henry was staying the night at a tavern in the town of Woodbury, where the woman in charge was "immoderately fond of a cherishing glass," and made a "clatter all night" with "the other domestics." When he tried to pay the bill the next morning, the woman was "much intoxicated with her morning draught, as well as evening debauch," and mistakenly gave him far too much money by way of change.[59]

Despite this anecdote, women often appear quite clever in the pages of Henry's narrative, and indeed, they are typically the ones who foil his conspiracies. In one instance, early on in Henry's career as a thief, he stole "a paper money bill" from a neighbor's house, only to be found out by the woman of the house who "missed her bill, [and] when calling to mind, that none else had been present, she placed her suspicions upon me." Upon being confronted, young Henry eventually confessed to the crime and returned the money. In another instance, later on in his life, a woman with whom Henry was having an affair became "fully convinced of my duplicity and intention to deceive her, and, being at this crisis, urged on by her friends, she went and entered a complaint before Esq. Butler, a neighboring magistrate."[60]

Another woman once thwarted Henry's plan to escape from military prison with a group of fellow deserters, and yet another called him out in church as an impostor while he was feigning to be a priest. In this instance, it was Henry's lecherousness that seemed to do him in. The woman apparently noticed him eyeballing her "in such a carnal way and manner, that [she] perceived he had the devil in his heart." She explained that "he first surveyed my face, then my feet, then my whole person," which Henry concedes "was literally true," and admits that he "could not but admire at the intuitive sagacity of the young gypsy, who was able to hit off, so adroitly, my real character."[61]

At other times though, Henry's narrative offers a peek into the more lustful side of gender relations, offering anecdotes that don't always reflect well on women's morality but at the same time illustrates their subtle rejection of patriarchy. At one point he met a woman named Sally Hall, and concedes that "lasciviousness ... was an original ingredient in my composition," so he "made love to this damsel, and continued the courtship, with ardour, for a time." He eventually impregnated her but had no intention of "healing the transgression by marriage," as he "had not the most exalted opinion" of Sally's "virtue and accomplishments." Nevertheless, Henry assured her that they would marry some day and they continued their secret affair.[62]

While some female characters in Henry's memoirs might appear promiscuous and others were more proper, virtually all of them shine through as independent and strong-minded individuals who do not shy away from speaking their minds. In this way, the interactions with women that Henry shares throughout the book demonstrate their capability, intelligence and competence, as well as the growing respect they commanded from men. The portrayals underscore their growing independence and the myriad ways in which they challenged traditional stereotypes, whether through exercising sexual freedom or personal assertiveness, recalling that while the norm prior to the revolution was for women to be treated as less than full citizens, increasingly republican ideas were being applied more equally. With the new spirit of republicanism that took hold following the revolution, exemplified by Henry's anecdotes and enabled by the increased access to education that women began to enjoy, it became more widely accepted that natural rights belonged not just to men, but to women as well.

14

Heroes, Anti-Heroes and Villains

A small, leatherbound book, Henry Tufts's autobiography was published in 1807 in Dover, New Hampshire, and has sometimes been erroneously referred to as the first full-length autobiography of an American criminal. In fact, those honors seem to belong to Stephen Burroughs's memoirs, which were first published a decade earlier and reprinted nearly 30 times over a period of 50 years, becoming something of a national best-seller.[1] Like Tufts, Burroughs was a thief and a counterfeiter who operated in New England in the late 18th century, and his narrative was heavy on entertaining anecdotes while free of moral pretenses. He was, however, quick to blame others and took pains to vindicate his name from the many exaggerated claims that had circulated about him in New England.

Conversely, Tufts did not attack his enemies in his narrative nor seek vindication. Far from a glorification of criminality or a self-serving defense of his actions, his autobiography candidly portrayed the difficulties and heartache of a vagabond's life, noting that "by sad experience, I can say, that the ways of wickedness are not pleasant."[2] Henry admitted that he was "subject to frequent remorse, and much disquiet, on the score of my past dissipation and glaring misdemeanors." Despite these caveats, however, the book's publication was somewhat scandalous, with New Englanders apparently objecting to its perceived celebration of vice and its undermining of the broader national mythology of a righteous revolution that had just been won. Some have even claimed that following the book's release, a mob of outraged citizens burned down the printing house that published it.

According to a contemporary account:

> This Wednesday evening, at 9¼ o'clock, the inhabitants of Dover were alarmed by the cry of fire. It commenced its destructive progress in a large building owned by Samuel Bragg, jr. printer, in the bindery on the lower floor, the

upper story of which was occupied by Mr. Bragg as a Printing Office and Bookstore.... The conflagration from room to room was rapid beyond conception and although the inhabitants who were in large numbers assembled in a few minutes made every exertion in the power of mortals to arrest the velocity of this devouring element, the whole building soon exhibited one column of flame, ascending in awful grandeur to the clouds.... Not a single article was saved from the Printing Office and Bookstore.[3]

This fire took place three years after the *Narrative* was published and although rumors have persisted that it was an act of arson in protest of Henry's book, there is actually no evidence that it was set intentionally much less that it was the act of an angry mob. Although proof is lacking, however, the longstanding assumption would be in keeping with the societal norms of the day and is not beyond the realm of possibility. At the time, mobs frequently targeted establishments that were considered a threat to the public good—such as brothels—sometimes with a wink and a nod from local magistrates who lacked the legal authority to take action on their own. Book burnings were also not unheard of, a New England tradition dating back to 1651 when all copies of William Pynchon's anti–Puritan tract, *The Meritorious Price of Our Redemption*, were publicly burned in Massachusetts.[4] Quaker books were also considered by the authorities to be "corrupt, heretical, and blasphemous doctrines contrary to the truth of the gospel," and were set ablaze in Boston's Market Square.[5]

So, with this historical context in mind and considering how intensely despised Henry was in New England, it wouldn't be a stretch to assume that there was some correlation between Henry's book and the inferno. It is noteworthy, however, that the contemporary sources don't mention an angry mob and those who have made this claim have never been able to provide evidence. Whether the fire was an accident or an act of arson intended to erase the book from existence, though, the book managed to survive. While nothing apparently was salvaged from the fire—and in spite of subsequent efforts by the Tufts family to suppress the book—a handful of copies remained in circulation, and lived on in the folklore of New England for generations.

Indeed, although "Henry Tufts" may not be a household name today, at one time it was so well-known that it would be incidentally mentioned in newspapers with the assumption being that readers would be familiar with him. The *Boston Herald*, for instance, made a passing reference to Henry in a 1904 article about a vigilante group called the White Caps. In tracing the origins of this group, the *Herald* noted that it "dated back to the days of Rainsford Rogers, an impostor and vagabond whose villainies outdid all the efforts of Henry Tufts."[6] That the newspaper would use his name so casually without explicating on the reference was a strong indication that his legacy was alive and well in Massachusetts more than a century after his neck had been saved by Samuel Adams—much to the chagrin of respectable New Englanders.

In her 1892 book *Landmarks in Ancient Dover, New Hampshire*, Mary Thompson emphasized the enduring infamy of Henry Tufts in the New Hampshire Seacoast region a century after his final jailbreak. She described him as a "shameless" man, but despite her assessment that his "pernicious book" held little to no historical or literary value, unfortunately she had to concede that it retained "a debasing popularity among the vulgar." Thompson attributed the enduring popularity of the book to the lamentable truth that "some people have a taste for nastiness, as the Zulus have for Ubomi—that is, for carrion with worms in it, a Ubominable mess indeed, as Henry Tufts' narrative is said to be."[7]

Another local history of Dover described Henry a bit less reproachfully, but also hinted at the lasting notoriety of his name even into the 20th century. The 1913 *Notable events in the history of Dover*, by George Wadleigh, called him "the most noted vagabond of his day [who] spent much of his time in Dover and other jails for the petty offences of which he was guilty."[8]

Likewise, a local history of Lee, New Hampshire, covering more than 250 years of oral tradition and primary sources, refers to Henry as something of a "Jessie [sic] James legend" and calls him "a man of ill repute" who "terrorized the townspeople with his nightly thefts." Collected by Martha Butterfield, this history offers anecdotes and memories passed down by several generations, noting that Henry "stirred up a lot of fear and anxiety in the Lee area" and suggested that his book should have been titled "The Terror of the Province."[9] In one story conveyed in Butterfield's book, a local woman who raised hens threatened to shoot Henry with buckshot if he came anywhere near her birds. Hearing a rumor of the threat, Henry decided to take her up on the challenge. As Butterfield describes it, he "stirred up her hens so they were squawking loudly; and when she leaned out her window to see what was going on, he grabbed her long nightie and pulled it over her head and proceeded to escape with a bag of chickens."

This story doesn't appear in Henry's *Narrative*, raising the possibility that he either intentionally left it out so as not to sully his image or that it was a fabrication intended to exaggerate the threat Henry posed. It's also possible, of course, that it was just one of many such incidents, as Henry concedes that his time in Lee resulted in many farmers "regret[ting] the loss of their fleecy tribes," as well as "the poultry, which were immolated daily." Rather than getting into detail about each and every theft, Henry said that he prefers to "pass over more trivial incidents," since an "endeavour to particularize the numerous tricks and villainies which first and last

I have practiced would be a vain and useless task."[10] In other words, Henry seemed to acknowledge his iniquities without exalting them, a subtlety that appeared lost on his many critics who have treated him as an unequivocal villain and his book as completely lacking any redeeming value.

* * *

There is one man, however, who lauded him as a hero and is probably more responsible than anyone for rescuing his name from infamy and disgrace. In the 1880s, Colonel Thomas Wentworth Higginson, a Unitarian minister and former member of the Secret Six committee that clandestinely supported anti-slavery radical John Brown, began lecturing about Henry and in 1888 published an article in *Harper's Magazine*[11] celebrating "the wholly disreputable and therefore most instructive career of Henry Tufts." As Higginson wrote, without his "reprobate" perspective, the history of the United States is "imperfectly understood." While most biographies highlight the lives of influential and important men, Henry's book "derives its worth from the very badness of the society into which it brings us; it reveals the existence, behind all that was decent and moral in that period, of a desperate and lawless minority."[12]

In an effort to spread his story far and wide, Col. Higginson spent decades regaling audiences with lectures that extolled Henry as a rebel and anti-conformist. In an account of one of Higginson's lectures, Tufts is described as a "hero" who reveals "the under side of New-England manners and morals about the time of the Revolution." Higginson dazzled his New York audience with stories of how this bandit "deserted from the army, and led his pursuers on a chase across the hills of Massachusetts, stealing horses for himself as often as he wanted a fresh mount," the *New York Times* reported on January 14, 1885. Higginson's tales of Tufts's exploits "were rich specimens of the quaint conceit and pomposity of this knight of rascals," according to the *Times*.[13]

A decade and a half later, Higginson was still telling Henry's story to anyone who would listen. At a meeting of the Society of Colonial Wars in 1903, Higginson recalled that Henry's life reveals "hardly a trace of honest industry, with the exception of his services in the Revolution," noting however that Henry was implicated in the distribution of counterfeit currency that subverted the cause.[14] Higginson also featured Tufts's story in a book he wrote titled *Travelers and Outlaws*, placing him alongside other early American rebels like Nat Turner, the leader of an 1831 slave revolt, and William Ellery, one of the 56 signers of the United States Declaration of Independence.[15]

With Higginson keeping Tufts's story alive into the 20th century, a librarian and writer named Edmund Pearson discovered it and decided to republish the autobiography, which was apparently very rare. (Both Higginson and Pearson claimed that they were only able to find a single copy each in New England libraries.) When Pearson's abridged version of Tufts's autobiography was republished in the early 1930s, a newspaper review praised it as "interesting reading, not only because of his candor and the quaintness of his style, but because he incidentally throws some light on the conditions of life in America in the closing decades of the eighteenth century." The review noted that Henry's memoirs also represent an early example of the true crime genre, coming out "long before modern publishers realized that truth is stranger than fiction, and began to compete with one another for the right to publish the confessions of real criminals."[16]

* * *

In the case of Tufts's book, though, it has always been hard to say with any certainty whether truth is stranger than fiction because it is sometimes hard to tell what is true and what isn't. Besides the fact that it celebrates the "misspent life" of a villain who some would rather forget about, one of the main criticisms of the book is that it is based on the recollections of a known liar and that some of the anecdotes seem to be embellished if not fabricated from whole cloth.

Its ending, in particular, has been questioned as implausible, raising doubts about much of the rest of the story—but in this case, at least, it appears that the historical record bolsters Henry's account. According to the book, after the commutation of his sentence by Adams and his escape from jail in Salem, Henry Tufts was never arrested again. "Since that period I have carried my dish pretty uprightly," Henry writes, and "have been guilty of few or no misdemeanors, but have persevered heroically in regular habits and virtuous resolutions."[17] He also claims that he "no longer dread[s] the scourge of future punishment," which begs the question: how could this man, who was ostensibly a fugitive from a life sentence, feel so confident in his standing that he would write a tell-all book that would bring attention to himself and provide all the necessary evidence to a prosecutor to have him once again sentenced to death?

As Daniel Allie, the editor of the 2017 reprint of Henry's narrative, writes, "For this to be true, one would have to accept that a man could escape from life imprisonment, and publicly advertise the fact later, under his own name, without any repercussions whatsoever. Yet this, it turns out, is exactly what happened."[18] Contemporary newspaper reports confirm, indeed, that Tufts broke out of jail after his commutation, and that he was never apprehended again.

Other details from his narrative have been bolstered by property records. As a nineteenth-century book explains, the cellar of the house where Henry once lived came to be owned by James McDaniel, and the name of "Hanary Tufts" is signed to a petition for the separation of Lee from Durham, November 18, 1765, corroborating at least a few facts Henry related in his memoirs. It is also noted that "the Tufts family of this vicinity has acquired an unenviable notoriety from the exploits of Henry Tufts (or 'Turf' as the name was generally called in his day)," noting that "the details of [his book] have never been supposed strictly true, but they undoubtedly present a faithful likeness of this depraved man."[19]

But while many have attempted to downplay his name and uplift the accomplishments of more reputable members of the Tufts family, Allie points out that it was precisely because of his transgressions that his story is worth studying. Citing his "anecdotes of jailbreaks, horse thefts, [and] quack doctoring," Allie points out that "Henry Tufts' perspective is completely unlike any of his contemporaries, and his book is all the better for it."[20]

Then again, perhaps it's not that his perspective is completely unlike any others, it's just that it is completely unlike any other *recorded* perspective. Members of the criminal underclass, including Henry's peers who may have shared a jail cell with him once or twice, probably did share his perspective in some ways but simply didn't have the gumption to write out their life stories for posterity. And if they had, perhaps their books would have been suppressed as well, as villains are expected to be not just remorseful but silent.

Nevertheless, at the end of his memoirs, Henry offers an apology to those he had wronged throughout his early life. As he entered his twilight years, he pledged to continue offering his services as a physician rather than applying his skills as a thief, "endeavoring to advance the benefit of my fellow creatures, and do all the good I can ... to make some little atonement, in the latter part of my life, for the many mischiefs and evils, which I brought upon myself, my family and others, in the earlier stages of it." He also conveys his hope that the "bitter misfortunes here recited, may be a caveat to others, and a mean of deterring them from such flagitious pursuits and diabolical devices." The path to happiness, Henry came to realize, is to "follow unerringly the golden rule, 'to do unto others, as he would wish to be done unto.'"[21]

Some critics have dismissed his expressions of atonement in the final pages of the book as disingenuous attempts to bolster the book's legitimacy, but a fair reading would have to give Henry at least some benefit of the doubt in his claims of remorse. Even if one doubts his sincerity, furthermore, it seems that whatever wrongs he committed he more than paid for in his incarceration at Castle Island, where, Henry explained, "it was impossible to see either peace or comfort." His "five disastrous years" in prison were spent sleeping on the floor, "with a tattered rug or blanket for a covering," and "each morning" being "turned out to perform our daily task of nail making." The food was nauseating and despite forcing himself to "swallow even a quantum sufficient for the sustenation of life," he was reduced to "nearly a skeleton." During his incarceration, Henry confides that he often longed "to end [his] complicated miseries by a speedy death."[22]

After years of this pitiful existence, however, Henry found redemption and a second chance in his escape from jail and his return to his first wife in Limington, Maine. After all of his trials and tribulations, Henry discovered Lydia, two of their sons and their families all in good health, with his other children off serving as apprentices. Although Henry didn't go into much detail about his reception upon this homecoming, by all appearances it seemed his children and wife forgave him for abandoning them years earlier. The reunion with his loved ones and their welcoming of him despite his transgressions must have had a deep impact on Henry, especially after spending years with the "dregs of human nature" at Castle Island.

While this was certainly a poignant moment, it was probably not just for its redemptive ending that Americans have enjoyed reading Henry's story over the years—whether the original printing that came out in the early 19th century or the reprint that appeared during the Great Depression. As an outsider who existed apart from the social structure, readers could decry his behavior while admiring the rogue's ability to create his own sense of justice and live by his own set of values. Rather than devoting himself to improving society—or like Samuel Adams, challenging systemic injustice through organized acts of rebellion—Henry Tufts simply sought to survive in what he called "an unfeeling world."[23]

In this way, there was probably something visceral that Americans in the early republic related to other than just his tales of turpitude. In a country that had rebelled against the authority of the Crown and fought a war against the world's most powerful empire to establish "natural rights," the individualistic and unfettered lifestyle of the vagabond surely resonated among many underdogs of society. Defiance of authority had become pervasive in the new republic, and Americans who had refused to accept the limitations placed on them by an English king displayed a growing willingness to pursue their own interests. Personal freedom, along with self-reliance and self-initiative, became widely celebrated ideals,[24] and despite his many personal flaws, Henry exhibited many of the republican virtues that Americans embraced.

In a nation still dizzy from its unlikely victory over the British Empire but also reeling from internal divisions, Henry's irreverent book may have also been a refreshing respite from the self-serving narratives celebrating the glory of the American Revolution and the endless tales touting the sacrifices of America's Founding Fathers. Regardless of how much truth there may be in the stories of courage surrounding the revolution—and there certainly was no shortage of them to celebrate, from the Midnight Ride and the Lexington muster to the crossing of the Delaware and the British surrender at the Battle of Yorktown—Americans may have desired an alternative that elevates the rogue rather than the revolutionary.

But at the same time, this alternative history undermined the efforts of patriots who were busy trying to unite the plucky young country and promote a coherent national identity based on righteousness and virtue. The story of a deserter and counterfeiter who was apathetic to the cause of independence would have to be suppressed and its protagonist marginalized as a liar and thief, but unfortunately for the mythmakers, these vices and sins may not be as rare as we would like to think, and for this reason there would remain a market for "pernicious books" like Henry's. Vice, indeed, has always featured as a central component of the national experience, from early Americans' love affair with alcohol to the opioid epidemic of today, and although as individuals, Americans might consider themselves virtuous, research has shown, in fact, that everyone has a natural tendency toward dishonesty.

* * *

A 2015 survey by the Pew Research Center found that Americans overwhelmingly view each other as patriotic and trustworthy, with majorities of 79 and 69 percent, respectively, agreeing with those descriptions,[25] but as Dan Ariely, a behavioral economist and bestselling author of *The (Honest) Truth About Dishonesty,* has shown through extensive social experiments, most people lie and cheat at least some. "Let me come right out and say it," Ariely writes in his book. "They cheat. You cheat. And yes, I also cheat from time to time."[26] This more unvarnished reality, ultimately, is what Henry Tufts reminds us of, and why the unyielding stance of Samuel Adams, who insisted on upholding a resolute commitment to virtue, may not have been feasible in the long run. The fact is, despite our carefully constructed self-image being bolstered by the heroes that we elevate—those we name cities after such as Washington and beers after such as Adams—the reality is that perhaps we all have a little bit of Henry Tufts in us.

Rather than acknowledge these frailties, however, or come to terms with our baked-in hypocrisies as a nation, there is a tendency to reaffirm America's goodness by identifying and isolating the villains. Finger-pointing and passing judgment at miscreants like Henry Tufts helps to distinguish the praiseworthy from the deplorable, and at the same time, acknowledging and celebrating national heroes helps firm up a sense of righteousness. But while elevating the Founding Fathers, it is worth remembering that many of them had serious shortcomings as well, with, for example, 41 of the 56 signers of the Declaration owning slaves, according to one study.[27] Thomas Jefferson is perhaps the most flagrant example of America's double standards, celebrated as the author of the Declaration of Independence and an indispensable Founding Father, but also seen by many as a walking contradiction because his professed beliefs are often contradicted by his actions. In particular, the fact that he was a lifelong slave-owner calls into question his sincerity when he declared that "all men are created equal," which by extension raises doubts about America's broader adherence to its fundamental values.

Jefferson's defenders are quick to point out that it is not fair to hold him to modern standards, that the general views of slavery have evolved over time and that although today we consider it a moral abomination, it was a widely accepted practice in the 18th century. While there might be some truth in this, it tends to ignore the fact that even within the context of the time, there were plenty of people who recognized it as distasteful at best or inherently evil at worst. Founders who vocally opposed slavery included John Adams, Roger Sherman, Gouverneur Morris, Alexander Hamilton, Benjamin Franklin, and Samuel Adams. These individuals never owned slaves, but even among slaveholders, there was a recognition that the practice was wrong. George Washington once described owning slaves as his life's "only unavoidable subject of regret,"[28] and Jefferson himself openly criticized slavery as a "hideous blot,"[29] claiming that "there [was] nothing I would not sacrifice to a practicable plan of abolishing every vestige of this moral and political depravity."[30]

According to his writings, Jefferson believed that slavery violated the laws of nature and presented a threat to the survival of the fledgling American Republic. Yet, despite publicly advocating for its eventual abolition, he owned more than 600 slaves during his lifetime,[31] more than any other American president, and was known to give them away as gifts, thoughtlessly breaking up families to impress his friends and relatives with human wedding presents. He even reneged on his own promises to free his slaves upon his death. Through the inconsistencies of his words and actions, the imperfect Thomas Jefferson perfectly personifies the contradictions of an American Revolution that championed the cause of "liberty" while systematically denying the most basic liberties to so many less fortunate people.

This hypocrisy, indeed, was apparent to many at the time. In a letter to her husband John Adams dated March 31, 1776, Abigail Adams questioned the commitment of Virginians such as Jefferson to the revolution due to their defense of slavery. "I have sometimes been ready to think that the passion for Liberty cannot be Eaquelly Strong in the Breasts of those who have been accustomed to deprive their fellow Creatures of theirs," Abigail Adams wrote.[32]

Abigail Adams, while perhaps more in tune with her moral core than most of her contemporaries, demonstrates that there were some who recognized the incongruities of the movement for American independence even in the throes of revolution. Yet, although she is widely celebrated for her high moral principles, which were undoubtedly held sincerely, she was also known to bend her ethical standards when necessary—using justifications for questionable actions that were not unlike the rationales used to justify slavery by some of her compatriots. For example, while her husband John was in Philadelphia serving in the Continental Congress and later as a diplomat in Europe, she was left in charge of running the family farm, which proved to be a daunting challenge. There was a labor shortage due to the war, which also brought inflation and high taxes, and at times it was a struggle to make ends meet. So, she decided to fire all the employees, expel the tenants and rent it out to two newly married brothers, who would split the harvest with her.

Relieved of daily farming duties and having kept close tabs on the rising price of goods over the years, Abigail focused her attention on profiting off of war-related inflation in the colonies. While John was serving the revolutionary cause in Europe, she would send him lists of items to ship her, which he would then dutifully gather and send back across the Atlantic. When the goods arrived, she would set aside the items that her family needed and sell the rest at marked-up prices to New England shopkeepers through intermediaries like Cotton Tufts to conceal her involvement in the price-gouging scheme.[33]

Although some people might call this "war profiteering," few would likely fault Abigail Adams for doing what she needed to do in order to survive during difficult times, and in fact we would probably admire her for her pragmatism, resourcefulness and cleverness. After all, in a complicated world fraught with difficulties, even someone of the unparalleled moral character of Abigail Adams would be justified in skimming some profits from the war in order to make ends meet.

But of course, these ethical compromises and moral ambiguities are not unlike the justifications that Henry Tufts would offer for his life of crime, or the rationales utilized by slavery's defenders—while acknowledging that it was perhaps objectionable, the Peculiar Institution was seen as a necessary evil in a world of adversity. Like Henry Tufts, who sometimes alluded in his memoirs to some invisible compulsion to continue his immoral ways even when he knew that his interests would be better served by giving up his vagabond life and settling down, many in the founding generation appeared compelled to maintain their slave-owning lifestyles despite knowing that slavery was wrong.

* * *

Although Samuel Adams never owned slaves and prided himself on living a virtuous life, he was also pragmatic and had a singularly focused devotion to the cause that may have blinded him to the double standards at the core of the American Revolution. While he at times expressed distaste for slavery and never personally participated in the practice, he certainly did not make abolitionism a cornerstone of his revolutionary ideals either. What troubled Adams far more than infringements of the rights of African Americans that slavery represented was the perceived contravention of colonists' rights that London's imposition of unfair taxes represented.

Besides this blind spot, some of his contemporaries saw him as overly rigid, unreasonable and even somewhat bigoted. He also had a malicious streak exemplified by a tendency to mercilessly tear down those he didn't like, some said. As the Rev. John Eliot wrote in 1809, "his manners were austere, his remarks never favourable to the rising generation."[34] Convinced that "the Puritans of New England were the men to set an example to the world," he was well-suited to resist a foreign occupation and help pull down a tyrannical government, but not as equipped to found a nation in line with modern sensibilities, his critics were quick to point out. As Eliot explained, "he did worthily in those times" of resisting the Intolerable Acts, but was unprepared for "building up a government suited to the condition of a people."[35] As someone rooted firmly in the past, his legacy would soon become distorted by a younger generation that was quickly losing touch with the Puritan world from which Adams had emerged.

One member of that younger generation was William Tudor, 57 years Adams's junior, who wrote in 1823 that the revolutionary was a "strict calvinist" of "too much sternness and pious bigotry." Tudor observed that "probably no individual of his day had so much the feelings of the ancient puritans."[36] To his critics, he was seen as someone who pretended to desire nothing more than the simple Puritan life, but revealed his violent and vindictive nature when rallying attacks against his enemies.

In this way, oddly enough, Adams was both a fanatical revolutionary and a staunch conservative, and thus he had trouble fitting into the paradigm that was emerging in the early 19th century of a progressive nation championing Enlightenment values and modernity. As a consequence, he was largely expunged from the national iconography that emerged following the revolution, and historians would have trouble reconciling his contradictions. Twentieth-century scholar Clifford Shipton, for example, wrote that Adams "preached hate to a degree without rival," alleging that he "taught his dog Queue to bite every Red Coat he saw, and took little children to the Commons to teach them to hate British soldiers."[37]

While Adams became known as among the more virulent of the anti-British agitators, his legacy was also influenced by his handling of Shays's Rebellion, which helped cement an image of a conservative rebel who only very selectively applied principles of fairness and justice. James Warren, an old revolutionary who supported the cause of the Shaysites, said that Adams's response to the rebellion revealed him as "the most arbitrary and despotic man in the Commonwealth." Although he rose to prominence in the 1760s and early 1770s as a champion of the little guy and an uncompromising voice for democratic ideals, with his harsh response to the anti-tax rebels in the state's backcountry, Adams had "forsaken all his old principles and professions," Warren wrote.[38] This is despite the fact that many of the participants in Shays's Rebellion had fought bravely in the revolution that Adams helped to spark. In this way, Adams made clear that his populism only went so far, and while he often leveled charges of hypocrisy at the Brits during the heyday of his revolutionary agitation, he might have been somewhat hypocritical himself.

Henry Tufts, for all his faults, was no hypocrite—he just didn't particularly care about society's concepts of right and wrong, nor did he pretend to. As slave-owners rationalized their actions, awkwardly attempting to square the circle of a revolution for liberty that overlooked the plight of those in bondage, and while radicals such as Adams rather hyperbolically compared taxation without representation to the status of slavery while ignoring the ordeal of overtaxed farmers and the injustice of chattel slavery, Henry simply went about his life, sometimes offering oblique justifications for his transgressions but more often just committing his crimes without overthinking issues of morality. "I have given," Henry wrote toward the end of his book, "with as much perspicuity and brevity, as was practicable, in my situation, a general account of the adventures, travels, sufferings and persecutions, which have attended me, first and last, through the boisterous vicissitudes of life."[39] There is something refreshing in that candor and openness.

* * *

What this all recalls is that assigning historical figures the labels of heroes and villains might not be possible in any objective sense because questions of ethics and morality are malleable and relative, and beyond that, commonly held assumptions and prevailing mythologies are often undermined by the actual evidence. When it comes to the American

Revolution, in particular, it is easy to be disappointed by national heroes failing to live up to their professed ideals, which reflects more broadly Americans' contradictory views about their own revolutionary past and a history tainted by slavery and conquest. In order to understand it, then, it is necessary to maintain a nuanced perspective, which applies not only to our cherished founders, but also for appreciating the contributions to history of those who have long been slandered as villains. This applies not only to vagabonds like Henry Tufts, but also other mixed bags like Benedict Arnold, Daniel Shays, King George III, and Thomas Gage. In the traditional telling of the American Revolution's story, these individuals tend to be assigned the role of villains, but upon closer examination they may not have been the unequivocal devils that they have made out to be.

While Samuel Adams harshly denounced Gage for his "perfidy,"[40] for example, and considered him "void of a Spark of Humanity,"[41] by many historical accounts he was a decent man driven by a commitment to law and the "common rights of mankind." He held a belief in liberty that was perhaps more hierarchical and aristocratic than the Boston radicals' views, insisting that too much power had been diffused to the masses who had been manipulated by duplicitous leaders, but under normal circumstances his differences with the patriots would probably not have been entirely irreconcilable. He conceded at one point in the escalating revolutionary crisis that, on the whole, the colonists were "not the despicable rabble too many have supposed them to be," but that "two or three worthless fellows at the head of the mobs" had misled them into rebellion.[42] He earnestly sought to avoid provoking violence and even his adversaries saw him as a man of peace who sought conciliation and not confrontation, with one calling him a "good and wise man … surrounded with difficulties."[43]

But ultimately, Gage would become something of a tragic figure who pursued a course in 1774 and 1775 that led directly to the occupation of Boston, the Powder Alarm, and the Battle of Lexington and Concord.[44] How much of this was personally his fault, however, is an open question. While Gage believed that he was acting in the best interests of the Crown and seeking to promote order and stability, he ultimately came to the conclusion that no matter what Britain had done, whether Parliament had adopted the Coercive Acts or taken a more lenient approach, the crisis would have escalated anyway because men like Samuel Adams were determined to use any pretext available to manipulate the situation.

Like General Gage, King George III was, of course, widely villainized in the revolutionary era, but a closer look reveals that he may not have been the tyrant typically seen in his depictions. As Andrew Roberts shows in *The Last King of America: The Misunderstood Reign of King George III*, the king was actually a rather enlightened constitutional monarch who celebrated the Magna Carta of 1215 as well as the Glorious Revolution of 1688 and denounced royalist tyranny at every opportunity.[45] And despite their personal attacks against the "mad king," there is a chance that some of the founders might have actually gotten along with him on a personal level if circumstances had been different.

Like many of the heroes of the revolution, the king was a man of the Enlightenment, a lover of music, architecture and art. He played the piano and violin, drew architectural designs, and collected artwork by Poussin and Raphael. He was also a collector of books with a personal library that was one of the finest in the world, and took great interest in astronomy. Following a meeting between the king and a poet and playwright named Samuel Johnson, who had just taken a guided tour of King George's library, Johnson remarked, "They may talk of the King as they will, but he is the finest gentleman I have ever seen." In short, King George had much in common with men such as Benjamin Franklin, Thomas Jefferson and Samuel Adams, and was far from the unhinged tyrant that he has been portrayed as. The "madness" of King George that he would long be remembered for, in fact, was probably caused by a hereditary disease called porphyria rather than mental illness.[46]

Although the king may have misjudged the situation during the early stages of the crisis and certainly made some questionable decisions that tended to escalate the conflict—and probably could have deescalated the situation by graciously accepting the Olive Branch Petition in 1775—some of the offenses he was blamed for were clearly exaggerated if not completely fabricated. In an early version of the Declaration of Independence, for instance, Jefferson included a 168-word passage that eloquently (if bizarrely) denounced slavery as one of the Crown's many transgressions against the colonies. Effectively blaming King George III for personally initiating and maintaining the transatlantic slave trade, Jefferson argued that the monarch had "waged cruel war against human nature itself." By "captivating & carrying [Africans] into slavery in another hemisphere or to incur miserable death in their transportation thither," Jefferson wrote, the king was guilty of "violating its most sacred rights of life & liberty in the persons of a distant people who never offended him." Slavery, Jefferson continued, was used as a weapon of "warfare of the Christian King of Great Britain" who was "determined to keep open a market where MEN should be bought & sold." In this way, King George "has prostituted his negative for suppressing every legislative attempt to prohibit or to restrain this execrable commerce: and that this assemblage of horrors might want no fact of distinguished die."[47]

The anti-slavery passage was removed and replaced with the more concise and innocuous "he has excited domestic insurrections amongst us," which was primarily a reference to Lord Dunmore's Proclamation that slaves who escaped masters to join the fight against the rebels would be granted their freedom. Jefferson's original language was dropped during the drafting and editing process sometime between July 1 and 3, 1776, out of an apparent desire to prevent unnecessary divisions over the contentious issue of slavery when what was needed at the time was unity. It's possible, also, that there was some recognition among the delegates that even within the context of a revolution largely characterized by double standards on concepts of liberty, adopting a document that denounced slavery while so many of the founders were slaveholders themselves may have been just a bridge too far.

As generally learned men, the signers of the Declaration may have found it somewhat ahistorical to blame King George for the transatlantic slave trade when everyone knew that the practice of shipping abducted Africans across the Atlantic predated the king's birth by more than a century—introduced by the British to Virginia way back in 1619. It also appears that far from being its initiator, King George was an opponent of slavery. In the late 1750s, while he was a teenager, George actually wrote an essay denouncing slavery and criticizing racism in general, arguing pointedly that the "pretexts used … for enslaving the New World were extremely curious." Identifying the motives for colonialism as "the propagation of the Christian religion" and justified on the basis that the indigenous peoples differed "in colour, manners and customs," a young Prince George observed that these justifications were "too absurd to take the trouble of refuting."[48] When it comes to enslaving Africans, he wrote that "the very reasons urged for it will be perhaps sufficient to make us hold such practice in execration." Unlike Jefferson, however, who wrote flowery denunciations of slavery while personally participating in it, George practiced what he preached. As his biographer Andrew Roberts pointed out in a 2021 interview, the American Founding Fathers "can't consider themselves to be morally superior to King George III, because George III never bought or sold a slave in his life."[49]

The same could not be said of Thomas Jefferson and George Washington, of course, who owned hundreds of slaves and had some questionable practices in how they treated them, having young boys whipped,[50] for instance, or extracting teeth for dentures.[51] While apologists would insist that these actions must be understood in the context of the time, it seems that less understanding is granted to common criminals like Henry Tufts. If the offenses committed by Founding Fathers are excused, however, shouldn't the same latitude be given to those who eked a living by stealing horses?

The difference that some might draw in this argument is that for all of their shortcomings, the Founding Fathers had considerable redeeming value while criminals like Henry Tufts had none. What redeems the founders' legacy and overshadows their shortcomings, ultimately, is that they changed the course of human history by challenging absolute monarchy and advancing democratic governance. They were astute political thinkers, innovators, and leaders, as well as farmers, inventors, and statesmen. Henry Tufts was none of these things, but what he was, certainly, was a rebel and a survivor. He may not have shared the greater sense of purpose of some of his contemporaries, but the way he lived his life may have been the best option that he saw for himself in a world full of hardship and challenge.

But regardless of what one might think of Henry Tufts, or for that matter, America's Founding Fathers or King George III, it is prudent, as a matter of historical inquiry, to maintain something of a dispassionate detachment from the subject. Just as dismissing historical figures as unworthy of attention due to their moral transgressions might limit perceptions of the past, placing them on pedestals is also a sure way to cloud understanding. Condemning historical figures as villains, at the end of the day, is as problematic as celebrating them as heroes.

15

Coming to Terms with the Revolution

It wasn't long after the American Revolution that many of its biggest proponents began expressing doubts about the democratic experiment that they had just launched. Alienation, disillusionment, and indeed pessimism ran rampant among the Founding Fathers, with Alexander Hamilton speaking for many when he wrote that "every day proves to me more and more that this American world was not made for me."[1] Hamilton, sadly, would pay the ultimate price for the growing divides in the post-revolutionary period, when his political and personal differences with Aaron Burr led to a duel that mortally wounded the nation's first Treasury Secretary.

While the Hamilton-Burr feud was perhaps somewhat exceptional for its intensity, it was representative of a general malaise that had fallen over the country's political class in the early 19th century. Divided by factionalism and ideological disputes, the elites seemed to agree on only one thing: the revolution's principles were being betrayed by incompetent and unprincipled men of the rival faction. The celebrations at the end of the war were replaced with recriminations, with Thomas Jefferson, for example, blaming New England federalists for most of the problems facing the new republic. In earlier years, Jefferson had expressed great faith in the people to meet any challenge, but a few decades after he wrote the Declaration of Independence, he began to doubt whether ordinary people were capable of being entrusted with the republic's future.[2]

Samuel Adams shared this sense of despair. Years after the revolution, he would regret that the spirit of patriotism that gave rise to the rebellion seemed to be waning and that too many Americans were distracted by the pursuit of wealth and the frivolities of entertainment rather than focusing on securing and advancing the cause of liberty. Adams saw threats to the new American republic everywhere, exhibited by a "Decay of publick Spirit" that was "more threatning to the Liberties of a Common Wealth than Hosts of foreign Enemies," as well as "the Want of publick Virtue," which "withhold[s] their Smiles from the wise and good as to bestow them on the wicked & unfaithful."[3] Alarmed by what appeared to him as a decline in morality, following the revolution, Adams took a firm stand against allowing women into gambling parlors and bringing theater to Boston, which he believed could open the door to a European-style court society setting root in America.

His opposition to lifting the theater ban, which had been in place in Boston since 1750, isolated him from the rising tide of public opinion, and when he took the floor at a town meeting at Faneuil Hall to denounce the theater as a "receptacle of the lewd and lazy," he was shouted down by his fellow citizens. "Some of the advocates for [the theater], did take advantage of their number to silence and bear down their opponents. Among those, thus silenced and borne down, was Mr. Samuel Adams," reported a stunned Abraham Bishop in the Democratic-Republican newspaper *Argus*. "Samuel Adams rose to speak in the midst of his fellow-citizens, and was silenced!"[4]

Clearly, times had changed since Adams rallied the patriots to dump tea in the Boston Harbor, and it seemed that in his old age he had grown out of touch with the "young men of the Revolution" who believed that by embracing drama and the arts they were "pushing back the boundaries of darkness," and continuing the implementation of Enlightenment values.[5] To the contrary, Adams considered the theater a "school of vice" that would encourage people to "forget their political duties." In the midst of the controversy in 1785, Samuel wrote to his cousin John that "too many of the Citizens thro' the Commonwealth ... are imitating the Britons in every idle Amusement & expensive Foppery which it is in their Power to invent for the Destruction of a young Country." He worried whether "our People expect to indulge themselves in the unbounded Use of every unmeaning & fantastick Extravagance because they would follow the Lead of Europeans, & not spend all their Money?" He rejected the growing materialism in American society, expressing dismay in particular over "the Equipage, the Furniture & expensive Living of too many, the Pride & Vanity of Dress which pervades thro every Class, confounding every Distinction between the Poor & the Rich and evincing the Want both of Example & Economy."[6]

John Adams, for his part, also worried about the direction of the nation, and especially fretted about the making of a new hereditary elite in the United States. But while troubled by some trends that he saw developing in the new republic, John, it seems, was a bit more sanguine and pragmatic than Samuel, writing that "promoting Education in Knowledge Virtue and Benevolence ... will confirm mankind in the opinion of the necessity of preserving and Strengthening the Dykes against the

Ocean, its Tides and Storms." That is to say, he believed that the "ocean" of vice should be contained but seemed to appreciate that it was foolish to think that it would ever be conquered. Human nature could never be fully tamed, in other words, and therefore the Puritan vision of a city on a hill, or Samuel Adams's hope for a Christian Sparta, were not realistic. "Human Appetites, Passions, Prejudices and self Love," John Adams wrote, "will never be conquered by Benevolence and Knowledge, alone introduced by human means."[7]

John Adams may have been more in touch with the real world and accepting of its shortcomings, but he, like Samuel, was also not fully satisfied with the republic that had been launched by their revolution, nor was he confident that the story of the revolution would ever be told properly. Stressing the importance of historical accuracy, he counselled artist John Trumbull as he painted the famous depiction of the moment that the Second Continental Congress's drafting committee—composed of John Adams, Roger Sherman, Robert Livingston, Thomas Jefferson, and Benjamin Franklin—submitted Jefferson's text for consideration. "Let not our Posterity be deluded by fictions under pretence of poetical or graphical Licenses," Adams wrote to Trumbull. He advised in general against placing too much emphasis on moments such as the signing of the Declaration of Independence, imploring Trumbull not to forget about other key events such as the day in March 1770, following the Boston Massacre, that Samuel Adams successfully led a crowd of thousands to demand the removal of British troops from Boston. "Who will paint Samuel Adams at the head of ten thousand Freemen and Volunteers," John Adams asked Trumbull, "with his quivering paralytic hands in the Counsel Chamber shaking the souls of Hutchinson and Dalrymple and driving down to the Castle the two offending Regiments, which Lord North ever afterwards called 'Sam. Adamses two Regiments'?"[8]

John Adams also appealed directly to his cousin to ensure that his place in history was preserved. In particular, John urged Samuel to collect and publish his four decades' worth of writing, so as not to cede the privilege of defining the legacy of the American Revolution to others.[9] While Samuel remained largely ambivalent about this, resigning himself to the belief that only God could judge him and the larger morality of the revolution that he helped launch, John remained persistently troubled in his twilight years about how this history would be told in the future. In an 1815 letter to Thomas Jefferson he asked, "Who shall write the history of the American revolution? Who can write it? Who will ever be able to write it?"[10] Jefferson, incidentally, didn't think that anyone would be able to write it properly, answering Adams's question with a simple response that "nobody" could tell the story of the American Revolution, "except merely it's external facts."[11]

In fact, as we now know, Adams and Jefferson were wrong. While some of the details of the debates in the Continental Congress may have been lost to history, there was still plenty of material to work with, and throughout the ages the story would be told and retold and retold again. Indeed, with the possible exception of the Civil War, there is no event in American history that has been studied and written about more than the American Revolution. Over the years, it has been examined from every possible angle, from every analytical framework, through the lens of every ideology conceivable. Historians have quibbled over details and debated issues such as the role of class and slavery but have nonetheless widely celebrated the selflessness, zeal and courage of the Founding Fathers and the citizen soldiers of the Continental Army. Both conservatives and liberals have embraced principles of the revolution, with those on the right stressing the founders' wisdom in establishing limited government, and progressives finding inspiration in their ideals that advanced the cause of human rights and equality.

Some revisionists and radical historians, on the other hand, have tended to emphasize the Founding Fathers' hypocrisy and questioned their true commitment to the values that they professed.

* * *

More critical analyses have described the reactionary nature of the revolution, with populist historian Howard Zinn writing in *A People's History of the United States* that its primary significance was that it established a useful narrative to "hold back a number of potential rebellions and create a consensus of popular support for the rule of a new, privileged leadership." By "creating a nation, a symbol, a legal unity called the United States, they could take over land, profits, and political power from favorites of the British Empire."[12]

Many progressives have been influenced by the Marxist analysis of the revolution, with Karl Marx writing in *Capital* that the American Revolution "sounded the tocsin for the European middle class,"[13] meaning that it served as a rallying cry to the bourgeoisie and provided inspiration for subsequent democratic revolutions, including the French Revolution that began in 1789. Through his prism of understanding history as a series of class struggles that would someday result in a classless, stateless utopia, Marx saw the Revolutionary War as a bourgeois movement rather than a revolt of the proletariat, and subsequent generations of scholars would come to question whether it could properly be called a revolution at all.[14] Since it did not result in a fundamental altering of class relationships or overhaul of economic power structures, it did not fit neatly into Marx's dialectical materialist concept of history.

15. Coming to Terms with the Revolution

In 1891, Friedrich Engels, co-author with Marx of the *Communist Manifesto*, observed that the ultimate result of the American Revolution was a system in which "politicians" would form a more separate, powerful section of the nation. "It is precisely in America that we see best how there takes place this process of the state power making itself independent in relation to society, whose mere instrument it was originally intended to be," he wrote. In the United States, "there exists no dynasty, no nobility, no standing army, beyond the few men keeping watch on the Indians." Despite this lack of a dynasty or nobility, the system came to be dominated by "two great gangs of political speculators," i.e., Democrats and Republicans, "who alternately take possession of the state power and exploit it by the most corrupt means and for the most corrupt ends—and the nation is powerless against these two great cartels of politicians, who are ostensibly its servants, but in reality exploit and plunder it."[15]

Samuel Adams died nine decades before Engels wrote this harsh assessment of the revolution's ultimate results, so it is purely a matter a speculation whether he would have agreed with it, but considering the pessimism he was expressing late in life and his unbending commitment to morality in government, there is a good chance he would have shared at least some of Engels's criticism. Although he affiliated himself with Jefferson's Democratic-Republicans, Adams had little patience for the factionalism that was dividing the political class into what would become America's two permanent parties, and more than anything, Adams dreaded disunity. "Neither religion nor liberty can long subsist in the tumult of altercation," he wrote to Thomas Paine in 1802, "and amidst the noise and violence of faction."[16] He also detested political corruption and would have been aghast at the rising tendency of politicians to enrich themselves by profiting off of public office.

Upon his death on October 2, 1803, minister Thomas Thacher gave a eulogy that aptly summarized Adams's anti-materialist worldview:

> God forbid! we sink in luxury and licentiousness; if our hearts are cankered with avarice, and we become dead to every noble and generous principle; if the torch of civil discord is blown up, and is permitted to blaze with increasing fury; if unbridled faction and unprincipled ambition are elevated to dominion, while true patriotism and genuine worth are thrown into obscurity, then we expect a total eclipse of our past and present glory.[17]

As a staunch opponent of luxury and licentiousness, which he closely associated with vice and corruption, Adams emphasized instead the power of virtue, and he had high expectations of the people to live up to the ideals of patriotism and liberty that so many in the revolution fought and died for. But unfortunately for him, and for the nation in general, not all Americans shared that zeal and commitment, and this, ultimately, is what may have undone the utopian vision of a Christian Sparta. The "uncommonly misspent life" of Henry Tufts—as well as his many likeminded associates and love interests—reminds us of the probable inevitability of this outcome.

* * *

Like so many of the revolutionary generation, Tufts seemed to understand that his lot in life would not be greatly affected by either an American victory or a British victory, so he—as did many Native American tribes—played both sides to his advantage. But while Tufts may have been

This work by Samuel Jennings is the first known American painting to address the issue of slavery and its abolition. Produced in the early 1790s, the painting features a Liberty figure surrounded by symbols of the Enlightenment, with a group of emancipated slaves at her feet. Outside, black people dance around a Liberty Pole. The painting underlines the fact that although the American Revolution did not abolish chattel slavery, it did bring to the forefront the incongruities of human bondage in a democratic republic (*Study for Liberty Displaying the Arts and Sciences, or the Genius of America Encouraging the Emancipation of the Blacks*, by Samuel Jennings, ca. 1791–92. Metropolitan Museum of Art, Karen Buchwald Wright Gift).

more forthright than most about his lack of ethical convictions, many others who were involved in the revolution also exhibited a propensity to self-aggrandizement, which, in some cases, may indeed have been their primary motivation.

To people like Benedict Arnold and other opportunists in the officer class, there was a clear desire to leverage the revolution as a means of career and class advancement, but even to the more seemingly idealistic of the founders, there was a combination of factors that spurred them to revolutionary action. Land acquisition and mercantilism were among the motivations of some Founding Fathers such as George Washington and John Hancock, and while their commitment to the cause of liberty may have been sincerely held, it was not the only factor in their thinking. The role that class played in this struggle was complex and nuanced, with aims of the revolution limited primarily to political and not economic change. "We did not declare our independence of George III in order to reform the land laws, change the criminal codes, spread popular education, or separate church and state," Richard B. Morris wrote in *The William and Mary Quarterly* in 1962. "We broke with England to achieve political independence, freedom from external controls, emancipation, if you will, of the bourgeoisie from mercantilist restraints."[18]

And then, of course, there is the issue of slavery, which some modern-day historical revisionists insist was the overriding concern of the founders—not to abolish slavery, they claim, but to maintain it. The view that the American Revolution was fought primarily to preserve and defend the institution of slavery from threats posed to it by the British has grown more prominent in recent years. It served as the central theme of a 2014 book by University of Houston historian Gerald Horne titled *The Counter-Revolution of 1776: Slave Resistance and the Origins of the United States of America* and was further popularized by the *New York Times*' 1619 Project, launched in August 2019 with the goal of "refram[ing] the country's history by placing the consequences of slavery and the contributions of Black Americans at the very center of the United States' national narrative."[19] In the introductory essay to the 1619 Project, Nikole Hannah-Jones asserted that "one of the primary reasons the colonists decided to declare their independence from Britain was because they wanted to protect the institution of slavery," leading to a torrent of criticism. Many historians from across the political spectrum have pointed out that the bold claims made by Gerald Horne and Nikole Hannah-Jones are simply not backed up by the facts and the explanations that they offer for the causes of the American Revolution are simplistic at best.

While it is obvious that the revolution did not end chattel slavery, it did set a course for its eventual abolition, with the First Continental

Congress pledging in October 1774 to refrain from participation in the African slave trade,[20] and northern states completely prohibiting human bondage after the revolution. More generally, the principles championed by the revolutionaries contributed to the intellectual environment for advancing the abolitionist cause, and with some explicitly denouncing slavery—including Thomas Jefferson in the first draft of the Declaration of Independence—the social and political environment enabling the Peculiar Institution was consistently undermined.

But of course, this doesn't mean that the motivations of the patriots who launched the revolution were not somewhat contradictory and sometimes hypocritical. It is clear from the paucity of statements that they made about slavery—at least in comparison to the diatribes issued against issues such as unfair taxes and British encroachments on the "natural rights" of colonists—that this was not their primary concern.

The reality is that slavery in general was not considered an important enough issue to merit the sustained attention of revolutionary leaders. They often likened British taxes to enslavement, but when it came to actual slavery, as in the state of bondage that blacks were subjected to in the colonies, they were far less concerned. The most common complaint against the British in this regard was not that they would end slavery in the colonies, but that they were inciting violence against slave-owners. Samuel Adams made this point in a speech celebrating the Declaration of Independence in 1776, reiterating one of the grievances that had been included in the document, namely that the British had inspired slave revolts in the colonies. "The men who now invite you to surrender your rights into their hands, are the men who ... have taught treachery to your slaves, and courted them to assassinate your wives and children," Adams said.[21] This, of course, was not a defense of slavery, just a criticism of the Brits instigating slave insurrections.

But Adams also avoided placing an inordinate amount of emphasis on this issue and urged fellow rebels to remember what really mattered the most, which he saw as liberty. In the same speech, he spoke hyperbolically about unfair taxation and restrictions on political rights and freedoms, drawing an analogy between London and a father who "would claim authority to make your child a slave because you had nourished him in his infancy" (a point that Henry Tufts, with his experience working for his father but then denied compensation, might have related to). "If ye love wealth better than liberty, the tranquility of servitude than the animating contest of freedom,—go from us in peace," Adams stated. "Crouch down and lick the hands which feed you. May your chains sit lightly upon you, and may posterity forget that ye were our countrymen!"[22]

15. Coming to Terms with the Revolution

* * *

While Adams's uncompromising approach to republican ideals may have been a necessary component of ensuring the revolution's success, it can also serve as a warning against ideology and fanaticism overtaking reason and prudence. His uncompromising stand against injustice, while perhaps needed to rally Americans in the cause of independence, led directly to a war that cost between 25,000 to 50,000 lives, which adjusting for population rates would be the equivalent of at least 2.5 million dying in a civil war today. Whether or not one considers this a price worth paying for independence and liberty, it should also serve as a reminder that being overly eager to take up arms can have dire, unforeseen consequences, and can sometimes set the stage for more violence to come. There is some irony in the fact that both the Revolutionary War and the following bloody rebellion led by Daniel Shays were direct results of previous wars. In the case of the revolution, what precipitated the crisis was the Crown's raising of taxes to pay for the costly French and Indian War of the 1750s and early '60s. Then, in order to pay debts incurred in the struggle against the British, the founders of the new American republic determined that it was necessary to impose harsh taxes, which led to more violence. With even this cursory understanding of early American history, it becomes clear that war has inherent difficulties, leads to a cycle of debt and instability, and produces unpredictable (or, perhaps, inevitable?) results.

It should also be appreciated that the war that Samuel Adams helped precipitate through his tireless advocacy for liberty would, funnily enough, pose a direct threat to that same liberty. In the mid-1770s, colonial society saw the rapid shutting down of nuanced debate and free speech, with loyalists and patriots hardening their positions, and those who wished to remain neutral forced to choose sides, often through violent coercion. Families were torn apart, communities divided, and the use of torture normalized. Whether or not he approved of such tactics as tarring and feathering, it is clear that Adams helped usher in the somewhat fanatical devotion to liberty that made such abuses permissible.

Many of those who lived through this period came to intimately appreciate the threat to liberty that war represented, which is one reason that the power to declare war was placed in the deliberative bodies of Congress rather than in the Executive Branch. As Founding Father James Madison explained in 1795, "Of all the enemies to public liberty, war is, perhaps, the most to be dreaded, because it comprises and develops the germ of every other." Not only does war spawn "debts and taxes," which he called "the known instruments for bringing the many under the domination of the few," but also it creates "the means of seducing the minds … of the people." War, he said, leads to "the inequality of fortunes, and the opportunities of fraud, growing out of a state of war, and in the degeneracy of manners and of morals, engendered by both." He also worried about the effects of maintaining a standing army and how war empowers the executive at the expense of other branches of government. "No nation could preserve its freedom in the midst of continual warfare," he concluded.[23]

Adams might take issue with the suggestion that there was anything untoward about the violence unleashed in the revolution, and would recall that what Americans fought for was a just cause. "The Romans fought for Empire," Adams wrote in 1782, drawing distinctions between imperial ambitions and the righteous American cause. "The Pride of that haughty People was to domineer over the rest of Mankind. But this is not our Object. We contend for the Liberty of our Country and the Rights of human Nature."[24] Henry Tufts, for what it's worth, shared this rosier view of the revolutionary period, writing in his memoirs that it was an "auspicious aera, which gave freedom to the western world."[25]

Although the Revolutionary War may have had altruistic goals, it was largely thanks to the righteous mission of the founders and the Puritans before them to establish a "city upon a hill," i.e., a virtuous democracy that would serve as a model to the world, that a rather messianic mission would take hold to bring the blessings of liberty to other peoples, sometimes at the barrel of a gun. The idealism of the founders, the convictions of individuals like Samuel Adams that the American cause was the cause of all mankind, and the certitude that comes with the belief that God is on the American side, led directly to expansionist policies throughout the 19th and 20th centuries—guided by ideologies such as Manifest Destiny and the White Man's Burden—and arguably continues to define U.S. foreign policy in the 21st. For all of the American revolutionaries' wonderful contributions to the world and the gratitude that is owed to that generation, it is hard to deny the direct line between the visionary republicanism that the patriots spearheaded and the imperialistic policies that modern neoconservatives and liberal interventionists continue to champion. This, in turn, requires constant attention to mythmaking and suppression of inconvenient realities.

* * *

Leo Strauss, a professor of political philosophy at the University of Chicago in the 1950s and '60s, influenced generations of U.S. political figures with his emphasis on the importance of fostering a national mythology to advance both liberal democracy and national security. His views were particularly attractive to the neoconservative movement that rose to prominence in the late 20th century but could be seen to play a role more broadly in providing practical solutions to complex contemporary problems, with an emphasis on developing an abstract legend of American history that would provide an intellectual basis for U.S. leadership on the global stage. Something of a cynic—or, as his supporters would call him, a realist—Strauss cited Machiavelli in arguing that every nation is founded on the brutal and illegal seizure of territory. Because all regimes are built on plunder, he argued, myths must be created to conceal this unpleasant and scandalous truth from the masses. "A self-respecting society," he wrote, "cannot become reconciled to the notion that its foundation was laid in crime."[26]

In the case of America, the notion that its foundation was laid in crime is a multilayered one, and is difficult to deny. Not only was land seizure from the Native Americans a motivating factor in the revolutionary cause, but crimes of various types played a central role in the revolution and the subsequent founding of the nation. Despite their high-minded rhetoric and ideals, the reality is that the radicals who kickstarted the Revolutionary War were committing numerous crimes through their acts of sedition and resistance to the British. From the smugglers who systematically avoided paying taxes to the sailors and ropemakers who punished informers by tarring and feathering them to the rioters who plundered the homes of customs officials to the minutemen who took up arms against the king's soldiers, the revolution was made possible by various forms of lawbreaking—some of it civil but much of it quite violent. This, of course, was acknowledged and justified by those who were involved, with political thinkers such as Samuel Adams providing the intellectual basis for breaking the law in the service of a higher good. In the context of the revolution, lawbreaking was necessary in order to achieve the goal of a democratic society based on liberty and justice—the ends justified the means, in other words.

The actions of Henry Tufts, of course, were more clearcut cases of lawbreaking, and condemning them is easy enough. The fact that he was a common criminal rather than a revolutionary means that he was the wrong kind of lawbreaker and, hence, did not help to advance the national narrative. If he had chosen to be a smuggler who defied the laws of Parliament and the king, rather than a common thief, he may have been held up as a hero, but because the victims of his crimes were fellow colonists, he was a villain.

The shame that Henry's story has elicited among some of his kinsmen is a reflection of the prejudices that Americans hold when it comes to issues pertaining to the founding of the American republic, and the impulse to protect the national consensus. While the notion of American exceptionalism has been questioned since the inception of the nation, a powerful rhetorical style in American historiography has simultaneously tried to shore up the national identity, and nowhere has this trend been stronger than in Henry Tufts's old stomping grounds of New England. As historian Deborah Madsen writes, "The great achievement of American Puritanism was the channeling of radical energies into the American national mythology."[27]

Today, the virtues of the revolution are so ingrained in our thinking that anyone with a Revolutionary War veteran in their family tree would proudly point this out in casual conversation, but those with a war deserter in our ancestry would only admit this with a certain degree of embarrassment—despite the fact that it may have been nearly as common for soldiers to desert than it was to actually fulfill their enlistments. Because Henry failed to perform his duties and declined to participate in the establishment of the nation's founding myth, he could find little redemption for the crimes that he committed.

Nevertheless, Henry humbly asked forgiveness in the concluding pages of his autobiography and openly acknowledged the pain he had caused through his life of crime—granting himself something of the redemption that his kinsmen might deny him. Although it does seem at times that he is more concerned with his own "sufferings," which had been endured over many years of life on the run, he eventually seemed to internalize the lesson that by committing crimes against his fellow man (and woman), he was condemning himself to a life of pain. "The wages of sin is death," he wrote, while "the wages of a vicious, dissolute life is punishment." Even if one manages to escape the retribution administered by the state, "punishment ... is still our certain doom, by the invisible hand of inexorable justice," he observed. He thus warned the "rising generation ... to avoid those quicksands of vice, on which I have been so often wrecked," explaining that his "iniquities have been regularly visited with pain, poverty and stripes." To achieve happiness, Tufts concluded, our actions "must be good; the contrary of which my own life most abundantly demonstrates."[28]

*   *   *

How, then, should these lessons be applied more broadly to the United States of America? If the wages of crime is punishment, then what would a nation founded in crime expect to reap? And if Henry Tufts continues to be condemned, could many of our founders expect to be perpetually held in judgment for their actions as slave-owners who routinely broke up families, denied human beings their rights, and physically abused children?

Of course, while Henry has generally found little sympathy, the Founding Fathers often get a pass and their ethical breaches are brushed aside or excused. In some cases, concepts such as universal morality are questioned as unrealistic in a complicated world, a relativist approach that is somewhat selectively applied. While ideally, virtues such as honesty and

15. Coming to Terms with the Revolution

integrity should apply equally across historical epochs, the reality is that these questions are often relative, subjective, and situational.

The parallel lives of Henry Tufts and Samuel Adams, linked forever by the act of mercy that gave Tufts a second chance, bring to the fore these contradictions and, in this way, illuminate the politics of inclusion and exclusion in the emerging democratic republic. While the patriotic sentiment typified by the American Revolution and the spirit of liberty manifested in the Declaration of Independence was certainly real, the story of Henry Tufts reminds us that not all Americans shared the sense of purpose, idealism and patriotic fervor that is often associated with the Revolutionary War era. Although many New Englanders demonstrated uncommon courage and fortitude in skirmishes such as the Battle of Bunker Hill, where an ill-equipped rabble had bravely fought the finest troops in the world, there were also plenty of people who couldn't be bothered with the cause.

In this lithograph produced in 1876, an elderly man points to a musket on the wall and tells a young boy, possibly his grandson, about his experience in the American Revolution. Initially an oral history with firsthand accounts passed along by participants, the story of the revolution became forged over time as something of a national mythology (created ca. 1876. Medium: lithograph. Library of Congress Prints and Photographs Division).

Nevertheless, it is the bravery of American patriots that has been remembered over the centuries and universally celebrated. Even at the time, some British leaders marveled at their sense of purpose and viewed the courage of the patriots as a sign of the righteousness of the American cause. In Parliament, George Johnstone gave a speech in 1775 that hailed the Battle of Bunker Hill as something of a watershed moment for humanity. "To see an irregular peasantry," an amazed Johnstone said, "opposed by every circumstance of cannon and bombs that could terrify minds, calmly waiting the attack ... who can reflect on such scenes, and not adore the Constitution of Government which could breed such men! Who is there that can dismiss all doubts on the justice of a cause which can inspire such conscious rectitude?"[29] This rectitude has continued to inspire revolutionary leaders throughout the ages. Even Vladimir Lenin, the Marxist political theorist who led the Russian Revolution in 1917, stood in awe of the bravery demonstrated in the American Revolution and praised the American people for giving the world "an example of a revolutionary war against feudal enslavement."[30]

But the story of Henry Tufts reminds us that the valor so widely celebrated was far from universal during the revolution and that to achieve independence, opportunism was also required. It highlights the social divisions that allowed certain colonists to consider the rights of man while others struggled to make a living and simply did not have the luxury to philosophize about liberty. While some saw independence as vital, others might have considered their interests better served by supporting the British, while some didn't care either way.

Henry Tufts's story recalls that the revolution was forged not only by the oratory of Patrick Henry or the organizing skills of Samuel Adams or the leadership of George Washington or the political acumen of John Adams or the writing abilities of Thomas Jefferson, but also by the sacrifices of those at the bottom dregs of society. The revolution was fought by patriots, yes, but also by reprobates. Therefore, as Americans reflect every Fourth of July on the virtuous nature of the revolution, with its high-minded commitment to liberty, it is worth considering the role that vice played in this struggle, as well as its continued influence on shaping the American political system. Whether it was the vice of greed compelling colonists to continue their pursuit of westward expansion in violation of the Royal Proclamation of 1763, or the vice of alcohol consumption prompting the rejection of the anti-smuggling measure known as the Sugar Act, it should be appreciated that iniquity—not just fortitude—played a significant role in America's founding.

The duality of virtue and vice is perfectly embodied by the figures of Samuel Adams and Henry Tufts, and while we may never know for certain why Adams took mercy on Tufts by granting the reprieve that spared his life, perhaps there was a recognition on some level of the value that even an incorrigible criminal can play in building the republic, and the enduring possibility for redemption.

As Adams explained to his wife in 1779, he deplored vices such as greed and detested those who sought only self-aggrandizement, but understood that such individuals have always existed and always will. The important thing for the republic is for virtuous people to stand in opposition to such figures and champion morality and honesty. "I do not think my Countrymen are ungrateful," Adams wrote, "but I am afraid there is a Faction among them, consisting of a few Men, who are under the Dominion of those Passions which have been the Bane of Society in all Ages—Ambition and Avarice." He also railed against "those who aimd at grasping Wealth and Power," underlining that he "wish[es] their Number may not increase." Adams, however, understood that "they ever will [exist] in this World of Vanity," which is why America, "when she was wise, was jealous of such Designs."[31]

Left unsaid by Adams is the fact that were it not for men of ambition and avarice who grasped for wealth and power, the revolution that he spearheaded might never have come to fruition. From the elite landowners and speculators to the lowly yeoman farmers and landless poor, from people like Henry Tufts who were apathetic about the cause and only joined the army for a payday to those in the officer class who only signed up to advance their careers, there is ample reason to believe that patriotic zeal was not always the primary incentive for the revolution.

While many of the elite set their sights on taking lands belonging to Native Americans, Henry's motivations for briefly joining the revolutionary cause were far simpler: to receive bounty and accoutrements. More fundamentally, though, what Henry sought was to live a happy life free of "vexing strife." It took him longer than most people to realize the path to this happiness, but towards the end of his "uncommonly misspent life," he seemed to finally get it. "The primary source of peace to the human mind is the consciousness of having travelled in the paths of uprightness," Henry wrote in the final pages of his book, "that, in proportion as a man's life is well or ill spent, his real happiness or misery may be calculated."

Whether he was ever redeemed in the eyes of his contemporaries, or welcomed by his kinsmen, seemed to be of little concern to Henry. He found contentment in putting his life of crime behind him and living his remaining days virtuously and righteously. "Still was I happy," he wrote in one of his poems, "still fair liberty and love inspir'd extatic bliss and glee."[32]

America, as a nation founded in both idealism and crime, in virtue and in vice, would do well to pause for a moment and ponder this vagabond's parting thoughts.

Chapter Notes

Preface

1. Tufts, Henry. *A Narrative of the Life, Adventures, Travels and Sufferings of Henry Tufts, Now Residing at Lemington, in the District of Maine In substance, as compiled from his own mouth.* Samuel Bragg, 1807, p. 117.
2. Stoll, Ira. *Samuel Adams: A Life.* Free Press, 2009, p. 262.
3. Alexander, John K. *Samuel Adams: America's Revolutionary Politician.* Rowman & Littlefield, 2004, p. 222.

Introduction

1. "Henry Tufts Wrote First American Criminal Autobiography." SeacoastNH.com. https://www.seacoastnh.com/henry-tufts-wrote-first-american-criminal-autobiography/. Accessed October 15, 2022.
2. Tufts, Thomas. "Henry Tufts; black sheep of an otherwise respectable family." *Tufts Genealogy*, October 25, 2012. https://tuftsgenealogy.blogspot.com/2012/10/henry-tufts-blacksheep-of-otherwise.html. Accessed October 15, 2022.
3. Tufts, Jay Franklin. *Tufts Family History: A True Account and History of Our Tufts Families, From and Before 1638–1963.* J.F. Tufts, 1963, p. 150.
4. Tufts, Thomas. "Henry Tufts; black sheep of an otherwise respectable family." *Tufts Genealogy*, October 25, 2012. https://tuftsgenealogy.blogspot.com/2012/10/henry-tufts-blacksheep-of-otherwise.html. Accessed October 15, 2022.
5. "Weymouth celebrates groundbreaking for New Tufts Library." Town of Weymouth, March 27, 2019. https://www.weymouth.ma.us/library-construction-committee/news/weymouth-celebrates-groundbreaking-for-new-tufts-library. Accessed August 4, 2022.
6. Tufts, Thomas W. "Tufts Soldiers to remember on Memorial Day." *Tufts Family Genealogy*, May 25, 2014. https://tuftsgenealogy.blogspot.com/2014/05/tufts-soldiers-to-remember-on-memorial.html.
7. Dewey, John, and Tufts, James Hayden. *Ethics.* Henry Holt and Company, 1908, p. 10.
8. Feffer, Andrew. *The Chicago Pragmatists and American Progressivism.* Cornell University Press, 1993, p. 232.
9. Tufts, Thomas. "Henry Tufts; black sheep of an otherwise respectable family." *Tufts Genealogy*, October 25, 2012. https://tuftsgenealogy.blogspot.com/2012/10/henry-tufts-blacksheep-of-otherwise.html. Accessed October 15, 2022.
10. Higginson, Thomas Wentworth. *Travelers and Outlaws*: Episodes in American History. Lee and Shepard Publishers, 1889, p. 89.
11. Allie, Daniel. "The Second Complete Edition: The How and Why of It." *The Online Henry Tufts Resource*, March 18, 2017. https://henrytufts.wordpress.com/2017/03/18/how-and-why/. Accessed October 15, 2022.
12. *Ibid.*
13. Keating, Neal. Foreword to *The Autobiography of a Criminal.* Breakout Productions, 1993.
14. Fischer, David Hackett. *Paul Revere's Ride.* Oxford University Press, 1995, pp. 124–125.
15. Tufts, Thomas W. "Zachariah Tufts Revolutionary soldier in Morgan's

sharpshooters." *Tufts Family Genealogy*, January 11, 2014. https://tuftsgenealogy.blogspot.com/2014/01/zachariah-tufts-revolutionary-soldier.html. Accessed March 15, 2023.

16. Tufts, Thomas W. "All the Tufts Revolutionary soldiers Frederick to James Tufts." *Tufts Family Genealogy*, March 14, 2014. https://tuftsgenealogy.blogspot.com/2014/01/zachariah-tufts-revolutionary-soldier.html. Accessed March 15, 2023.

17. McCullough, David. *John Adams*. Simon & Schuster, 2001, p. 66.

18. "Adams Family Papers." Massachusetts Historical Society. https://www.masshist.org/adams/adams-family-papers. Accessed September 27, 2022.

19. Maier, Pauline. "Coming to Terms with Samuel Adams." *The American Historical Review*, vol. 81, no. 1, Feb. 1976, p. 12.

20. *Ibid.*, p. 14.

21. *Ibid.*

22. Rakove, Jack. *Revolutionaries: A New History of the Invention of America*. Houghton Mifflin Harcourt, 2010, p. 38.

23. Schiff, Stacy. *The Revolutionary: Samuel Adams*. Little, Brown, 2022, p. 277.

24. Maier, Pauline. "Coming to Terms with Samuel Adams." *The American Historical Review*, vol. 81, no. 1, Feb. 1976, pp. 12–37.

25. "From John Adams to William Tudor, Sr., 5 June 1813." *Founders Online, National Archives*. https://founders.archives.gov/documents/Adams/99-02-02-6054. Accessed August 13, 2023.

26. Maier, Pauline. "Coming to Terms with Samuel Adams." *The American Historical Review*, vol. 81, no. 1, Feb. 1976, p. 14.

27. *Ibid.*

28. Warren, Mercy Otis. *History of the Rise, Progress, and Termination of the American Revolution interspersed with Biographical, Political and Moral Observations—Volume 1*. Liberty Fund, 1805, p. 211.

29. Stoll, Ira. *Samuel Adams: A Life*. Free Press, 2009, p. 261.

30. Raphael, Ray. *Founding Myths: Stories That Hide Our Patriotic Past*. The New Press, 2014, p. 27.

31. Schiff, Stacy. *The Revolutionary: Samuel Adams*. Little, Brown, 2022, p. 323.

32. Stoll, Ira. *Samuel Adams: A Life*. Free Press, 2009, p. 261.

33. Wells, William V. *The Life and Public Services of Samuel Adams*. Little, Brown, 1865, p. 410.

34. Allison, Robert J. *The Boston Tea Party*. Commonwealth Editions, 2007, p. 14.

35. Stoll, Ira. *Samuel Adams: A Life*. Free Press, 2009, p. 263.

36. Scee, Trudy Irene. *Rogues, Rascals, and Other Villainous Mainers*. Down East Books, 2014, p. 11.

37. "The Many Loves of Henry Tufts: Original Colonial Badboy." New England Historical Society. https://newenglandhistoricalsociety.com/henry-tufts-original-colonial-badboy/. February 13, 2023.

38. Pierce, Bessie L. *Public Opinion and the Teaching of History in the United States*. Alfred A. Knopf, 1926, pp. 329–330.

39. Loewen, James W. *Lies My Teacher Told Me: Everything Your American History Textbook Got Wrong*. Simon & Schuster, 1995, p. 18.

40. Fischer, David Hackett. *Paul Revere's Ride*. Oxford University Press, 1995, pp. 327–328.

41. Bailey, Thomas. *Essays Diplomatic and Undiplomatic of Thomas A. Bailey*. Appleton-Century-Crofts, 1969, p. 18.

Chapter 1

1. Reynolds, David. *America: Empire of Liberty*. Penguin, 2010, p. 31.

2. *Ibid.*, p. 32.

3. Tufts, Henry. *A Narrative of the Life, Adventures, Travels and Sufferings of Henry Tufts, Now Residing at Lemington, in the District of Maine In substance, as compiled from his own mouth*. Samuel Bragg, 1807, p. 9.

4. *Ibid.*, p. 10.

5. Corey, Deloraine P. *The History of Malden, Massachusetts, 1633–1785*. W.S. Hills, 1899, p. 331.

6. *Ibid.*, p. 120.

7. Schiff, Stacy. *The Revolutionary: Samuel Adams*. Little, Brown, 2022, p. 160.

8. Adams, Samuel. *The Writings of Samuel Adams—Volume 1*. Edited by Harry Alonzo Cushing. G.P. Putnam's Sons, 1904, p. 77.

Notes—Chapter 1

9. Maier, Pauline. *The Old Revolutionaries: Political Lives in the Age of Samuel Adams.* Knopf, 1980, p. 309.

10. Schiff, Stacy. *The Revolutionary: Samuel Adams.* Little, Brown, 2022, p. 34.

11. "To John Adams from Samuel Adams, 25 November 1790." *Founders Online, National Archives.* https://founders.archives.gov/documents/Adams/06-20-02-0257.

12. Letter from John Adams to Abigail Adams, 26 January 1794. Massachusetts Historical Society.

13. "1765. December. 23d. Monday." *Founders Online, National Archives.* https://founders.archives.gov/documents/Adams/01-01-02-0009-0005-0006. [Original source: *The Adams Papers, Diary and Autobiography of John Adams, vol. 1, 1755–1770.* Edited by L.H. Butterfield. Harvard University Press, 1961, pp. 270–273.]

14. Schiff, Stacy. *The Revolutionary: Samuel Adams.* Little, Brown, 2022, p. 30.

15. Newcomb, Alyssa. "Abigail Adams Lost Letter Shares Future First Lady's Views on U.S. Politics, Life Abroad." ABC News, June 15, 2011. https://abcnews.go.com/U.S./lost-abigail-adams-letter-donated-massachusetts-museum/story?id=13848810. Accessed August 8, 2022.

16. Tufts, Henry. *A Narrative of the Life, Adventures, Travels and Sufferings of Henry Tufts, Now Residing at Lemington, in the District of Maine In substance, as compiled from his own mouth.* Samuel Bragg, 1807, p. 20.

17. Shammas, Carole. "English Inheritance Law and Its Transfer to the Colonies." *American Journal of Legal History*, 1987.

18. *Ibid.*

19. Wood, Gordon S. *The Radicalism of the American Revolution.* Vintage, 1993, pp. 46–47.

20. Tufts, Henry. *A Narrative of the Life, Adventures, Travels and Sufferings of Henry Tufts, Now Residing at Lemington, in the District of Maine In substance, as compiled from his own mouth.* Samuel Bragg, 1807, p. 20.

21. *Ibid.*

22. Thompson, Mary. *Landmarks in Ancient Dover, New Hampshire.* Concord Republican Press Association, 1892, p. 257.

23. Tufts, Henry. *A Narrative of the Life, Adventures, Travels and Sufferings of Henry Tufts, Now Residing at Lemington, in the District of Maine In substance, as compiled from his own mouth.* Samuel Bragg, 1807, p. 21.

24. *Ibid.*, p. 22.

25. Cable, Mary. *The Little Darlings: A History of Child Rearing in America.* Scribner, 1975, p. viii.

26. Wood, Gordon S. *The Radicalism of the American Revolution.* Vintage, 1993, p. 147.

27. *Ibid.*

28. Diggins, John Patrick. *John Adams: The American Presidents Series: The 2nd President, 1797–1801.* Times Books, 2003, p. 140.

29. Langguth, A.J. *Patriots: The Men Who Started the American Revolution.* Simon & Schuster, 1989, p. 30.

30. *Ibid.*, p. 31.

31. Puls, Mark. *Samuel Adams: Father of the American Revolution.* Palgrave Macmillan, 2009, p. 26.

32. Wells, William V. *The Life and Public Services of Samuel Adams: Being a Narrative of his Acts and Opinions, and of His Agency in Producing and Forwarding the American Revolution. With Extracts From His Correspondence, State Papers, and Political Essays, Volume 2.* Little, Brown, 1865, p. 28.

33. Buckingham, Joseph T. *Specimens of newspaper literature: with personal memoirs, anecdotes, and reminiscences.* Redding and Co., 1852, p. 14.

34. Schiff, Stacy. *The Revolutionary: Samuel Adams.* Little, Brown, 2022, p. 65.

35. Adams, Samuel. To the Representatives of Boston, May 24, 1764. Adams, Samuel. *The Writings of Samuel Adams—Volume 1, 1764–1769.* Collected and edited by Harry Alonzo Cushing. G.P. Putnam, 1904, p. 3.

36. Wood, Gordon S. *The American Revolution: A History.* Modern Library, 2003, p. 8.

37. *Ibid.*, p. 9.

38. Smith, Richard Norton. *Patriarch: George Washington and the New American Nation.* Houghton Mifflin, 1993, p. 2.

39. "From George Washington to George Mercer, 7 November 1771." *Founders Online, National Archives.* https://founders.archives.gov/documents/Washington/02-8-02-0359. [Original

source: *The Papers of George Washington, Colonial Series*, Vol. 8, 24 June 1767–25 December 1771. Edited by W.W. Abbot and Dorothy Twohig. University Press of Virginia, 1993, pp. 541–545.]
   40. Adams, Samuel. *The Writings of Samuel Adams—Volume 1*. Collected and edited by Harry Alonzo Cushing. G.P. Putnam, 1904, p. 9.
   41. *Ibid.*, p. 10.
   42. Morgan, Edmund S. *The Birth of the Republic, 1763–89*. University of Chicago Press, 2012, p. 8.
   43. Tufts, Henry. *A Narrative of the Life, Adventures, Travels and Sufferings of Henry Tufts, Now Residing at Lemington, in the District of Maine In substance, as compiled from his own mouth*. Samuel Bragg, 1807, p. 33.
   44. *Ibid.*, p. 14.
   45. *Ibid.*, p. 121.
   46. *Ibid.*, p. 114.
   47. *Ibid.*, p. 28.
   48. *Ibid.*, p. 14.

Chapter 2

   1. Tufts, Henry. *A Narrative of the Life, Adventures, Travels and Sufferings of Henry Tufts, Now Residing at Lemington, in the District of Maine In substance, as compiled from his own mouth*. Samuel Bragg, 1807, p. 316.
   2. "America's first murderer was executed for killing fellow Plymouth settler." Mayflower 400. https://www.mayflower400uk.org/education/who-were-the-pilgrims/2020/may/john-billington/. Accessed October 16, 2022.
   3. Hearn, Daniel Allen. *Legal Executions in New England: A Comprehensive Reference, 1623–1960*. McFarland, 2008, p. 6.
   4. *Ibid.*, p. 7.
   5. *Records of the Court of Assistants of the Colony of the Massachusetts Bay, 1630–1692*. County of Suffolk, 1901.
   6. Winthrop, John. *The Journal of John Winthrop, 1630–1649*. Harvard University Press, 1996, p. 1.
   7. Mather, Cotton. *The valley of Hinnom. The terrours of hell demonstrated and the methods of escaping the terrible miseries of the punishments on the wicked there, declared. In a sermon preached in the hearing, and at the request, of a man under a sentence of death for a murder; just before the execution of the sentence; and upon a text by himself assigned for the sermon to insist upon*. Boston, 13.d. IV.m. 1717, p. 3.
   8. Wood, Gordon S. *The American Revolution: A History*. Modern Library, 2003, p. 9.
   9. "The Planter, No. II." *The American Magazine and Monthly Chronicle for the British Colonies*, November 1757, p. 83.
   10. Nicolazzo, Sal. *Vagrant Figures: Law, Literature, and the Origins of the Police*. Yale University Press, 2021, p. 4.
   11. *Early American Indian Documents: Treaties and Laws, 1607–1789*. 20 vols. Edited by Alden T. Vaughan. University Publications of America, 1979. Vol. 17: *New England and Middle Atlantic Laws*, p. 168.
   12. "Index by State: Massachusetts—1630–1800." https://deathpenaltyusa.org/usa1/state/massachusetts1.htm. Accessed March 10, 2023.
   13. *Journal of Lieutenant Isaac Bangs, April 1 to July 29, 1776*, p. 29 https://tile.loc.gov/storage-services/public/gdcmassbookdig/journaloflieuten00bang/journaloflieuten00bang.pdf. Accessed January 19, 2023.
   14. Schenawolf, Harry. "Holy Ground: New York City's Red Light District During the American Revolutionary War." *Revolutionary War Journal*, October 10, 2015. https://www.revolutionarywarjournal.com/holy-ground/. Accessed January 19, 2023.
   15. Lenney, Christopher J. *Sightseeking: Clues to the Landscape History of New England*. University Press of New England, 2005, p. 33.
   16. McCullough, David. *1776*. Simon & Schuster, 2006, p. 27.
   17. Fraser, Antonia. *The Weaker Vessel: Woman's Lot in Seventeenth-Century England*. Weidenfeld and Nicolson, 1984.
   18. Linnane, Fergus. *Madams: Bawds and Brothel-Keepers of London*. The History Press, 2009, p. 1.
   19. Clarke, R.J. "The land of the 'free': Criminal transportation to America." *The History Press*. https://www.thehistorypress.co.uk/articles/the-land-of-the-free-criminal-transportation-to-america/. Accessed January 17, 2023.

20. "Felons and Rattlesnakes, 9 May 1751." *Founders Online, National Archives.* https://founders.archives.gov/documents/Franklin/01-04-02-0040. [Original source: *The Papers of Benjamin Franklin*, vol. 4, July 1, 1750, through June 30, 1753. Edited by Leonard W. Labaree. Yale University Press, 1961, pp. 130–133.]

21. Rozbicki, Michal Jan. *The Complete Colonial Gentleman: Cultural Legitimacy in Plantation America.* University of Virginia Press, 1998, p. 92.

22. Vaver, Anthony. *Bound with an Iron Chain: The Untold Story of How the British Transported 50,000 Convicts to Colonial America.* Pickpocket Publishing, 2011, p. 249.

23. Clarke, R.J. "The land of the 'free': Criminal transportation to America." *The History Press.* https://www.thehistorypress.co.uk/articles/the-land-of-the-free-criminal-transportation-to-america/. Accessed January 17, 2023.

24. Vaver, Anthony. *Bound with an Iron Chain: The Untold Story of How the British Transported 50,000 Convicts to Colonial America.* Pickpocket Publishing, 2011, p. 6.

25. *Ibid.*, p. 3.

26. Vaver, Anthony. "'Human Serpents sent us by our Mother Country': The Transformation of Anthony Lamb, Transported Convict." *Readex Report*, vol. 5, issue 1, February 2010. https://www.readex.com/readex-report/issues/volume-5-issue-1/human-serpents-sent-us-our-mother-country-transformation. Accessed January 17, 2023.

27. Johnson, Ben. "The Amazing Escapes of Jack Sheppard." *Historic UK.* https://www.historic-uk.com/HistoryUK/HistoryofEngland/The-Amazing-Escapes-of-Jack-Sheppard/. Accessed March 20, 2023.

28. *The Recorder* (Richmond, Virginia), June 2, 1802, p. 3.

29. Thompson, Mary. *Landmarks in Ancient Dover, New Hampshire.* Concord Republican Press Association, 1892, p. 257.

30. Tufts, Henry. *A Narrative of the Life, Adventures, Travels and Sufferings of Henry Tufts, Now Residing at Lemington, in the District of Maine In substance, as compiled from his own mouth.* Samuel Bragg, 1807, p. 11.

31. Butterfield, Martha. *The Land in Our Hands—Burley-Demeritt Farm in Lee, NH: Its History.* Lulu.com, 2016, p. 41.

32. Tufts, Henry. *A Narrative of the Life, Adventures, Travels and Sufferings of Henry Tufts, Now Residing at Lemington, in the District of Maine In substance, as compiled from his own mouth.* Samuel Bragg, 1807, p. 44.

33. *Ibid.*, p. 50.

34. *Ibid.*, p. 57.

35. *Ibid.*, p. 58.

36. *Ibid.*, p. 132.

37. *Ibid.*, p. 311.

38. Adams, Samuel. *The Writings of Samuel Adams—Volume 4.* Edited by Harry Alonzo Cushing. G.P. Putnam's Sons, 1908, p. 352.

39. *Ibid.*

40. Rush, Benjamin. *Letters of Benjamin Rush: Volume II: 1793–1813.* Edited by Lyman Henry Butterfield. Princeton University Press, 1951, p. 762.

41. Franklin, Benjamin. *A Dissertation on Liberty and Necessity, Pleasure and Pain.* Printed in the Year mdccxxv. Yale University Library, https://founders.archives.gov/documents/Franklin/01-01-02-0028. Accessed February 27, 2023.

42. Wollaston, William. *The Religion of Nature Delineated.* J. Beecroft, et al., 1750 reprint of 1722 original, p. 33.

43. Tufts, Henry. *A Narrative of the Life, Adventures, Travels and Sufferings of Henry Tufts, Now Residing at Lemington, in the District of Maine In substance, as compiled from his own mouth.* Samuel Bragg, 1807, p. 11.

44. *Ibid.*, p. vii.

45. *Ibid.*

46. Wood, Gordon S. *The Radicalism of the American Revolution.* Vintage, 1993, p. 193.

47. di Beccaria, Cesare Bonesana. *An Essay on Crimes and Punishments (1764) A New Edition Corrected.* W.C. Little & Co., 1872, p. 18.

48. Tufts, Henry. *A Narrative of the Life, Adventures, Travels and Sufferings of Henry Tufts, Now Residing at Lemington, in the District of Maine In substance, as compiled from his own mouth.* Samuel Bragg, 1807, p. 11.

49. Mather, Cotton. *Pillars of salt. An history of some criminals executed in this land, for capital crimes. : With some of their*

dying speeches; collected and published, for the warning of such as live in destructive courses of ungodliness. : Whereto is added, for the better improvement of this history, a brief discourse about the dreadful justice of God, in punishing of sin, with sin.* Printed by B. Green and J. Allen, 1699, p. 12.

50. White, Alexander. *A narrative of the life and conversion of Alexander White, aet. 23. Who was executed at Cambridge, November 18, 1784, for the murder of a Captain White, at sea. : Containing extracts from his manuscripts, and some letters written by him a short time before his execution.* Powars and Willis, 1784, p. 15.

51. Burroughs, Stephen. *Memoirs of the Notorious Stephen Burroughs: Containing Many Incidents in the Life of this Wonderful Man Never Before Published.* Charles Gaylord Printing House, 1835, p. vi.

52. Oliver, Peter. *Peter Oliver's Origin and Progress of the American Rebellion: A Tory View.* Edited by Douglass Adair and John A. Schutz. Stanford University Press, 1961, p. 39.

53. "Thomas Hobbes: Methodology." *Internet Encyclopedia of Philosophy.* https://iep.utm.edu/hobmeth/. Accessed October 2, 2022.

54. Locke, John. *The Two Treatises of Civil Government.* Edited by Thomas Hollis. A. Millar et al., 1689.

55. Adams, Samuel. *The Rights of the Colonists: The Report of the Committee of Correspondence to the Boston Town Meeting,* November 20, 1772. Old South Leaflets no. 173. Directors of the Old South Work, 1906, p. 417.

56. Wood, Gordon S. *The Radicalism of the American Revolution.* Vintage, 1993, p. 229.

Chapter 3

1. Wood, Gordon S. *The American Revolution: A History.* Modern Library, 2003, p. 35.

2. Rutland, Robert. "Bills of Rights and the First Ten Amendments to the Constitution." *A Companion to the American Revolution.* Edited by Jack P. Greene and J.R. Pole. Blackwell, 2000, p. 265.

3. Wood, Gordon S. *The American Revolution: A History.* Modern Library, 2003, p. 9.

4. Adams, Samuel. *The Writings of Samuel Adams—Volume 2.* Edited by Harry Alonzo Cushing. G.P. Putnam's Sons, 1906, p. 174.

5. O'Toole, James M. "The Historical Interpretations of Samuel Adams." *The New England Quarterly,* vol. 49, no. 1, 1976, p. 82.

6. Raphael, Ray. *The American Revolution: A People's History: How Common People Shaped the Fight for Independence.* Profile, 2002, p. 12.

7. Matson, Cathy. "The Atlantic Economy in an Era of Revolutions: An Introduction." *The William and Mary Quarterly,* Third Series, vol. 62, no. 3, July 2005, pp. 357–364.

8. Schiff, Stacy. *The Revolutionary: Samuel Adams.* Little, Brown, 2022, p. 114.

9. Adams, Samuel. Instructions to Boston's Representatives, May 28, 1764. https://www.revolutionary-war-and-beyond.com/instructions-to-bostons-representatives-may-28-1764.html. Accessed March 4, 2023.

10. Adams, Samuel. *The Writings of Samuel Adams—Volume 1.* Edited by Harry Alonzo Cushing. G.P. Putnam's Sons, 1904, p. 9.

11. Bailyn, Bernard. *The Ordeal of Thomas Hutchinson.* Belknap Press, 1976, pp. 64–65.

12. Schiff, Stacy. *The Revolutionary: Samuel Adams.* Little, Brown, 2022, p. 88.

13. *Ibid.,* p. 135.

14. *Ibid.,* p. 83.

15. Jensen, Merrill. *The Founding of a Nation: A History of the American Revolution, 1763–1776.* Hackett, 2004, p. 142.

16. Raphael, Ray. *Founding Myths: Stories That Hide Our Patriotic Past.* The New Press, 2014, p. 34.

17. Schiff, Stacy. *The Revolutionary: Samuel Adams.* Little, Brown, 2022, p. 90.

18. Stoll, Ira. *Samuel Adams: A Life.* Free Press, 2009, pp. 44–45.

19. Schiff, Stacy. *The Revolutionary: Samuel Adams.* Little, Brown, 2022, p. 111.

20. Gage, Thomas. *The Correspondence of General Thomas Gage.* Edited by Clarence Edwin Carter. Yale University Press, 1931, p. 67.

21. Schiff, Stacy. *The Revolutionary: Samuel Adams.* Little, Brown, 2022, p. 82.

22. Stoll, Ira. *Samuel Adams: A Life*. Free Press, 2009, p. 43.
23. Fowler, William M. *Samuel Adams: Radical Puritan*. Longman, 1997, p. 66.
24. Brookhiser, Richard. "Samuel Adams: Puritan. Patriot. Protestor." *History Net*, October 13, 2020. https://www.historynet.com/samuel-adams-puritan-patriot-protestor/. Accessed September 26, 2022.
25. Adams, Samuel. Article in the *Boston Gazette*, October 1768. http://www.samuel-adams-heritage.com/documents/article-in-boston-gazette.html. Accessed April 24, 2023.
26. Locke, John. *Second Treatise on Government*. 1689. https://housedivided.dickinson.edu/sites/teagle/texts/john-locke-second-treatise-on-government-1689/. Accessed September 2, 2022.
27. Tufts, Henry. *A Narrative of the Life, Adventures, Travels and Sufferings of Henry Tufts, Now Residing at Lemington, in the District of Maine In substance, as compiled from his own mouth*. Samuel Bragg, 1807, p. 13.
28. Wood, Gordon S. *The American Revolution: A History*. Modern Library, 2003, p. 33.
29. Tucker, Spencer C. *American Revolution: The Definitive Encyclopedia and Document Collection*. ABC-CLIO, 2018, p. 870.
30. McCullough, David. *John Adams*. Simon & Schuster, 2001, p. 66.
31. *Ipswich Journal*, January 4, 1777.
32. Legal Papers of *John Adams*, Volume 1. Massachusetts Historical Society. https://www.masshist.org/publications/adams-papers/index.php/view/ADMS-05-01-02-0002-0001-0002. Accessed September 30, 2022.
33. Young, Alfred F., and Kaye, Harvey J. *Liberty Tree: Ordinary People and the American Revolution*. New York University Press, 2006, p. 156.
34. *Ibid*.
35. Stoll, Ira. "Bring Forth the Tar and Feathers." *New York Sun*, March 11, 2008. https://www.nysun.com/article/arts-bring-forth-the-tar-and-feathers. Accessed July 27, 2023.
36. *Pennsylvania Gazette*, June 29, 1774.
37. Schiff, Stacy. *The Revolutionary: Samuel Adams*. Little, Brown, 2022, p. 150.
38. Alexander, John K. *Samuel Adams: America's Revolutionary Politician*. Rowman & Littlefield, 2004, p. 80.
39. John Adams to Thomas Jefferson. *The Works of John Adams*, Vol. 10. Jazzybee Verlag, 2015, p. 143.
40. Stoll, Ira. *Samuel Adams: A Life*. Free Press, 2009, p. 86.
41. *John Adams'* Argument for the Defense, December 3–4, 1770. https://founders.archives.gov/documents/Adams/05-03-02-0001-0004-0016. Accessed March 9, 2023.
42. Fowler, William M., and Handlin, Oscar. *Samuel Adams: Radical Puritan*. Longman, 1997, p. 190.
43. Zavala, Cesar. "The Incident on King Street: The Boston Massacre of 1770." StMU Research Scholars, March 24, 2017. https://stmuscholars.org/the-incident-on-king-street/. Accessed September 2, 2022.
44. Stoll, Ira. *Samuel Adams: A Life*. Free Press, 2009, p. 86.
45. Andrews, Evan. "Remembering the Boston Massacre." *History.com*, August 30, 2018. https://www.history.com/news/the-boston-massacre-245-years-ago. Accessed September 2, 2022.
46. Tufts, Henry. *A Narrative of the Life, Adventures, Travels and Sufferings of Henry Tufts, Now Residing at Lemington, in the District of Maine In substance, as compiled from his own mouth*. Samuel Bragg, 1807, p. 45.
47. *Ibid*., p. 46.
48. "Dover's First Hanging." Dover Public Library. https://www.dover.nh.gov/government/city-operations/library/research-learn/history/dovers-first-hanging/ Accessed June 11, 2023.

Chapter 4

1. Adams, Samuel. Essay in the *Boston Gazette*, October 14, 1771.
2. Adams, Samuel. *The Rights of the Colonists: The Report of the Committee of Correspondence to the Boston Town Meeting*, November 20, 1772. Old South Leaflets no. 173. Directors of the Old South Work, 1906, p. 417.
3. Wood, Gordon S. *The Radicalism of the American Revolution*. Vintage, 1993, p. 13.
4. *Ibid*., p. 14.

5. "John Adams to Abigail Adams, 6 July 1774." *Founders Online, National Archives.* https://founders.archives.gov/documents/Adams/04-01-02-0086. [Original source: *The Adams Papers, Adams Family Correspondence, Vol. 1, December 1761–May 1776.* Edited by Lyman H. Butterfield. Harvard University Press, 1963, pp. 126–128.]

6. Letter from John Adams to Abigail Adams, 6 July 1774, "Mobs are the trite Topick..."

7. Samuel Adams to Elbridge Gerry, Boston, March 25, 1774. [J.T. Austin, *Life of Elbridge Gerry, Vol. 1,* pp. 36–39.] https://www.gutenberg.org/cache/epub/2093/pg2093.html. Accessed September 26, 2022.

8. *Ibid.*

9. Fischer, David Hackett. *Paul Revere's Ride.* Oxford University Press, 1995, p. 26.

10. *Ibid.,* p. 37.

11. *New-Hampshire Gazette,* November 8, 1771.

12. Carp, Benjamin L. "Did Dutch Smugglers Provoke the Boston Tea Party?" *Early American Studies,* vol. 10, no. 2, Special Issue: Anglo-Dutch Revolutions, Spring 2012, pp. 335–359.

13. Raphael, Ray. "Tea Party Myths." *American History,* June 2010.

14. Adams, Samuel. "Resolutions of the Town of Boston." *The Writings of Samuel Adams—Volume 3.* Edited by Harry Alonzo Cushing. G.P. Putnam's Sons, 1907, pp. 67–69.

15. Schiff, Stacy. *The Revolutionary: Samuel Adams.* Little, Brown, 2022, p. 239

16. Fradin, Dennis Brindell. *The Boston Tea Party.* Cavendish Square Publishing, 2008, p. 23.

17. Schiff, Stacy. *The Revolutionary: Samuel Adams.* Little, Brown, 2022, p. 244.

18. Allison, Robert J., ed. *The Boston Tea Party.* Commonwealth Editions, 2007, pp. 41–42.

19. Thatcher, Benjamin Bussey. *Traits of the Tea Party: Being a Memoir of George R.T. Hewes, one of the last of its survivors; with a history of that transaction: reminiscences of the massacre, and the siege, and other stories of old times.* Harper & Brothers, 1835, p. 176.

20. Fischer, David Hackett. *Paul Revere's Ride.* Oxford University Press, 1995, p. 26.

21. John Andrews to William Barrell, letter regarding the Boston Tea Party, December 18, 1773. https://cdnsm5-ss1.sharpschool.com/UserFiles/Servers/Server_10640642/File/bugge/Chapter%205/Letter%20Regarding%20the%20Boston%20Tea%20Party%201773.pdf. Accessed May 25, 2023.

22. Raphael, Ray. "Debunking Tea Party Myths." *History Net,* April 1, 2010. https://www.historynet.com/debunking-boston-tea-party-myths/. Accessed May 25, 2023.

23. Schiff, Stacy. *The Revolutionary: Samuel Adams.* Little, Brown, 2022, p. 248.

24. Fischer, David Hackett. *Paul Revere's Ride.* Oxford University Press, 1995, p. 31.

25. Looff, Kathryn M. "The Perils of Power: Thomas Hutchinson, Thomas Gage, and the Perception of Authority, 1770–1775." Baylor University, https://hdl.handle.net/2104/11852. Accessed February 18, 2023.

26. "The Boston Port Act: March 31, 1774." Avalon Project—Great Britain: Parliament. Yale University, Lilian Goldman Law Library. http://avalon.law.yale.edu/18th_century/boston_port_act.asp. Accessed September 30, 2022.

27. Stoll, Ira. *Samuel Adams: A Life.* Free Press, 2009, p. 120.

28. Fischer, David Hackett. *Paul Revere's Ride.* Oxford University Press, 1995, p. 42.

29. "The Massachusetts Government Act: May 20, 1774." Avalon Project—Great Britain: Parliament. Yale University, Lilian Goldman Law Library. http://avalon.law.yale.edu/18th_century/mass_gov_act.asp. Accessed September 30, 2022.

30. "Administration of Justice Act." May 20, 1774. https://www.ushistory.org/declaration/related/aja.html. Accessed February 19, 2023.

31. "The Quartering Act: June 2, 1774." Avalon Project—Great Britain: Parliament. Yale University, Lilian Goldman Law Library. http://avalon.law.yale.edu/18th_century/quartering_act_1774.asp. Accessed September 30, 2022.

32. George Washington to Bryan Fairfax, July 4, 1774. *Founders Online, National Archives.* Last modified June 13, 2018. http://founders.archives.gov/documents/

Washington/02-10-02-0075. Accessed September 30, 2022.

33. Schiff, Stacy. *The Revolutionary: Samuel Adams*. Little, Brown, 2022, p. 268.

34. *Warren-Adams Letters, being chiefly a Correspondence among John Adams, Samuel Adams, and James Warren. Volume I, 1743–1777*. Massachusetts Historical Society, 1917, p. 72.

35. Rust, Randal. "Powder Alarm Summary." *American History Central*, April 2, 2021. https://www.americanhistorycentral.com/entries/powder-alarm-1774-massachusetts/. Accessed February 15, 2023.

36. Fischer, David Hackett. *Paul Revere's Ride*. Oxford University Press, 1995, p. 47.

37. Rust, Randal. "Powder Alarm Summary." *American History Central*, April 2, 2021. https://www.americanhistorycentral.com/entries/powder-alarm-1774-massachusetts/. Accessed February 15, 2023.

38. Johnston, Patrick. "The Powder Alarm and Mobilization of the New England Countryside, 1774–1775." *Historical Journal of Massachusetts*, vol. 37, no. 1, Spring 2009.

39. Raphael, Ray. "When Rabble-Rousing Samuel Adams Slowed Down the Revolution." *Journal of the American Revolution*, September 16, 2015. https://allthingsliberty.com/2015/09/when-rabble-rousing-samuel-adams-slowed-down-the-revolution/. Accessed February 19, 2023.

40. Samuel Adams to James Warren, writing from Philadelphia, fall of 1774. *Warren-Adams Letters*, Massachusetts Historical Society, 1917, 26.

41. Oliver, Peter. *Peter Oliver's Origin and Progress of the American Rebellion: A Tory View*. Edited by Douglass Adair and John A. Schutz. Stanford University Press, 1961, p. 116.

42. Raphael, Ray. "When Rabble-Rousing Samuel Adams Slowed Down the Revolution." *Journal of the American Revolution*, September 16, 2015. https://allthingsliberty.com/2015/09/when-rabble-rousing-samuel-adams-slowed-down-the-revolution/. Accessed February 19, 2023.

43. Fischer, David Hackett. *Paul Revere's Ride*. Oxford University Press, 1995, p. 195.

44. Nelson, James L. *Benedict Arnold's Navy: The Ragtag Fleet That Lost the Battle of Lake Champlain but Won the American Revolution*. McGraw Hill, 2006, p. 3.

45. Fischer, David Hackett. *Paul Revere's Ride*. Oxford University Press, 1995, p. 257.

46. *Ibid.*, p. 183.

47. Copeland, Travis. "North Carolina's Response to the Battles of Lexington and Concord." *Journal of the American Revolution*, July 5, 2021. https://allthingsliberty.com/2021/07/north-carolinas-response-to-the-battles-of-lexington-and-concord/. Accessed December 15, 2022.

48. Paine, Thomas. *Common Sense*, 3rd ed. 1776, p. 15.

49. Fischer, David Hackett. *Paul Revere's Ride*. Oxford University Press, 1995, p. 263.

50. Joseph Warren to Towns, April 20, 1775. https://www.drjosephwarren.com/2014/04/barbarous-murders-committed-on-our-innocent-brethren/. Accessed February 21, 2023.

51. Langdon, Samuel. *Government corrupted by vice, and recovered by righteousness. A sermon preached before the honorable Congress of the colony of the Massachusetts-Bay in New England, assembled at Watertown, on Wednesday the 31st day of May, 1775. Being the anniversary fixed by charter for the election of counsellors*. Printed by Benjamin Edes, 1775.

52. Stoll, Ira. *Samuel Adams: A Life*. Free Press, 2009, pp. 162–163.

53. "General Thomas Gage Proclamation." *Revolutionary War and Beyond*, June 12, 1775. https://www.revolutionary-war-and-beyond.com/general-thomas-gage-proclamation-june-12-1775.html. Accessed February 17, 2023.

54. Wood, Gordon S. *The American Revolution: A History*. Modern Library, 2003, p. 54.

55. Fischer, David Hackett. *Paul Revere's Ride*. Oxford University Press, 1995, p. 247.

56. "Olive Branch Petition," July 8, 1775. https://www.digitalhistory.uh.edu/disp_textbook.cfm?smtID=3&psid=3881. Accessed February 17, 2023.

57. Letter from Abigail Adams to John Adams, November 12, 1775. https://www.masshist.org/digitaladams/archive/

doc?id=L17751112aa. Accessed February 17, 2023.
58. Stoll, Ira. *Samuel Adams: A Life.* Free Press, 2009, p. 164.
59. Oliver, Peter. *Peter Oliver's Origin and Progress of the American Rebellion: A Tory View.* Edited by Douglass Adair and John A. Schutz. Stanford University Press, 1961, p. 39.

Chapter 5

1. Tufts, Henry. *A Narrative of the Life, Adventures, Travels and Sufferings of Henry Tufts, Now Residing at Lemington, in the District of Maine In substance, as compiled from his own mouth.* Samuel Bragg, 1807, p. 66.
2. Ibid., p. 67.
3. Ghere, David L. "The 'Disappearance' of the Abenaki in Western Maine: Political Organization and Ethnocentric Assumptions." *American Indian Quarterly*, vol. 17, no. 2, Spring 1993, p. 196.
4. Tufts, Henry. *A Narrative of the Life, Adventures, Travels and Sufferings of Henry Tufts, Now Residing at Lemington, in the District of Maine In substance, as compiled from his own mouth.* Samuel Bragg, 1807, p. 73.
5. Ibid., p. 76.
6. Ibid., p. 77.
7. Day, Gordon M. "Henry Tufts as a Source on the Eighteenth Century Abenakis." *Ethnohistory*, vol. 21, no. 3, Summer 1974, p. 189.
8. Calloway, Colin G. *The Western Abenakis of Vermont, 1600–1800: War, Migration, and the Survival of an Indian People.* University of Oklahoma Press, 1994, p. 201.
9. Ghere, David L. "The 'Disappearance' of the Abenaki in Western Maine: Political Organization and Ethnocentric Assumptions." *American Indian Quarterly*, vol. 17, no. 2, Spring 1993, p. 202.
10. Nies, Judith. *Native American History: A Chronology of a Culture's Vast Achievements and Their Links to World Events.* Ballantine, 1996, p. 76.
11. Ibid., p. 77.
12. Dixon, David. *Never Come to Peace Again: Pontiac's Uprising and the Fate of the British Empire in North America.* University of Oklahoma Press, 2014.
13. Ghere, David L. "The 'Disappearance' of the Abenaki in Western Maine: Political Organization and Ethnocentric Assumptions." *American Indian Quarterly*, vol. 17, no. 2, Spring 1993, p. 199.
14. Nies, Judith. *Native American History: A Chronology of a Culture's Vast Achievements and Their Links to World Events.* Ballantine, 1996, p. 76.
15. Ibid., p. 135.
16. Aron, Stephen. "The Making of the First American West and the Unmaking of Other Realms." *A Companion to the American West.* Edited by William Deverell. Blackwell, 2004, p. 9.
17. White, Richard. *The Middle Ground: Indians, Empires, and Republics in the Great Lakes Region, 1650–1815.* Cambridge University Press, 1991.
18. Aron, Stephen. "The Making of the First American West and the Unmaking of Other Realms." *A Companion to the American West.* Edited by William Deverell. Blackwell, 2004, p. 9.
19. Ghere, David L. "The 'Disappearance' of the Abenaki in Western Maine: Political Organization and Ethnocentric Assumptions." *American Indian Quarterly*, vol. 17, no. 2, Spring 1993, p. 193.
20. Senier, Siobhan. "All This/Is Abenaki Country." *Studies in American Indian Literatures*, 2010, p. 3.
21. Ghere, David L. "The 'Disappearance' of the Abenaki in Western Maine: Political Organization and Ethnocentric Assumptions." *American Indian Quarterly*, vol. 17, no. 2, Spring 1993, p. 194.
22. Ibid., p. 198.
23. Nelson, James L. *Benedict Arnold's Navy: The Ragtag Fleet That Lost the Battle of Lake Champlain but Won the American Revolution.* McGraw Hill, 2006, p. 257.
24. Tufts, Henry. *A Narrative of the Life, Adventures, Travels and Sufferings of Henry Tufts, Now Residing at Lemington, in the District of Maine In substance, as compiled from his own mouth.* Samuel Bragg, 1807, p. 186
25. Ibid. pp. 186–187.
26. Ibid., p. 69.
27. "Molly Ockett and Her World." Bethel Historical Society. https://www.bethelhistorical.org/legacy-site/Molly_Ockett_and_Her_World.html. Accessed March 2, 2023.
28. Tufts, Henry. *A Narrative of the*

Life, Adventures, Travels and Sufferings of Henry Tufts, Now Residing at Lemington, in the District of Maine In substance, as compiled from his own mouth. Samuel Bragg, 1807, p. 70.

29. Jay, Robert. *The Trade Card in Nineteenth-Century America.* University of Missouri Press, 1987, p. 71.

30. *Ibid.*

31. Weatherford, Jack. *Indian Givers: How Native Americans Transformed the World.* Broadway Books, 2010, p. 236.

32. David Bellin, Joshua. "Taking the Indian Cure: Thoreau, Indian Medicine, and the Performance of American Culture." *The New England Quarterly*, vol. 79, no. 1, March 2006, p. 10.

33. Weatherford, Jack. *Indian Givers: How Native Americans Transformed the World.* Broadway Books, 2010, pp. 227–228.

34. *Ibid.*, pp. 233–234.

35. Tufts, Henry. *A Narrative of the Life, Adventures, Travels and Sufferings of Henry Tufts, Now Residing at Lemington, in the District of Maine In substance, as compiled from his own mouth.* Samuel Bragg, 1807, p. 271.

36. Hinderaker, Eric. "The Amerindian Population in 1763." *A Companion to the American Revolution.* Edited by Jack P. Greene and J.R. Pole. Blackwell, 2000, p. 95.

37. Marshall, Peter. "The West and the Amerindians, 1756–1776." *A Companion to the American Revolution.* Edited by Jack P. Greene and J.R. Pole. Blackwell, 2000, p. 157.

38. Aron, Stephen. "The Making of the First American West and the Unmaking of Other Realms." *A Companion to the American Revolution.* Edited by Jack P. Greene and J.R. Pole. Blackwell, 2000, pp. 8–9.

39. Ghere, David L. "The 'Disappearance' of the Abenaki in Western Maine: Political Organization and Ethnocentric Assumptions." *American Indian Quarterly*, vol. 17, no. 2, Spring 1993, pp. 201–202.

40. Williamson, William Durkee. *The History of the State of Maine: From Its First Discovery, A.D. 1602, to the Separation, A.D. 1820.* Glazier, Masters & Company, 1832, p. 605.

41. Marshall, Peter. "The West and the Amerindians, 1756–1776." *A Companion to the American Revolution.* Edited by Jack P. Greene and J.R. Pole. Blackwell, 2000, p. 158.

42. Perdue, Theda. *Cherokee Women: Gender and Culture Change, 1700–1835 (Indians of the Southeast).* Bison Books, 1999, p. 88.

43. Hinderaker, Eric. "The Amerindian Population in 1763." *A Companion to the American Revolution*, edited by Jack P. Greene and J.R. Pole. Blackwell, 2000, p. 95.

44. Bentinck, Rudolph. *Bentinck's Journal: Seven Years' War with George Washington, 1756–1762.* https://cdm16923.contentdm.oclc.org/digital/collection/p16923coll6/id/3728. Accessed March 5, 2023.

45. Shannon, Timothy J. "French and Indian Cruelty? The Fate of the Oswego Prisoners of War, 1756–1758." *The Cupola*, Summer 2014.

46. Starbuck, David R. "The 'Massacre' at Fort William Henry: History Archaeology, and Re-enactment." *Expedition*, vol. 50, issue 1. https://www.penn.museum/sites/expedition/the-massacre-at-fort-william-henry/. Accessed March 5, 2023.

47. "French and Indian War." *History.com*, November 9, 2009, last updated August 29, 2003. https://www.history.com/topics/native-american-history/french-and-indian-war. Accessed October 26, 2022.

48. Cave, Alfred A. *The French and Indian War.* Bloomsbury Academic, 2004, pp. 117–118.

49. Hinderaker, Eric. "The Amerindian Population in 1763." *A Companion to the American Revolution.* Edited by Jack P. Greene and J.R. Pole. Blackwell, 2000, p. 94.

50. *Ibid.*, p. 95.

51. *Ibid.*, p. 94.

52. *Ibid.*, p. 96.

53. Humphreys, R.A. "Lord Shelburne and the Proclamation of 1763." *The English Historical Review* 49, no. 194, 1934, p. 242.

54. Dixon, David. *Never Come to Peace Again: Pontiac's Uprising and the Fate of the British Empire in North America.* University of Oklahoma Press, 2014.

55. Adams, Samuel. *The Writings of Samuel Adams—Volume 2.* Edited by Harry Alonzo Cushing. G.P. Putnam's Sons, 1906, pp. 368–369.

56. Ghere, David L. "The 'Disappearance' of the Abenaki in Western Maine: Political Organization and Ethnocentric Assumptions." *American Indian Quarterly*, vol. 17, no. 2, Spring 1993, p. 202.

57. Hinderaker, Eric. "The Amerindian Population in 1763." *A Companion to the American Revolution*. Edited by Jack P. Greene and J.R. Pole. Blackwell, 2000, p. 95.

58. Adams, Samuel. *The Writings of Samuel Adams—Volume 4*. Edited by Harry Alonzo Cushing. G.P. Putnam's Sons, 1908, p. 377.

59. Letter from Benjamin Franklin to James Parker, March 20, 1751. https://founders.archives.gov/documents/Franklin/01-04-02-0037. Accessed March 13, 2023.

60. Lafitau, Joseph Francois. *Customs of the American-Indians Compared with the Customs of Primitive Time*. Edited by William N. Fenton and Elizabeth L. Moore. The Champlain Society, 1974, p. 87.

61. Crytzer, Brady J. "Longhouse Lost: The Battle of Oriskany and the Iroquois Civil War." *Journal of the American Revolution*, July 30, 2020. https://allthingsliberty.com/2020/07/longhouse-lost-the-battle-of-oriskany-and-the-iroquois-civil-war/. Accessed March 2, 2023.

62. Paxton, James. *Joseph Brant and His World: 18th Century Mohawk Warrior and Statesman*. James Lormier & Company, 2008, pp. 40–42.

63. Crytzer, Brady J. "Longhouse Lost: The Battle of Oriskany and the Iroquois Civil War." *Journal of the American Revolution*, July 30, 2020. https://allthingsliberty.com/2020/07/longhouse-lost-the-battle-of-oriskany-and-the-iroquois-civil-war/. Accessed March 2, 2023.

64. "From George Washington to Major General John Sullivan, 31 May 1779." *Founders Online, National Archives*. https://founders.archives.gov/documents/Washington/03-20-02-0661. [Original source: *The Papers of George Washington, Revolutionary War Series, Vol. 20, 8 April–31 May 1779*. Edited by Edward G. Lengel. University of Virginia Press, 2010, pp. 716–719.]

65. Ghere, David L. "The 'Disappearance' of the Abenaki in Western Maine: Political Organization and Ethnocentric Assumptions." *American Indian Quarterly*, vol. 17, no. 2, Spring 1993, p. 202.

66. Calloway, Colin G. *The Western Abenakis of Vermont, 1600–1800: War, Migration, and the Survival of an Indian People*. University of Oklahoma Press, 1994, p. 208.

67. Calloway, Colin G. *The Indian World of George Washington: The First President, the First Americans, and the Birth of the Nation*. Oxford University Press, 2018, p. 133.

68. Tufts, Henry. *A Narrative of the Life, Adventures, Travels and Sufferings of Henry Tufts, Now Residing at Lemington, in the District of Maine In substance, as compiled from his own mouth*. Samuel Bragg, 1807, p. 91.

Chapter 6

1. Calhoon, Robert. "Loyalism and Neutrality." *A Companion to the American Revolution*. Edited by Jack P. Greene and J.R. Pole. Blackwell, 2000, p 235.

2. Ibid.

3. Flick, Alexander Clarence. *Loyalism in New York During the American Revolution*. Macmillan, 1901.

4. Herrera, Ricardo A. "The King's Friends: Loyalists in British Strategy." *Strategy in the American War of Independence: A Global Approach*. Edited by Donald Stoker, Kenneth J. Hagan and Michael T. McMaster. Routledge, 2010, p. 109.

5. McCullough, David. *1776*. Simon & Schuster, 2006, p. 118.

6. Ibid., p. 101.

7. Johnson, Samuel. "Taxation No Tyranny: An Answer to the Resolutions and Address of the American Congress." *The Works of Samuel Johnson*. Pafraets & Company, 1913. https://www.samueljohnson.com/tnt.html. Accessed September 8, 2022.

8. Gilbert, Alan. *Black Patriots and Loyalists: Fighting for Emancipation in the War for Independence*. University of Chicago Press, 2012, p. 1.

9. Gara, Donald J. "Loyal Subjects of the Crown: The Queen's Own Loyal Virginia Regiment and Dunmore's Ethiopian Regiment, 1775–76." *Journal of the Society*

for *Army Historical Research*, vol. 83, no. 333 (Spring 2005), pp. 30–42.

10. Jasanoff, Maya. *Liberty's Exiles: American Loyalists in the Revolutionary World*. Vintage, 2012, p. 352.

11. Nell, William Cooper. *The Colored Patriots of the American Revolution: With Sketches of Several Distinguished Colored Persons: To Which is Added a Brief Survey of the Conditions and Prospects of Colored Americans*. Robert F. Wallcut, 1855, p. 29.

12. Blanck, Emily. "Seventeen Eighty-Three: The Turning Point in the Law of Slavery and Freedom in Massachusetts." *New England Quarterly*, 2002, pp. 24–51.

13. Nell, William Cooper. *The Colored Patriots of the American Revolution: With Sketches of Several Distinguished Colored Persons: To Which is Added a Brief Survey of the Conditions and Prospects of Colored Americans*. Robert F. Wallcut, 1855, p. 25.

14. Tufts, Henry. *A Narrative of the Life, Adventures, Travels and Sufferings of Henry Tufts, Now Residing at Lemington, in the District of Maine In substance, as compiled from his own mouth*. Samuel Bragg, 1807, p. 154.

15. Ellefson, C. Ashley. "Seven Hangmen of Colonial Maryland," Chapter 6, "Character and Competence," http://aomol.net/megafile/ msa/speccol/sc2900/sc2908/000001/000819/html/index.html.

16. Miller, John Chester. *The Wolf by the Ears: Thomas Jefferson and Slavery*. University of Virginia Press, 1991, p. 41.

17. Stoll, Ira. *Samuel Adams: A Life*. Free Press, 2009, p. 117.

18. *Ibid*.

19. Adams, Samuel. *The Writings of Samuel Adams—Volume 2*. Edited by Harry Alonzo Cushing. G.P. Putnam's Sons, 1906, p. 65.

20. Adams, Samuel. *The Life and Public Services of Samuel Adams—Volume 1*. Edited by William V. Wells. Little, Brown, 1865, p. 407.

21. Adams, Samuel. *The Writings of Samuel Adams—Volume 2*. Edited by Harry Alonzo Cushing. G.P. Putnam's Sons, 1906, p. 319.

22. *Ibid*., p. 324.

23. Adams, Samuel. *The Writings of Samuel Adams—Volume 1*. Edited by Harry Alonzo Cushing. G.P. Putnam's Sons, 1904, p. 5.

24. *Ibid*., p. 18.

25. Schiff, Stacy. *The Revolutionary: Samuel Adams*. Little, Brown, 2022, p. 162.

26. *A Narrative, of the excursion and ravages of the King's troops under the command of General Gage, on the nineteenth of April, 1775. Together with the depositions taken by order of Congress, to support the truth of it*. Massachusetts, Provincial Congress, 1775, p. 3.

27. Journals of the Continental Congress—Petition to the King; July 8, 1775. https://avalon.law.yale.edu/18th_century/contcong_07-08-75.asp. Accessed August 25, 2023.

28. Wood, Gordon S. *The American Revolution: A History*. Modern Library, 2003, p. 65.

29. Price, Richard. "Observations on the importance of the American Revolution, and the means of making it a benefit to the world." Royal Society of London, and of the Academy of Arts and Sciences in New-England. https://quod.lib.umich.edu/e/evans/N14780.0001.001/1:3?rgn=div1;view=fulltext. Accessed April 12, 2023.

30. Tufts, Henry. *A Narrative of the Life, Adventures, Travels and Sufferings of Henry Tufts, Now Residing at Lemington, in the District of Maine In substance, as compiled from his own mouth*. Samuel Bragg, 1807, p. 100.

31. *Ibid*., p. 307.

32. *Ibid*., p. 101.

33. Paine, Thomas. *The Works of Thomas Paine: Common sense. The crisis. Public good. Letter addressed to the Abbe Raynal. Dissertations on government, the affairs of the bank, and paper-money. Miscellaneous pieces, in prose and verse; published in the Pennsylvania magazine, in the year 1775*. James Carey, 1797, p. 46.

34. Oliver, Peter. "An Address to the Soldiers of Massachusetts Bay who are now in Arms against the Laws of their Country." *The Massachusetts Gazette & Boston Weekly News-Letter*, January 11, 1776. https://americainclass.org/sources/makingrevolution/war/text2/oliveraddresssoldiers.pdf. Accessed September 30, 2022.

35. Klein, Christopher. "10 Reasons Why Gouverneur Morris Was the Oddest Founding Father." *History.com*, January 24, 2020. https://www.history.com/news/10-things-you-may-not-know-about-

the-oddest-founding-father. Accessed September 22, 2022.

36. Sheppard, Si. *Patriot vs. Loyalist: American Revolution 1775–83*. Bloomsbury, 2022, p. 32.

37. Brink, Benjamin Myer. "The Lineage of the Clinton Family." *Olde Ulster: An Historical and Genealogical Magazine*, vol. 2, 1905, pp. 53–60.

38. Bell, J.L. "Isaac Royall and 'the very Day the battle happen'd.'" *Boston 1775*. https://boston1775.blogspot.com/2016/04/isaac-royall-and-very-day-battle-happend.html. Accessed August 26, 2023.

39. Cotton Tufts to Abigail Adams, January 12, 1786. *Founders Online, National Archives*. https://founders.archives.gov/documents/Adams/04-07-02-0005. Accessed February 28, 2023.

40. Tufts, Henry. *A Narrative of the Life, Adventures, Travels and Sufferings of Henry Tufts, Now Residing at Lemington, in the District of Maine In substance, as compiled from his own mouth*. Dover: Samuel Bragg, 1807, p. 101

41. *Tufts Kinsmen—Volume 1*. Edited by Herbert Freeman Adams. Tufts Kinsmen Association, 2010, p. 201

42. Massachusetts, Office of the Secretary of State. *Massachusetts Soldiers and Sailors of the Revolutionary War*. Wright and Potter Printing Co., State Printers, 1896, p. 151.

43. Wild, Helen Tilden. *Medford in the Revolution: military history of Medford, Massachusetts, 1765–1783: also list of soldiers and civil officers, with genealogical and biographical notes*. J.C. Miller, Jr., 1903, p. 50

44. Tufts, Tom. "William Tuffs History or Mystery?" *Tufts Genealogy*, March 21, 2013. https://tuftsgenealogy.blogspot.com/2013/03/william-tuffs-history-or-mystery.html. Accessed August 19, 2023.

45. Tufts, Tom. "Nova Scotia Tufts; Chapter 5, Reverend Joshua Tufts' story and families of his first son John." *Tufts Genealogy*, March 13, 2015. https://tuftsgenealogy.blogspot.com/2015/03/nova-scotia-tufts-chapter-5-reverend.html. Accessed August 19, 2023.

46. Hatfield, Stuart. "Faking It: British Counterfeiting During the American Revolution." *Journal of the American Revolution*, October 7, 2015. https://allthingsliberty.com/2015/10/faking-it-british-counterfeiting-during-the-american-revolution/. Accessed September 24, 2022.

47. Thies, Clifford F. "Not Worth a Continental." American Institute for Economic Research, November 3, 2021. https://www.aier.org/article/not-worth-a-continental/. Accessed June 4, 2023.

48. Description of counterfeit bills, which were done in imitation of the true ones ordered by the Honorable the Continental Congress, bearing date 20th May, 1777, and 11th April, 1778. https://www.loc.gov/resource/bdsdcc.05501/?sp=1. Accessed May 3, 2023.

49. Tufts, Henry. *A Narrative of the Life, Adventures, Travels and Sufferings of Henry Tufts, Now Residing at Lemington, in the District of Maine In substance, as compiled from his own mouth*. Samuel Bragg, 1807, p. 178.

50. *Ibid.*, p. 120.

51. *Ibid.*, p. 179.

52. Hatfield, Stuart. "Faking It: British Counterfeiting During the American Revolution." *Journal of the American Revolution*, October 7, 2015. https://allthingsliberty.com/2015/10/faking-it-british-counterfeiting-during-the-american-revolution/. Accessed September 24, 2022.

53. Blanchard, Amos. *American Military Biography: Containing the Lives, Characters, and Anecdotes of the Officers of the Revolution, who Were Most Distinguished in Achieving Our National Independence. Also, the Life of Gilbert Motier La Fayette*. Roberts & Burr, 1825, p. 548.

54. Wells, William V. *The Life and Public Services of Samuel Adams: Being a Narrative of his Acts and Opinions, and of His Agency in Producing and Forwarding the American Revolution. With Extracts From His Correspondence, State Papers, and Political Essays, Volume 2*. Little, Brown, 1865, p. 193.

55. *Ibid.*, p. 422.

56. McCullough, David. *1776*. Simon & Schuster, 2006, p. 258.

57. Ranlet, Philip "Tory David Sproat of Pennsylvania and the Death of American Prisoners of War." *Pennsylvania History*, vol. 61, no. 2, April 1994, pp. 185–205.

58. Freneau, Philip. *The British Prison-Ship: A Poem*. F. Bailey, 1781, p. 8.

59. Oehler, Markus. "The Punishment of Thirty-Nine Lashes (2 Corinthians

11:24) and the Place of Paul in Judaism." *Journal of Biblical Literature*, vol. 140, no. 3, 2021.
   60. Raphael, Ray. *A People's History of the American Revolution: How Common People Shaped the Fight for Independence*. Perennial, 2002, pp. 214–215.
   61. Davis, Robert Scott. "Portraits of Southern Partisans: Likenesses of Thomas Brown and Elijah Clarke." *Journal of the American Revolution*, April 15, 2013. https://allthingsliberty.com/2013/04/portraits-of-southern-partisans-likenesses-of-thomas-brown-and-elijah-clarke/. Accessed May 5, 2023.
   62. Smith, Merril D., ed. *The World of the American Revolution: A Daily Life Encyclopedia*, 2 vols. ABC-CLIO, 2015, p. 547.
   63. Schenawolf, Harry. "Trinity Church: Home to the Holy Ground and New York City's 'Red-Light' District." *Revolutionary War Journal*, June 29, 2015. https://www.revolutionarywarjournal.com/trinity-church/. Accessed January 19, 2023.
   64. Gutridge, Molly. *Broadside*, 1779. National Humanities Center, 2010/2013. americainclass.org/. Early American Imprints, Doc. 43671.

Chapter 7

   1. Underdal, Stanley J., ed. "Military History of the American Revolution." The Proceedings of the 6th Military History Symposium United States Air Force Academy, 10–11 October 1974. Air Force Academy Office, 1976.
   2. George Washington to Joseph Reed, January 14, 1776. William B. Reed, Reprint of the original letters from Washington to Joseph Reed, during the American Revolution. Referred to in the pamphlets of Lord Mahon and Mr. Sparks (A. Hart, Late Carey and Hart, 1852), p. 44.
   3. *Ibid.*, pp. 36–37.
   4. Middlekauff, Robert. *This Glorious Cause: The American Revolution, 1763–1789*. Oxford University Press, 2005, p. 372.
   5. McCullough, David. *1776*. Simon & Schuster, 2006, p. 34.
   6. *Warren-Adams Letters, being chiefly a Correspondence among John Adams, Samuel Adams, and James Warren. Volume I, 1743–1777*. Massachusetts Historical Society, 1917, p. 275.
   7. Tufts, Henry. *A Narrative of the Life, Adventures, Travels and Sufferings of Henry Tufts, Now Residing at Lemington, in the District of Maine In substance, as compiled from his own mouth*. Samuel Bragg, 1807, p. 101.
   8. *Ibid.*, p. 103.
   9. Schenawolf, Harry. "Battle of Mamaroneck, New York—'A Pretty Affair' in the American Revolutionary War." *Revolutionary War Journal*, March 5, 2013. https://www.revolutionarywarjournal.com/battle-of-mamaroneck/. Accessed September 16, 2022.
   10. Ward, Harry M. *George Washington's Enforcers: Policing the Continental Army*. Southern Illinois University Press, 2006, p. 13.
   11. "From George Washington to John Hancock, 25 September 1776." Founders Online, National Archives. https://founders.archives.gov/documents/Washington/03-06-02-0305. [Original source: *The Papers of George Washington, Revolutionary War Series, Vol. 6, 13 August 1776–20 October 1776*. Edited by Philander D. Chase and Frank E. Grizzard, Jr. University Press of Virginia, 1994, pp. 393–401.]
   12. Orders to Major General Israel Putnam, 25 August 1776. Founders Online, National Archives. https://founders.archives.gov/documents/Washington/03-06-02-0113. Accessed March 16, 2023.
   13. McCullough, David. *1776*. Simon & Schuster, 2006, p. 41.
   14. *Ibid.*, p. 64.
   15. Orders to Major General Israel Putnam, 25 August 1776. Founders Online, National Archives. https://founders.archives.gov/documents/Washington/03-06-02-0113. Accessed March 16, 2023.
   16. McCullough, David. *1776*. Simon & Schuster, 2006, p. 41.
   17. *Ibid.*, p. 250.
   18. *Ibid.*, p. 225.
   19. Schenawolf, Harry. "Battle of Mamaroneck, New York—'A Pretty Affair' in the American Revolutionary War." *Revolutionary War Journal*, March 5, 2013. https://www.revolutionarywarjournal.

com/battle-of-mamaroneck/. Accessed September 16, 2022.
20. McCullough, David. *1776*. Simon & Schuster, 2006, p. 249.
21. *Ibid.*, p. 243.
22. *Ibid.*, p. 249.
23. *Ibid.*, p. 227.
24. Boyle, Joseph Lee. "Revolutionary War Desertions" from the introduction of *'He Loves a Good Deal of Rum': Military Desertions during the American Revolution, 1775-1783—Volume One*. Genealogical Publishing Company, 2009.
25. Tufts, Henry. *A Narrative of the Life, Adventures, Travels and Sufferings of Henry Tufts, Now Residing at Lemington, in the District of Maine In substance, as compiled from his own mouth*. Samuel Bragg, 1807, p. 157.
26. *Ibid.*, pp. 220–223.
27. McCullough, David. *1776*. Simon & Schuster, 2006, p. 37.
28. McDonnell, Michael A. "Resistance to the American Revolution." *A Companion to the American Revolution*. Edited by Jack P. Greene and J.R. Pole. Blackwell, 2000, p. 345.
29. McCullough, David. *1776*. Simon & Schuster, 2006, p. 37.
30. *Ibid.*, p. 31.
31. Holzwarth, Larry. "This Is What Life was Like for Soldiers of the Continental Army During the American Revolution." *History Collection*, April 10, 2019. https://historycollection.com/this-is-what-life-was-like-for-soldiers-of-the-continental-army-during-the-american-revolution/5/.
32. McDonnell, Michael A. "Resistance to the American Revolution." *A Companion to the American Revolution*. Edited by Jack P. Greene and J.R. Pole. Blackwell, 2000, p. 347.
33. McCullough, David. *1776*. Simon & Schuster, 2006, p. 29.
34. Tufts, Henry. *A Narrative of the Life, Adventures, Travels and Sufferings of Henry Tufts, Now Residing at Lemington, in the District of Maine In substance, as compiled from his own mouth*. Samuel Bragg, 1807, p. 106.
35. Boyle, Joseph Lee. "Revolutionary War Desertions" from the introduction of *'He Loves a Good Deal of Rum': Military Desertions during the American Revolution, 1775-1783—Volume One*. Genealogical Publishing Company, 2009.
36. Tufts, Henry. *A Narrative of the Life, Adventures, Travels and Sufferings of Henry Tufts, Now Residing at Lemington, in the District of Maine In substance, as compiled from his own mouth*. Samuel Bragg, 1807, p. 104.
37. *Ibid.*, p. 141.
38. Haw, James. *John & Edward Rutledge of South Carolina*. University of Georgia Press, 1997, p. 71.
39. McCullough, David. *1776*. Simon & Schuster, 2006, p. 55.
40. *Ibid.*, p. 54.
41. Gordon, William. *The History of the Rise, Progress, and Establishment, of the Independence of the United States of America—Volume 1*. Books for Libraries Press, 1969, p. 347.
42. Stoll, Ira. *Samuel Adams: A Life*. Free Press, 2009, p. 181.
43. *Ibid*.
44. Adams, Samuel. *The Rights of the Colonists: The Report of the Committee of Correspondence to the Boston Town Meeting*. November 20, 1772. Old South Leaflets no. 173, p. 417.
45. Thomas Jefferson to Henry Lee, May 8, 1825. https://teachingamericanhistory.org/document/letter-to-henry-lee/. Accessed September 1, 2022.
46. Adams, Samuel. *The Writings of Samuel Adams—Volume 2*. Edited by Harry Alonzo Cushing. G.P. Putnam's Sons, 1906, p. 259
47. Paine, Thomas. *Common Sense*, 3rd ed. 1776, p. 15.
48. Travers, Len. *Celebrating the Fourth: Independence Day and the Rites of Nationalism in the Early Republic*. University of Massachusetts Press, 1997, p. 28.
49. "To George Washington from John Hancock, 6 July 1776." *Founders Online, National Archives*. https://founders.archives.gov/documents/Washington/03-05-02-0153. [Original source: *The Papers of George Washington, Revolutionary War Series*, Vol. 5, 16 June 1776–12 August 1776. Edited by Philander D. Chase. University Press of Virginia, 1993, pp. 219–221.]
50. Maier, Pauline. *American Scripture: Making the Declaration of Independence*. Alfred A. Knopf, 1997, p. 156.
51. John H. Hazelton, *The Declaration*

of Independence: Its History. Dodd, Mead, 1906.

52. Simner, Marvin L. "The Use of the Declaration of Independence as a Military Recruitment Tool." *Journal of the American Revolution*, March 31, 2022. https://allthingsliberty.com/2022/03/the-use-of-the-declaration-of-independence-as-a-military-recruitment-tool/. Accessed September 1, 2022.

53. Adams, Samuel. "American Independence." Speech, August 1, 1776. https://www.revolutionary-war-and-beyond.com/american-independence-speech-by-samuel-adams-august-1-1776.html. Accessed September 11, 2022.

54. Journal of Ambrose Serle, July 12, 1776. https://ndar-history.org/?q=node/6025. Accessed September 4, 2022.

55. Cole, Jones T. "'The rage of tory-hunting': Loyalist Prisoners, Civil War, and the Violence of American Independence." *Journal of Military History*, vol. 81, issue 3, July 2017, pp. 719–746.

56. Journal of Ambrose Serle, July 12, 1776. https://ndar-history.org/?q=node/6025. Accessed September 4, 2022.

57. Simner, Marvin L. "The Use of the Declaration of Independence as a Military Recruitment Tool." *Journal of the American Revolution*, March 31, 2022. https://allthingsliberty.com/2022/03/the-use-of-the-declaration-of-independence-as-a-military-recruitment-tool/. Accessed September 1, 2022.

58. Edgar, Walter B. *South Carolina: A History*. University of South Carolina Press, 1998, p. 231.

59. Simner, Marvin L. "The Use of the Declaration of Independence as a Military Recruitment Tool." *Journal of the American Revolution*, March 31, 2022. https://allthingsliberty.com/2022/03/the-use-of-the-declaration-of-independence-as-a-military-recruitment-tool/. Accessed September 1, 2022.

60. Letter from Alexander Hamilton to Lieutenant Colonel John Laurens, June 30, 1780. *Founders Online*, National Archives. https://founders.archives.gov/documents/Hamilton/01-02-02-0742. Accessed October 4, 2022.

61. Simner, Marvin L. "The Use of the Declaration of Independence as a Military Recruitment Tool." *Journal of the American Revolution*, March 31, 2022. https://allthingsliberty.com/2022/03/the-use-of-the-declaration-of-independence-as-a-military-recruitment-tool/. Accessed September 1, 2022.

62. George Washington to George Lewis, January 11, 1778, *The Papers of George Washington. Revolutionary War Series*, 13:202, and William Smallwood to George Washington, January 26, 1778, *The Papers of George Washington. Revolutionary War Series*, 13:355.

63. George Washington to James Mitchell Varnum, March 20, 1778, *The Papers of George Washington. Revolutionary War Series*, 14:247.

64. "From George Washington to the Commanding Officer at Morristown, 30 December 1776." *Founders Online*, National Archives. https://founders.archives.gov/documents/Washington/03-07-02-0385. [Original source: *The Papers of George Washington, Revolutionary War Series, Vol. 7, 21 October 1776–5 January 1777*. Edited by Philander D. Chase. University Press of Virginia, 1997, pp. 490–491.]

65. McCullough, David. *1776*. Simon & Schuster, 2006, p. 286.

66. "To George Washington from Jacob Duché, 8 October 1777." *Founders Online*, National Archives. https://founders.archives.gov/documents/Washington/03-11-02-0452. [Original source: *The Papers of George Washington, Revolutionary War Series, Vol. 11, 19 August 1777–25 October 1777*. Edited by Philander D. Chase and Edward G. Lengel. University Press of Virginia, 2001, pp. 430–437.]

67. Stoll, Ira. *Samuel Adams: A Life*. Free Press, 2009, p. 187.

Chapter 8

1. Smith, Abbott Emerson. *Colonists in Bondage: White Servitude and Convict Labor in America, 1607–1776*. Omohundro Institute of Early American History and Culture and the University of North Carolina Press, 1947, p. 245.

2. Tufts, Henry. *A Narrative of the Life, Adventures, Travels and Sufferings of Henry Tufts, Now Residing at Lemington, in the District of Maine In substance, as compiled from his own mouth*. Samuel Bragg, 1807, p. 320.

3. *Ibid.*, p. 61.
4. *Ibid.*
5. *Ibid.*, p. 22.
6. *Ibid.*, p. 169.
7. *Ibid.*, p. 154.
8. Wells, William V. *The Life and Public Services of Samuel Adams: Being a Narrative of his Acts and Opinions, and of His Agency in Producing and Forwarding the American Revolution. With Extracts From His Correspondence, State Papers, and Political Essays, Volume 1.* Little, Brown, 1865, pp. 53–54.
9. Schiff, Stacy. "The Noble Fury of Samuel Adams." *Smithsonian Magazine*, October 2022. https://www.smithsonianmag.com/history/noble-fury-samuel-adams-180980758/. Accessed March 21, 2023.
10. Wood, Gordon S. *The Radicalism of the American Revolution.* Vintage, 1993, p. 23.
11. Otis, James. *Collected Political Writings of James Otis.* Edited by Richard Samuelson. Liberty Fund, 2015, p. 50.
12. Zinn, Howard. *A People's History of the United States.* HarperPerennial, 1995, p. 61.
13. Whittenburg, James. "Planters, Merchants, and Lawyers: Social Change and the Origins of the North Carolina Regulation." *The William and Mary Quarterly*, 1977.
14. Zinn, Howard. *A People's History of the United States.* HarperPerennial, 1995, p. 63.
15. Bassett, John S. "The Regulators of North Carolina, 1765–1771." *Annual Report of the American Historical Association for the Year 1894.* Government Printing Office, 1895, 209–242.
16. Zinn, Howard. *A People's History of the United States.* HarperPerennial, 1995, p. 68.
17. *Ibid.*
18. Thompson, Peter. *Rum Punch & Revolution: Taverngoing & Public Life in Eighteenth-Century Philadelphia.* University of Pennsylvania Press, 1998, p. 166.
19. McCullough, David. *1776.* Simon & Schuster, 2006, pp. 157–158.
20. *Ibid.*, p. 167.
21. *Ibid.*, p. 158.
22. Lindert, Peter H., and Williamson, Jeffrey G. "American Colonial Incomes, 1650–1774." Working Paper 19861, National Bureau of Economic Research, January 2014. http://www.nber.org/papers/w19861. Accessed January 11, 2023.
23. *Ibid.*
24. Sellers, Charles. *The Market Revolution: Jacksonian America, 1815–1846.* Oxford University Press, 1991, p. 4.
25. Tufts, Henry. *A Narrative of the Life, Adventures, Travels and Sufferings of Henry Tufts, Now Residing at Lemington, in the District of Maine In substance, as compiled from his own mouth.* Samuel Bragg, 1807, p. 154.
26. De Crevecoeur, J. Hector St. John. *Letters from an American Farmer and Sketches of Eighteenth-Century America.* Penguin Classics, 1981, p. 72.
27. *Ibid.*, p. 85.
28. Fischer, David Hackett. *Paul Revere's Ride.* Oxford University Press, 1995, p. 39.
29. Zucker, A.E. *General de Kalb, Lafayette's Mentor.* University of North Carolina Press, 1966, p. 117.
30. Camp, Phineas. *The Life of General Lafayette, Marquis of France, General in the United States Army, Etc.* C.M. Saxton, 1856, p. 31.
31. Wood, Gordon S. *The Radicalism of the American Revolution.* Vintage, 1993, p. 112.
32. "From George Washington to Catharine Sawbridge Macaulay Graham, 9 January 1790." *Founders Online*, National Archives. https://founders.archives.gov/documents/Washington/05-04-02-0363. [Original source: *The Papers of George Washington, Presidential Series, Vol. 4, 8 September 1789–15 January 1790*, edited by Dorothy Twohig. University Press of Virginia, 1893, pp. 551–554.]
33. Headle, Lura E. "Grants of Land by the United States to our Soldiers of Past Wars." *Advocate of Peace through Justice*, vol. 84, no. 5, May 1922, p. 176.
34. Bounty-Land Warrants for Military Service, 1775–1855. *National Archives* and Records Administration. https://www.archives.gov/files/research/military/bounty-land-1775-1855.pdf. Accessed June 4, 2023.
35. Main, Jackson Turner. *Social Structure of Revolutionary America.* Princeton University Press, 1969, p. 9.
36. "Who Voted in Early America?" Constitutional Rights Foundation. https://

www.crf-usa.org/bill-of-rights-in-action/bria-8-1-b-who-voted-in-early-america. Accessed October 6, 2022.

37. "From George Washington to Benjamin Harrison, 18–30 December 1778." *Founders Online*, National Archives. https://founders.archives.gov/documents/Washington/03-18-02-0510.

38. Cogliano, Francis D. *Revolutionary America, 1763–1815: A Political History*. Taylor & Francis, 2016, p. 107.

39. McDonnell, Michael A. "Resistance to the American Revolution." *A Companion to the American Revolution*. Edited by Jack P. Greene and J.R. Pole. Blackwell, 2000, p. 346.

40. *Ibid.*, p. 345.

41. Countryman, Edward. "Confederation: State Governments and Their Problems." *A Companion to the American Revolution*. Edited by Jack P. Greene and J.R. Pole. Blackwell, 2000, p. 366.

42. McDonnell, Michael A. "Resistance to the American Revolution." *A Companion to the American Revolution*. Edited by Jack P. Greene and J.R. Pole. Blackwell, 2000, p. 345.

43. *Ibid.*, p. 346.

44. *Ibid.*

45. *Ibid.*, p. 343.

46. Bly, Antonio T., and Ingerick, Ryan. "'Able and willing to bear Arms': Indentured Servants and the Coming of the American Revolution in Virginia." *Configurações* 26, December 15, 2020. http://journals.openedition.org/; configuracoes/9963; DOI: https://doi.org/10.4000/configuracoes.9963. Accessed April 20, 2023.

47. *Ibid.*

48. *Ibid.*

49. McDonnell, Michael A. "Resistance to the American Revolution." *A Companion to the American Revolution*. Edited by Jack P. Greene and J.R. Pole. Blackwell, 2000, p. 342.

50. *Ibid.*, p. 347.

51. Tufts, Henry. *A Narrative of the Life, Adventures, Travels and Sufferings of Henry Tufts, Now Residing at Lemington, in the District of Maine In substance, as compiled from his own mouth*. Dover: Samuel Bragg, 1807, p. 105

52. McDonnell, Michael A. "Resistance to the American Revolution," *A Companion to the American Revolution*. Edited by Jack P. Greene and J.R. Pole. Blackwell, 2000, p. 345.

53. "From George Washington to Henry Laurens, 23 December 1777." *Founders Online*, National Archives. https://founders.archives.gov/documents/Washington/03-12-02-0628. [Original source: *The Papers of George Washington, Revolutionary War Series, Vol. 12, 26 October 1777–25 December 1777*. Edited by Frank E. Grizzard, Jr., and David R. Hoth. Charlottesville: University Press of Virginia, 2002, pp. 683–687.]

54. Nagy, John A. *Rebellion in the Ranks: Mutinies of the American Revolution*. Westholme, 2007, p. 78.

55. McClellan, Joseph. "Diary of the Revolt of the Pennsylvania Line, January 1781." Pennsylvania Archives, Second Series, Volume XI. Lane S. Hart, State Printer, 1880, p. 631

56. "Diary of the Revolt of the Pennsylvania Line, January 1781." Pennsylvania Archives, Second Series, Volume XI. Lane S. Hart, State Printer, 1880, pp. 633–634.

57. Reed, William Bradford. *Life and correspondence of Joseph Reed, military secretary of Washington, at Cambridge*. Lindsay and Blakiston, 1847, p. 320.

58. *Journals of the Continental Congress, 1774–1789, Volume XIX, January 1–April 23, 1781*. Government Printing Office, 1912, p. 80.

59. Schellhammer, Michael. "Mutiny of the Pennsylvania Line." *Journal of the American Revolution*, January 14, 2014. https://allthingsliberty.com/2014/01/mutiny-pennsylvania-line/. Accessed April 19, 2023.

60. Nagy, John A. *Rebellion in the Ranks: Mutinies of the American Revolution*. Westholme, 2007, p. 65.

61. Shy, John. *A People Numerous and Armed: Reflections on the Military Struggle for American Independence*. Rev. ed. University of Michigan Press, 1990, p. 168.

62. McDonnell, Michael A. "Resistance to the American Revolution," *A Companion to the American Revolution*. Edited by Jack P. Greene and J.R. Pole. Blackwell, 2000, p. 342.

63. *Ibid.*, p. 345.

64. Clark, J.C.D. "The Unexpected Revolution: America, 1774–1787," *Thomas Paine: Britain, America, and France in the Age of Enlightenment and*

Revolution. Oxford Academic, February 15, 2018. https://doi.org/10.1093/oso/9780198816997.003.0005. Accessed August 4, 2023.

65. "From John Adams to Patrick Henry, 3 June 1776." Founders Online, National Archives. https://founders.archives.gov/documents/Adams/06-04-02-0102. [Original source: The Adams Papers, Papers of John Adams, Vol. 4, February–August 1776. Edited by Robert J. Taylor. Harvard University Press, 1979, pp. 234–235.]

66. Adams, Samuel. The Writings of Samuel Adams—Volume 4. Edited by Harry Alonzo Cushing. G.P. Putnam's Sons, 1908, p. 115.

67. Wood, Gordon S. The American Revolution: A History. Modern Library, 2003, p. 125.

68. Ibid., p. 121.

Chapter 9

1. Schiff, Stacy. The Revolutionary: Samuel Adams. Little, Brown, 2022, p. 25.

2. Miller, John C. Sam Adams: Pioneer in Propaganda. Little, Brown, 1936, p. 39.

3. Bell, J.L. "You Won't Believe How Samuel Adams Recruited Sons of Liberty." Journal of the American Revolution, February 5, 2014. https://allthingsliberty.com/2014/02/you-wont-believe-how-samuel-adams-recruited-sons-of-liberty/. Accessed March 13, 2023.

4. Alexander, John K. Samuel Adams: America's Revolutionary Politician. Rowman & Littlefield, 2002, p. 111.

5. Cregeau, Damien. "'Spirits of Independence': Ten Taverns of the Revolutionary War Era." Journal of the American Revolution, April 29, 2021. https://allthingsliberty.com/2021/04/spirits-of-independence-ten-taverns-of-the-revolutionary-war-era/. Accessed March 18, 2023.

6. Fischer, David Hackett. Paul Revere's Ride. Oxford University Press, 1995, p. 125

7. Tufts, Henry. A Narrative of the Life, Adventures, Travels and Sufferings of Henry Tufts, Now Residing at Lemington, in the District of Maine In substance, as compiled from his own mouth. Samuel Bragg, 1807, p. 276.

8. "Revolutionary Taverns." American Antiquarian Society. https://www.americanantiquarian.org/Exhibitions/Reading/revolutionary.htm. Accessed March 18, 2023.

9. A Guide Book for Williamsburg, Virginia. Colonial Williamsburg, Incorporated, 1936, p. 15.

10. Dawson, Henry. Westchester County, New York, During the American Revolution. H.B. Dawson, 1886, pp. 7–8.

11. Stoll, Ira. Samuel Adams: A Life. Free Press, 2009, p. 146.

12. Fischer, David Hackett. Paul Revere's Ride. Oxford University Press, 1995, p. 193.

13. Thompson, Peter. Rum Punch & Revolution: Taverngoing & Public Life in Eighteenth-Century Philadelphia. University of Pennsylvania Press, 1998, p. 151.

14. Ibid., pp. 151–152.

15. From George Washington to Major General Nathanael Greene, August 1, 1777. https://founders.archives.gov/documents/Washington/03-10-02-0476. Accessed March 18, 2023.

16. "General Orders, 5 August 1777." Founders Online, National Archives. https://founders.archives.gov/documents/Washington/03-10-02-0524. [Original source: The Papers of George Washington, Revolutionary War Series, Vol. 10, 11 June 1777–18 August 1777. Edited by Frank E. Grizzard, Jr. Charlottesville: University Press of Virginia, 2000, p. 508.]

17. Klein, Christopher. "How Samuel Adams Became Linked to Beer." History.com, January 27, 2015. https://www.history.com/news/the-sudsy-history-of-samuel-adams. Accessed March 18, 2023.

18. Massachusetts Gazette and Boston News-Letter, no. 3268, May 22, 1766.

19. "General Orders, 18 April 1783." Founders Online, National Archives. https://founders.archives.gov/documents/Washington/99-01-02-11097. Accessed April 19, 2023.

20. Kitman, Marvin. George Washington's Expense Account. Grove Press, 2001, p. 143.

21. Rupp, Rebecca. "Rum: The Spirit That Fueled a Revolution." National Geographic, April 10, 2015. https://www.nationalgeographic.com/culture/article/rum-the-spirit-that-fueled-a-revolution. Accessed March 23, 2023.

Notes—Chapter 9

22. Rorabaugh, W.J. "Alcohol in America." *OAH Magazine of History*, vol. 6, no. 2, Fall 1991, p. 17.
23. Nissenbaum, Stephen. *The Battle for Christmas: A Social and Cultural History of Our Most Cherished Holiday*. Vintage, 1997, p. 261,
24. Rudin, Max. "Beer and America." *American Heritage*, vol. 53, issue 3, 2002. https://www.americanheritage.com/beer-and-america. Accessed March 23, 2023.
25. Smith, Gregg. *Beer in America: The Early Years—1587–1840*. Brewers Publications, 1998, pp. 11–12.
26. Mather, Cotton. *Pillars of salt. An history of some criminals executed in this land, for capital crimes. : With some of their dying speeches; collected and published, for the warning of such as live in destructive courses of ungodliness. : Whereto is added, for the better improvement of this history, a brief discourse about the dreadful justice of God, in punishing of sin, with sin*. Printed by B. Green, and J. Allen, 1699, p. 67.
27. Ibid., p. 72.
28. Rudin, Max. "Beer and America." *American Heritage*, vol. 53, issue 3, 2002. https://www.americanheritage.com/beer-and-america. Accessed March 23, 2023.
29. Rupp, Rebecca. "Rum: The Spirit That Fueled a Revolution." *National Geographic*, April 10, 2015. https://www.nationalgeographic.com/culture/article/rum-the-spirit-that-fueled-a-revolution. Accessed March 23, 2023.
30. "The Sugar Act of 1764." American History Central. https://www.americanhistorycentral.com/entries/sugar-act/. Accessed March 18, 2023.
31. Adams, Samuel. "Instructions to Boston's Representatives." May 28, 1764. https://www.revolutionary-war-and-beyond.com/instructions-to-bostons-representatives-may-28-1764.html. Accessed March 19, 2023.
32. "Seizure of Hancock's Sloop, 1768–1769." *Founders Online*, National Archives. https://founders.archives.gov/documents/Adams/01-03-02-0016-0021. [Original source: *The Adams Papers, Diary and Autobiography of John Adams, Vol. 3, Diary, 1782–1804*; Autobiography, Part One to October 1776, edited by L.H. Butterfield. Harvard University Press, 1961, pp. 305–306.]
33. *Boston News-Letter*, June 16, 1768.
34. Deposition of Harrison, June 11, 1768, Treas. 1:465, fol. 74, National Archives of the United Kingdom.
35. Adams, Samuel. *The Writings of Samuel Adams—Volume 1*. Edited by Harry Alonzo Cushing. G.P. Putnam's Sons, 1904, p. 245.
36. Warren, Mercy Otis. *History of the Rise, Progress, and Termination of the American Revolution interspersed with Biographical, Political and Moral Observations—Volume 1*. Liberty Fund, 1805, p. 211.
37. Schiff, Stacy. "The Noble Fury of Samuel Adams." *Smithsonian Magazine*, October 2022. https://www.smithsonianmag.com/history/noble-fury-samuel-adams-180980758/. Accessed March 21, 2023.
38. Thompson, Peter. *Rum Punch & Revolution: Taverngoing & Public Life in Eighteenth-Century Philadelphia*. University of Pennsylvania Press, 1998, p. 1.
39. "The Drinker's Dictionary, 13 January 1737." *Founders Online*, National Archives. https://founders.archives.gov/documents/Franklin/01-02-02-0029. [Original source: *The Papers of Benjamin Franklin, Vol. 2, January 1, 1735, through December 31, 1744*. Edited by Leonard W. Labaree. Yale University Press, 1961, pp. 173–178.]
40. Franklin, Benjamin. "The Drinker's Dictionary." January 13, 1737. *Founders Online*, National Archives. https://founders.archives.gov/documents/Franklin/01-02-02-0029. Accessed March 24, 2023.
41. Franklin, Benjamin. *Memoirs of the Life and Writings of Benjamin Franklin Volume 5*. Edited by William Templeton and Franklin. H. Colburn, 1819, p. 286.
42. Ibid., p. 291.
43. Rorabaugh, W.J. "Alcohol in America." *OAH Magazine of History*, vol. 6, no. 2, Fall 1991, p. 17.
44. Tufts, Henry. *A Narrative of the Life, Adventures, Travels and Sufferings of Henry Tufts, Now Residing at Lemington, in the District of Maine In substance, as compiled from his own mouth*. Samuel Bragg, 1807, p. 174.
45. Griffin, Patrick. *American Leviathan: Empire, Nation, and Revolutionary Frontier*. Hill and Wang, 2008, p. 61.

46. "The Royal Proclamation." October 7, 1763. https://avalon.law.yale.edu/18th_century/proc1763.asp. Accessed March 23, 2023.

47. Griffin, Patrick. *American Leviathan: Empire, Nation, and Revolutionary Frontier.* Hill and Wang, 2008.

48. *The Scotch-Irish in America: proceedings and addresses of the 1st-10th congress, 1889–1901 Volume 3.* Scotch-Irish Society of America, 1901, p. 240.

49. Silver, Peter. *Our Savage Neighbors: How Indian War Transformed Early America.* W.W. Norton, 2009, p. 203.

50. Withers, Alexander Scott. *Chronicles of Border Warfare: A History of the Settlement by the Whites, of Northwestern Virginia, and of the Indian Wars and Massacres, in That Section of the State.* The Robert Clarke Company, 1895, p. 149.

51. Howe, Henry. *Historical Collections of Ohio: Containing a Collection of the Most Interesting Facts, Traditions, Biographical Sketches, Anecdotes, Etc., Relating to Its General and Local History: with Descriptions of Its Counties, Principal Towns and Villages; Illustrated by 177 Engravings.* Derby, Bradley & Company, 1847, pp. 266–267.

52. Wittenberg, Eric J. "Lord Dunmore's War: The Opening of the American Revolution." *Emerging Revolutionary War*, December 3, 2015. https://emergingrevolutionarywar.org/2015/12/03/lord-dunmores-war-the-opening-of-the-american-revolution/. Accessed March 24, 2023.

53. Tyler, John W. "'Such Ruins Were Never Seen in America': The Looting of Thomas Hutchinson's House at the Time of the Stamp Act Riots." *Boston Furniture: 1700–1900.* Colonial Society of Massachusetts, 2016, p. 163

54. Fischer, David Hackett. *Paul Revere's Ride.* Oxford University Press, 1995, p. 140.

55. Rupp, Rebecca. "Rum: The Spirit That Fueled a Revolution." *National Geographic*, April 10, 2015. https://www.nationalgeographic.com/culture/article/rum-the-spirit-that-fueled-a-revolution. Accessed March 23, 2023.

56. Curtis, Wayne. *And a Bottle of Rum: A History of the New World in Ten Cocktails.* Broadway Books, 2007, p. 93.

57. *Ibid.*, p. 95.

58. Fischer, David Hackett. *Paul Revere's Ride.* Oxford University Press, 1995, p. 341.

59. Gleason, Hall. "Captain Isaac Hall." Medford Historical Society, March 20, 1905. https://www.perseus.tufts.edu/hopper/text?doc=Perseus%3Atext%3A2005.05.0008%3Achapter%3D23. Accessed March 24, 2023.

60. Wren, Christopher S. *Those Turbulent Sons of Freedom: Ethan Allen's Green Mountain Boys and the American Revolution.* Simon & Schuster, 2018, p. 26.

61. Stryker, William S. *The Battles of Trenton and Princeton.* Houghton, Mifflin, 1898, p. 361.

62. "The Battle of Trenton." *American Revolutionary War Battles for 1776.* https://revolutionarywar.us/year-1776/battle-of-trenton/. Accessed April 5, 2023.

63. Lengel, Edward G. *General George Washington: A Military Life.* Random House, 2005, p. 186.

64. McCullough, David. *1776.* Simon & Schuster, 2006, p. 282.

65. *The Detail and Conduct of the American War, under Generals Gage, Howe, Burgoyne, and Vice Admiral Lord Howe.* 3rd ed. War College Series, 1780, p. 40.

66. McCullough, David. *1776.* Simon & Schuster, 2006, p. 282.

67. Fischer, David Hackett. *Washington's Crossing.* Oxford University Press, 2006, p. 257.

68. *Ibid.*, p. 256.

69. *Ibid.*, pp. 124–125.

70. "General Orders, 25 July 1776." *Founders Online*, National Archives. https://founders.archives.gov/documents/Washington/03-05-02-0333. [Original source: *The Papers of George Washington, Revolutionary War Series, Vol. 5, 16 June 1776–12 August 1776.* Edited by Philander D. Chase. Charlottesville: University Press of Virginia, 1993, pp. 457–458.]

71. Johnston, Henry Phelps. *The Campaign of 1776 around New York and Brooklyn.* Long Island Historical Society, 1878, p. 86.

72. Harris, Michael C. *Germantown: A Military History of the Battle for Philadelphia, October 4, 1777.* Savas Beatie, 2020, p. 445.

73. Taaffe, Stephen R. *Washington's Revolutionary War Generals.* University of Oklahoma Press, 2019, p. 123.

74. Rorabaugh, W.J. *The Alcoholic Republic: An American Tradition.* Oxford University Press, 1981, pp. 5–6.

75. Kendall, Joshua. "The First Children Who Led Sad Lives." *Smithsonian Magazine*, February 11, 2016. https://www.smithsonianmag.com/history/first-children-who-led-sad-lives-180958099/. Accessed March 25, 2023.

76. "Abigail Adams to John Quincy Adams, 29 January 1801." Founders Online, National Archives. https://founders.archives.gov/documents/Adams/04-14-02-0248. [Original source: *The Adams Papers, Adams Family Correspondence, Vol. 14, October 1799–February 1801.* Edited by Hobson Woodward, Sara Martin, Christopher F. Minty, Amanda M. Norton, Neal E. Millikan, Gwen Fries, and Sara Georgini. Harvard University Press, 2019, pp. 547–551.]

77. Todd, Charles Burr, ed. *Life and Letters of Joel Barlow, LL.D., poet, statesman, philosopher with extracts from his works and hitherto unpublished poems.* G.P. Putnam's Sons, 1886, p. 237.

78. Deedy, John. "Tom Paine Would Drink to New Rochelle." *The New York Times*, April 22, 1973,

Chapter 10

1. Arendt, Hannah. *The New Yorker*, September 12, 1970.

2. Bullen, Daniel. *Daniel Shays's Honorable Rebellion: An American Story.* Westholme, 2021, p. 11.

3. Taylor, Robert J. "Construction of the Massachusetts Constitution." American Antiquarian Society, Worcester, MA, 1980, p. 326,

4. Ibid.

5. "Constitution of Massachusetts." October 25, 1780. https://consource.org/document/constitution-of-massachusetts-1780-10-25/20130122075650/. Accessed August 20, 2023.

6. "To John Adams from Samuel Adams, 10 July 1780." Founders Online, National Archives. https://founders.archives.gov/documents/Adams/06-09-02-0305. [Original source: *The Adams Papers, Papers of John Adams, Vol. 9, March 1780–July 1780.* Edited by Gregg L. Lint and Richard Alan Ryerson. Harvard University Press, 1996, pp. 507–508.]

7. Stoll, Ira. *Samuel Adams: A Life.* Free Press, 2009, p. 221.

8. Balik, Shelby M. "'Persecuted in the Bowels of a Free Republic': Samuel Ely and the Agrarian Theology of Justice, 1768–1797." *Massachusetts Historical Review*, vol. 15, 2013, pp. 89–122.

9. Tufts, Henry. *A Narrative of the Life, Adventures, Travels and Sufferings of Henry Tufts, Now Residing at Lemington, in the District of Maine In substance, as compiled from his own mouth.* Samuel Bragg, 1807, p. 170

10. Vaughan, Alden T. "The 'Horrid and Unnatural Rebellion' of Daniel Shays." *American Heritage*, vol. 17, issue 4, June 1966. https://www.americanheritage.com/horrid-and-unnatural-rebellion-daniel-shays. Accessed December 10, 2022.

11. Bullen, Daniel. *Daniel Shays's Honorable Rebellion: An American Story.* Westholme, 2021, pp. 20–21.

12. Petition of the Worcester County Convention, 28 September 1786, Shays Rebellion Collection, American Antiquarian Society.

13. George Minot to Thomas Ward, Box 6, Folder 1, Ward Family Papers, AAS; Worcester County Gaol Petition, 7 December 1785, Box 3, Folder 4, Worcester County, MA papers, AAS.

14. "Why Is Shays' Rebellion Important?" *History in Charts.* September 7, 2021.

15. Vaughan, Alden T. "The 'Horrid and Unnatural Rebellion' of Daniel Shays." *American Heritage*, vol. 17, issue 4, June 1966. https://www.americanheritage.com/horrid-and-unnatural-rebellion-daniel-shays. Accessed December 10, 2022.

16. *The Hampshire Gazette*, September 26, 1786.

17. Bullen, Daniel. *Daniel Shays's Honorable Rebellion: An American Story.* Westholme, 2021, xiii.

18. Wells, Frederic Palmer. *History of Newbury, Vermont, from the discovery of the Coös country to present time. With genealogical records of many families.* Caledonian Company, 1902, pp. 121-122.

19. Bullen, p. 107.

20. Ibid., p. 75.

21. Ibid., p. 96.

22. Szatmary, David P. *Shays' Rebellion: The Making of an Agrarian Insurrection.*

University of Massachusetts Press, 1980, pp. 84–86.

23. Declaration of the General Court that a Rebellion Exists. Massachusetts General Court. February 4, 1787. https://shaysrebellion.stcc.edu/shaysapp/artifact_trans.do?shortName=declaration_rebellion4feb87&page=back. Accessed December 10, 2022.

24. Bullen, Daniel. *Daniel Shays's Honorable Rebellion: An American Story*. Westholme, 2021, p. 77.

25. Ibid.

26. Ibid., p. 76.

27. Ibid., p. 77.

28. Maier, Pauline. *Ratification: The People Debate the Constitution, 1787–1788*. Simon & Schuster, 2011, p. 16.

29. Holton, Woody. "Abigail Adams, Bond Speculator." *William and Mary Quarterly*, vol. 64, no. 4, October 2007.

30. Bullen, Daniel. *Daniel Shays's Honorable Rebellion: An American Story*. Westholme, 2021, p. 93.

31. Letter to George Washington from Henry Knox, October 23, 1786. *Founders Online*, National Archives. https://founders.archives.gov/documents/Washington/04-04-02-0274. Accessed January 12, 2023.

32. George Washington to David Humphreys, 22 October 1786. The Papers of George Washington Digital Edition.

33. George Washington to Henry Knox, 25 February 1787. The Papers of George Washington Digital Edition.

Chapter 11

1. Wood, Gordon S. *The American Revolution: A History*. Modern Library, 2003, p. 140.

2. "From George Washington to Henry Knox, 3 February 1787." *Founders Online*, National Archives. https://founders.archives.gov/documents/Washington/04-05-02-0006. [Original source: *The Papers of George Washington, Confederation Series, Vol. 5, 1 February 1787–31 December 1787*. Edited by W.W. Abbot. Charlottesville: University Press of Virginia, 1997, pp. 7–9.]

3. Beard, Charles. *An Economic Interpretation of the Constitution of the United States*. The Free Press, 1913, p. 52

4. Bullen, Daniel. *Daniel Shays's Honorable Rebellion: An American Story*. Westholme, 2021, p. 226.

5. "From George Washington to John Jay, 15 August 1786," *Founders Online*, National Archives. https://founders.archives.gov/documents/Washington/04-04-02-0199. [Original source: *The Papers of George Washington, Confederation Series, Vol. 4, 2 April 1786–31 January 1787*. Edited by W.W. Abbot. Charlottesville: University Press of Virginia, 1995, pp. 212–213.]

6. Adams, Samuel. *The Writings of Samuel Adams—Volume 4*. Edited by Harry Alonzo Cushing. G.P. Putnam's Sons, 1908, p. 332.

7. Ellis, Joseph J. *The Quartet: Orchestrating the Second American Revolution, 1783–1789*. Vintage, 2016, pp. 145–146.

8. Dickinson, John. Notes for a speech, July 9, 1787. https://housedivided.dickinson.edu/sites/teagle/texts/constitutional-convention-1787/. Accessed June 6, 2023.

9. Debates and proceedings in the Convention of the commonwealth of Massachusetts, held in the year 1788, and which finally ratified the Constitution of the United States. Massachusetts. Convention, Peirce, Bradford [Kinney], 1819–1889, Hale, Charles, 1831–1882, Massachusetts. General Court, p. 209.

10. Lee, Richard Henry. "Antifederalist No. 36: Representation and Internal Taxation." http://resources.utulsa.edu/law/classes/rice/Constitutional/AntiFederalist/36.htm. Accessed February 5, 2023.

11. Bullen, Daniel. *Daniel Shays's Honorable Rebellion: An American Story*. Westholme, 2021, p. 230.

12. Forkosch, Morris D. "Who are the 'People' in the Preamble to the Constitution." *Case Western Reserve Law Review* 19, no. 644, 1968.

13. Farrand, Max, ed. *The Records of the Federal Convention of 1787*. Yale University Press, 1966, p. 137.

14. Brookhiser, Richard. *Gentleman Revolutionary: Gouverneur Morris, the Rake Who Wrote the Constitution*. Free Press, 2008, pp. 90–91.

15. Ibid.

16. Speech of Patrick Henry, June 5, 1788. https://www.let.rug.nl/usa/documents/1786-1800/the-anti-federalist-papers/-

speech-of-patrick-henry-(june-5-1788).php. Accessed November 1, 2022.

17. Samuel Adams letter to *John Adams*, November 20, 1790. *The Life And Public Services of Samuel Adams—Volume Three*. Edited by William V. Wells. Little, Brown, 1865, p. 308.

18. Wood, Gordon S. *The American Revolution: A History*. Modern Library, 2003, p. 94.

19. Constitution of Virginia (1776). https://encyclopediavirginia.org/entries/the-constitution-of-virginia-1776/. Accessed March 4, 2023.

20. "Vices of the Political System of the United States, April 1787." *Founders Online*, National Archives. https://founders.archives.gov/documents/Madison/01-09-02-0187.

21. Articles of Confederation; March 1, 1781. Miscellaneous Papers of the Continental Congress, 1774–1789; Records of the Continental and Confederation Congresses and the Constitutional Convention, Record Group 360; *National Archives Building*, Washington, D.C.

22. "Madison Debates," May 31, 1787. Yale Law School Lillian Goldman Law Library. https://avalon.law.yale.edu/18th_century/debates_531.asp#1. Accessed October 30, 2022.

23. Tufts, Henry. *A Narrative of the Life, Adventures, Travels and Sufferings of Henry Tufts, Now Residing at Lemington, in the District of Maine In substance, as compiled from his own mouth*. Samuel Bragg, 1807, p. 240.

24. Brookhiser, Richard. *Gentleman Revolutionary: Gouverneur Morris, the Rake Who Wrote the Constitution*. Free Press, 2008, p. 84.

25. "Madison Debates," May 31, 1787. Yale Law School Lillian Goldman Law Library. https://avalon.law.yale.edu/18th_century/debates_531.asp#1. Accessed October 30, 2022.

26. *Ibid.*

27. Hamilton, Alexander. Federalist No. 35. https://guides.loc.gov/federalist-papers/text-31-40. Accessed July 30, 2023.

28. Dry, Murray. "The Debate Over Ratification of the Constitution." *A Companion to the American Revolution*. Edited by Jack P. Greene and J.R. Pole. Blackwell, 2000, p. 486.

29. *Ibid.*, p. 487.

30. "The Founding Fathers: Elbridge Gerry, Massachusetts." *National Archives*. https://www.archives.gov/founding-docs/founding-fathers-massachusetts#gerry. Accessed October 9, 2022.

31. Letter of the President of the Federal Convention, Dated September 17, 1787, to the President of Congress, Transmitting the Constitution. https://avalon.law.yale.edu/18th_century/translet.asp. Accessed October 9, 2022.

32. *Ibid.*

33. Bullen, Daniel. *Daniel Shays's Honorable Rebellion: An American Story*. Westholme, 2021, p. 227.

34. *Ibid.*

35. George Washington's First Inaugural Address, April 30, 1789. https://www.archives.gov/legislative/features/gw-inauguration. Accessed October 9, 2022.

36. Militia Act of 1792, Second Congress, Session I. Chapter XXVIII. Passed May 2, 1792, providing for the authority of the President to call out the Militia. https://www.constitution.org/1-Activism/mil/mil_act_1792.htm?utm_content=cmp-true. Accessed August 26, 2023.

37. Letter from Thomas Jefferson to Marie-Joseph-Paul-Yves-Roch-Gilbert du Motier, Marquis de Lafayette, November 4, 1823. *Founders Online*, National Archives. https://founders.archives.gov/documents/Jefferson/98-01-02-3843. Accessed January 27, 2023.

38. "To John Adams from Samuel Adams, 25 November 1790." *Founders Online*, National Archives. https://founders.archives.gov/documents/Adams/06-20-02-0257. [Original source: *The Adams Papers, Papers of John Adams, Vol. 20, June 1789–February 1791*. Edited by Sara Georgini, Sara Martin, R. M. Barlow, Gwen Fries, Amanda M. Norton, Neal E. Millikan, and Hobson Woodward. Harvard University Press, 2020, pp. 434–439.]

39. Adams, Samuel. *The Writings of Samuel Adams—Volume 4*. Edited by Harry Alonzo Cushing. G.P. Putnam's Sons, 1908, p. 229.

40. Wood, Gordon S. *The American Revolution: A History*. Modern Library, 2003, p. 101.

41. "Madison Debates," May 31, 1787. Yale Law School Lillian Goldman Law Library. https://avalon.law.yale.

edu/18th_century/debates_531.asp#1. Accessed October 30, 2022.
42. "VI. To the Inhabitants of the Colony of Massachusetts-Bay, 27 February 1775," *Founders Online*, National Archives. https://founders.archives.gov/documents/Adams/06-02-02-0072-0007. [Original source: *The Adams Papers, Papers of John Adams, vol. 2, December 1773–April 1775*, edited by Robert J. Taylor. Harvard University Press, 1977, pp. 288–307.]
43. Tufts, Henry. *A Narrative of the Life, Adventures, Travels and Sufferings of Henry Tufts, Now Residing at Lemington, in the District of Maine In substance, as compiled from his own mouth*. Samuel Bragg, 1807, p. 250.
44. Ibid., p. 252.
45. Thompson, Roger. *Sex in Middlesex: Popular Mores in a Massachusetts County, 1649–1699*. University of Massachusetts Press, 1986, p. 37.
46. Gutierrez, Michael Keenan. "The Trial and Execution of Ruth Blay." *We're History*, June 12, 2015. https://werehistory.org/ruth-blay/. Accessed January 19, 2023.
47. Tufts, Henry. *A Narrative of the Life, Adventures, Travels and Sufferings of Henry Tufts, Now Residing at Lemington, in the District of Maine In substance, as compiled from his own mouth*. Samuel Bragg, 1807, p. 254.
48. Ibid., p. 255.
49. Ibid., p. 254.
50. Ibid., p. 257.
51. "Washington's Farewell Address 1796." https://avalon.law.yale.edu/18th_century/washing.asp. Accessed June 22, 2023.
52. Tufts, Henry. *A Narrative of the Life, Adventures, Travels and Sufferings of Henry Tufts, Now Residing at Lemington, in the District of Maine In substance, as compiled from his own mouth*. Samuel Bragg, 1807, p. 333.

Chapter 12

1. Adams, Samuel. *The Writings of Samuel Adams—Volume 4*. Edited by Harry Alonzo Cushing. G.P. Putnam's Sons, 1908, p. 210.
2. Bullen, Daniel. *Daniel Shays's Honorable Rebellion: An American Story*. Westholme, 2021, p. 218.
3. Feer, Robert A. *Shay's Rebellion*. Garland, 1988, p. 416; Mass., *Acts and Laws, 1786-1787*, p. 994.
4. "Pardon for Henry McCulloch & Jason Parmenter." September 12, 1787. https://www.shaysrebellion.stcc.edu/shaysapp/artifact.do?shortName=mcculloch_pardon. Accessed February 3, 2023.
5. DiCamillo, Michael. "'They Crucified Two Thieves': The Executions of John Bly and Charles Rose, Shays's Rebels." *The Histories* vol. 5, issue 2, article 2. https://digitalcommons.lasalle.edu/the_histories/vol5/iss2/2. Accessed February 4, 2023.
6. "Cotton Tufts to *John Adams*, 30 June 1787." *Founders Online*, National Archives. https://founders.archives.gov/documents/Adams/04-08-02-0041. [Original source: *The Adams Papers, Adams Family Correspondence, vol. 8, March 1787- December 1789*. Edited by C. James Taylor, Margaret A. Hogan, Jessie May Rodrique, Gregg L. Lint, Hobson Woodward, and Mary T. Claffey. Harvard University Press, 2007, pp. 101–104.]
7. Samuel Adams to Arthur Fenner, governor of Rhode Island, December 6, 1794. Samuel Adams Papers, New York Public Library.
8. Peres Fobes, *A Sermon Preached Before His Excellency Samuel Adams, May 27, 1795*. Mercury Press, by Yount and Minns, 1795, p. 38.
9. "From John Adams to John Jay, 25 August 1785," *Founders Online*, National Archives. https://founders.archives.gov/documents/Adams/06-17-02-0196. [Original source: *The Adams Papers, Papers of John Adams, Vol. 17, April–November 1785*. Edited by Gregg L. Lint, C. James Taylor, Sara Georgini, Hobson Woodward, Sara B. Sikes, Amanda A. Mathews, and Sara Martin. Harvard University Press, 2014, pp. 354–362.]
10. Wells, William V. *The Life and Public Services of Samuel Adams Volume 3*. Little, Brown, 1865, pp. 324–328.
11. Tufts, Henry. *A Narrative of the Life, Adventures, Travels and Sufferings of Henry Tufts, Now Residing at Lemington, in the District of Maine In substance, as compiled from his own mouth*. Samuel Bragg, 1807, p. 282.
12. Ibid., p. 213.
13. Ibid., pp. 289–290.

14. Pearson, Edmund. *The Autobiography of a Criminal.* Duffield & Company, 1930, pp. 347–357.
15. Tufts, Henry. *A Narrative of the Life, Adventures, Travels and Sufferings of Henry Tufts, Now Residing at Lemington, in the District of Maine In substance, as compiled from his own mouth.* Samuel Bragg, 1807, p. 218.
16. Pearson, Edmund. *The Autobiography of a Criminal.* Duffield & Company, 1930, pp. 347–357.
17. Tufts, Henry. *A Narrative of the Life, Adventures, Travels and Sufferings of Henry Tufts, Now Residing at Lemington, in the District of Maine In substance, as compiled from his own mouth.* Samuel Bragg, 1807, p. 219.
18. *Ibid.*, p. 292.
19. *Ibid.*, p. 219.
20. *Ibid.*, p. 304.
21. Pearson, Edmund. *The Autobiography of a Criminal.* Duffield & Company, 1930, pp. 347–357.
22. Williams, Daniel E. "Doctor, Preacher, Soldier, Thief: A New World of Possibilities in the Rogue Narrative of Henry Tufts." *Early American Literature* XIX, 1984, p. 4.
23. *Dunlap and Claypoole's American Daily Advertiser* (Philadelphia, Pennsylvania), September 23, 1794.
24. Friedman, Lawrence M. *Crime and Punishment in American History.* Basic Books, 1994, p. 44.
25. *Newburyport Herald*, vol. XXIV, issue 97, March 6, 1821, p. 1.
26. *The Diary of Matthew Patten of Bedford, NH from 1754 to 1788.* Rumford Press, 1903, p. 308.
27. *Boston Evening Post*, October 9, 1769.
28. Hamlin, Hannibal. *Psalm Culture and Early Modern English Literature.* Cambridge University Press, 2004, p. 174.
29. Williams, Daniel E. "Doctor, Preacher, Soldier, Thief: A New World of Possibilities in the Rogue Narrative of Henry Tufts." *Early American Literature* XIX, 1984, p. 5.
30. Tufts, Henry. *A Narrative of the Life, Adventures, Travels and Sufferings of Henry Tufts, Now Residing at Lemington, in the District of Maine In substance, as compiled from his own mouth.* Samuel Bragg, 1807, p. 188.
31. *Ibid.*, p. 195.
32. "Notable events in the history of Dover, New Hampshire, from the first settlement in 1623 to 1865." https://archive.org/stream/notableeventsinh00wadl/notableeventsinh00wadl_djvu.txt. Accessed August 2, 2022.
33. Tufts, Henry. *A Narrative of the Life, Adventures, Travels and Sufferings of Henry Tufts, Now Residing at Lemington, in the District of Maine In substance, as compiled from his own mouth.* Samuel Bragg, 1807, p. 213.
34. *Ibid.*, p. 247.
35. *Ibid.*, p. 167.
36. *Ibid.*, p. 303.
37. *Acts and Laws of the Commonwealth of Massachusetts.* Wright & Potter, 1896, p. 600.
38. Tufts, Henry. *A Narrative of the Life, Adventures, Travels and Sufferings of Henry Tufts, Now Residing at Lemington, in the District of Maine In substance, as compiled from his own mouth.* Samuel Bragg, 1807, p. 289.
39. Stamper, Peta. "The Death Penalty: When Was Capital Punishment Abolished in Britain?" History Hit, December 10, 2021. https://www.historyhit.com/the-history-of-capital-punishment-in-britain/. Accessed August 2, 2022.
40. Werin, Lars. *Economic Behavior and Legal Institutions: An Introductory Survey.* World Scientific Publishing Co., 2003, p. 191.
41. The House of Representatives of Massachusetts to the Governor, January 26, 1773. [Massachusetts State Papers, pp. 351–364; also printed in the *Boston Gazette*, February 1, 1773, and in *The Speeches of His Excellency Governor Hutchinson* (Boston, 1773), pp. 33–58].
42. Adams, Samuel. *The Writings of Samuel Adams—Volume 4.* Edited by Harry Alonzo Cushing. G.P. Putnam's Sons, 1908, p. 393.
43. Letter from Benjamin Franklin to Benjamin Vaughan, March 14, 1785. *Founders Online*, National Archives. https://founders.archives.gov/documents/Franklin/01-43-02-0335. Accessed January 22, 2023.
44. Hostettler, John. *Cesare Beccaria: The Genius of "On Crimes and Punishments."* Waterside Press, 2011, p. 132.
45. di Beccaria, Cesare. *An Essay on*

Crimes and Punishments. John Exshaw, 1767, p. 39.

46. "Adams' Argument for the Defense: 3–4 December 1770." *Founders Online*, National Archives. https://founders.archives.gov/documents/Adams/05-03-02-0001-0004-0016. [Original source: *The Adams Papers, Legal Papers of John Adams, Vol. 3, Cases 63 and 64: The Boston Massacre Trials*. Edited by L. Kinvin Wroth and Hiller B. Zobel. Harvard University Press, 1965, pp. 242–270.]

47. Jefferson, Thomas. *Legal Commonplace Book, 1762–1767*. https://www.loc.gov/item/mtjbib026466/.

48. "History of the Death Penalty: The Abolitionist Movement." Death Penalty Information Center. https://deathpenaltyinfo.org/facts-and-research/history-of-the-death-penalty/the-abolitionist-movement. Accessed January 22, 2023.

49. Wood, Gordon S. *The American Revolution: A History*. Modern Library, 2003, p. 125.

50. Adams, Samuel. *The Writings of Samuel Adams—Volume 4*. Edited by Harry Alonzo Cushing. G.P. Putnam's Sons, 1908, p. 380.

51. *Ibid.*, p. 381.

52. Loeb, R.H. *Crime and Capital Punishment*, 1986. https://www.ojp.gov/ncjrs/virtual-library/abstracts/crime-and-capital-punishment-1. Accessed September 6, 2022.

53. Tufts, Henry. *A Narrative of the Life, Adventures, Travels and Sufferings of Henry Tufts, Now Residing at Lemington, in the District of Maine In substance, as compiled from his own mouth*. Samuel Bragg, 1807, pp. 318–319

54. "Seacoast Fortification—First System." GlobalSecurity.org https://www.globalsecurity.org/military/facility/coastal-forts-first-system.htm. Accessed May 22, 2023.

55. Address to the Legislature of Massachusetts. June 4, 1794. *Independent Chronicle*, June 5, 1794.

56. Tufts, Henry. *A Narrative of the Life, Adventures, Travels and Sufferings of Henry Tufts, Now Residing at Lemington, in the District of Maine In substance, as compiled from his own mouth*. Samuel Bragg, 1807, p. 321

57. "Broke Jail, in Salem." *Salem Gazette*, vol. XII, issue 761, November 20, 1798, p. 4.

Chapter 13

1. Tufts, Henry. *A Narrative of the Life, Adventures, Travels and Sufferings of Henry Tufts, Now Residing at Lemington, in the District of Maine In substance, as compiled from his own mouth*. Samuel Bragg, 1807, p. 161.

2. Schiff, Stacy. *The Revolutionary: Samuel Adams*. Little, Brown, 2022, p. 35.

3. Adams, Samuel. *The Writings of Samuel Adams—Volume 4*. Edited by Harry Alonzo Cushing. G.P. Putnam's Sons, 1908, p. 351.

4. Schiff, Stacy. *The Revolutionary: Samuel Adams*. Little, Brown, 2022, p. 27.

5. Puls, Mark. *Samuel Adams: Father of the American Revolution*. New York: Palgrave Macmillan, 1994, p. 27.

6. Miller, John C. *Sam Adams: Pioneer in Propaganda*. Stanford University Press, 1936, p. 16.

7. Neem, Johann N. *Democracy's Schools: The Rise of Public Education in America (How Things Worked)*. Johns Hopkins University Press, 2017, p. 5.

8. Adams, Samuel. *The Writings of Samuel Adams—Volume 4*. Edited by Harry Alonzo Cushing. G.P. Putnam's Sons, 1908, p. 238.

9. Wood, Gordon S. *The Radicalism of the American Revolution*. Vintage, 1993, p. 199.

10. *Ibid.*, p. 197.

11. Wood, Gordon S. *The American Revolution: A History*. Modern Library, 2003, p. 102.

12. De Crevecoeur, J. Hector St. John. *Letters from an American Farmer and Sketches of Eighteenth-Century America*. Penguin Classics, 1981, p. 243.

13. Brackenridge, H.H. "A poem, on the rising glory of America being an exercise Delivered at the Public Commencement at Nassau-Hall, September 25, 1771."

14. Adams, Samuel. *The Writings of Samuel Adams—Volume 4*. Edited by Harry Alonzo Cushing. G.P. Putnam's Sons, 1908, p. 351.

15. Massachusetts Constitution. The

General Court of the Commonwealth of Massachusetts. https://malegislature.gov/Laws/Constitution.

16. Wood, Gordon S. *The American Revolution: A History*. Modern Library, 2003, p. 123.

17. *Ibid.*, p. 124.

18. Wood, Gordon S. *The Radicalism of the American Revolution*, Vintage Books, 1993, p. 100.

19. Wood, Gordon S. *The American Revolution: A History*. Modern Library, 2003, p. 132.

20. Tufts, Henry. *A Narrative of the Life, Adventures, Travels and Sufferings of Henry Tufts, Now Residing at Lemington, in the District of Maine In substance, as compiled from his own mouth*. Samuel Bragg, 1807, p. 279.

21. *Ibid.*, p. 219.

22. Wood, Gordon S. *The American Revolution: A History*. Modern Library, 2003, pp. 132–133.

23. "Religion and the Founding of the American Republic." Library of Congress. https://www.loc.gov/exhibits/religion/rel07.html. Accessed June 3, 2023.

24. *The Oxford Handbook of Evangelical Theology*. Oxford University Press, 2013, p. 473.

25. *Ibid.*, p. 231.

26. Noll, Mark A. "The American Revolution and Protestant Evangelicalism." *The Journal of Interdisciplinary History*, vol. 23, no. 3, Winter 1993, p. 615.

27. Tufts, Henry. *A Narrative of the Life, Adventures, Travels and Sufferings of Henry Tufts, Now Residing at Lemington, in the District of Maine In substance, as compiled from his own mouth*. Samuel Bragg, 1807, p. 340.

28. *Ibid.*, pp. 109–110.

29. Adams, Samuel. *The Writings of Samuel Adams—Volume 4*. Edited by Harry Alonzo Cushing. G.P. Putnam's Sons, 1908, p. 51.

30. *Ibid.*, p. 34.

31. Wood, Gordon S. *The Radicalism of the American Revolution*. Vintage, 1993, p. 367.

32. Gilreath, James. *Thomas Jefferson and the Education of a Citizen*. Library of Congress, 1999, p. 80.

33. Letter to Charles Yancey, January 6, 1816. *Founders Online*, National Archives. https://founders.archives.gov/documents/Jefferson/03-09-02-0209. Accessed February 28, 2023.

34. Letter to John Adams, October 28, 1813. https://cooperative-individualism.org/jefferson-thomas_correspondence-aristocracy-of-talent-1813.htm. Accessed February 27, 2023.

35. Adams, Samuel. *The Writings of Samuel Adams—Volume 4*. Edited by Harry Alonzo Cushing. G.P. Putnam's Sons, 1908, p. 124.

36. Wells, William V. *The Life and Public Services of Samuel Adams—Volume 3*. Little, Brown, 1865, pp. 324–328.

37. Adams, Samuel. *The Writings of Samuel Adams—Volume 4*. Edited by Harry Alonzo Cushing. G.P. Putnam's Sons, 1908, p. 371.

38. *Ibid.*, p. 379.

39. Wood, Betty. "The Impact of the Revolution on the Role, Status, and Experience of Women." *A Companion to the American Revolution*. Edited by Jack P. Greene and J.R. Pole. Blackwell, 2000, p. 421.

40. Schiff, Stacy. *The Revolutionary: Samuel Adams*. Little, Brown, 2022, p. 75.

41. Wells, William V. *The Life and Public Services of Samuel Adams*. Little, Brown, 1865, p. 53.

42. Skemp, Sheila L. "Women and Politics in the Era of the American Revolution." *Oxford Research Encyclopedia of American History* 09. Oxford University Press. Accessed April 27, 2023, https://oxfordre.com/americanhistory/view/10.1093/acrefore/9780199329175.001.0001/acrefore-9780199329175-e-216.

43. Wike, Sudie Doggett. *Women in the American Revolution*. McFarland, 2018, p. 59.

44. Raphael, Ray. "Marblehead Woman." *Journal of the American Revolution*, May 7, 2014. https://allthingsliberty.com/2014/05/marblehead-woman/. Accessed May 26, 2023.

45. Mayer, Holly A. *Belonging to the Army: Camp Followers and Community During the American Revolution*. University of South Carolina Press, 1999, p. 1.

46. Raphael, Ray. "Marblehead Woman." *Journal of the American Revolution*, May 7, 2014. https://allthingsliberty.com/2014/05/marblehead-woman/. Accessed May 26, 2023.

47. Murray, Judith Sargent. *Selected*

Writings of Judith Sargent Murray. Oxford University Press, 1995, pp. 3–15.

48. Kerber, Linda. "The Republican Mother: Women and the Enlightenment-An American Perspective." *American Quarterly*, vol. 28, no. 2, Summer 1976, pp. 187–205.

49. Wollstonecraft, Mary. *A Vindication of the Rights of Women*. Prometheus Books, 1989, p. 30.

50. *Ibid.*, p. 16.

51. Wood, Betty. "The Impact of the Revolution on the Role, Status, and Experience of Women." *A Companion to the American Revolution*. Edited by Jack P. Greene and J. R. Pole. Blackwell, 2000, p. 426

52. Zagarri, Rosemarie. "The Rights of Man and Woman in Post-Revolutionary America." *The William and Mary Quarterly*, vol. 55, no. 2, April 1998, pp. 203–230,

53. Wood, Gordon S. *The Radicalism of the American Revolution*. Vintage, 1993, p. 7.

54. *Ibid.*, p. 49.

55. "Abigail Adams to John Adams, 31 March 1776." *Founders Online*, National Archives. https://founders.archives.gov/documents/Adams/04-01-02-0241.

56. Tufts, Henry. *A Narrative of the Life, Adventures, Travels and Sufferings of Henry Tufts, Now Residing at Lemington, in the District of Maine In substance, as compiled from his own mouth*. Samuel Bragg, 1807, p. 362.

57. *Ibid.*, p. 27.

58. *Ibid.*, pp. 265–266.

59. *Ibid.*, p. 122.

60. *Ibid.*, p. 24.

61. *Ibid.*, p. 111.

62. *Ibid.*, p. 24.

Chapter 14

1. Williams, Daniel E. "Rogues, Rascals and Scoundrels: The Underworld Literature of Early America." *American Studies*, vol. 24, no. 2. Fall 1983, p. 14.

2. Tufts, Henry. *A Narrative of the Life, Adventures, Travels and Sufferings of Henry Tufts, Now Residing at Lemington, in the District of Maine In substance, as compiled from his own mouth*. Samuel Bragg, 1807, p. 363.

3. Wadleigh, George. *Notable events in the history of Dover, New Hampshire, from the first settlement in 1623 to 1865*. 1913, pp. 197–198.

4. Bremer, Francis J., and Webster, Tom. *Puritans and Puritanism in Europe and America: A Comprehensive Encyclopedia*. ABC-CLIO, 2006, p. 183, 209.

5. Bowden, James. *The History of the Society of Friends in America, Volume 1*. Franklin Classics, 2018, p. 33.

6. "Origin of 'White Caps.'" *Evening Star* (Washington, D.C.), May 25, 1904. Reprinted from the *Boston Herald*.

7. Thompson, Mary. *Landmarks in Ancient Dover, New Hampshire*. Concord Republican Press Association, 1892, p. 257.

8. Wadleigh, George. *Notable events in the history of Dover, New Hampshire, from the first settlement in 1623 to 1865*. 1913, p. 185.

9. Butterfield, Martha. *The Land in Our Hands—Burley-Demeritt Farm in Lee, NH: Its History*. Lulu.com, 2016, p. 41.

10. Tufts, Henry. *A Narrative of the Life, Adventures, Travels and Sufferings of Henry Tufts, Now Residing at Lemington, in the District of Maine In substance, as compiled from his own mouth*. Samuel Bragg, 1807, p. 53

11. Higginson, Thomas Wentworth. "A New England Vagabond." *Harper's Magazine*, vol. 76, 1888, pp. 605–611.

12. Higginson, Thomas Wentworth. *Travelers and Outlaws: Episodes in American History*. Lee and Shepard Publishers, 1889, p. 89.

13. "An Ancient Vagabond." *The New York Times*, January 14, 1885,

14. "Henry Tufts the Vagabond." *The Boston Globe*, October 28, 1903.

15. Higginson, Thomas Wentworth. *Travellers and Outlaws: Episodes in American History*. Lee and Shepard, 1889.

16. "A Criminal's Confessions." *The Age*, November 14, 1931

17. Tufts, Henry. *A Narrative of the Life, Adventures, Travels and Sufferings of Henry Tufts, Now Residing at Lemington, in the District of Maine In substance, as compiled from his own mouth*. Samuel Bragg, 1807, p. 363

18. Allie, Daniel. "When Lies Are Found to be Truth: Henry Tufts' Final Escape." HenryTufts.com, https://henrytufts.wordpress.com/2017/08/17/when-lies-are-found-to-be-truth/. Accessed August 5, 2022.

Notes—Chapter 14

19. Thompson, Mary. *Landmarks in Ancient Dover, New Hampshire*. Concord Republican Press Association. 1892, p. 257.

20. Allie, Daniel. "Henry Tufts was a villain." *Tufts Family Genealogy*. https://tuftsgenealogy.blogspot.com/2017/03/henry-tufts-was-villian.html. Accessed January 15, 2023.

21. Tufts, Henry. *A Narrative of the Life, Adventures, Travels and Sufferings of Henry Tufts, Now Residing at Lemington, in the District of Maine In substance, as compiled from his own mouth*. Samuel Bragg, 1807, pp. 363–364.

22. *Ibid.*, p. 308.

23. *Ibid.*, p. 32.

24. Williams, Daniel E. "Rogues, Rascals and Scoundrels: The Underworld Literature of Early America." *American Studies*, vol. 24, no. 2, Fall 1983, p. 13.

25. Smith, Samantha. "Patriotic, honest and selfish: How Americans describe … Americans." Pew Research Center, December 11, 2015. https://www.pewresearch.org/short-reads/2015/12/11/patriotic-honest-and-selfish-how-americans-describe-americans/. Accessed August 7, 2023.

26. Ariely, Dan. *The (Honest) Truth About Dishonesty: How We Lie to Everyone—Especially Ourselves*. Harper, 2012, p. 7.

27. Andrews, Colman. "These are the 56 people who signed the Declaration of Independence." USA Today, July 3, 2019. www.usatoday.com/story/money/2019/07/03/july-4th-the-56-people-who-signed-the-declaration-of-independence/39636971/. Accessed December 18, 2022.

28. Comment by George Washington, recorded by David Humphries, in the latter's biography of Washington, now in the Rosenbach Library in Philadelphia, quoted in Charles C. Wall, "Housing and Family Life of the Mount Vernon Negro," unpublished paper prepared for the Mount Vernon Ladies' Association, May 1962, prefatory note.

29. Letter of Thomas Jefferson to William Short, September 8, 1823, Thomas Jefferson Papers, Earl Gregg Swem Library, College of William and Mary. *Founders Online*, National Archives. https://founders.archives.gov/documents/Jefferson/98-01-02-3750. Accessed August 9, 2022.

30. Letter of Thomas Jefferson to Thomas Cooper, September 10, 1814. National Archives. *Founders Online* https://founders.archives.gov/documents/Jefferson/03-07-02-0471. Accessed August 9, 2022.

31. "Jefferson & Slavery." *Monticello*. https://www.monticello.org/thomas-jefferson/jefferson-slavery/. Accessed August 9, 2022.

32. Letter of Abigail Adams to *John Adams*. March 31, 1776. Founders Online, National Archives. https://founders.archives.gov/documents/Adams/04-01-02-0241. Accessed August 9, 2022.

33. Young, Emily. "By Any Means Necessary: An Examination of Abigail Adams's Survival During the American Revolution." *Recounting the Past—A Student Journal of Historical Studies*, 2019, pp. 106–107.

34. Eliot, John. *A Biographical Dictionary: Containing a Brief Account of the First Settlers, and Other Eminent Characters Among the Magistrates, Ministers, Literary and Worthy Men, in New-England*. Cushing and Appleton, Salem, and Edward Oliver, 1809, p. 6.

35. *Ibid.*, p. 7.

36. Tudor, William. *The Life of James Otis, of Massachusetts: Containing Also, Notices of Some Contemporary Characters and Events, from the Year 1760 to 1775*. Wells and Lilly, 1823, pp. 274–275.

37. Shipton, Clifford. *Sibley's Harvard Graduates: Biographical Sketches of Those Who Attended Harvard College Volume 10*. Massachusetts Historical Society, 1958, p. 434

38. "To John Adams from James Warren, 18 May 1787." *Founders Online*, National Archives. https://founders.archives.gov/documents/Adams/06-19-02-0055. [Original source: *The Adams Papers, Papers of John Adams, Vol. 19, February 1787–May 1789*. Edited by Sara Georgini, Sara Martin, R. M. Barlow, Amanda M. Norton, Neal E. Millikan, and Hobson Woodward. Harvard University Press, 2016, pp. 75–77.]

39. Tufts, Henry. *A Narrative of the Life, Adventures, Travels and Sufferings of Henry Tufts, Now Residing at Lemington, in the District of Maine In substance, as compiled from his own mouth*. Samuel Bragg, 1807, p. 364.

40. Adams, Samuel. *The Writings of Samuel Adams—Volume 4*. Edited by

Harry Alonzo Cushing. G.P. Putnam's Sons, 1908, p. 223.
  41. *Ibid.*, p. 194.
  42. Schiff, Stacy. *The Revolutionary: Samuel Adams.* Little, Brown, 2022, p. 297.
  43. Fischer, David Hackett. *Paul Revere's Ride.* Oxford University Press, 1995, p. 36.
  44. *Ibid.*, pp. xvi–xvii.
  45. Roberts, Andrew. *The Last King of America: The Misunderstood Reign of George III.* Viking, 2021.
  46. McCullough, David. *1776.* Simon & Schuster, 2006, pp. 5–6.
  47. "Declaring Independence." https://www.digitalhistory.uh.edu/disp_textbook.cfm?smtID=3&psid=112. Accessed December 18, 2022.
  48. Roberts, Andrew. "In Defense of King George." *Smithsonian Magazine*, November 2021. https://www.smithsonianmag.com/history/in-defense-of-king-george-180978852/. Accessed December 19, 2022.
  49. Chotiner, Isaac. "Why Andrew Roberts Wants Us to Reconsider King George III." *The New Yorker*, November 9, 2021. https://www.newyorker.com/news/q-and-a/why-andrew-roberts-wants-us-to-reconsider-king-george-iii. Accessed December 19, 2022.
  50. Wiencek, Henry. *Master of the Mountain: Thomas Jefferson and His Slaves.* Farrar, Straus and Giroux, 2012, p. 119.
  51. Wiencek, Henry. *An Imperfect God: George Washington, His Slaves, and the Creation of America.* Farrar, Straus and Giroux, 2003, p. 112.

Chapter 15

  1. Alexander Hamilton to Gouverneur Morris, January 27, 1802. https://www.alexanderhamiltonexhibition.org/letters/01_27.html. Accessed May 1, 2023.
  2. Wood, Gordon S. *The Radicalism of the American Revolution.* Vintage, 1993, p. 367.
  3. Adams, Samuel. *The Writings of Samuel Adams—Volume 4.* Edited by Harry Alonzo Cushing. G.P. Putnam's Sons, 1908, p. 239.
  4. McFarland, Bridget. "'This Affair of a Theatre': The Boston Theatre Controversy and the Americanization of the Stage." *Theatre History*, vol. 38, 2019, p. 28.
  5. Wood, Gordon S. *The Radicalism of the American Revolution.* Alfred A. Knopf, 1992, p. 191.
  6. Adams, Samuel. *The Writings of Samuel Adams—Volume 4.* Edited by Harry Alonzo Cushing. G.P. Putnam's Sons, 1908, pp. 315–316.
  7. "From John Adams to Samuel Adams, 18 October 1790." *Founders Online*, National Archives. https://founders.archives.gov/documents/Adams/06-20-02-0254. [Original source: *The Adams Papers, Papers of John Adams, Vol. 20, June 1789–February 1791*. Edited by Sara Georgini, Sara Martin, R. M. Barlow, Gwen Fries, Amanda M. Norton, Neal E. Millikan, and Hobson Woodward. Harvard University Press, 2020, pp. 424–429.]
  8. "From John Adams to John Trumbull, 18 March 1817." *Founders Online*, National Archives. https://founders.archives.gov/documents/Adams/99-02-02-6730.
  9. Schiff, Stacy. *The Revolutionary: Samuel Adams.* Little, Brown, 2022, p. 322.
  10. "John Adams to Thomas Jefferson, 30 July 1815," *Founders Online*, National Archives. https://founders.archives.gov/documents/Jefferson/03-08-02-0507. [Original source: *The Papers of Thomas Jefferson, Retirement Series, vol. 8, 1 October 1814 to 31 August 1815.* Edited by J. Jefferson Looney. Princeton: Princeton University Press, 2011, pp. 625–626.]
  11. "Thomas Jefferson to John Adams, 10 August 1815." *Founders Online*, National Archives. https://founders.archives.gov/documents/Jefferson/03-08-02-0533. [Original source: *The Papers of Thomas Jefferson, Retirement Series, Vol. 8, 1 October 1814 to 31 August 1815.* Edited by J. Jefferson Looney. Princeton: Princeton University Press, 2011, pp. 656–659.]
  12. Zinn, Howard. *A People's History of the United States.* HarperPerennial, 1995, p. 59
  13. Marx, Karl. *Capital: A Critical Analysis of Capitalist Production—Volume 1.* Lawrence & Wishart, 1974, p. 20.
  14. Boorstin, Daniel J. *The Genius of American Politics*, 1953, p. 68.
  15. Engels, Friedrich. "The Civil War in France." https://www.marxists.org/archive/marx/works/1871/civil-war-france/postscript.htm. Accessed August 7, 2023.

16. Wells, William V. *The Life and Public Services of Samuel Adams: Being a Narrative of his Acts and Opinions, and of His Agency in Producing and Forwarding the American Revolution. With Extracts From His Correspondence, State Papers, and Political Essays, Volume 3.* Little, Brown, 1865, p. 373.

17. *Ibid.*, p. 398.

18. Morris, Richard B. "Class Struggle and the American Revolution." *The William and Mary Quarterly*, vol. 19, no. 1, January 1962, p. 26.

19. "The 1619 Project." *The New York Times*, August 17, 2019. https://www.nytimes.com/interactive/2019/08/14/magazine/1619-america-slavery.html. Accessed August 13, 2023.

20. McBurney, Christian. "The First Efforts to Limit the African Slave Trade Arise in the American Revolution: Part 3 of 3, Congress Bans the African Slave Trade." *Journal of the American Revolution*, September 15, 2020.

21. Adams, Samuel. "American Independence" Speech. August 1, 1776. https://www.revolutionary-war-and-beyond.com/american-independence-speech-by-samuel-adams-august-1-1776.html. Accessed September 11, 2022.

22. Wells, William V. *The Life and Public Services of Samuel Adams: Being a Narrative of His Acts and Opinions, and of His Agency in Producing and Forwarding the American Revolution. With Extracts from His Correspondence, State Papers, and Political Essays* Little, Brown, 1865, p. 415.

23. "Political Observations, 20 April 1795." *Founders Online*, National Archives. https://founders.archives.gov/documents/Madison/01-15-02-0423. [Original source: *The Papers of James Madison, vol. 15, 24 March 1793-20 April 1795.* Edited by Thomas A. Mason, Robert A. Rutland, and Jeanne K. Sisson. University Press of Virginia, 1985, pp. 511–534.]

24. Adams, Samuel. *The Writings of Samuel Adams—Volume 4.* Edited by Harry Alonzo Cushing. G.P. Putnam's Sons, 1908, p. 272.

25. Tufts, Henry. *A Narrative of the Life, Adventures, Travels and Sufferings of Henry Tufts, Now Residing at Lemington, in the District of Maine In substance, as compiled from his own mouth.* Samuel Bragg, 1807, p. 311.

26. Drury, Shadia B. *Political Ideas of Leo Strauss.* Palgrave Macmillan, 1988, p. 120.

27. Madsen, Deborah L. "The Sword or the Scroll: The Power of Rhetoric in Colonial New England." *American Studies*, vol. 33, no. 1, Spring 1992, pp. 45–61.

28. Tufts, Henry. *A Narrative of the Life, Adventures, Travels and Sufferings of Henry Tufts, Now Residing at Lemington, in the District of Maine In substance, as compiled from his own mouth.* Samuel Bragg, 1807, p. 365.

29. McCullough, David. *1776.* Simon & Schuster, 2006, p. 16.

30. Wood, Gordon S.. and Wood, Louise G., eds. *Russian-American Dialogue on the American Revolution.* University of Missouri Press, 1995, p. 69.

31. Adams, Samuel. *The Writings of Samuel Adams—Volume 4.* Edited by Harry Alonzo Cushing. G.P. Putnam's Sons, 1908, p. 138.

32. Tufts, Henry. *A Narrative of the Life, Adventures, Travels and Sufferings of Henry Tufts, Now Residing at Lemington, in the District of Maine In substance, as compiled from his own mouth.* Samuel Bragg, 1807, p. 320.

Bibliography

Adams, Samuel. *The Writings of Samuel Adams.* Edited by Harry Alonzo Cushing. G.P. Putnam's Sons, 1904.
Alexander, John K. *Samuel Adams: America's Revolutionary Politician.* Rowman & Littlefield, 2004.
Allison, Robert J. *The Boston Tea Party.* Commonwealth Editions, 2007.
Bailyn, Bernard. *The Ordeal of Thomas Hutchinson.* Belknap Press, 1976.
Beard, Charles. *An Economic Interpretation of the Constitution of the United States.* The Free Press, 1913.
Bell, J.L. "You Won't Believe How Samuel Adams Recruited Sons of Liberty." *Journal of the American Revolution*, February 5, 2014.
Bullen, Daniel. *Daniel Shays's Honorable Rebellion: An American Story.* Westholme, 2021.
Calloway, Colin G. *The Western Abenakis of Vermont, 1600–1800: War, Migration, and the Survival of an Indian People.* University of Oklahoma Press, 1994.
Cave, Alfred A. *The French and Indian War.* Bloomsbury Academic, 2004.
Clark, J.C.D. "The Unexpected Revolution: America, 1774–1787." *Thomas Paine: Britain, America, and France in the Age of Enlightenment and Revolution.* Oxford Academic, February 15, 2018.
Cole, Jones T. "'The rage of tory-hunting': Loyalist Prisoners, Civil War, and the Violence of American Independence." *Journal of Military History*, vol. 81, issue 3, July 2017.
Crytzer, Brady J. "Longhouse Lost: The Battle of Oriskany and the Iroquois Civil War." *Journal of the American Revolution*, July 30, 2020.
Day, Gordon M. "Henry Tufts as a Source on the Eighteenth Century Abenakis." *Ethnohistory*, vol. 21, no. 3, Summer 1974.
De Crevecoeur, J. Hector St. John. *Letters from an American Farmer and Sketches of Eighteenth-Century America.* Penguin Classics, 1981.
di Beccaria, Cesare Bonesana. *An Essay on Crimes and Punishments (1764) A New Edition Corrected.* W.C. Little & Co., 1872.
Diggins, John Patrick. *John Adams: The American Presidents Series: The 2nd President, 1797–1801.* Times Books, 2003.
Dixon, David. *Never Come to Peace Again: Pontiac's Uprising and the Fate of the British Empire in North America.* University of Oklahoma Press, 2014.
Fischer, David Hackett. *Paul Revere's Ride.* Oxford University Press, 1995.
Flick, Alexander Clarence. *Loyalism in New York During the American Revolution.* Macmillan, 1901.
Friedman, Lawrence M. *Crime and Punishment in American History.* Basic Books, 1994.
Gage, Thomas. *The Correspondence of General Thomas Gage.* Edited by Clarence Edwin Carter. Yale University Press, 1931.
Ghere, David L. "The 'Disappearance' of the Abenaki in Western Maine: Political Organization and Ethnocentric Assumptions." *American Indian Quarterly*, vol. 17, no. 2, Spring 1993.
Gilreath, James. *Thomas Jefferson and the Education of a Citizen.* Library of Congress, 1999.

Greene, Jack P., and Pole, J.R., eds. *A Companion to the American Revolution*. Blackwell, 2000.

Griffin, Patrick. *American Leviathan: Empire, Nation, and Revolutionary Frontier*. Hill and Wang, 2008.

Hatfield, Stuart. "Faking It: British Counterfeiting During the American Revolution." *Journal of the American Revolution*, October 7, 2015.

Hearn, Daniel Allen. *Legal Executions in New England: A Comprehensive Reference, 1623–1960*. McFarland, 2008.

Herrera, Ricardo A. "The King's Friends: Loyalists in British Strategy." *Strategy in the American War of Independence: A Global Approach*. Edited by Donald Stoker, Kenneth J. Hagan and Michael T. McMaster. Routledge, 2010.

Higginson, Thomas Wentworth. "A New England Vagabond." *Harper's Magazine*, Vol. 76, 1888.

Higginson, Thomas Wentworth. *Travelers and Outlaws: Episodes in American History*. Lee and Shepard Publishers, 1889.

Holzwarth, Larry. "This Is What Life was Like for Soldiers of the Continental Army During the American Revolution." *History Collection*, April 10, 2019.

Jasanoff, Maya. *Liberty's Exiles: American Loyalists in the Revolutionary World*. Vintage, 2012.

Jensen, Merrill. *The Founding of a Nation: A History of the American Revolution, 1763–1776*. Hackett, 2004.

Lafitau, Joseph Francois. *Customs of the American-Indians Compared with the Customs of Primitive Time*. Edited by William N. Fenton and Elizabeth L. Moore. The Champlain Society, 1974.

Langguth, A.J. *Patriots: The Men Who Started the American Revolution*. Simon & Schuster, 1989.

Locke, John. *The Two Treatises of Civil Government*. Edited by Thomas Hollis. A. Millar et al., 1689.

Loewen, James W. *Lies My Teacher Told Me: Everything Your American History Textbook Got Wrong*. Simon & Schuster, 1995.

Maier, Pauline. "Coming to Terms with Samuel Adams." *The American Historical Review*, vol. 81, no. 1, 1976.

Maier, Pauline. *The Old Revolutionaries: Political Lives in the Age of Samuel Adams*. Knopf, 1980.

Maier, Pauline. *Ratification: The People Debate the Constitution, 1787–1788*. Simon & Schuster, 2011.

Main, Jackson Turner. *Social Structure of Revolutionary America*. Princeton University Press, 1969.

Matson, Cathy. "The Atlantic Economy in an Era of Revolutions: An Introduction." *The William and Mary Quarterly*, Third Series, vol. 62, no. 3, July 2005.

McCullough, David. *John Adams*. Simon & Schuster, 2001.

McCullough, David. *1776*. Simon & Schuster, 2006.

Miller, John C. *Sam Adams: Pioneer in Propaganda*. Little, Brown, 1936.

Miller, John Chester. *The Wolf by the Ears: Thomas Jefferson and Slavery*. University of Virginia Press, 1991.

Morgan, Edmund S. *The Birth of the Republic, 1763–89*. University of Chicago Press, 2012.

Morris, Richard B. "Class Struggle and the American Revolution." *The William and Mary Quarterly*, vol. 19, no. 1, January 1962.

Nagy, John A. *Rebellion in the Ranks: Mutinies of the American Revolution*. Westholme, 2007.

Neem, Johann N. *Democracy's Schools: The Rise of Public Education in America (How Things Worked)*. Johns Hopkins University Press, 2017.

Nell, William Cooper. *The Colored Patriots of the American Revolution: With Sketches of Several Distinguished Colored Persons: To Which is Added a Brief Survey of the Conditions and Prospects of Colored Americans*. Robert F. Wallcut, 1855.

Nies, Judith. *Native American History: A Chronology of a Culture's Vast Achievements and Their Links to World Events*. Ballantine, 1996.

Bibliography

Oliver, Peter. *Peter Oliver's Origin and Progress of the American Rebellion: A Tory View.* Edited by Douglass Adair and John A. Schutz. Stanford University Press, 1961.

Otis, James. *Collected Political Writings of James Otis.* Edited by Richard Samuelson. Liberty Fund, 2015.

Paine, Thomas. *Common Sense.* 3rd ed. 1776.

Rakove, Jack. *Revolutionaries: A New History of the Invention of America.* Houghton Mifflin Harcourt, 2010.

Raphael, Ray. *Founding Myths: Stories That Hide Our Patriotic Past.* The New Press, 2014.

Raphael, Ray. "When Rabble-Rousing Samuel Adams Slowed Down the Revolution." *Journal of the American Revolution,* September 16, 2015.

Reynolds, David. *America: Empire of Liberty.* Penguin, 2010.

Roberts, Andrew. *The Last King of America: The Misunderstood Reign of George III.* Viking, 2021.

Rorabaugh, W.J. "Alcohol in America." *OAH Magazine of History,* vol. 6, no. 2, Fall 1991.

Scee, Trudy Irene. *Rogues, Rascals, and Other Villainous Mainers.* Down East Books, 2014.

Schiff, Stacy. "The Noble Fury of Samuel Adams." *Smithsonian Magazine,* October 2022.

Schiff, Stacy. *The Revolutionary: Samuel Adams.* Little, Brown, 2022.

Senier, Siobhan. "All This Is Abenaki Country." *Studies in American Indian Literatures,* 2010.

Sheppard, Si. *Patriot vs Loyalist: American Revolution 1775–83.* Bloomsbury, 2022.

Shy, John. *A People Numerous and Armed: Reflections on the Military Struggle for American Independence.* Rev. ed. University of Michigan Press, 1990.

Silver, Peter. *Our Savage Neighbors: How Indian War Transformed Early America.* W.W. Norton, 2009.

Simner, Marvin L. "The Use of the Declaration of Independence as a Military Recruitment Tool." *Journal of the American Revolution,* March 31, 2022.

Smith, Abbott Emerson. *Colonists in Bondage: White Servitude and Convict Labor in America, 1607–1776.* Omohundro Institute of Early American History and Culture and the University of North Carolina Press, 1947.

Smith, Merril D., ed. *The World of the American Revolution: A Daily Life Encyclopedia,* 2 vols. ABC-CLIO, 2015.

Smith, Richard Norton. *Patriarch: George Washington and the New American Nation.* Houghton Mifflin, 1993.

Stoll, Ira. *Samuel Adams: A Life.* Free Press, 2009.

Szatmary, David P. *Shays' Rebellion: The Making of an Agrarian Insurrection.* University of Massachusetts Press, 1980.

Thompson, Mary. *Landmarks in Ancient Dover, New Hampshire.* Concord Republican Press Association, 1892.

Thompson, Peter. *Rum Punch & Revolution: Taverngoing & Public Life in Eighteenth-Century Philadelphia.* University of Pennsylvania Press, 1998.

Travers, Len. *Celebrating the Fourth: Independence Day and the Rites of Nationalism in the Early Republic.* University of Massachusetts Press, 1997.

Tucker, Spencer C. *American Revolution: The Definitive Encyclopedia and Document Collection.* ABC-CLIO, 2018.

Tufts, Henry. *The Narrative of Henry Tufts: Second Complete Edition.* Edited by Daniel Allie. CreateSpace, 2017.

Vaver, Anthony. *Bound with an Iron Chain: The Untold Story of How the British Transported 50,000 Convicts to Colonial America.* Pickpocket Publishing, 2011.

Warren, Mercy Otis. *History of the Rise, Progress, and Termination of the American Revolution interspersed with Biographical, Political and Moral Observations—Volume 1.* Liberty Fund, 1805.

Weatherford, Jack. *Indian Givers: How Native Americans Transformed the World.* Broadway Books, 2010.

Wells, William V. *The Life and Public Services of Samuel Adams.* Little, Brown, 1865.

White, Richard. *The Middle Ground: Indians, Empires, and Republics in the Great Lakes Region, 1650–1815.* Cambridge University Press, 1991.

Wiencek, Henry. *An Imperfect God: George Washington, His Slaves, and the Creation of America*. Farrar, Straus and Giroux, 2003.

Wiencek, Henry. *Master of the Mountain: Thomas Jefferson and His Slaves*. Farrar, Straus and Giroux, 2012.

Wike, Sudie Doggett. *Women in the American Revolution*. McFarland, 2018.

Williams, Daniel E. "Doctor, Preacher, Soldier, Thief: A New World of Possibilities in the Rogue Narrative of Henry Tufts." *Early American Literature XIX*, 1984.

Williams, Daniel E. "Rogues, Rascals and Scoundrels: The Underworld Literature of Early America." *American Studies*, vol. 24, no. 2, Fall 1983.

Williamson, William Durkee. *The History of the State of Maine: From Its First Discovery, A.D. 1602, to the Separation, A.D. 1820*. Glazier, Masters & Company, 1832.

Wood, Gordon S. *The American Revolution: A History*. Modern Library, 2003.

Wood, Gordon S. *The Radicalism of the American Revolution*. Vintage, 1993.

Wood, Gordon S., and Wood, Louise G., eds. *Russian-American Dialogue on the American Revolution*. University of Missouri Press, 1995.

Young, Alfred F., and Kaye, Harvey J. *Liberty Tree: Ordinary People and the American Revolution*. New York University Press, 2006.

Zagarri, Rosemarie. "The Rights of Man and Woman in Post-Revolutionary America." *The William and Mary Quarterly*, vol. 55, no. 2, April 1998.

Zinn, Howard. *A People's History of the United States*. HarperPerennial, 1995.

Index

Abenaki Nation *see* Native Americans, Abenaki
Act for the Impartial Administration of Justice 72
Adams, Abigail 12, 23, 79, 106, 159, 169, 201, 216, 227–228
Adams, Charles Francis 12, 158–159
Adams, Charles Francis II 12
Adams, Elizabeth 27
Adams, Henry (John Adams's descendant) 12
Adams, Henry (Samuel Adams's ancestor) 21
Adams, John 11–14, 22–23, 25, 58, 62–63, 66–67, 74, 102, 105, 115, 118, 143, 146, 150, 158, 162–163, 178–179, 186, 192–193, 203, 209, 216, 227, 236–237, 248; and the Constitutional Convention 178–179; as a defense attorney 58–59, 62–63, 203; and the drafting of the Massachusetts Constitution 162–163, 209; in the First Continental Congress 74; and Samuel Adams 11–14, 22, 237; in the Second Continental Congress 102, 237; views on alcohol of 158; views on democracy of 186, 236–237; views on mob violence of 58, 66–67, 150; views on patriarchy of 25; views on slavery of 227
Adams, John Quincy 12, 159
Adams, Louisa Catherine 12
Adams, Samuel ix-x, 1–3, 5, 10–14, 17, 21–23, 26–27, 29, 40–43, 46–47, 49–56, 59–63, 65, 67–72, 74–80, 91–92, 99–102, 108–109, 113–115, 120–121, 124–125, 127–128, 131, 133, 136, 138, 143–145, 148–150, 160–164, 166–169, 174–176, 178–179, 183–184, 186, 190–198, 201–207, 211–213, 225–227, 229–232, 235–237, 239, 242–245, 247–249; and the Articles of Confederation 174–175; and the Battle of Lexington and Concord 75–76; and beer brewing 144, 148; and the Boston Massacre 63; and the Boston Tea Party 69–70; and the Boston theater controversy 236; British attempt to bribe 108–109; and the Circular Letter 57; and commutation of Henry Tufts's death sentence 5, 193–204, 221, 248; conservative views of 161, 229; and the Constitutional Convention 176, 178–179, 183–184; family background of 21–23, 26, 144; in the First Continental Congress 74; and Henry Tufts 10, 20, 22–23, 179, 193, 221, 247–248, 191–192; and John Adams 11–14, 237; and John Hancock 76; and John Locke 56; legacy of 13–14, 229–230, 237, 243; and the Liberty Affair 150; and the Massachusetts Constitution 162–163; and mob violence 14, 54–56, 59–60, 67–68, 74, 144, 150; as president of the Massachusetts Senate 163; and the Riot Act 169; in the Second Continental Congress 79, 102; and Shays's Rebellion 160–161, 166, 168–169, 191, 202; and the Stamp Act 52 56; and the Sugar Act 51 149; and taverns 145; and Thomas Gage 78, 231; and Thomas Hutchinson 50, 52, 62, 70–71; views on criminal justice of 43, 193, 201–204; views on the death penalty of 168, 201–202; views on education of 206, 212–213; views on independence of 57, 121, 124; views on liberty of 40, 47; views on religion of 211; views on slavery of 99, 176, 229, 242; views on wealth of 131, 143, 236, 249; views on white-Indian relations of 29, 91–92
Admiralty Court 52, 58
Agatha, Mary *see* Ockett, Molly
The Age of Reason (Paine) 159
Albany Congress 92–93
alcoholism 158–159
Allen, Ethan 155
Allen, James 133

289

Index

Allie, Daniel ix, 9, 223
America: Empire of Liberty (Reynolds) 12
The American Bloody Register (Russell) 44
American Indian Quarterly 82
American Legion 15–16
American Philosophical Association 8
American Revolution Podcast ix
America's First Dynasty: The Adamses (Brookhiser) 55
And a Bottle of Rum: A History of the New World in Ten Cocktails (Curtis) 154
Andrews, John 70
Androscoggin River 86
Annapolis, Maryland 54, 145, 175
Anti-Saloon League 158
Arendt, Hannah 161
Argus 236
Ariely, Dan 226
Arnold, Benedict 94, 105, 155, 231, 241
Articles of Confederation 93, 121, 170, 174–177, 180–183; *see also* Constitutional Convention
Atkins, James 119
Autobiography of a Criminal (Tufts, Pearson) 9

Bailey, Thomas A. 16
Baker, Joshua 152–153
Baldwin, James 16
Bancroft, George 131, 213
Bass, Henry 53
Battle of Bloody Brook 6
Battle of Bunker Hill 78–79, 102, 104, 106, 120, 127, 142, 247–248
Battle of Fort Oswego 90
Battle of Fort Ticonderoga *see* Fort Ticonderoga
Battle of Germantown 158
Battle of Guadalcanal 8
Battle of Lexington and Concord 10, 75–78, 93, 101, 120, 127, 155, 196, 231
Battle of Long Island 110
Battle of Oriskany 93
Battle of Trenton 114, 126, 155–159
Battle of Valcour Island 94
Battle of Yorktown 226
Becancour 84
Beccaria, Cesare 43–44, 202–203
beer 10, 144–148, 150, 155
Bell, J.L. x, 145
benefit of clergy 63, 199; *see also* capital punishment
Bentinck, Rudolph 89
Bermuda 96
Bernard, Francis 57
Berniere, Henry de 75

Bethel, Maine 81
Bickford, Lydia 5, 31, 38–39, 225
Billington, John 33
Bitting, Adam 141
Bishop, Abraham 236
Blackburn, Henry 199
Bly, John 192
Boston 1775 x
Boston Beer Company 10
Boston Caucus *see* Caucus Club of Boston
Boston Evening Post 60
Boston Gazette 27, 54, 61, 131
Boston Herald 220
Boston, Massachusetts 10, 14, 21–22, 29, 32, 53, 55, 57–63, 68–78, 91, 101, 106, 116, 121, 133, 140, 144–150, 153–155, 162, 165, 168, 191, 196, 199, 201, 203–205, 220, 231, 236–237; adoption of *The Rights of the Colonists* by 91, 121; and alcohol 153–155; closing the port of 71, 146; growth in the 18th century of 29; Henry Tufts's incarceration at Castle William in 196, 199, 205; Henry Tufts's stationing in during the Revolutionary War 116, 140; as an immigration entry point in the 17th century 21–22; and the Liberty Affair 57, 149–150; Market Square of 220; as merchant and financial hub 69, 168; mob rule in 63; occupation of 32, 60, 75, 101, 145, 231, 237; prostitution in 35; resistance to the Stamp Act in 53–54; resistance to the Tea Act in 69–70; siege of 75–76, 155; tar-and-featherings in 59; taverns of 144, 146; and tea smuggling 69; theater ban in 236
Boston Massacre 2, 12, 61–63, 78, 203–204, 237; Samuel Adams's agitation regarding 63, 237; trial of British soldiers for 62–63, 203,
Boston Port Act 71–72
Boston Tea Party 14, 68–72, 106, 146, 149, 168
Boston Town Meeting 51, 53, 69–70, 121, 236
Bound with an Iron Chain: The Untold Story of How the British Transported 50,000 Convicts to Colonial America (Vaver) 37
Bowdoin, James 162, 165, 168, 191
Bowles, Charles 97
Bradlee, David 59
branding 63, 98, 198–199; *see also* benefit of clergy
Brant, Joseph 93
Bridgetown, New Jersey 123
British Army 68, 70, 78, 89, 94, 97, 104–105, 134, 141

Index

The British Prison Ship (Freneau) 110
Brookhiser, Richard 55, 178
Brown, John (American abolitionist) 222
Brown, John (British Army Captain) 75
Brown, William 205
Bullen, Daniel x
Burgoyne, John 77, 104
Burke, Edmund 72, 98–99
Burr, Aaron 14, 235
Burroughs, Stephen 46, 219
Butler's Rangers 93
Butterfield, Martha 221

Calloway, Colin G. 82
Canada 30, 32, 51, 76–77, 81, 93, 96, 102, 200
Capital (Marx) 238
capital punishment 5, 33–34, 37, 44, 57, 64, 110, 148, 168–169, 188, 191, 196–204, 207
Cartier, Jacques 87
Castle Island 57, 62, 73, 196, 198–199, 201, 204–205, 224–225
Castle William *see* Castle Island
Catholics 83
Caucus Club of Boston 26, 145
Chalmers, James 29
Charleston, South Carolina 29, 58
Charlestown, Massachusetts 73, 204
Chester, New Hampshire 24
Chicago School of Pragmatism 8
Christmas 155, 157, 199
City Tavern 145
Civil War 15, 104
Clark, Lauren 147
Clinton, George 11, 104–105
Clinton, Henry 77, 104, 141
Clinton, James 104
Coercive Acts 71–72, 74, 229, 231
The Colored Patriots of the American Revolution (Nell) 97
Committees of Correspondence 74, 121, 145
Common Sense (Paine) 103, 113, 122, 159
Communist Manifesto (Engels and Marx) 239
Concord, Massachusetts 10, 75, 77, 93, 101, 120, 127, 155, 166, 196, 231
Conestoga River 152
Confiscation Act 138
Congress of the Confederation 169–170, 174, 181
Connecticut 53, 76, 110, 137–138, 140
Connecticut Compromise *see* Great Compromise
Connecticut River 39

Constitution of the United States 104, 175–186, 192, 203
Constitutional Convention 175–185
Continental Army 9, 94, 97, 105–111, 115–116, 119–121, 124–126, 134, 140–142, 146, 154, 157–158, 167, 190, 200, 214, 238; African-American participation in 97; alcohol consumption in 154, 157–158; and Benedict Arnold 105; desertion from 119, 190; discipline problems in 116, 119, 140, 157–158; recruitment difficulties of 115, 124; Tufts family participation in 106
Continental Congress: First 74–75, 146; Second 77, 79, 101, 116, 123, 127, 237
Continental currency 8, 107–108, 120, 228
convict transport 36–37
Coombs, Isaac 199
Cooper, Samuel 121
counterfeiting 107–108, 190
The Counter-Revolution of 1776: Slave Resistance and the Origins of the United States of America (Horne) 241
Crafty Bastards: Beer in New England from the Mayflower to Modern Day (Clark) 147
criminal justice 43, 179–181, 198, 202–205; *see also* benefit of clergy; branding; capital punishment
Curtis, Wayne 154
Cushing, Thomas 165

Dalrymple, William 62, 237
Daniel Morgan's Riflemen 10
Daniel Shays's Honorable Rebellion: An American Story (Bullen) x
Dartmouth 69
Davis, James 31
Day, Gordon 82, 84
Day, Luke 191
Declaration of Independence 11, 104–105, 112, 114, 121–124, 127, 136, 138, 168, 185, 211, 222, 227, 232, 235, 237, 242, 247
Delaware River 155, 157
Democratic-Republicans 239
Devonshire, England 21
Dewey, John 8
Dickinson, John 79, 176
A Dissertation on Liberty and Necessity, Pleasure and Pain (Franklin) 42
Dodge, John 196
Dorchester Heights, Massachusetts 154
Dover, New Hampshire 37, 200, 219, 221
Duché, Jacob 127
Dunlap and Claypoole's American Daily Advertiser 198
Dunmore, Lord 28, 97, 139, 146, 153, 233

Early American Literature 198
East Cambridge, Massachusetts 10
East India Company 69, 71
education 8, 10, 15–16, 24, 29, 40, 51, 92, 144, 176, 206–218, 236, 241
Eliot, John 229
Ellery, William 222
Ellis, Joseph J. 14
Ely, Samuel 163–164
Emerson, Smith 11
Engels, Friedrich 239
England 20–21, 36–37, 60, 68, 69, 77, 94, 96, 102–106, 109, 122, 131, 146, 149, 241; crime in 36–37; parliamentary debates on colonial crisis in 60; response to Boston Tea Party of 146
Enlightenment 25, 29, 40–43, 50, 124, 179, 207, 209, 229, 232, 236, 240
Ethiopian Regiment 97
Ethnohistory 82

Falmouth, Maine 63
Faneuil Hall 11, 53–54, 62, 69, 146, 168, 236
Fenner, Arthur 192
Fenton, John 109–110
Fifield, Maria 21
Fischer, David Hackett 10, 146, 154
flash lingo 32
Florida 28, 90
Fort Duquesne 89
Fort Frontenac 90
Fort Lee 156
Fort Ticonderoga 127, 155
Fort William Henry 90
Fosdick, Elizabeth 21
Fowler, William, Jr. 55
Franklin, Benjamin 11, 14, 36, 42, 71, 77, 92–93, 151, 202, 227, 232, 237; and alcohol 151; and the Boston Tea Party 71; and the Iroquois Confederacy 92–93; and the Second Continental Congress 237; and slavery 227; views on convict transport of 36; views on criminal justice of 202
Fraunces Tavern 145–146
French and Indian War 28–29, 51, 68, 84, 89–90, 243
Freneau, Philip 110
Fryeburg, Maine 86

Gadsden, Christopher 13
Gage, Thomas 55, 68, 71–78, 101, 109–110, 135, 231
Gailer, George 59
Gambell, David 108
George III, King of England 25, 49, 51, 53, 65–66, 71, 75, 79, 100–102, 107, 109–110, 121–122, 231–234
Gerry, Elbridge 67, 182–183, 186, 207
Ghere, David 82
Government Act 72
Grande Hermyne 87
Great Barrington, Massachusetts 166–167
Great Compromise 183–184; *see also* Constitutional Convention
Great Lakes 90
Great Migration 20
Greathouse, Daniel 153
Green Dragon Tavern 145–146
Green Mountain Boys 155
Greene, Nathanael 157
Greene and Delaware Moral Society 158
Griffin's Wharf 70; *see also* Boston Tea Party

Hagen, Tumkin 82
Haiti 37
Halifax, New Brunswick 105–106
Hall, Ebenr 155
Hall, Isaac 154–155
Hallowell, Benjamin 150
Hallywell, James 205
Hamilton, Alexander 14, 125, 138, 174, 177, 179, 183, 186, 227; and Aaron Burr 235; views on criminal justice 179; views on democracy of 183, 186; views on slavery 227; views on taxation of 138, 177
Hampshire County, Massachusetts 164
Hampshire Herald 166
Hancock, John 10, 47, 57, 59–60, 72, 75–79, 115–116, 123, 144, 147, 149, 165, 184–185, 191–192, 241; and the Battle of Lexington and Concord 75–76; and the Boston Tea Party 72; and the Constitutional Convention 184–185; and George Washington 123; as governor of Massachusetts 165, 191–192; and the Liberty Affair 57, 149; as president of the Provincial Congress 77; as president of the Second Continental Congress 79, 116, 123; and Samuel Adams 76; views on mob violence of 59–60
Hannah-Jones, Nikole 241
Harnett, Cornelius 13
Harper's Magazine 222
Harrison, Joseph 150
Harvard College 26, 103, 145, 196, 206–207, 213
Hawley, Joseph 164
Hawthorne, Nathaniel 32, 95
HBO (Home Box Office) 11, 59
Henry, Patrick 143, 178–179, 248

Index

HenryTufts.com ix
Hessians 97, 155–156, 159
Higginson, Thomas Wentworth 8, 222–223
Hillsborough, Lord 57
Hillsborough County, New Hampshire 199
History of the Rise, Progress, and Termination of the American Revolution (Warren) 13
Hobbes, Thomas 46–47, 50
Hochelaga village 87
The (Honest) Truth About Dishonesty (Ariely) 226
Horne, Gerald 241
Howe, Lord 109
Howe, William 77, 104
Humphrey, William 111
Hutchinson, Thomas 14, 26, 50, 52–53, 55, 60, 62, 64, 70, 71, 78, 108, 153, 202, 204, 237

impressment 57–58, 114, 134
The Independent Advertiser 26
Indian Givers: How Native Americans Transformed the World (Weatherford) 87
Indians *see* Native Americans
Inglis, Charles 110–111
Intolerable Acts *see* Coercive Acts
Ipswich, Massachusetts 194, 197–198
Ireland 134–135
Island of Heads 85

Jamaica 96
James, Jessie 221
Jay, John 175, 193, 207
Jay, Robert 86
Jefferson, Thomas 11–12, 14, 29, 43, 105, 121–123, 179, 186, 203, 207, 211–212, 227–228, 232–233, 235, 237–238, 242, 248; and the Declaration of Independence 121–123; and Samuel Adams 12, 43, 122; and slavery 227–228, 232–233, 242; views on criminal justice of 203; views on democracy of 186, 235; views on education of 212; views on religion of 211
Jersey 110
Jesuits 84, 93
John Adams (McCullough) 12
Johnson, Samuel 97, 232
Johnstone, George 248
Journal of the American Revolution x, 124, 145
Judd, Enoch 39
jury trials 49, 52, 179, 181, 203

Keating, Neal ix, 9, 154
Kelly, Andrew 139
Kennison, Abigail 145, 187–189, 197
King George's War 84
King Philip's War 6, 84
King Street Tavern 146
King's American Dragoons 96
King's Royal Regiment of New York 96
Knox, Henry 170
Korean War 8

Lafayette, Adrienne 136
Lafayette, Marquis de 136
Lafitau, Joseph 93
Land Bank 26, 166
Landmarks in Ancient Dover, New Hampshire (Thompson) 37, 221
Langdon, Samuel 77, 81
Langguth, A.J. 13
The Last King of America: The Misunderstood Reign of King George III (Roberts) 231
Lee, Henry 169
Lee, New Hampshire 31, 38, 63–64, 118, 221
Lee, Richard Henry 11, 77, 102, 120–121, 176
Legal Commonplace Book (Jefferson) 203
Leitch, Andrew 139
Lemington, Maine *see* Limington, Maine
Lenin, Vladimir 248
Lewis, John 97
Lexington, Massachusetts 10, 16, 75–77, 93, 101–102, 120, 127, 145–146, 154–155, 159, 196, 226, 231
Liberty (John Hancock's ship) 149–150
Liberty! (PBS series) 13–14
Liberty Tree 53
Limington, Maine 225
Lincoln, Benjamin 167, 169
Livingston, Robert 237
Locke, John 46–47, 50, 55–56, 79, 122, 207
Lord Dunmore's Proclamation 97, 139, 233
Lord Dunmore's War 153
Loyal Nine 53, 101
loyalists 51, 64, 93, 96, 104, 109–113, 122–124, 133, 139, 142–143, 243; *see also* Tories

Macaulay, Catharine 136
Machiavelli, Niccolò 245
Madeira, Portugal 149–150
Madeira wine 147, 149
Madison, James 14, 105, 174, 179–181, 207, 243–244; views on criminal justice of

180; views on democracy of 181; views on war of 243–244
Magna Carta 49, 66, 102, 232
Maier, Pauline 12, 123
Maine 28, 30, 63, 81, 83–88, 106, 154, 225
Mandamus Council 73
Marblehead, Massachusetts 15, 57–58, 112–114, 127, 196
Marx, Karl 238–239
Maryland 49, 89, 119, 123, 138, 145, 175, 177
Mason, George 138, 180, 182
Massachusetts 5–6, 15, 20–21, 26, 33, 50, 57–58, 65, 68, 71–78, 83, 92, 101, 105–106, 112–114, 118, 123, 127, 145, 154, 161–170, 175, 181–185, 192, 196–205, 209, 220–223; and alcohol 148–149; backcountry of 73, 154, 162; and capital punishment 188, 196–203; charter of 68; and the Coercive Acts 71; Constitution of 162–164, 209; and the Constitutional Convention 175, 181–185; and criminal justice reform 203–204; emigration to 6, 20; Executive Council of 197–198; General Court of 26, 57, 100, 163, 201; Henry Tufts and 15, 114, 196, 164, 222; and John Adams 162–163, 209; and John Hancock 165, 191–192; Land Bank affair in 26, 166; and loyalists 105; mob rule in 72; and Native Americans 92, 94; Riot Act of 169, 185; rum distilling industry of 51, 149–150, 154; and Samuel Adams 75–76, 101, 145, 160–163, 169, 166, 168–169, 188, 191, 202; Shays's Rebellion in 161–170; and slavery 99–100; Superior Court of 66; Thomas Hutchinson and 50
Massachusetts Act 105
Massachusetts Bay Colony 20–21, 33, 44, 101, 148
Massachusetts Body of Liberties 49
Massachusetts Compromise 184
Massachusetts Council *see* Massachusetts, General Court
The Massachusetts Gazette & Boston Weekly News-Letter 104
Massachusetts Historical Society 12
Massachusetts House of Representatives *see* Massachusetts, General Court
Massachusetts legislature *see* Massachusetts, General Court
Massachusetts Soldiers and Sailors of the Revolutionary War 10, 106
Mason, George 138, 180, 182
Massacre Day 63
Mather, Cotton 21–22, 34, 44–45, 148
Mather, Increase 21
Mauroy, Viscount de 135–136
Mayflower 147–148

Mayflower Compact 33
McClellan, Joseph 141
McCulloch, Henry 191
McCullough, David 12, 119
McDonnell, Michael 138
Medford, Massachusetts 21, 105–106, 154
Medford in the Revolution (Wild) 106
Meeting of Commissioners to Remedy Defects of the Federal Government 175
Menotomy, Massachusetts 76, 145
The Meritorious Price of Our Redemption (Pynchon) 220
Merrimack River 33
Meserve, George 68
Middlesex County, Massachusetts 75
Midnight Ride 10, 16, 76, 154, 226
Milford, Connecticut 53
Militia Act 169
Miller, John C. 55, 144–145
Mississippi River 28, 90
Molasses Act 149
Molineux, William 14
Monday Night Club 51
Montagu, John 70
Montesquieu, Baron de 46, 207
Montreal, Quebec 87
Morgan, Edmund S. 13, 29
Morris, Gouverneur 104, 178, 182, 184, 227
Morris, Lewis 104
Morris, Richard B. 241
Morris, Robert 126–127
Mount Vernon 138
Mystic River 21

Nagy, John A. 140
The Narrative of Henry Tufts (Allie, Tufts) 9, 223
The Narrative of the Excursion and Ravages of the King's Troops Under the Command of General Gage, on the Nineteenth of April 1775 101
A Narrative of the Life, Adventures, Travels and Sufferings of Henry Tufts (Tufts) 5, 8, 32, 40, 43–44, 86, 139, 216, 219, 221–225, 246
A Narrative of the Life and Conversion of Alexander White (White) 44
Native Americans 10, 28, 70, 77, 81–94, 102, 111, 152–153, 210, 239, 245, 249; Abenaki 9, 81–88, 94, 151; alliances with whites of 88, 93–94; Amoskeag 83; Androscoggin 83; beaver wars of 88; brutal reputation of 88–91; Catawba 89; Cayuga 93; Cherokee 89, 125; Coosuk 83; Conestoga 152;

cultural exchanges with whites of 86–88, 92; displacement of 94; healing techniques of 86–87; Huron 83–84, 87–88; Iroquois 83–84, 87, 89, 92–94; Kennebec 83; Mahican 84; Malacites 83; Micmacs 83; Mingo 89, 152; Missisquoi 83; Mohawk 70, 85, 93; Nashaway 83; Nipmuc 84; Norridgewock 83; Onondaga 93; Ossipee 83; participation in the Revolutionary War of 93–94; Passamaquoddy 83; Pawtucket 83; Penacook 83; Penobscot 83; Pigwacket 83, 86, 94; Pocomtuc 84; Seneca 93; Shawnee 89; Sokoki 83–84; Squakheag 83; Susquehannock 152; Wampanoag 84; Wawenoc 83; Winnipesaukee 83; Winooski 83; Wyandot 89
Navigation Acts 162
Nell, William Cooper 97
New England 1, 5, 9, 16–17, 21–23, 28, 32, 37, 44, 50–51, 57, 60, 63–64, 74, 77, 79, 83, 88, 94, 97–98, 106, 109, 117, 119, 123, 126, 147–149, 154, 169, 192, 200, 210–213, 219–223, 228–229, 235, 246–247
New England Historical Society 15
New France colony 83
New Hampshire 6, 24, 28, 37–39, 53, 63, 68, 83–84, 92, 118, 185, 188, 200, 219, 221, 224
New Jersey Volunteers 96
New Netherlands colony 83
New York 76, 90, 93–94, 96, 104–105, 111, 118, 127, 138, 200
New York, New York 29, 35, 69, 77, 96, 110, 123, 133, 146, 157, 222
New York Times 222, 241
Newark, New Jersey 117
Newbury, Massachusetts 33, 118
Newbury, Vermont 166
Newburyport Herald 199
Newcomen, John 33
Newgate Prison 37
Newport, Rhode Island 29
North Carolina Regulators 132, 167
North End Club 51
Northampton, Massachusetts 164
Norwich, Connecticut 137
Notable events in the history of Dover (Wadleigh) 221
Nova Scotia 28

Ockett, Molly 86
Ohio Valley 88–89
Olive Branch Petition 79, 101, 232
Oliver, Andrew 53
Oliver, Peter 46, 74, 79, 103–104
Oliver, Thomas 74

On Crimes and Punishments (Beccaria) 43, 202
Otis, James 58, 132, 149, 207

Paine, Elizabeth 21
Paine, Thomas 29, 76, 103, 122, 125, 159, 215, 239
Panton, Henry Gibson 58
Parker, Oliver 106
Parliament 26, 27, 49–50–57, 65, 68–69, 71–72, 100, 109, 119, 162, 231, 245, 248; adoption of the Boston Port Act by 71–72; adoption of the Coercive Acts by 71; adoption of the Government Act by 72; adoption of the Navigation Acts by 162; adoption of the Stamp Act by 53; adoption of the Sugar Act by 27; adoption of the Tea Act by 69; adoption of the Townshend Acts by 57; repeal of the Stamp Act by 55
Parmenter, Jason 191
Parsons, Eli 191
Parsons, James 139
Pascataquack, Massachusetts 33
Patriots: The Men Who Started the American Revolution (Langguth) 13
Patten, John 199
Paul Revere's Ride (Fischer) 146, 154
Paxton Boys 152
PBS (Public Broadcasting System) 13
Pearson, Edmund 9, 222–223
Pennsylvania 28, 49, 89–90, 94, 127, 140–141, 152, 177, 203; backcountry of 89, 94, 152; and capital punishment 203; Great Lakes region of 90; Supreme Executive Council of 141
Pennsylvania Gazette 36, 152
Pennsylvania Line Mutiny 140–141
A People Numerous and Armed (Shy) 142
A People's History of the United States (Zinn) 238
Petite Hermyne 87
Pew Research Center 226
Philadelphia, Pennsylvania 13, 29, 69, 70, 72, 74, 77, 91, 123, 133, 140, 145–147, 150, 175, 187, 189, 191, 194, 228
Phillips Exeter Academy 6
Pickering, John, Jr. 99
Pillars of Salt: An History of Some Criminals Executed in This Land for Capital Crimes (Mather) 44–45, 148
Pitt, William 90
Pitt Packet 57
Plymouth Colony 20, 86, 147–148
Plymouth Rock 148
Pontiac, chief of Ottawa tribe 90–91
Pontiac's Rebellion 91

Index

Portsmouth, New Hampshire 53, 68, 188, 199
Powder Alarm 74, 231
Preston, Thomas 63
primogeniture laws 23, 143
prostitution 33, 35–36, 220
Provincial Congress 75, 77
Puls, Mark x, 207
Puritanism 2, 12, 22, 25, 32, 34–35, 210, 229, 237, 246
Putnam, Israel 116–117
Pynchon, William 220

Quakers 79, 211, 220
Quartering Act 51, 56, 72

Rakove, Jack 12
Raleigh Tavern 145
Rall, Johann 156
Randolph, Edmund 177
Reed, Joseph 116, 141
The Religion of Nature Delineated (Wollaston) 42
Resolution 68
Revere, Paul 10, 16, 61–62, 75, 144, 146, 154, 159
The Revolutionary: Samuel Adams (Schiff) x
Revolutionary War 6, 10, 28, 35, 64, 93–94, 96–98, 104–107, 111, 114–120, 138–141, 147, 154–158, 161, 163, 166–167, 212, 239, 243–248; and African Americans 97; class divisions in 132–134; as economic conflict 107, 137; Henry Tufts's service in 11, 102, 111, 114–120, 127, 140; mutinies in 141–142; and Native Americans 93–94; New York campaign of 118, 126, 133; and slavery 98; Tufts family participation in 106
Revolutionary War Journal x
Reynolds, David 12
Reynolds Tavern 145
Rhode Island 192
Richardson, Ebenezer 60
Rights of the Colonists, The (Adams) 47, 91, 121
Riley, Miles 205
Roberts, Andrew 231
Roberts, John 58
Rogers, Rainsford 220
Rogues, Rascals, and Other Villainous Mainers (Scee) 15
Rose, Charles 191–192
Rousseau, Jean Jacques 46
Royal American Regiment 89
Royal Navy 57, 70–71, 73, 90, 104
Royal Proclamation Act 28, 51, 91, 152, 248
Royall, Isaac 105
rum 27, 51, 60, 64, 82, 87–88, 119, 147–158
Rush, Benjamin 42, 207
Rutledge, John 120

St. Francis mission 84
St. John de Crèvecoeur, J. Hector 134
Salem, Massachusetts 5, 21, 199, 205, 223
Salem Gazette 205
Salem Witch Trials 21
Savannah, Georgia 53
Savannah Tom 89
Scarlet Letter (Hawthorne) 32
Scee, Trudy Irene 15
Schenawolf, Harry x
Schiff, Stacy x, 14, 22, 27, 131
Schooler, William 33
Scotland 134
Scott, William 142
Second Treatise on Government (Locke) 56
Seider, Christopher 60–62
Seven Years' War *see* French and Indian War
Shays's Rebellion 8–9, 160–175, 185, 191–192, 198, 202, 230–231, 243
Sheppard, Jack 37
Sherman, Roger 182, 227
Sherman Compromise *see* Great Compromise
Sholy, Mary 33
Shy, John 142
Simner, Marvin L. 124
Simpson, John 196
Six Nations *see* Native Americans, Iroquois
slavery 15, 96–100, 139, 176, 207, 222, 227–233, 238, 240–242
Smith, James 39
Society of Colonial Wars 222
Somerville, Massachusetts 6
Sons of Liberty 14, 51, 53–54, 101, 103, 144–145
South Carolina 34, 58, 97, 120, 125
South Carolina General Assembly 125
South Carolina Royalists 96
Springfield, Massachusetts 167
Stamp Act 14, 32, 51–56, 132, 147, 153
Stephen, Adam 158
Stewart, John 15, 194, 196
Stoll, Ira x, 14, 59
Stono, South Carolina 97
Strauss, Leo 244–245
Stuart, John 88
Sudbury, Canada 81
Sudbury, Massachusetts 145
Suffolk County, Massachusetts 75

Sugar Act 27, 51–52, 149, 248
Susap, Polly 82
Susquehanna River 28
Swillaway, Henry 21

tar-and-featherings 14, 58–60, 62, 65, 110, 243, 245
Taunton, Massachusetts 166
Taxation No Tyranny (Johnson) 97
Tea Act 69, 133
Thacher, Thomas 239
Thomas, Elisha 64
Thomson, Charles 13
Tolbert, Samuel 141
Tories 74, 79, 96–97, 105, 110, 133, 138, 143, 145, 146, 186, 214; *see also* loyalists
Travelers and Outlaws (Higginson) 222
Treadwell, Jacob 92
Treaty of Paris (1763) 90
Treaty of Paris (1783) 35, 161–162, 166
Trinity Church 110
Troy, Michael ix
Trumbull, John 11
Tudor, William 229
Tuffs, William 106
Tufts, Aaron 6
Tufts, Abigail *see* Kennison, Abigail
Tufts, Adam 6
Tufts, Arthur 8
Tufts, Cato 106
Tufts, Charles 6
Tufts, Cotton 23, 76, 105, 192, 201, 228
Tufts, Henry ix, 1–3, 5–11, 15–17, 20–25, 28–34, 37–40, 42–44, 47, 49–50, 56–57, 63–65, 70, 75–76, 80–82, 84–87, 92, 94, 102, 105–108, 111, 114–120, 122, 127, 129–130, 134, 137, 139–140, 143–145, 151, 164, 169, 179, 186–190, 193–206, 210–212, 216–226, 228, 230–231, 233–234, 240, 242, 244–249; and the Abenaki Indians 9, 81–82, 86–87, 94–95, 98, 102; and Samuel Adams 10, 20, 22–23, 179, 193–198, 221, 247–248; and alcohol 151; autobiography of 5, 8, 32, 40, 43–44, 86, 139, 216, 219, 221–225, 246; as a counterfeiter 107–108; death sentence of 193–198; education of 206; family background of 20–23, 75–76, 105–106; as a historical source 82, 84; incarceration of 30, 164, 187, 204–205; legacy of 37, 82, 220–225, 233–234; military service of 11, 102, 111, 114–120, 127, 140; poetry of 40, 189–190; reprieve and commutation of 198–204; and Shays's Rebellion 166; and the silver spoons incident 194–196; and slavery 98; and taverns 145, 217; time in Exeter, New Hampshire, of 187–189; time in Lee, New Hampshire, of 31, 38, 63–64, 118, 221; time in Marblehead, Massachusetts, of 15, 114, 196; time in Newbury, Massachusetts 164; time in Virginia 30, 98; trustworthiness of 3, 15, 197–198; views on the Revolutionary War of 106, 244; views on religion of 210–211; wives of 5, 31, 38–39, 187–189, 197, 217, 225
Tufts, Ichabod 8
Tufts, James 6
Tufts, James Arthur 6
Tufts, James Hayden 8
Tufts, Jay Franklin 6
Tufts, Jesse 8
Tufts, Julie ix
Tufts, Lydia *see* Bickford, Lydia
Tufts, Peter 6, 8, 21, 23
Tufts, Samuel 10, 75–76
Tufts, Simeon 5
Tufts, Simon, Jr. 105
Tufts, Simon, Sr. 105
Tufts, Stanley 8
Tufts, Thomas (genealogist) ix, 6, 8, 106
Tufts, Thomas (Henry Tufts's grandfather) 21
Tufts, William (Revolutionary War veteran) 8
Tufts, William (War of 1812 veteran) 8
Tufts, Zachariah 10
Tufts Family Genealogy ix
Tufts Tavern 145
Tufts University 6
Turner, Nat 222

The United States Criminal Calendar 44
University of Chicago 8

Valley Forge, Pennsylvania 97, 127, 140
Vaver, Anthony 37
Vermont 28, 82–84, 118
Vietnam War 8
Virginia 28, 32, 49, 79, 87, 89–90, 98, 102, 119, 130, 132, 137–139, 145–146, 151–153, 167–170, 176–182, 203, 208, 212, 214, 228, 233; and alcohol 151; backcountry of 89, 152–153; and capital punishment 203; and the Constitutional Convention 177; and George Washington 90, 170; and Henry Tufts 30, 32, 98; insurrection of 1775–76 in 138; insurrection of 1781 in 137; militia of 119; and the Second Continental Congress 79; and Shays's Rebellion 167; and slavery 98, 130, 228, 233

Wadleigh, George 221
Warren, James 74, 115, 143, 230

Warren, Joseph 14, 73, 77, 144
Warren, Mercy Otis 13, 73, 150
Washington, George 8, 14, 28, 68, 71–72, 77, 90, 94, 96, 108, 115–118, 120, 123, 125–127, 136, 140–141, 146–147, 155–159, 170, 175, 184–186, 189–190, 205, 207, 227, 233, 241, 248; as commander of the Continental Army 8, 115–118, 123, 125–127, 140–141, 155–157; and the Constitutional Convention 170, 175, 184–185; First Inaugural Address of 185; and the French and Indian War 68, 90; and Henry Tufts 8, 189–190; and John Hancock 123; and Native Americans 94; response to the Coercive Acts of 72; and Samuel Adams 77, 205; and slavery 227, 233; and Thomas Paine 159; views on land of 28, 241; views on religion of 189; views on the Boston Tea Party of 71–72
Watertown, Massachusetts 77
Wayne, Anthony 140–141
Wayside Inn 145
Weatherford, Jack 87
Wells, Hannah 109
Wells, Maine 30
Wells, William V. 109
Wehnam, Massachusetts 196
The Western Abenakis of Vermont, 1600–1800: War, Migration, and the Survival of an Indian People (Calloway) 82
Weymouth, Massachusetts 6

Whigs 16, 43, 47, 59, 73–76, 97, 102, 133, 144, 186, 192
Whiskey Rebellion 160
White, Alexander 44
White, Mark 119
White Caps 220
Whiting, William 168
Whittemore, Samuel 76
Wilkins, Israel 199
Willard, Archibald 112
The William and Mary Quarterly 241
Williams, Daniel E. 198
Williams, John 33
Williams, Richard 35
Williamsburg, Virginia 145
Williamson, William Durkee 88
Winthrop, John 21, 33–34
Woburn, Massachusetts 76
Wollaston, William 42
Woman's Christian Temperance Union 158
Wood, Gordon S. 143, 215
Worcester County, Massachusetts 75–76, 165–166, 192
World War II 8

Yarmouth, Maine 106
Yellow Creek Massacre 153
Young, Alfred 59

Zinn, Howard 238

www.ingramcontent.com/pod-product-compliance
Ingram Content Group UK Ltd.
Pitfield, Milton Keynes, MK11 3LW, UK
UKHW041937210426
5322IPUK00016B/232